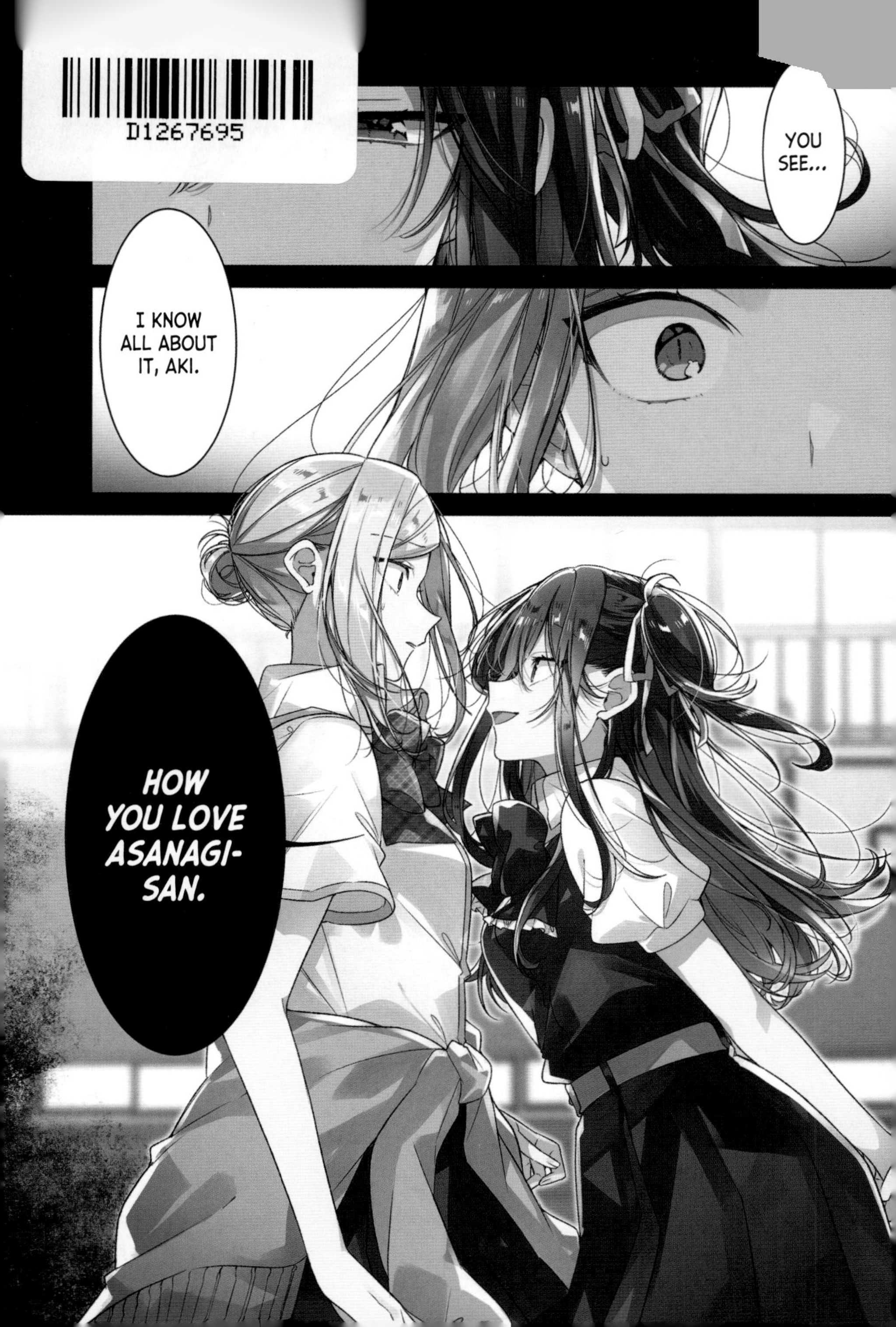
YOU SEE...
I KNOW ALL ABOUT IT, AKI.
HOW YOU LOVE ASANAGI-SAN.

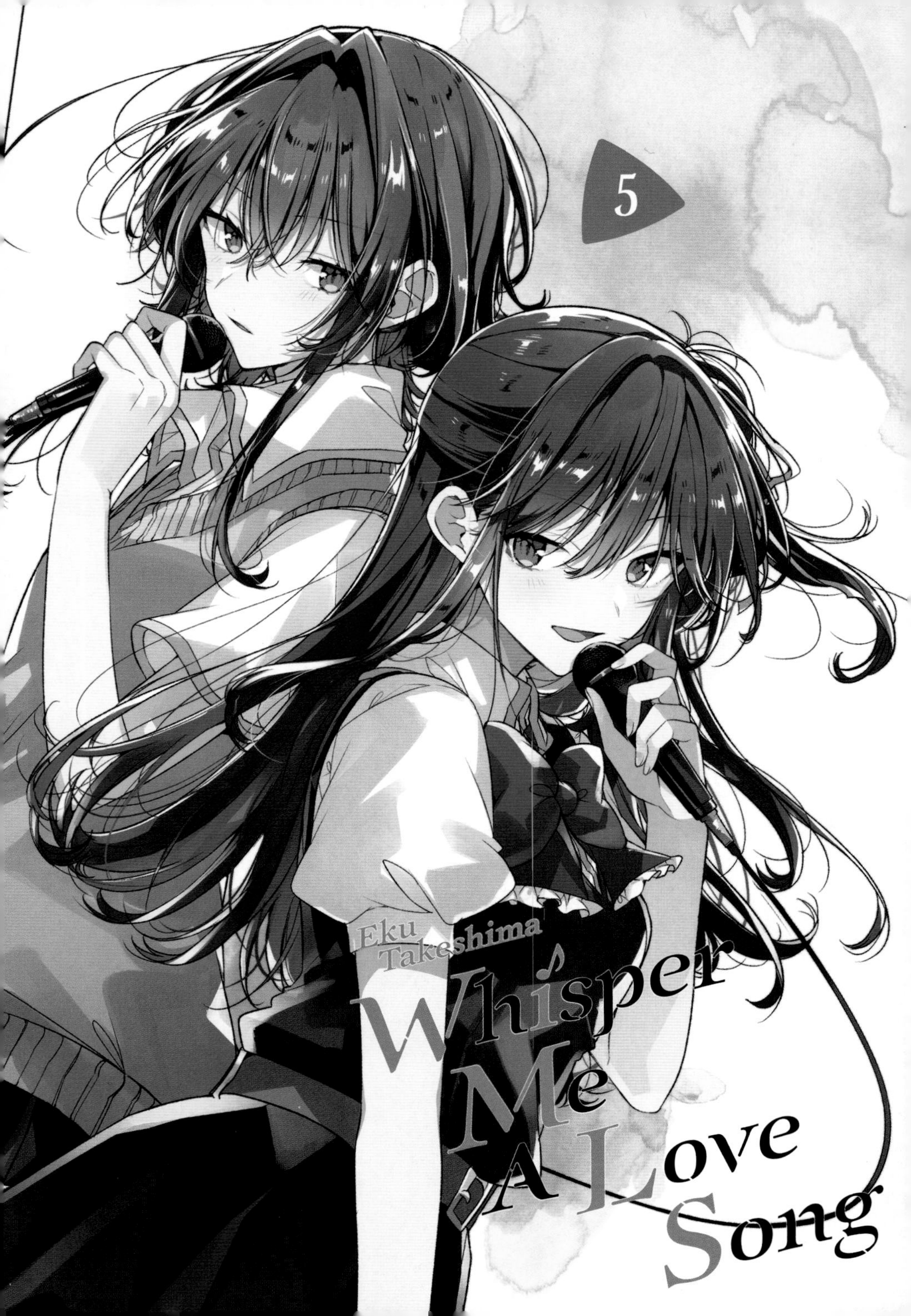
5
Eku Takeshima
Whisper Me A Love Song

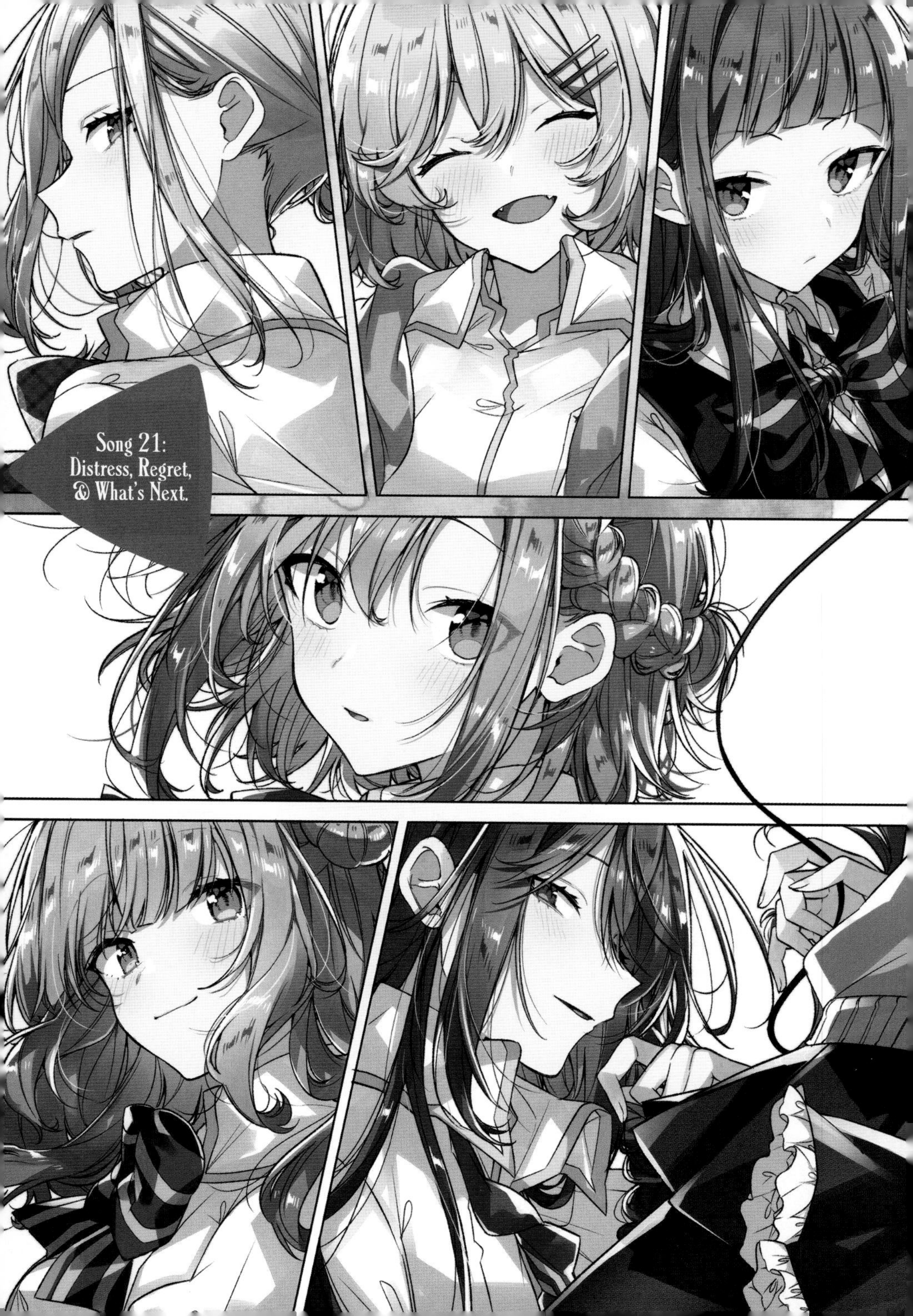
Song 21:
Distress, Regret,
& What's Next.

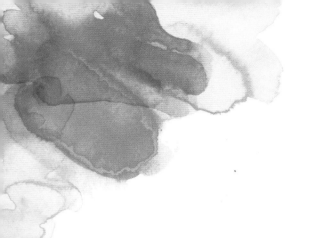

contents

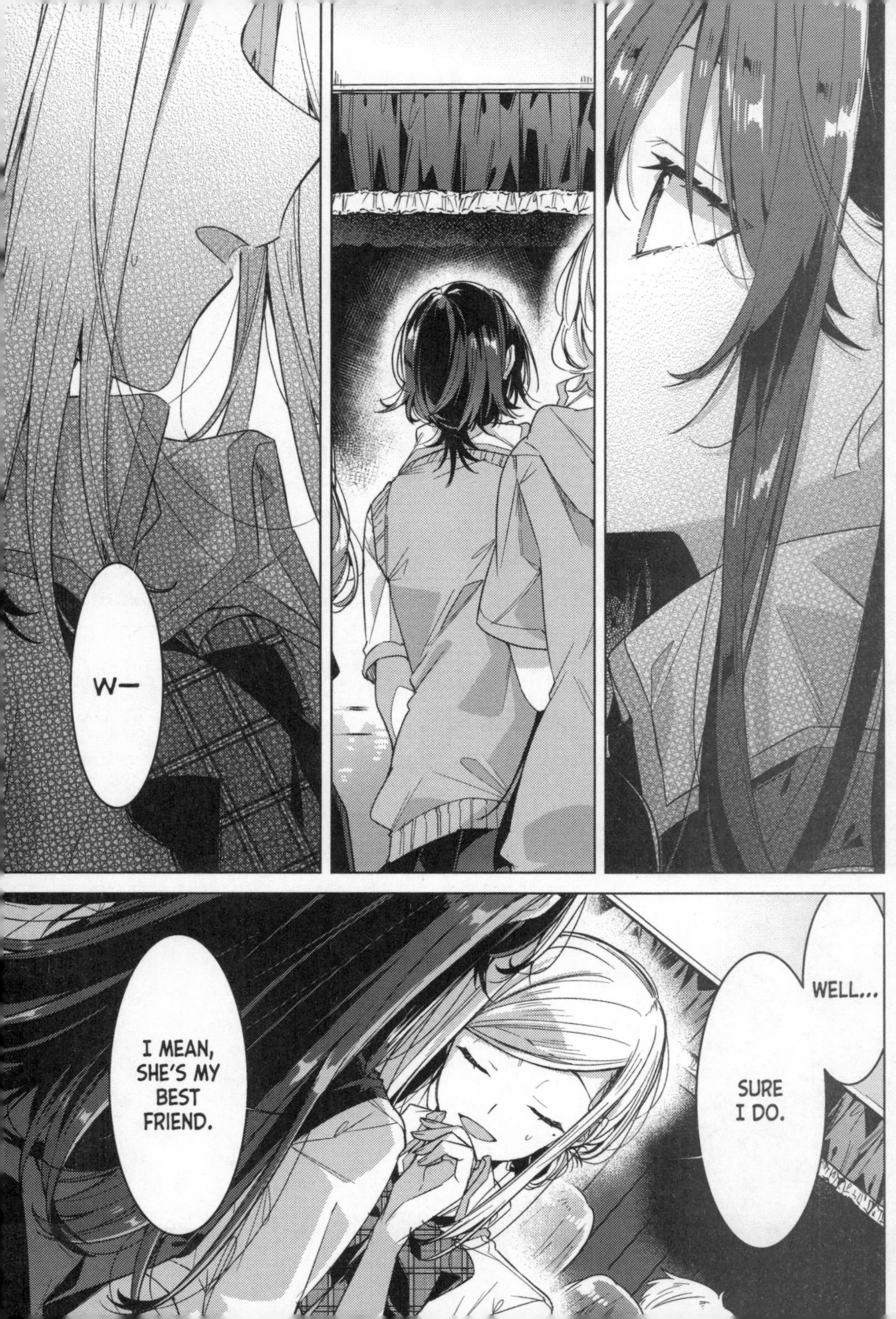
W—
WELL...
SURE I DO.
I MEAN, SHE'S MY BEST FRIEND.

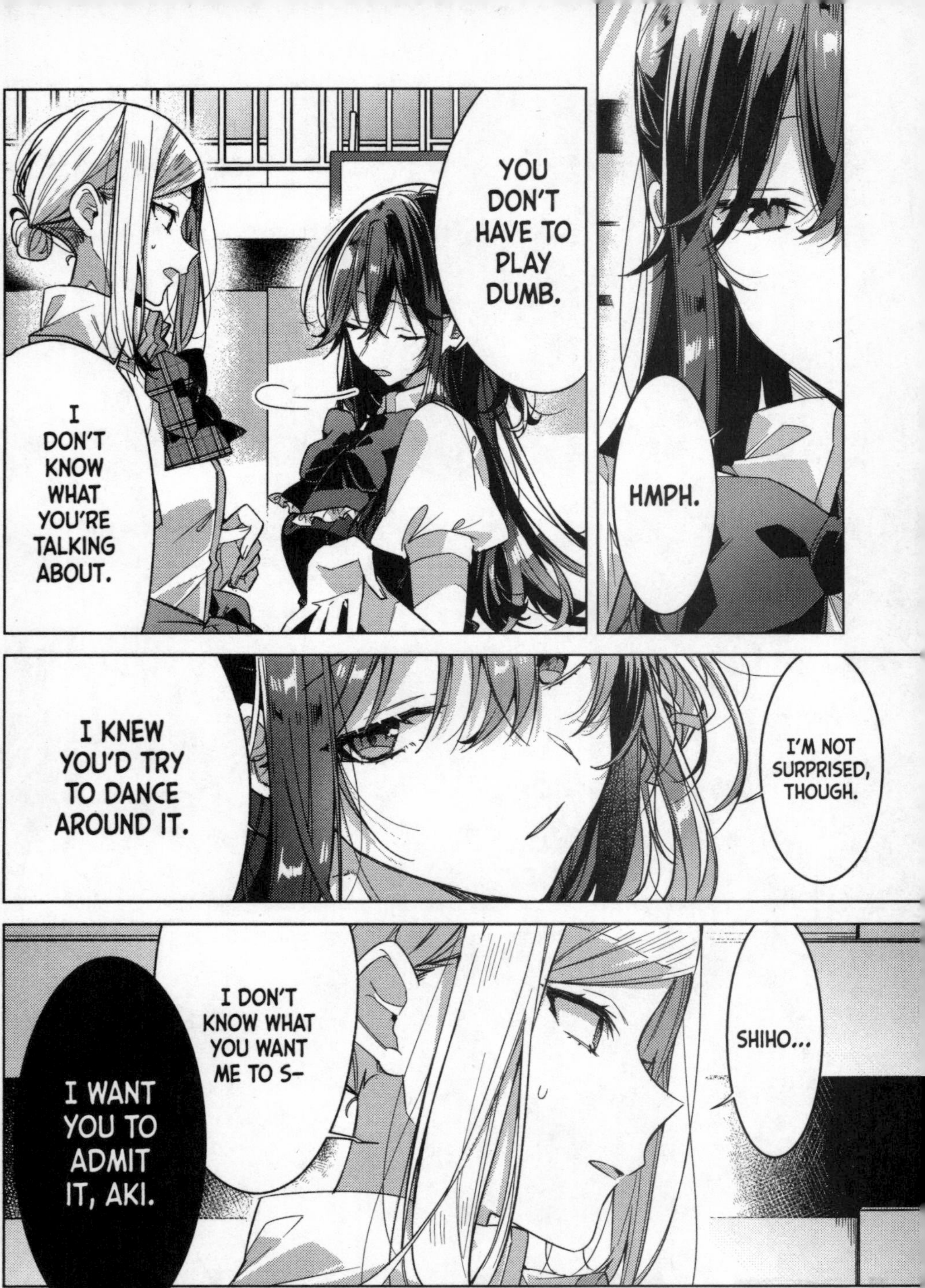
HMPH.
YOU DON'T HAVE TO PLAY DUMB.
I DON'T KNOW WHAT YOU'RE TALKING ABOUT.
I'M NOT SURPRISED, THOUGH.
I KNEW YOU'D TRY TO DANCE AROUND IT.
SHIHO...
I DON'T KNOW WHAT YOU WANT ME TO S–
I WANT YOU TO ADMIT IT, AKI.

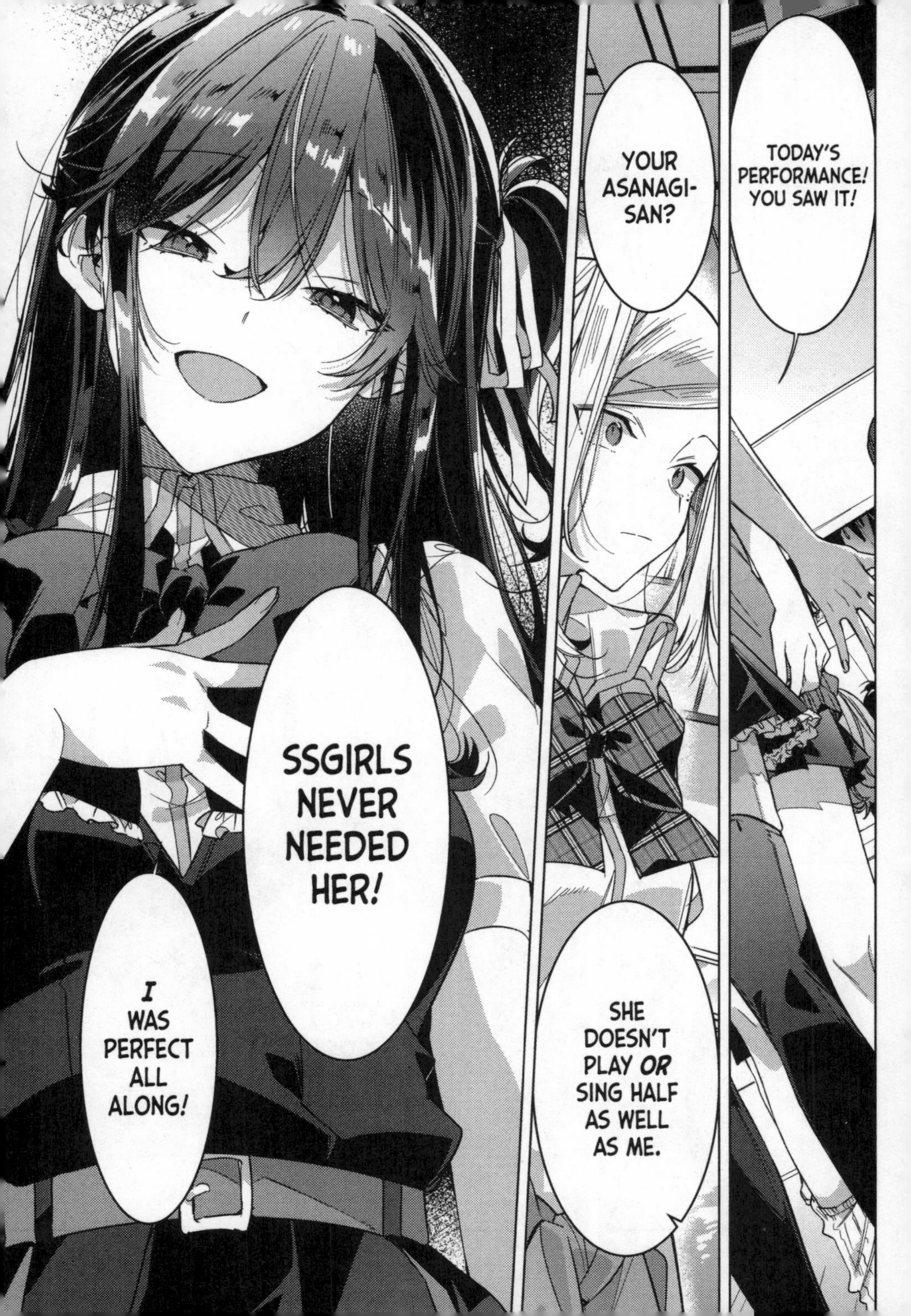
TODAY'S PERFORMANCE! YOU SAW IT!
YOUR ASANAGI-SAN?
SHE DOESN'T PLAY *OR* SING HALF AS WELL AS ME.
SSGIRLS NEVER NEEDED HER!
I WAS PERFECT ALL ALONG!

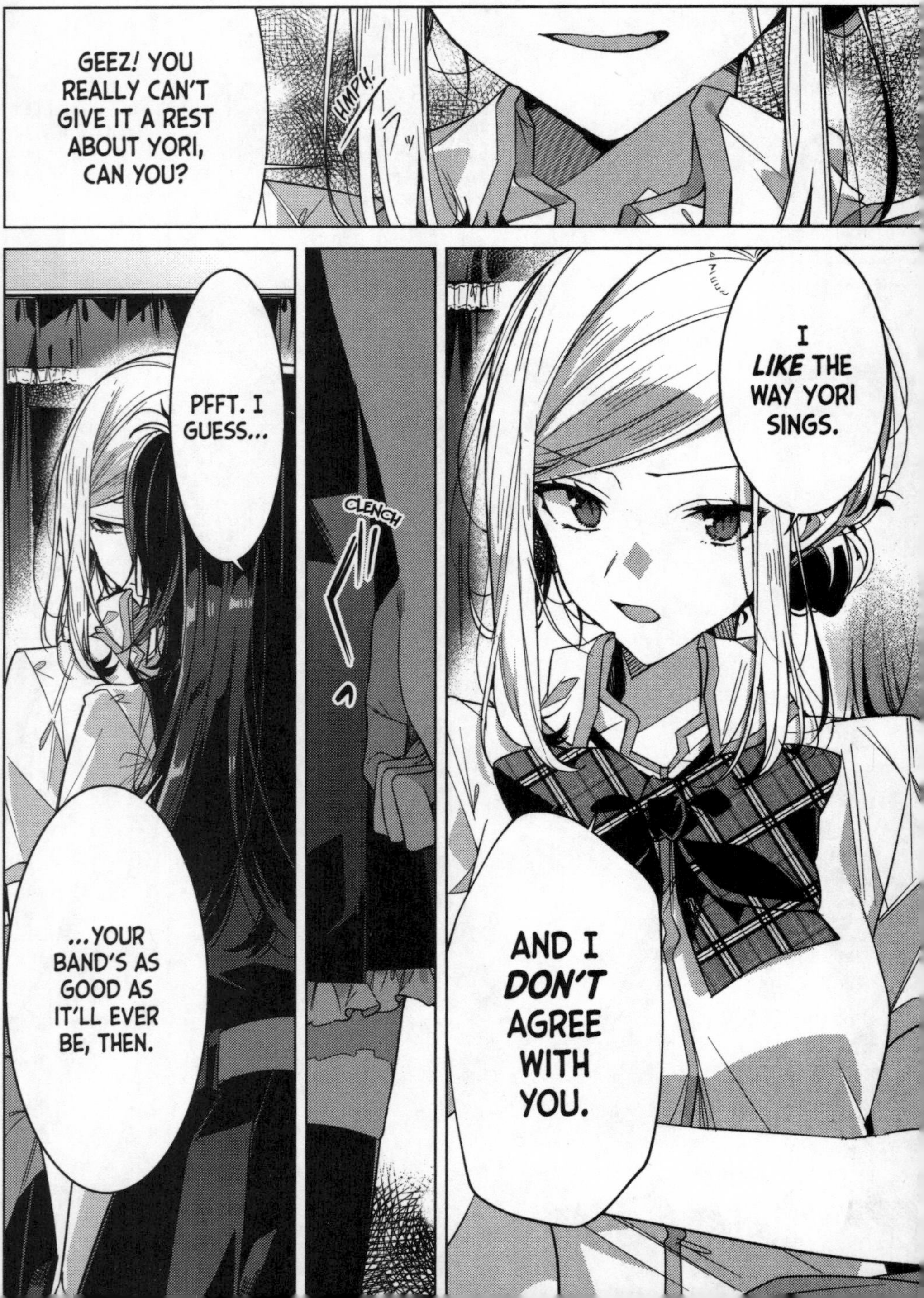
GEEZ! YOU REALLY CAN'T GIVE IT A REST ABOUT YORI, CAN YOU?
HMPH!
I *LIKE* THE WAY YORI SINGS.
AND I *DON'T* AGREE WITH YOU.
CLENCH
PFFT. I GUESS...
...YOUR BAND'S AS GOOD AS IT'LL EVER BE, THEN.

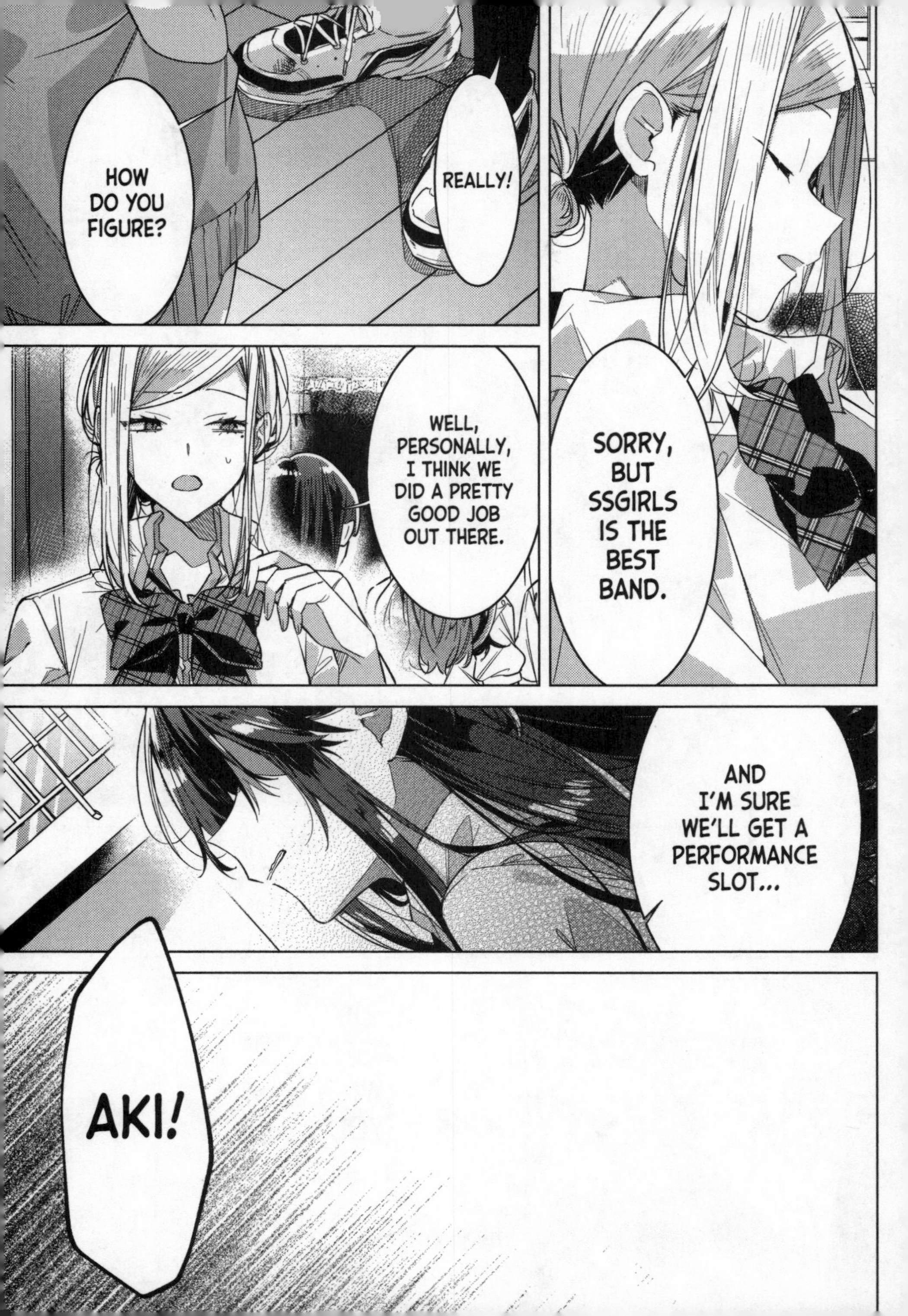
SORRY, BUT SSGIRLS IS THE BEST BAND.
REALLY!
HOW DO YOU FIGURE?
WELL, PERSONALLY, I THINK WE DID A PRETTY GOOD JOB OUT THERE.
AND I'M SURE WE'LL GET A PERFORMANCE SLOT...
AKI!

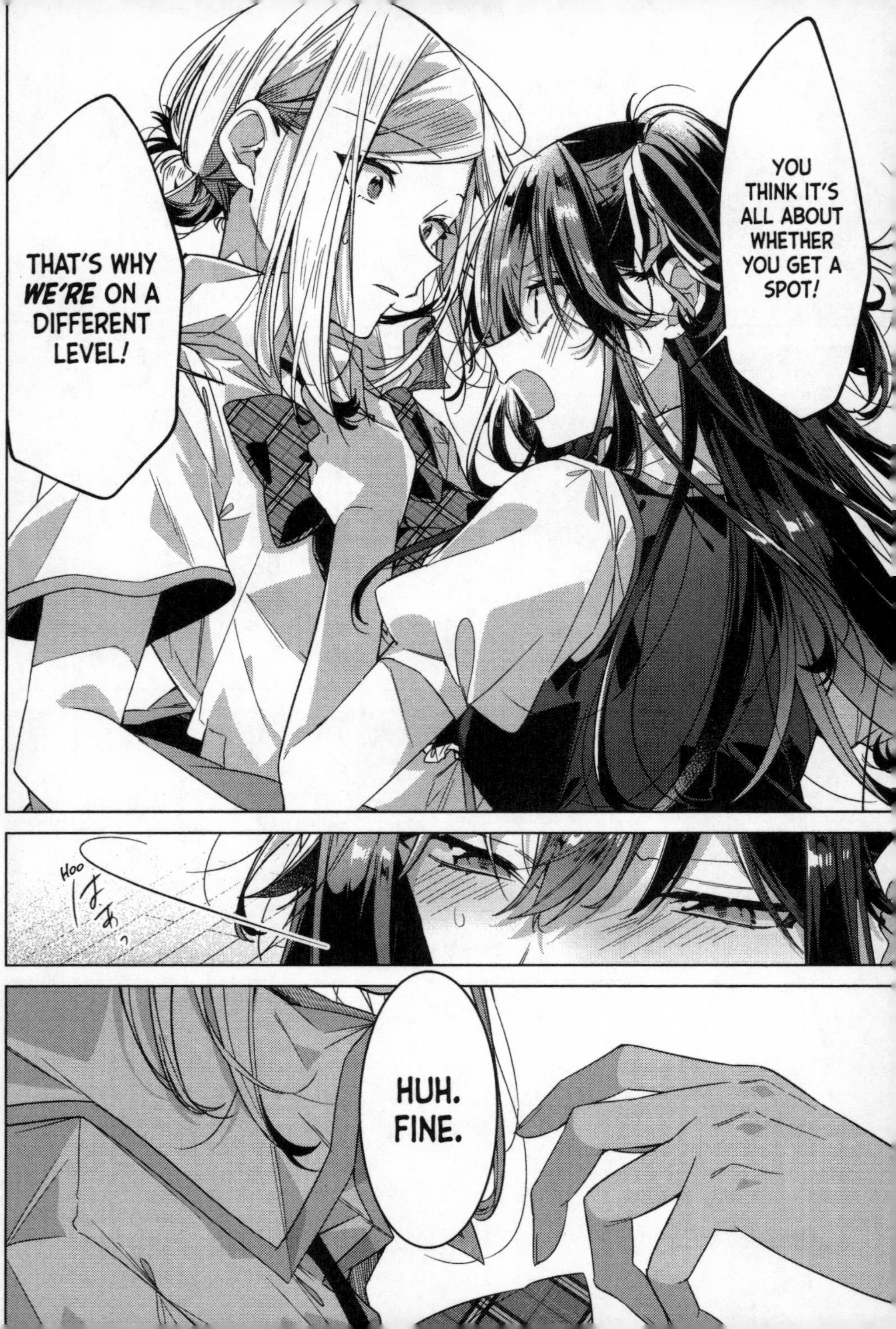
YOU THINK IT'S ALL ABOUT WHETHER YOU GET A SPOT!
THAT'S WHY *WE'RE* ON A DIFFERENT LEVEL!
Hoo
はぁっ
HUH. FINE.

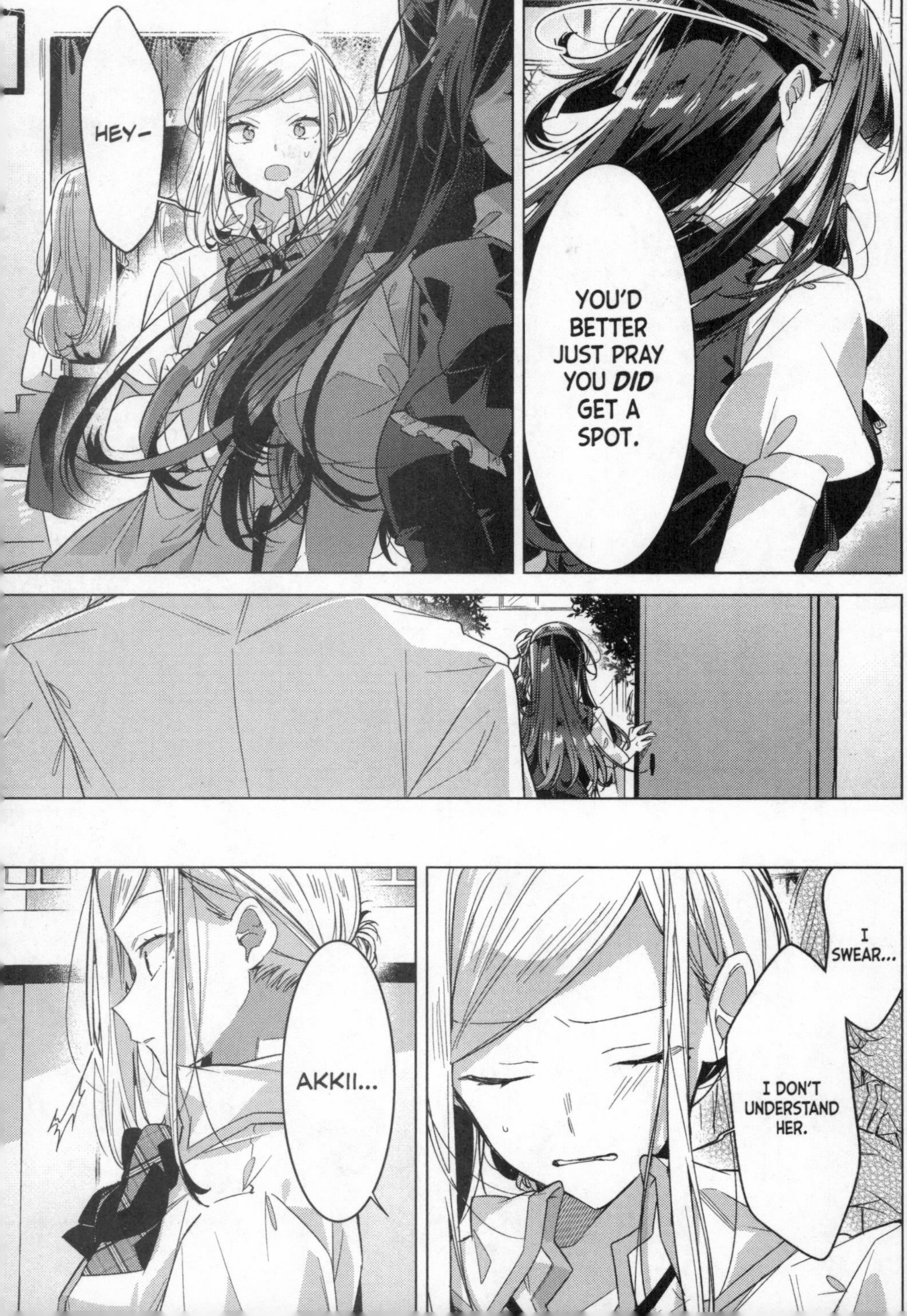
YOU'D BETTER JUST PRAY YOU *DID* GET A SPOT.
HEY–
I SWEAR...
I DON'T UNDERSTAND HER.
AKKII...

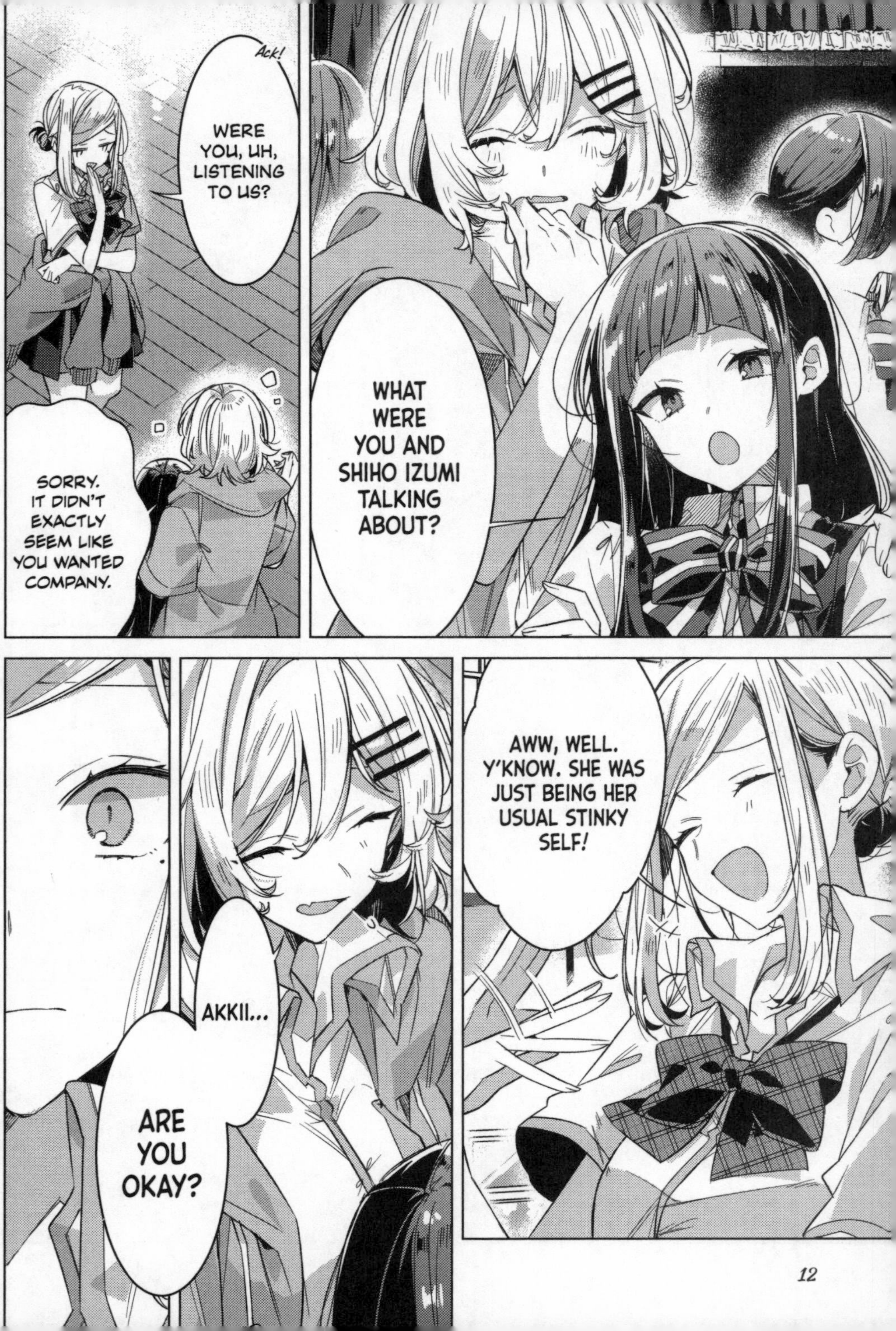
WHAT WERE YOU AND SHIHO IZUMI TALKING ABOUT?
Ack!
WERE YOU, UH, LISTENING TO US?
SORRY. IT DIDN'T EXACTLY SEEM LIKE YOU WANTED COMPANY.
AWW, WELL. Y'KNOW. SHE WAS JUST BEING HER USUAL STINKY SELF!
AKKII...
ARE YOU OKAY?

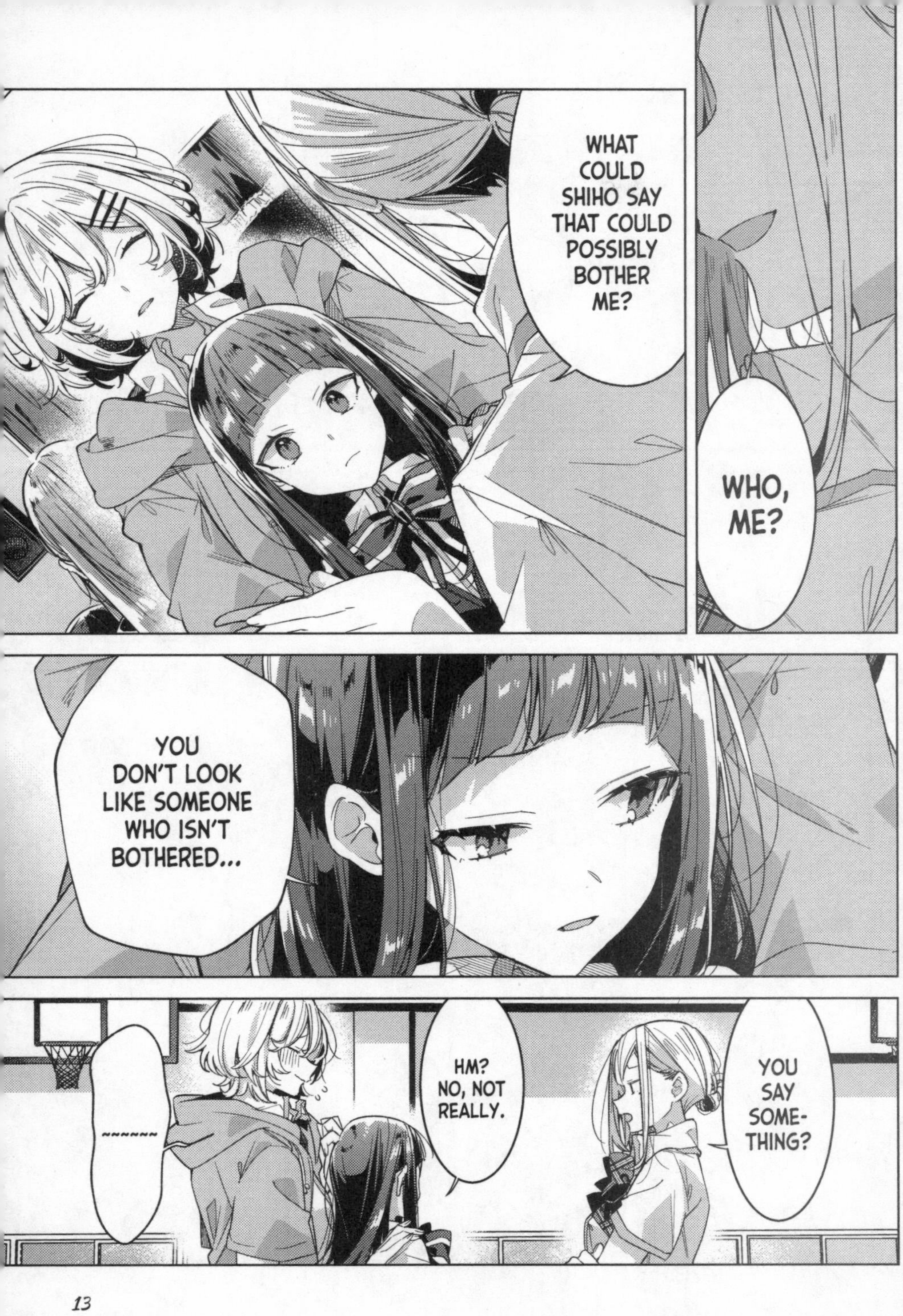
WHO, ME?
WHAT COULD SHIHO SAY THAT COULD POSSIBLY BOTHER ME?
YOU DON'T LOOK LIKE SOMEONE WHO ISN'T BOTHERED...
YOU SAY SOME-THING?
HM? NO, NOT REALLY.
~~~~~~
~~~~~~

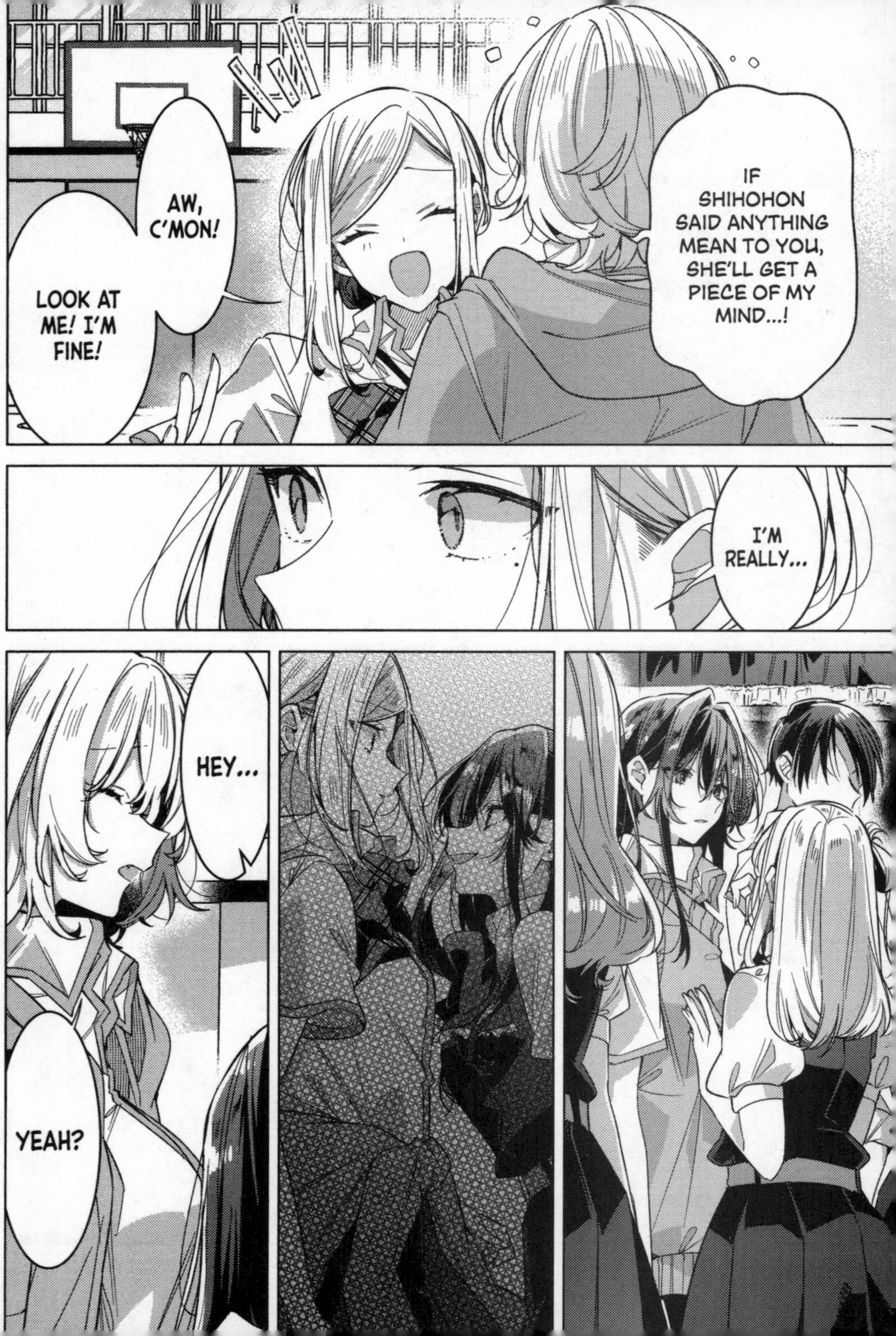
IF SHIHOHON SAID ANYTHING MEAN TO YOU, SHE'LL GET A PIECE OF MY MIND...!
AW, C'MON!
LOOK AT ME! I'M FINE!
I'M REALLY...
HEY...
YEAH?

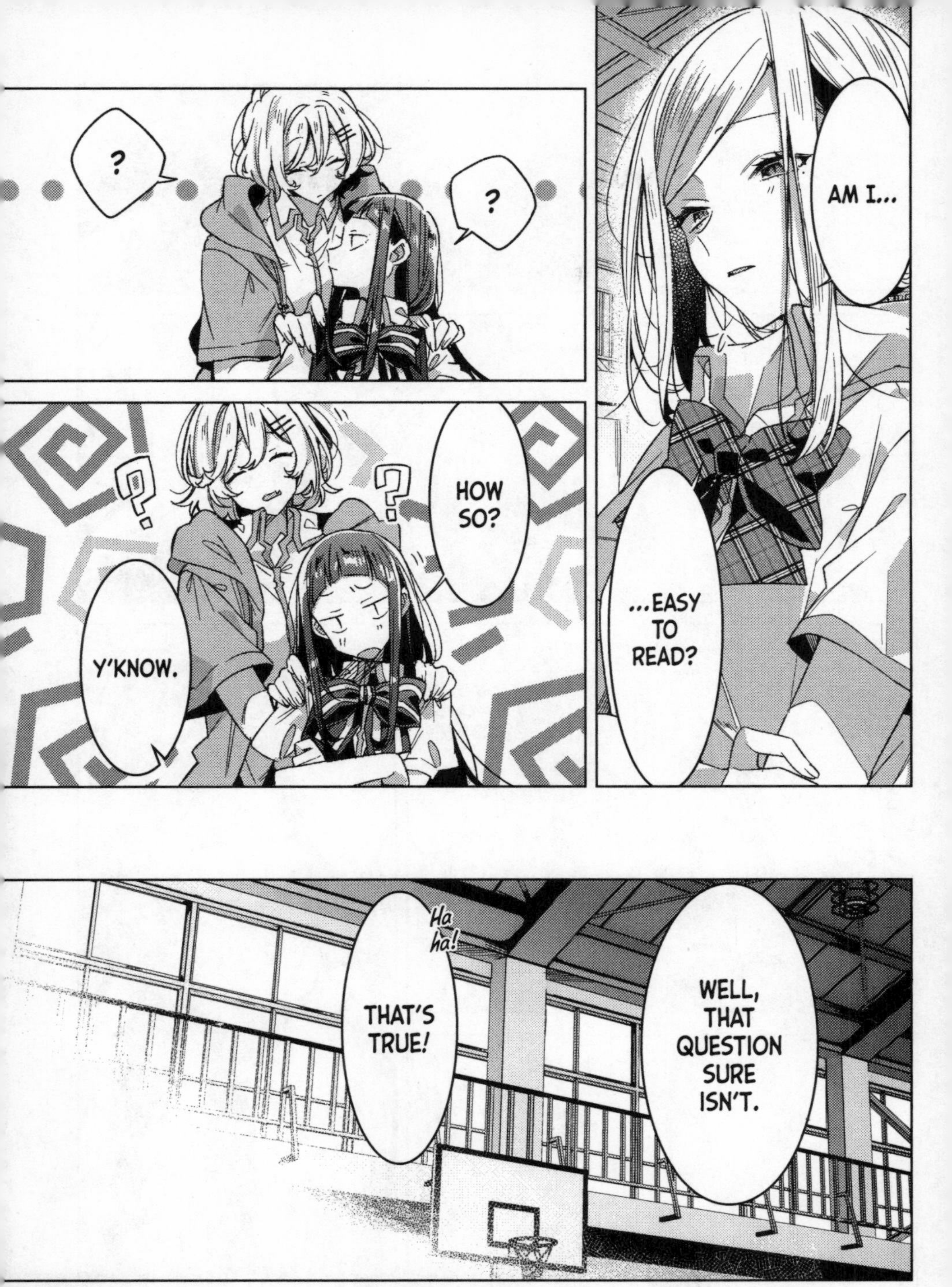
AM I...
...EASY TO READ?
?
?
HOW SO?
Y'KNOW.
WELL, THAT QUESTION SURE ISN'T.
Ha ha!
THAT'S TRUE!

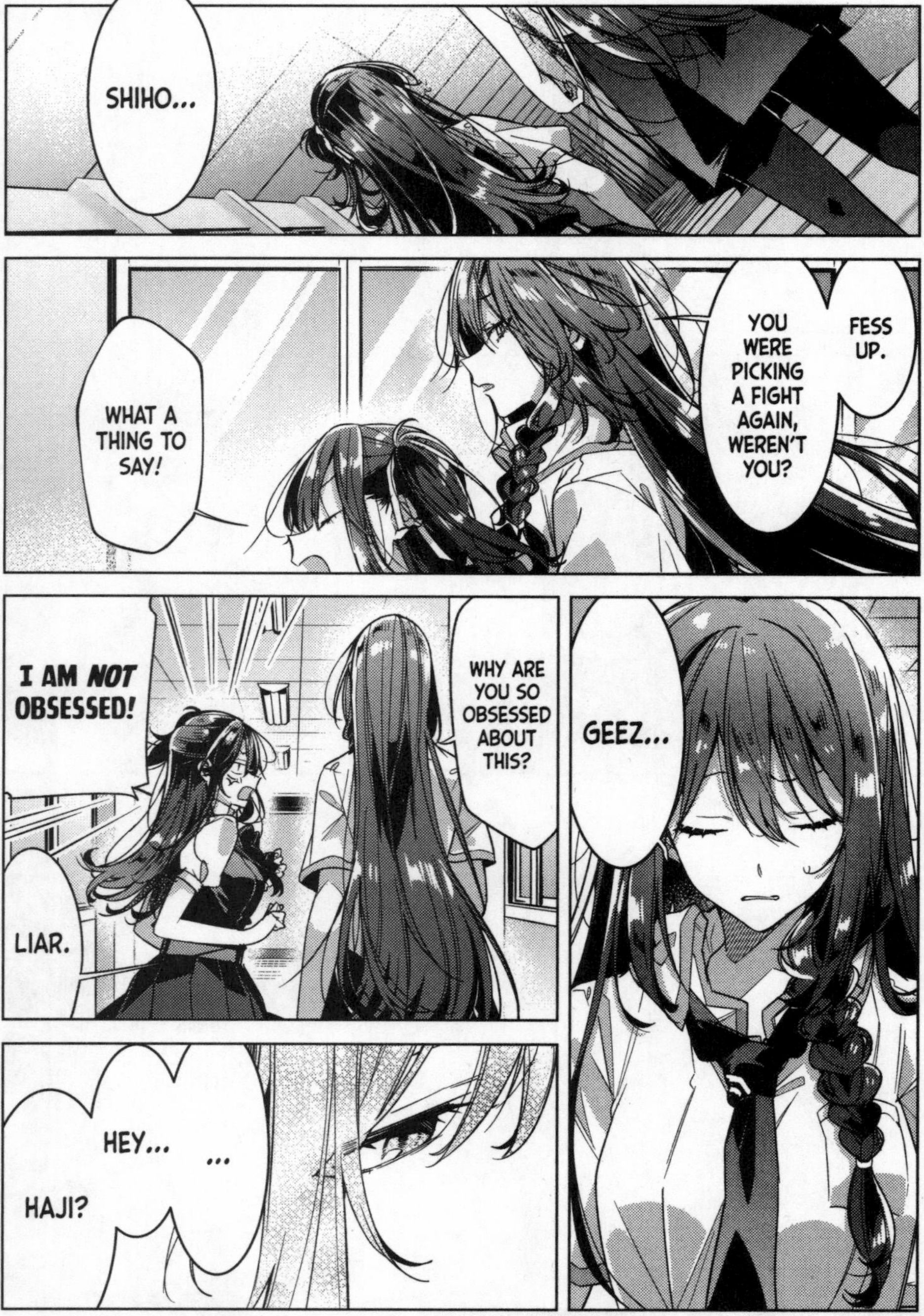
SHIHO...
FESS UP.
YOU WERE PICKING A FIGHT AGAIN, WEREN'T YOU?
WHAT A THING TO SAY!
GEEZ...
WHY ARE YOU SO OBSESSED ABOUT THIS?
I AM ***NOT*** OBSESSED!
LIAR.
HEY... ... HAJI?

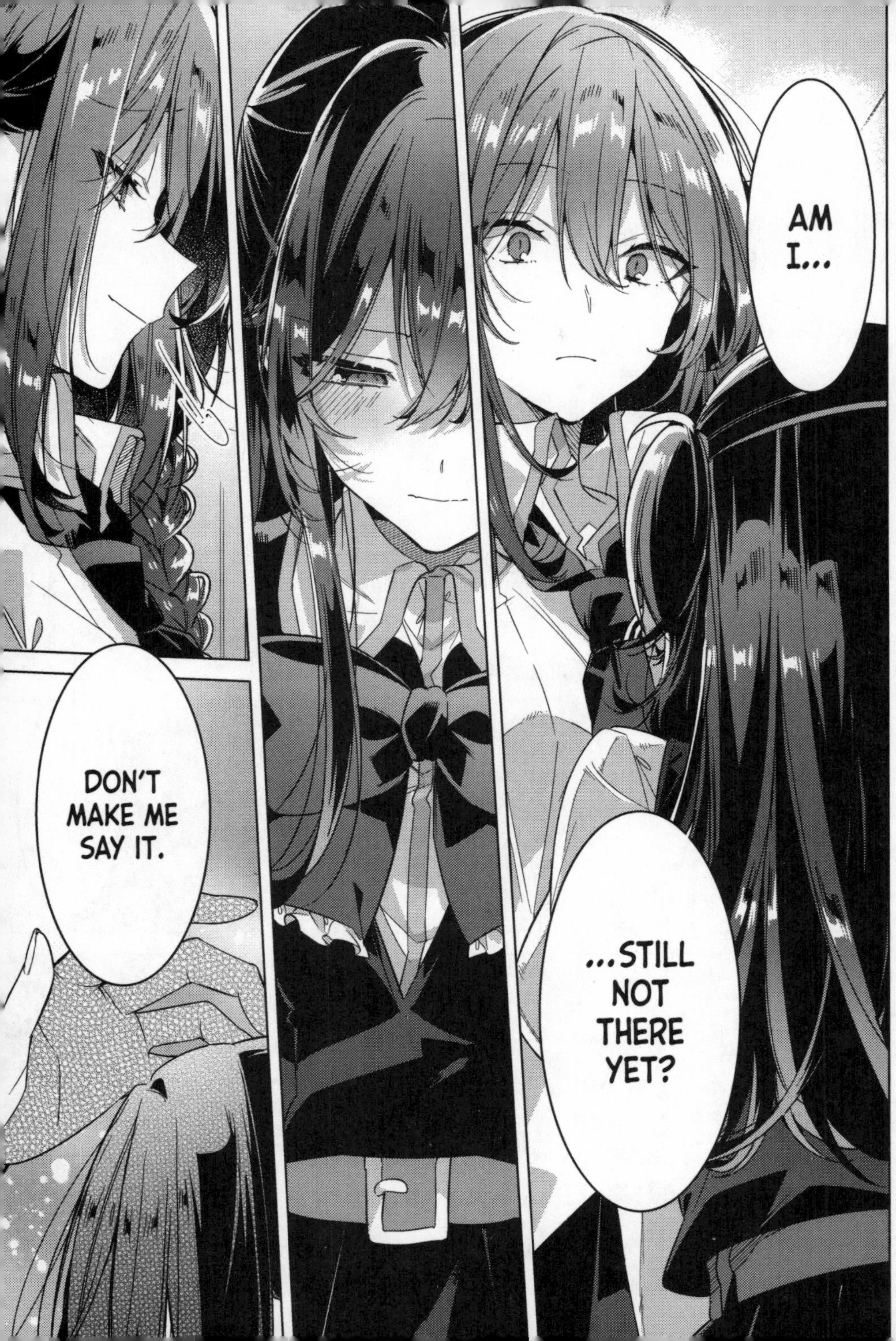
AM I...
...STILL NOT THERE YET?
DON'T MAKE ME SAY IT.

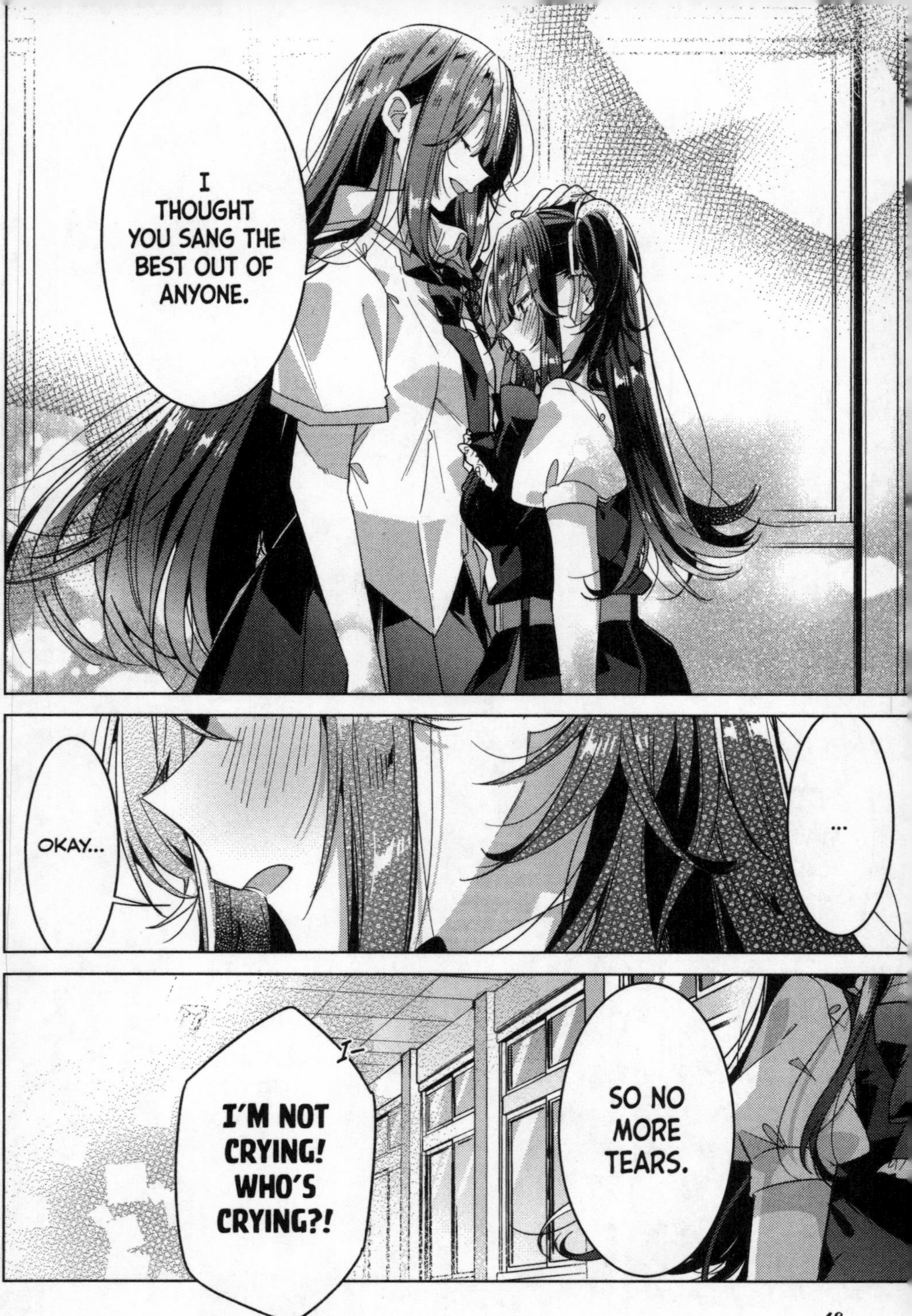
I THOUGHT YOU SANG THE BEST OUT OF ANYONE.
...
OKAY...
SO NO MORE TEARS.
I—
I'M NOT CRYING! WHO'S CRYING?!

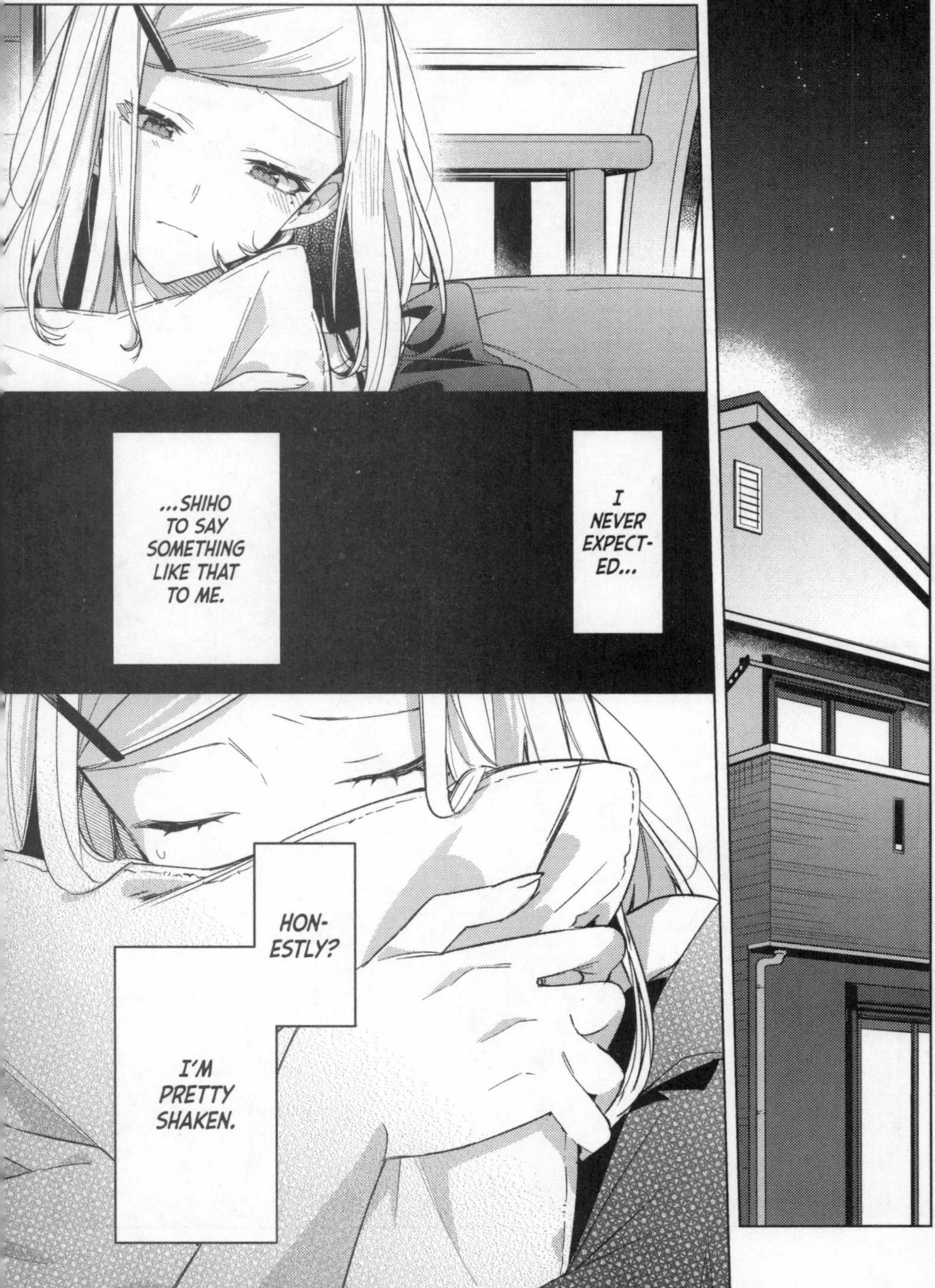
I NEVER EXPECTED...
...SHIHO TO SAY SOMETHING LIKE THAT TO ME.
HONESTLY?
I'M PRETTY SHAKEN.

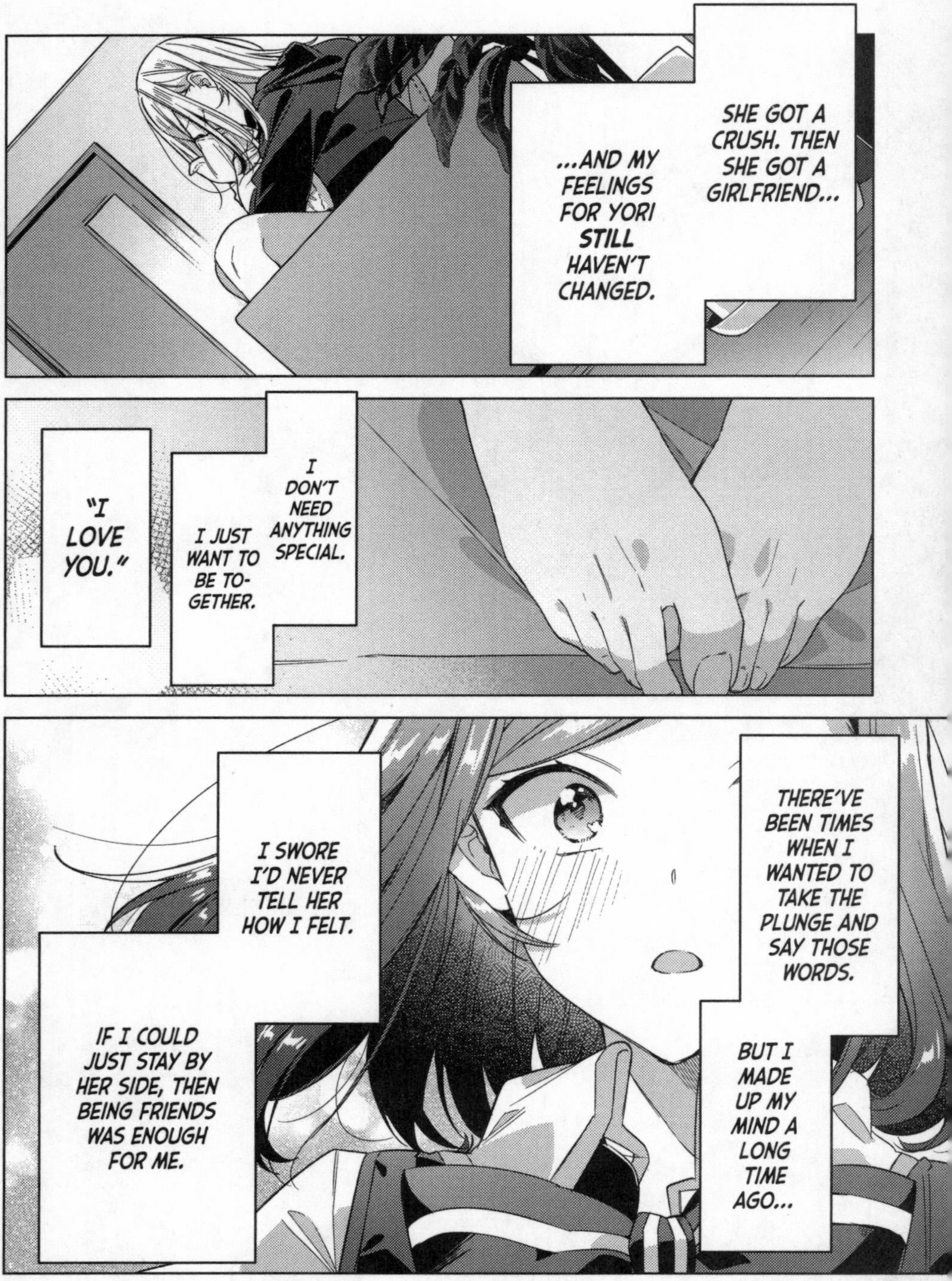
SHE GOT A CRUSH. THEN SHE GOT A GIRLFRIEND...
...AND MY FEELINGS FOR YORI STILL HAVEN'T CHANGED.
I DON'T NEED ANYTHING SPECIAL.
I JUST WANT TO BE TO-GETHER.
"I LOVE YOU."
THERE'VE BEEN TIMES WHEN I WANTED TO TAKE THE PLUNGE AND SAY THOSE WORDS.
BUT I MADE UP MY MIND A LONG TIME AGO...
I SWORE I'D NEVER TELL HER HOW I FELT.
IF I COULD JUST STAY BY HER SIDE, THEN BEING FRIENDS WAS ENOUGH FOR ME.

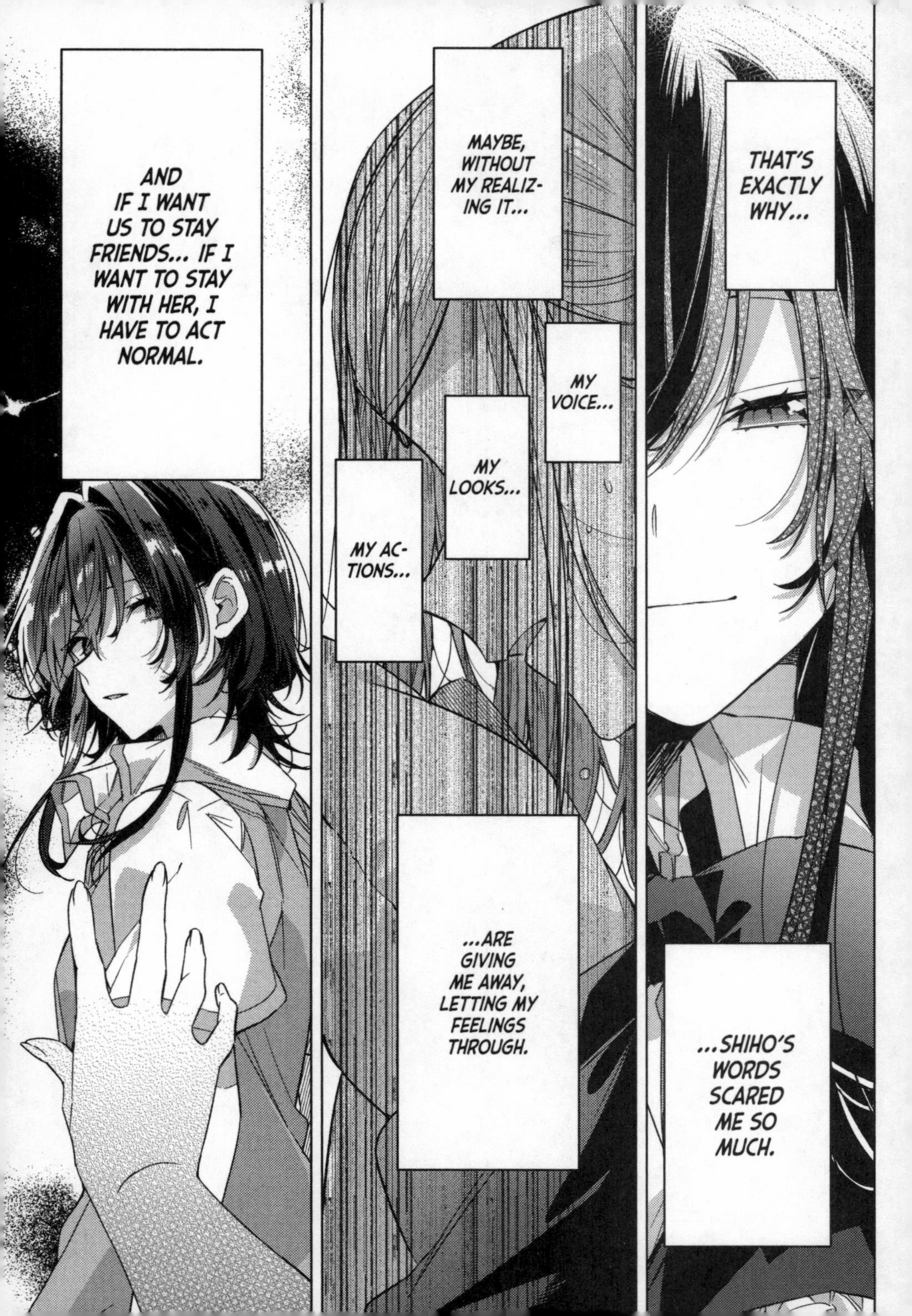
THAT'S EXACTLY WHY...
...SHIHO'S WORDS SCARED ME SO MUCH.
MAYBE, WITHOUT MY REALIZ-ING IT...
MY VOICE...
MY LOOKS...
MY AC-TIONS...
...ARE GIVING ME AWAY, LETTING MY FEELINGS THROUGH.
AND IF I WANT US TO STAY FRIENDS... IF I WANT TO STAY WITH HER, I HAVE TO ACT NORMAL.

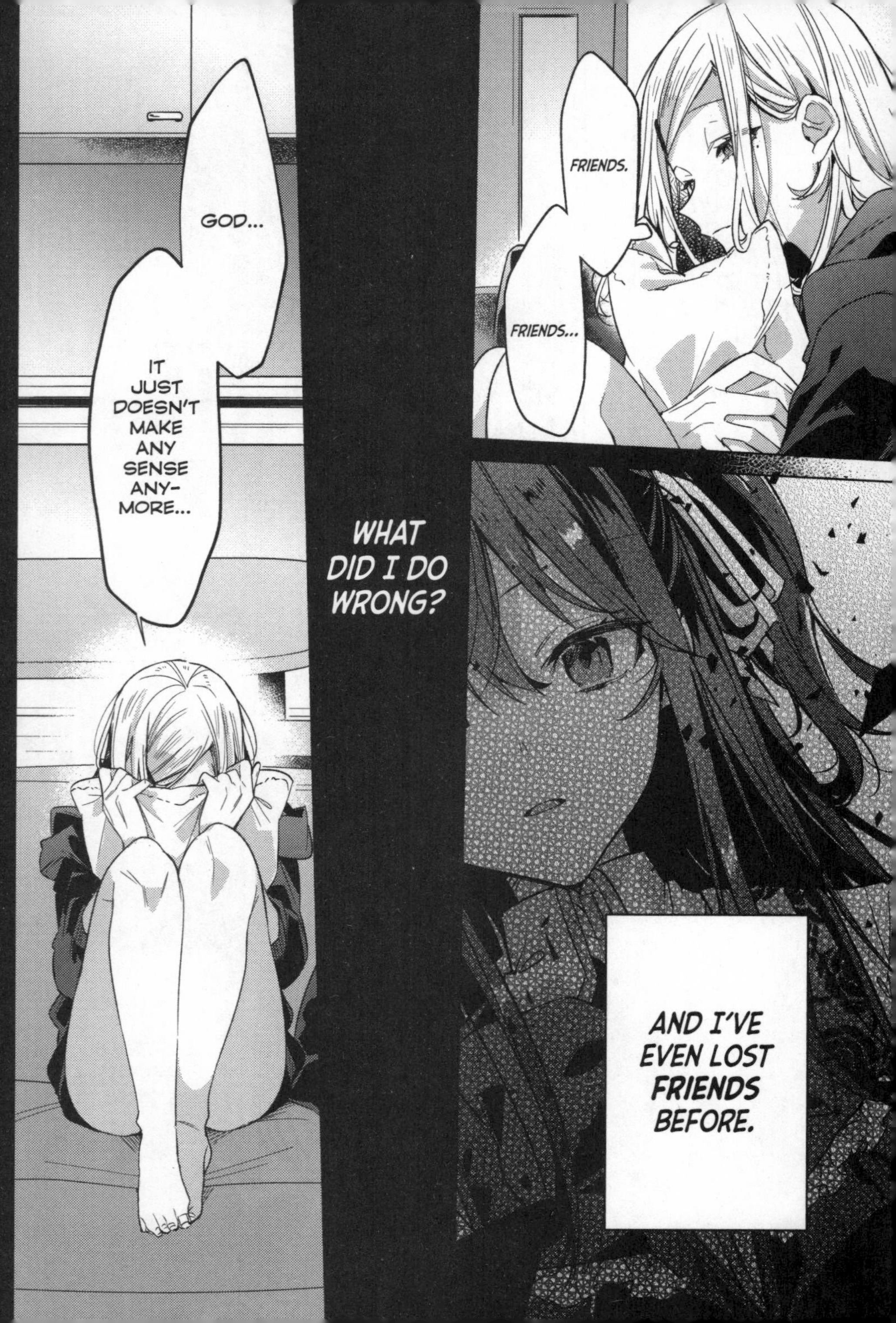
FRIENDS.
FRIENDS...
AND I'VE EVEN LOST FRIENDS BEFORE.
WHAT DID I DO WRONG?
GOD...
IT JUST DOESN'T MAKE ANY SENSE ANY-MORE...

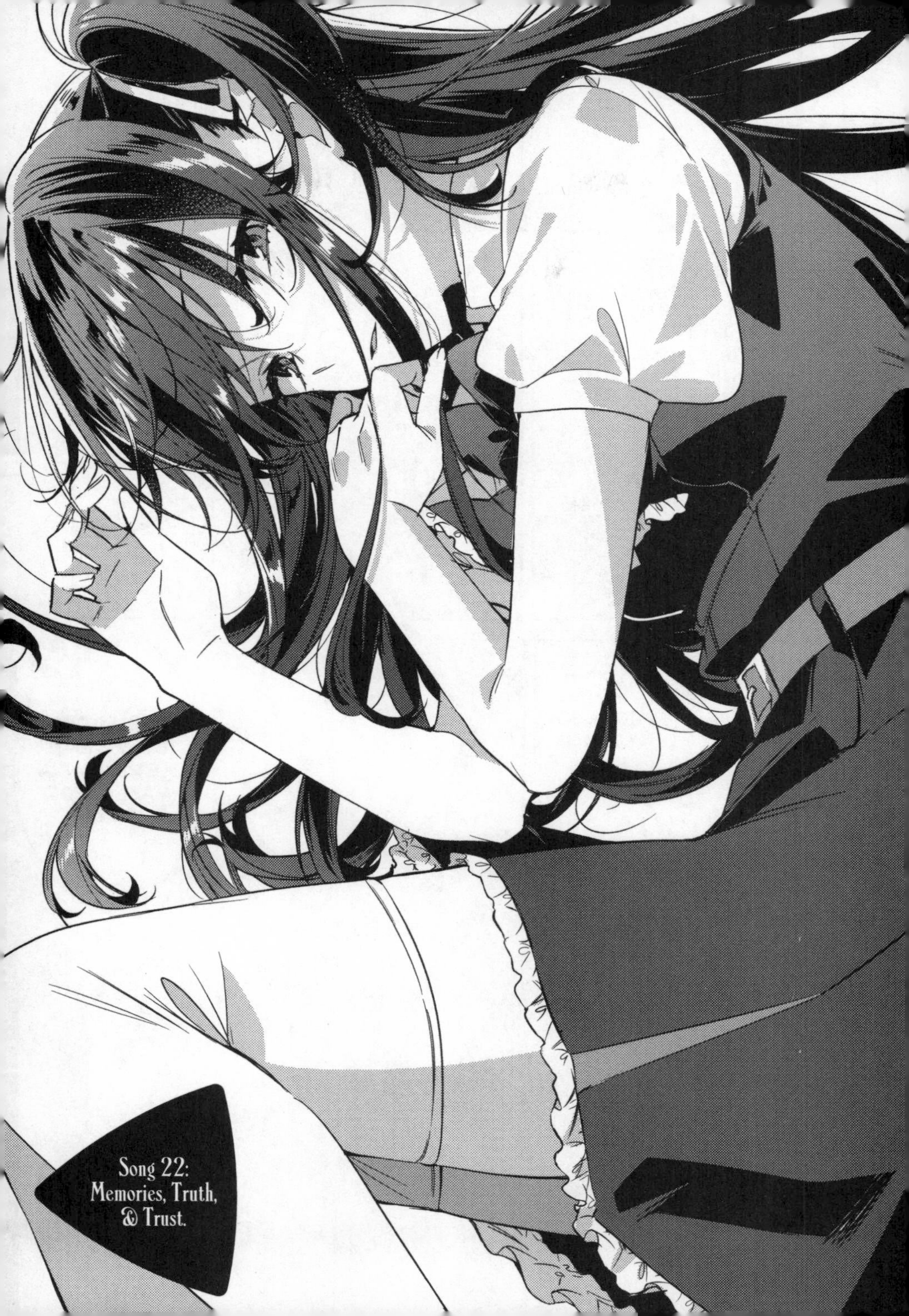
Song 22:
Memories, Truth,
& Trust.

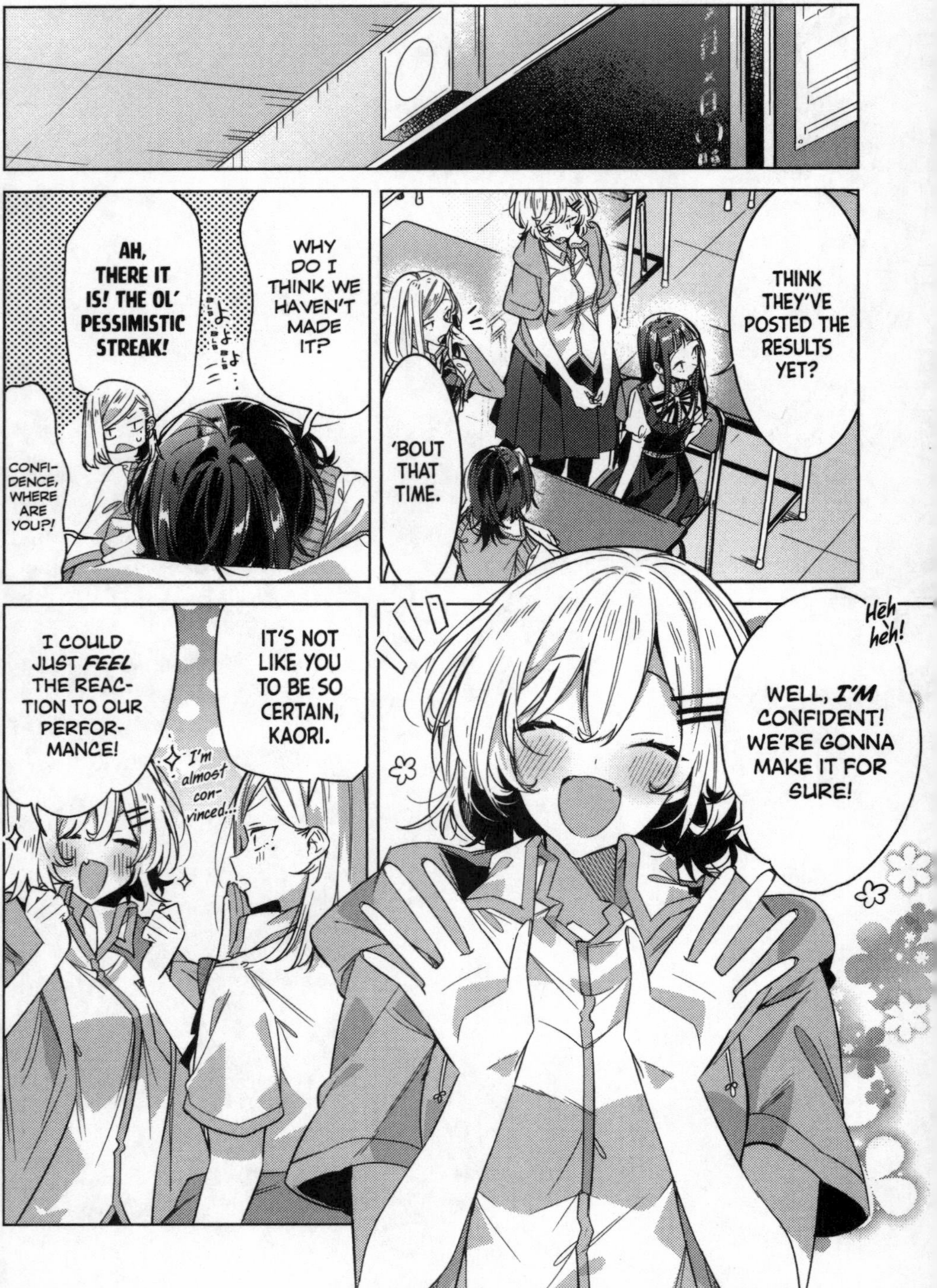
THINK THEY'VE POSTED THE RESULTS YET?
'BOUT THAT TIME.
WHY DO I THINK WE HAVEN'T MADE IT?
AH, THERE IT IS! THE OL' PESSIMISTIC STREAK!
CONFIDENCE, WHERE ARE YOU?!
Hēh hēh!
WELL, *I'M* CONFIDENT! WE'RE GONNA MAKE IT FOR SURE!
IT'S NOT LIKE YOU TO BE SO CERTAIN, KAORI.
I COULD JUST *FEEL* THE REACTION TO OUR PERFORMANCE!
I'm almost convinced...

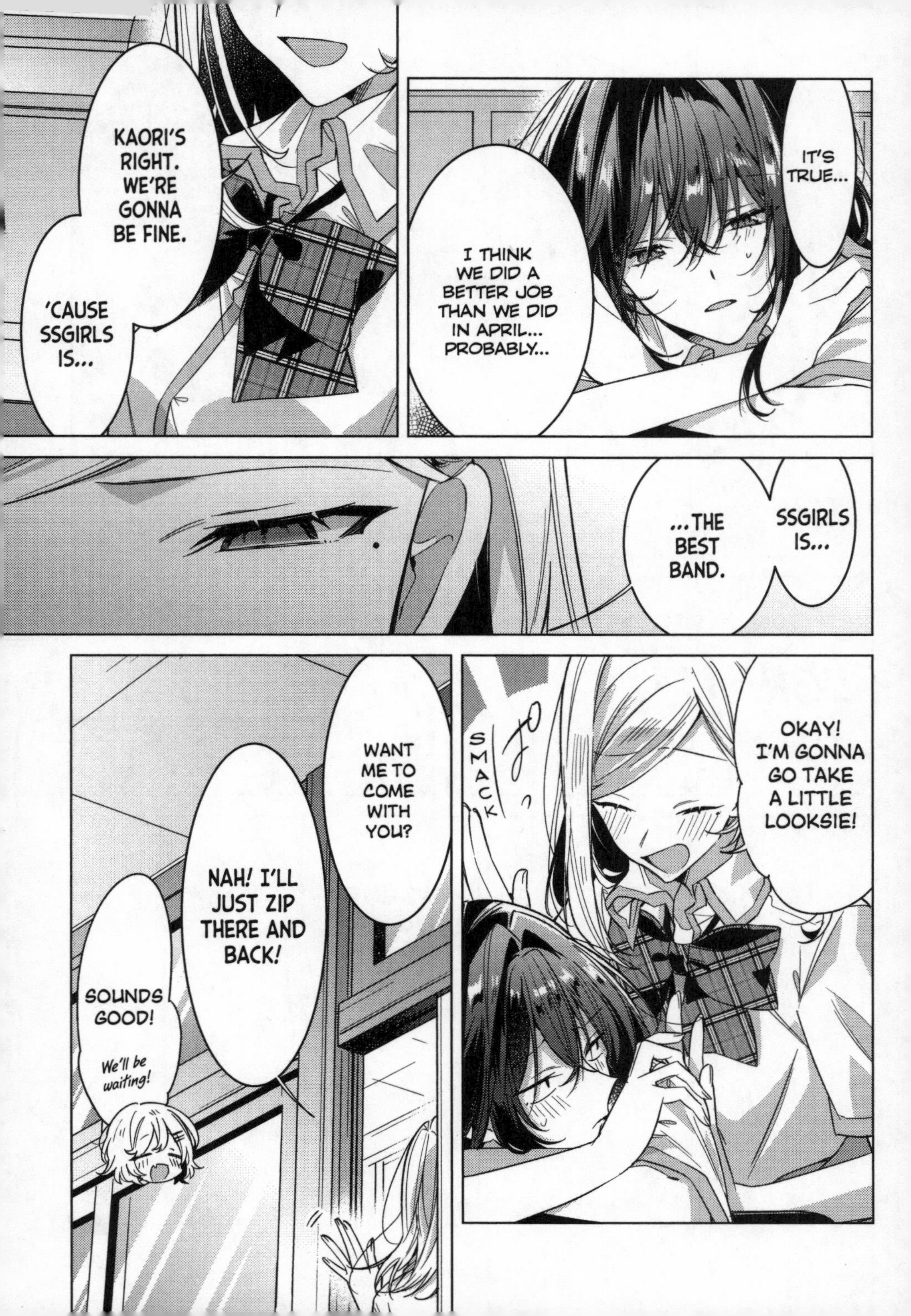
IT'S TRUE...
I THINK WE DID A BETTER JOB THAN WE DID IN APRIL... PROBABLY...
KAORI'S RIGHT. WE'RE GONNA BE FINE.
'CAUSE SSGIRLS IS...
SSGIRLS IS...
...THE BEST BAND.
OKAY! I'M GONNA GO TAKE A LITTLE LOOKSIE!
SMACK
WANT ME TO COME WITH YOU?
NAH! I'LL JUST ZIP THERE AND BACK!
SOUNDS GOOD!
We'll be waiting!

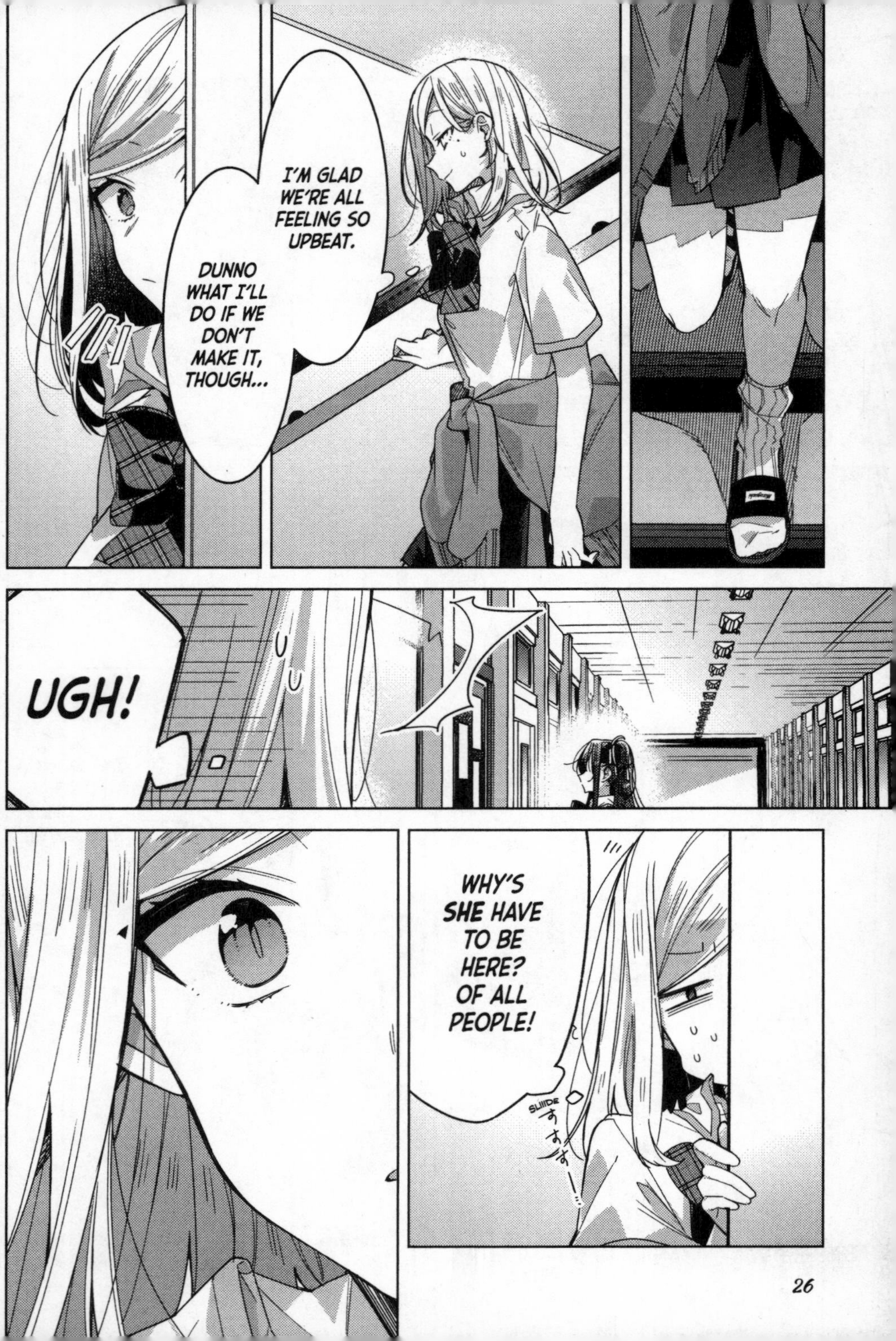
I'M GLAD WE'RE ALL FEELING SO UPBEAT.
DUNNO WHAT I'LL DO IF WE DON'T MAKE IT, THOUGH...
UGH!
WHY'S SHE HAVE TO BE HERE? OF ALL PEOPLE!
SLIIDE

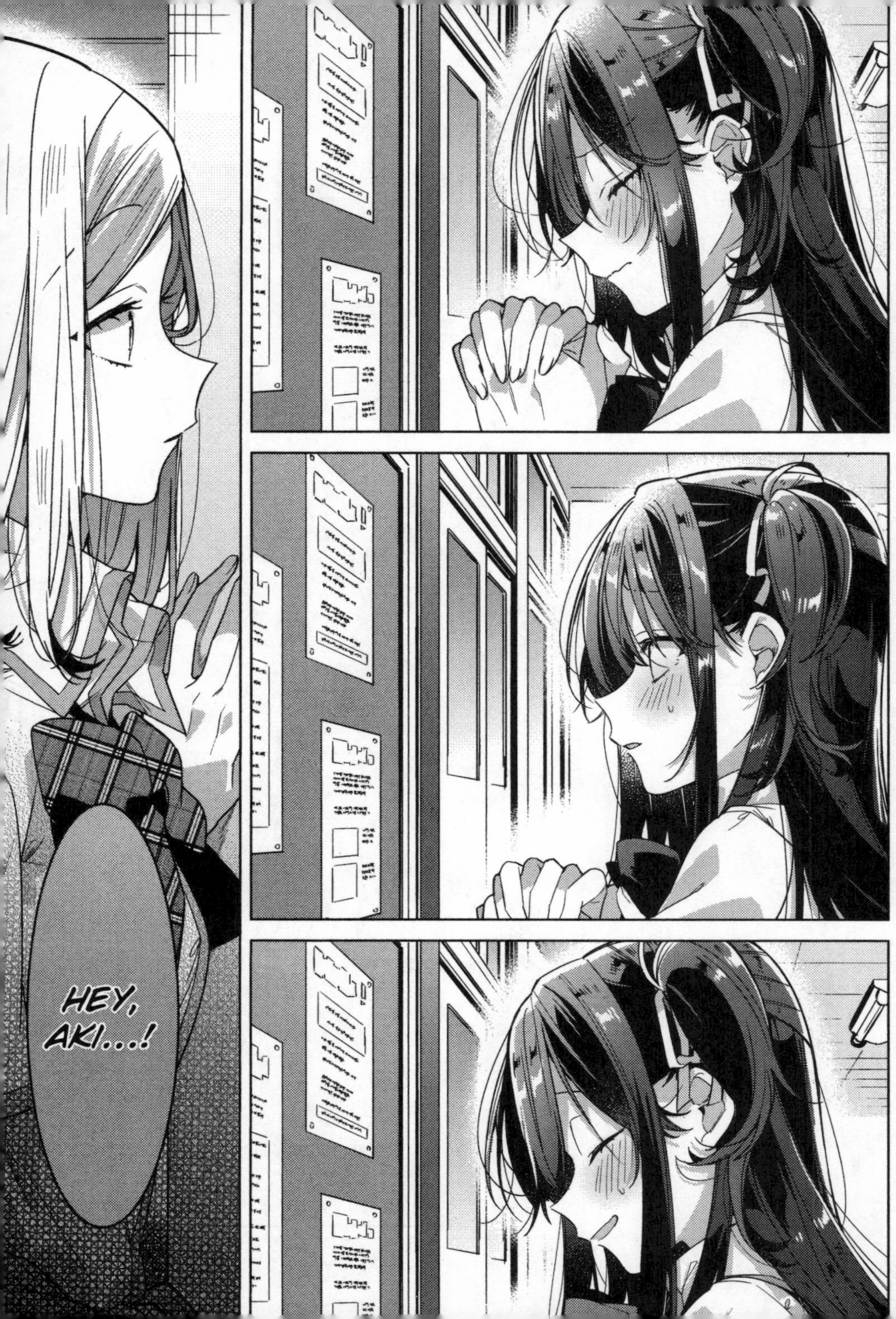
HEY, AKI...!

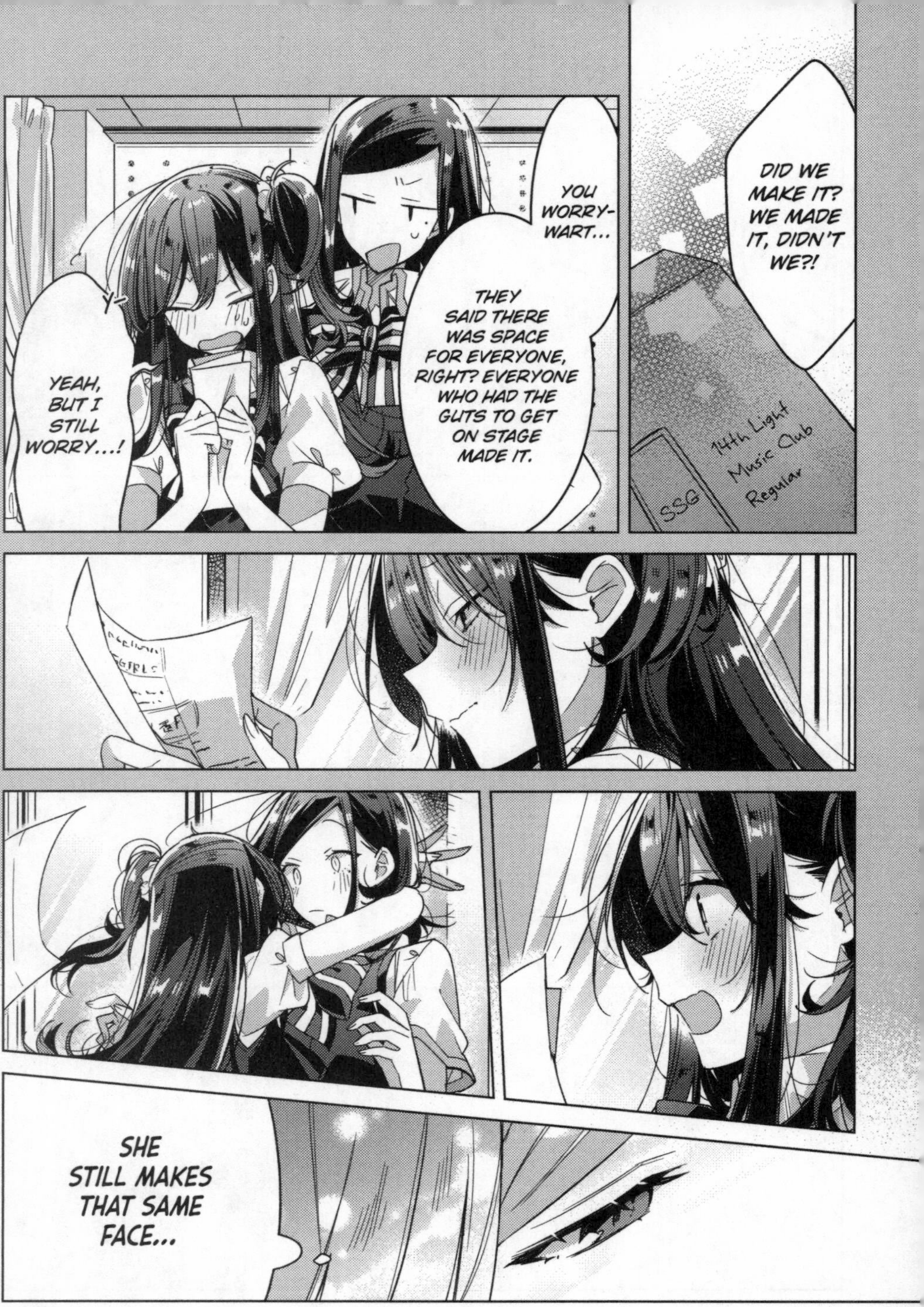
DID WE MAKE IT? WE MADE IT, DIDN'T WE?!
SSG
14th Light Music Club Regular
YOU WORRY-WART...
THEY SAID THERE WAS SPACE FOR EVERYONE, RIGHT? EVERYONE WHO HAD THE GUTS TO GET ON STAGE MADE IT.
Y—
YEAH, BUT I STILL WORRY...!
SHE STILL MAKES THAT SAME FACE...

BADUM
ドキ
BADUM
ドキ
SSGIRLS...
BADUM
ドキ

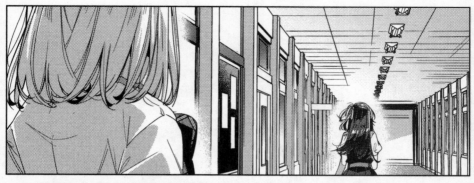

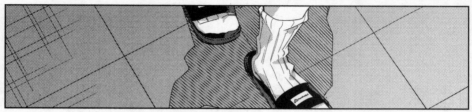

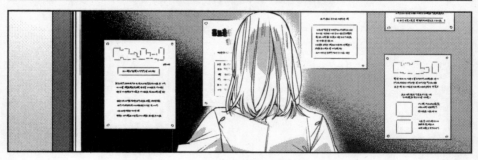

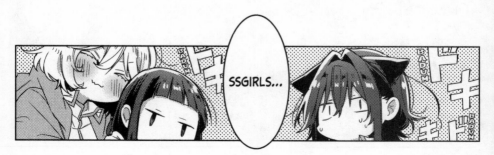

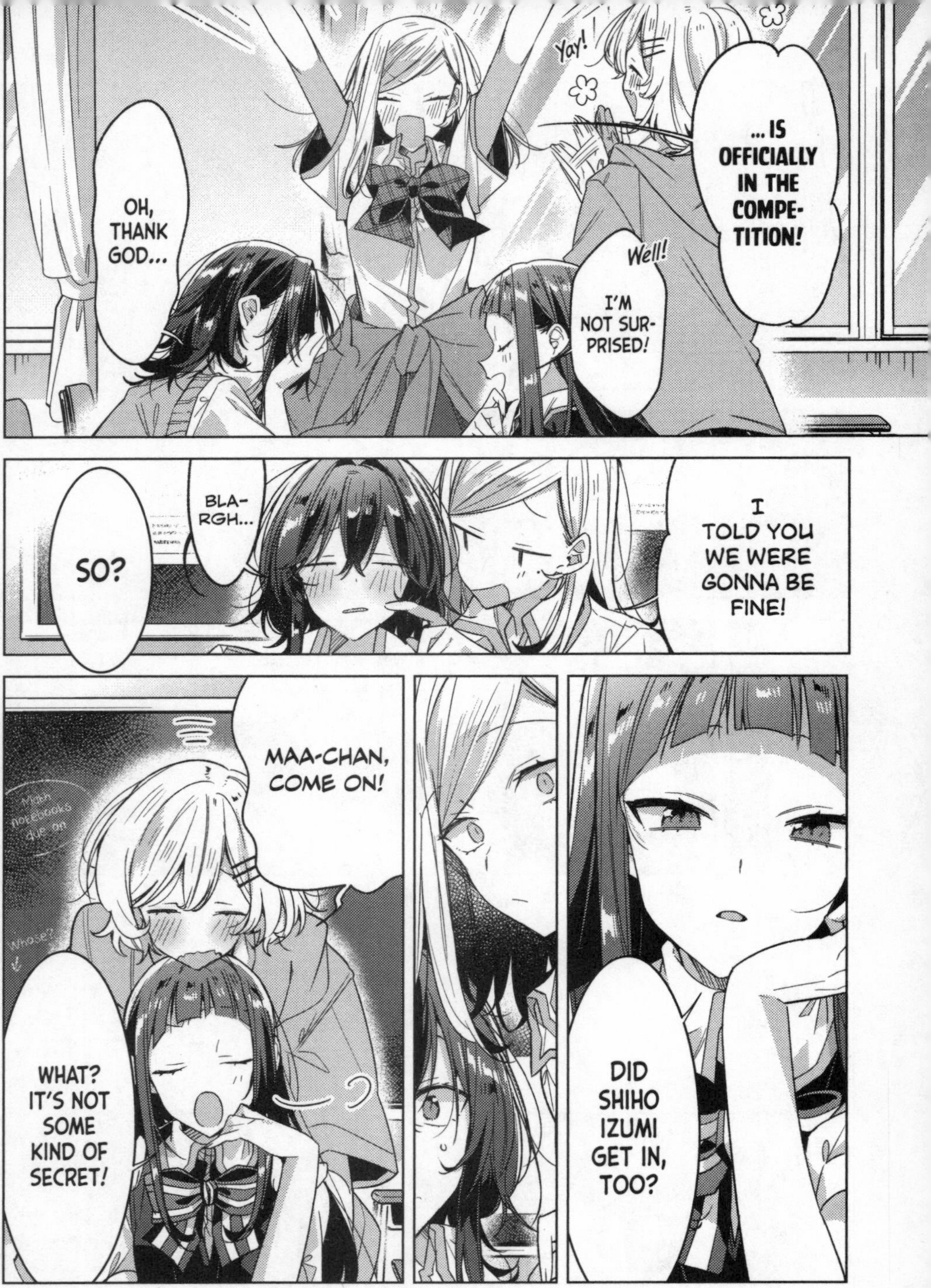
...IS OFFICIALLY IN THE COMPETITION!
Yay!
Well!
I'M NOT SURPRISED!
OH, THANK GOD...
I TOLD YOU WE WERE GONNA BE FINE!
BLA-RGH...
SO?
DID SHIHO IZUMI GET IN, TOO?
MAA-CHAN, COME ON!
WHAT? IT'S NOT SOME KIND OF SECRET!

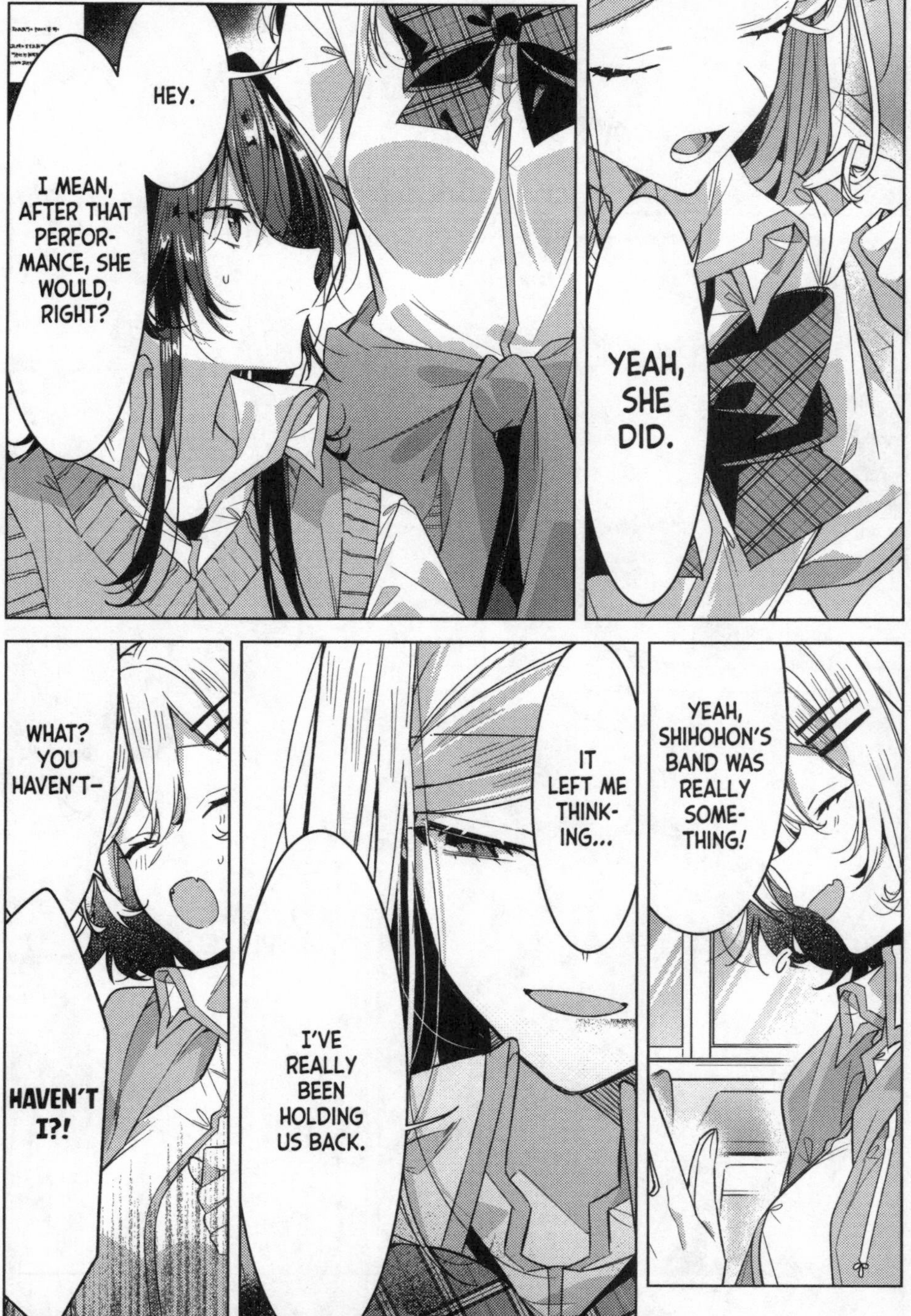
YEAH, SHE DID.
HEY.
I MEAN, AFTER THAT PERFORMANCE, SHE WOULD, RIGHT?
YEAH, SHIHOHON'S BAND WAS REALLY SOMETHING!
IT LEFT ME THINKING...
I'VE REALLY BEEN HOLDING US BACK.
WHAT? YOU HAVEN'T-
HAVEN'T I?!

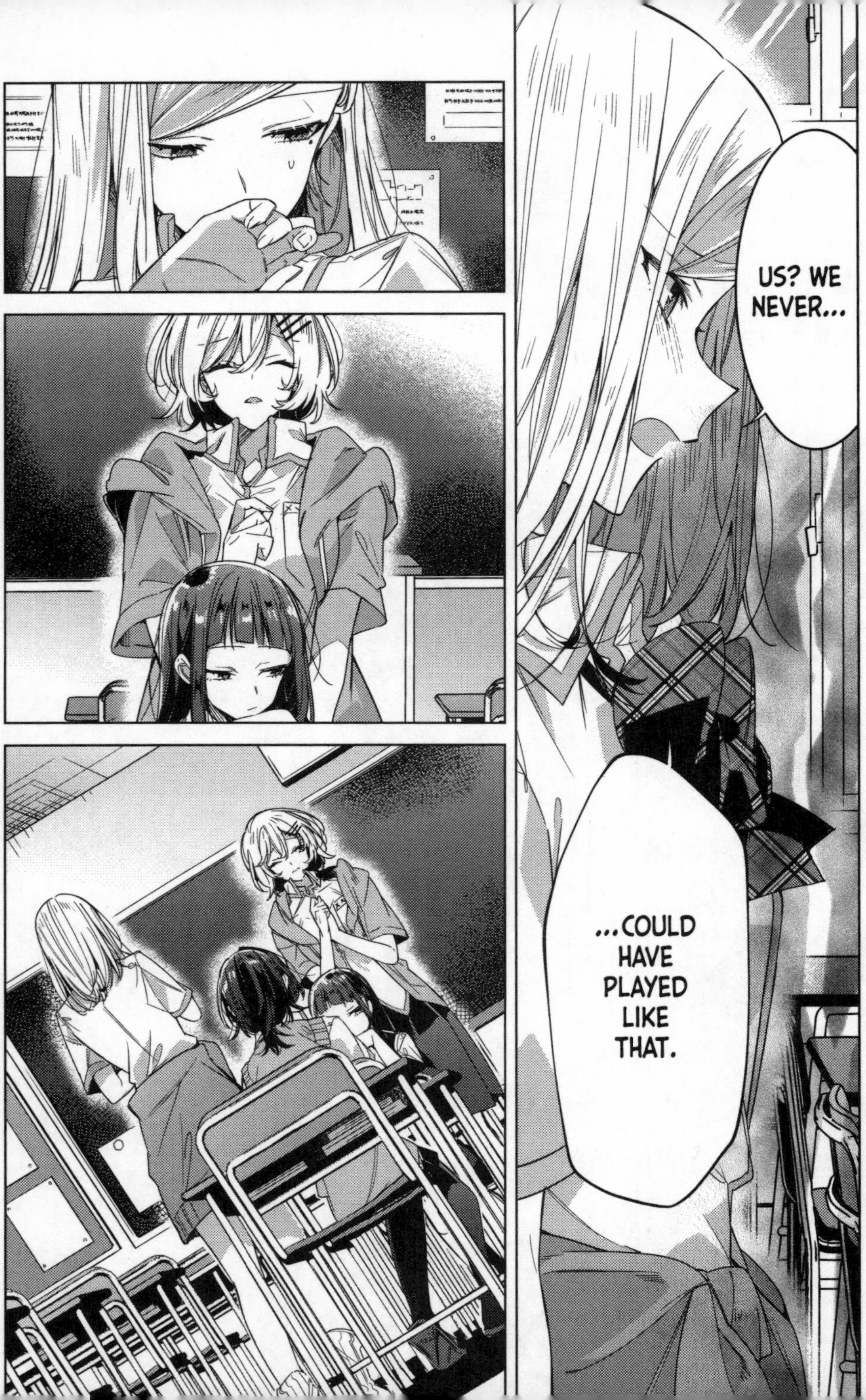
US? WE NEVER...
...COULD HAVE PLAYED LIKE THAT.

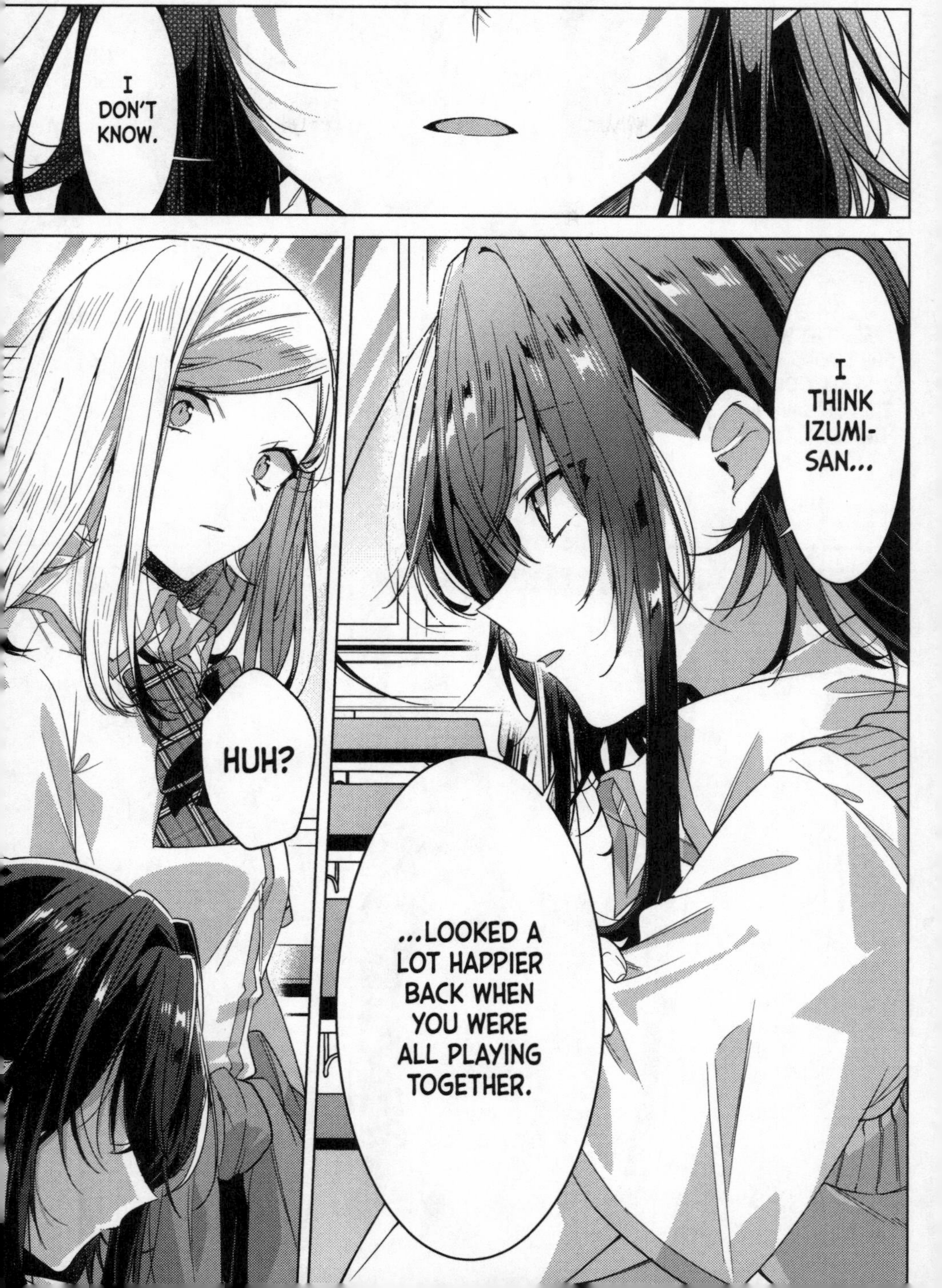
I DON'T KNOW.
I THINK IZUMI-SAN...
...LOOKED A LOT HAPPIER BACK WHEN YOU WERE ALL PLAYING TOGETHER.
HUH?

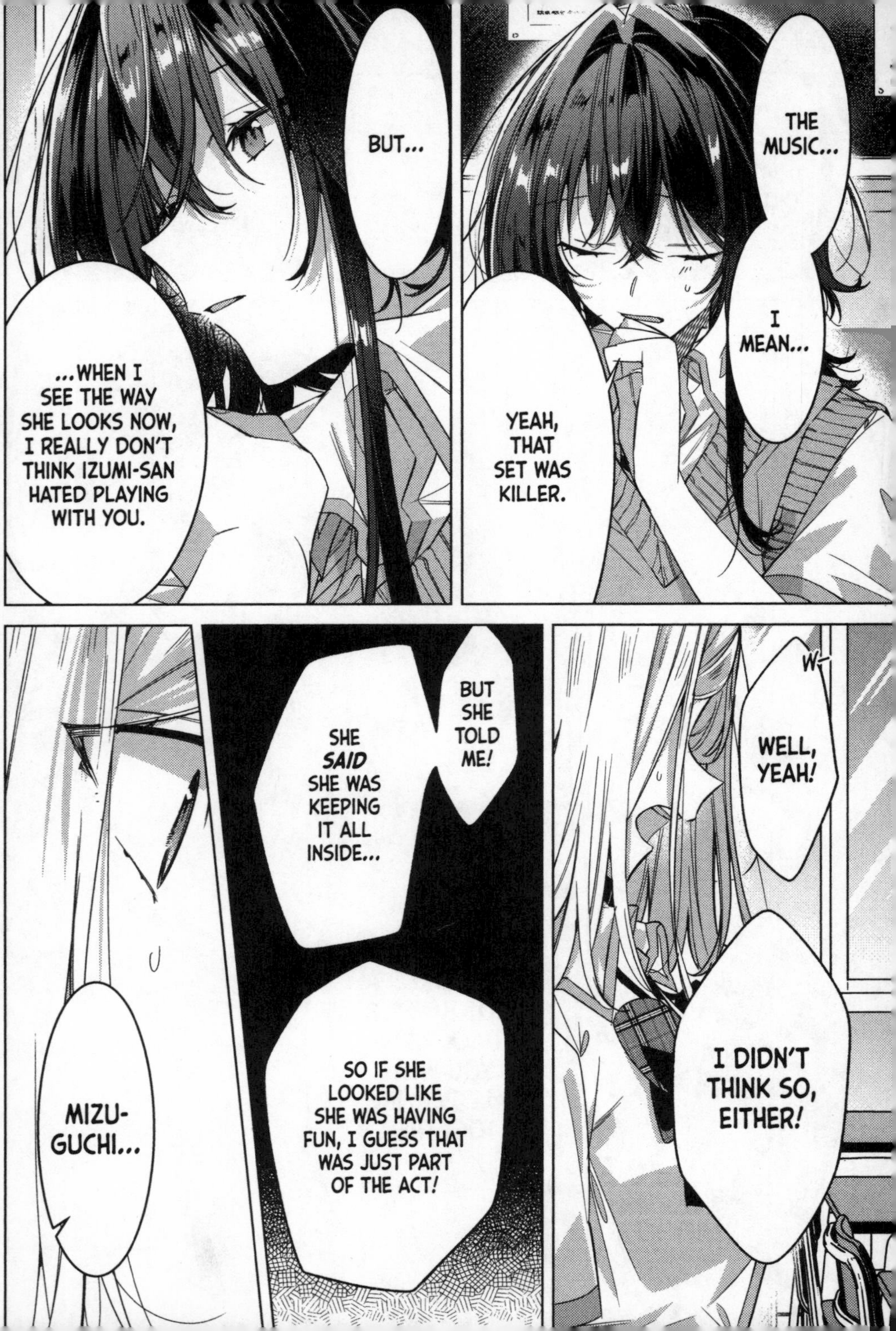
THE MUSIC...
I MEAN...
YEAH, THAT SET WAS KILLER.
BUT...
...WHEN I SEE THE WAY SHE LOOKS NOW, I REALLY DON'T THINK IZUMI-SAN HATED PLAYING WITH YOU.
W—
WELL, YEAH!
I DIDN'T THINK SO, EITHER!
BUT SHE TOLD ME!
SHE *SAID* SHE WAS KEEPING IT ALL INSIDE...
SO IF SHE LOOKED LIKE SHE WAS HAVING FUN, I GUESS THAT WAS JUST PART OF THE ACT!
MIZU-GUCHI...

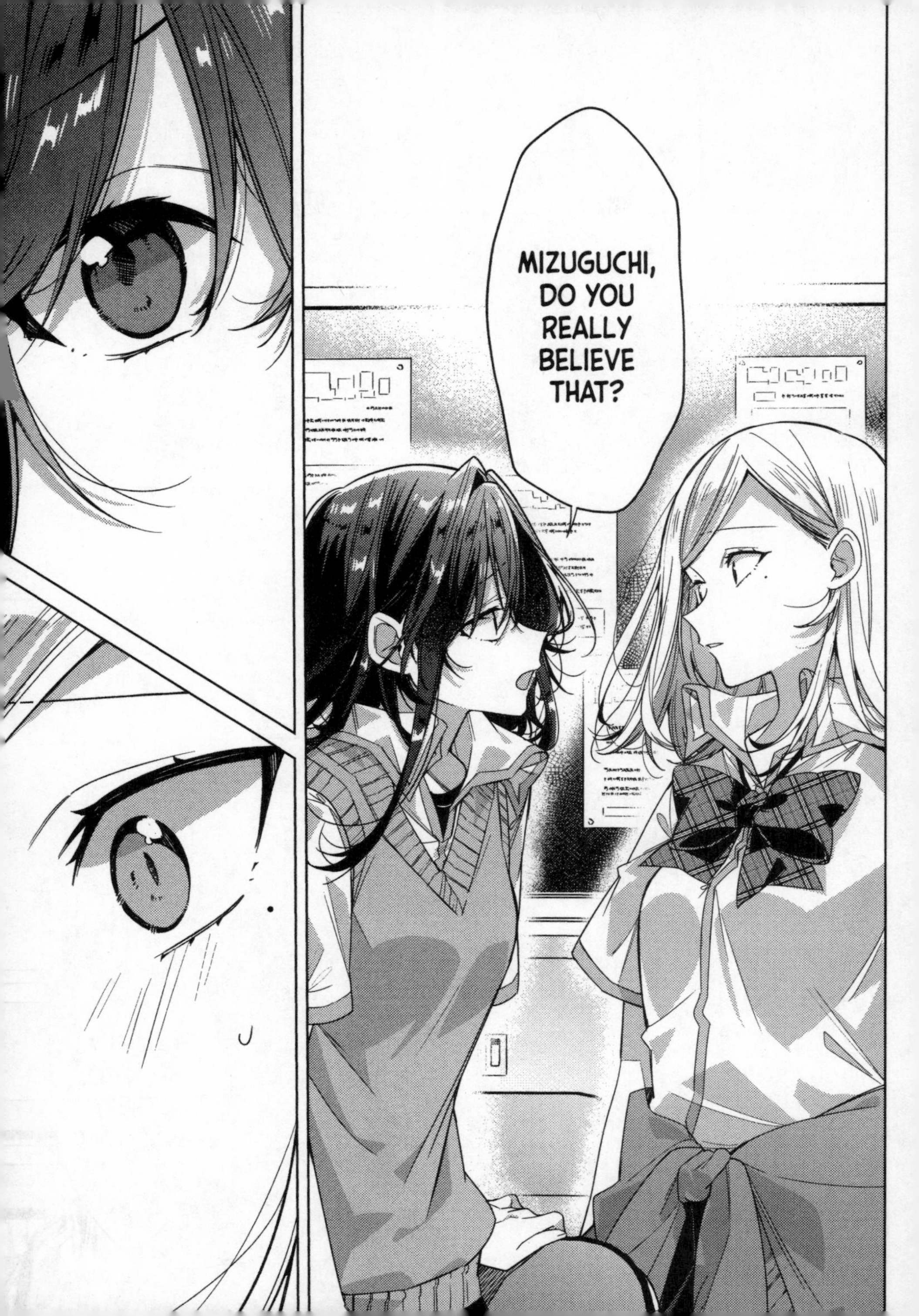
MIZUGUCHI, DO YOU REALLY BELIEVE THAT?

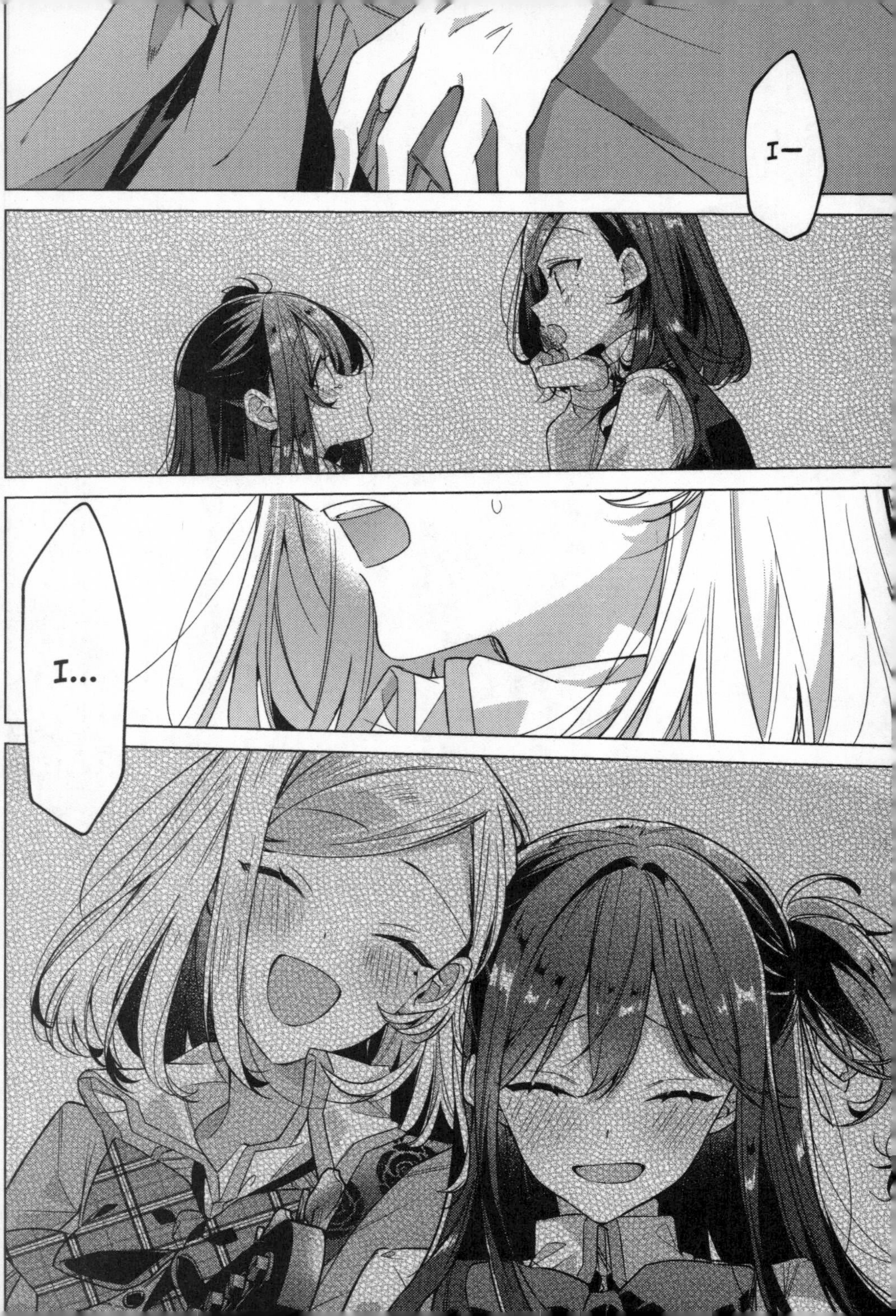
I—
I...

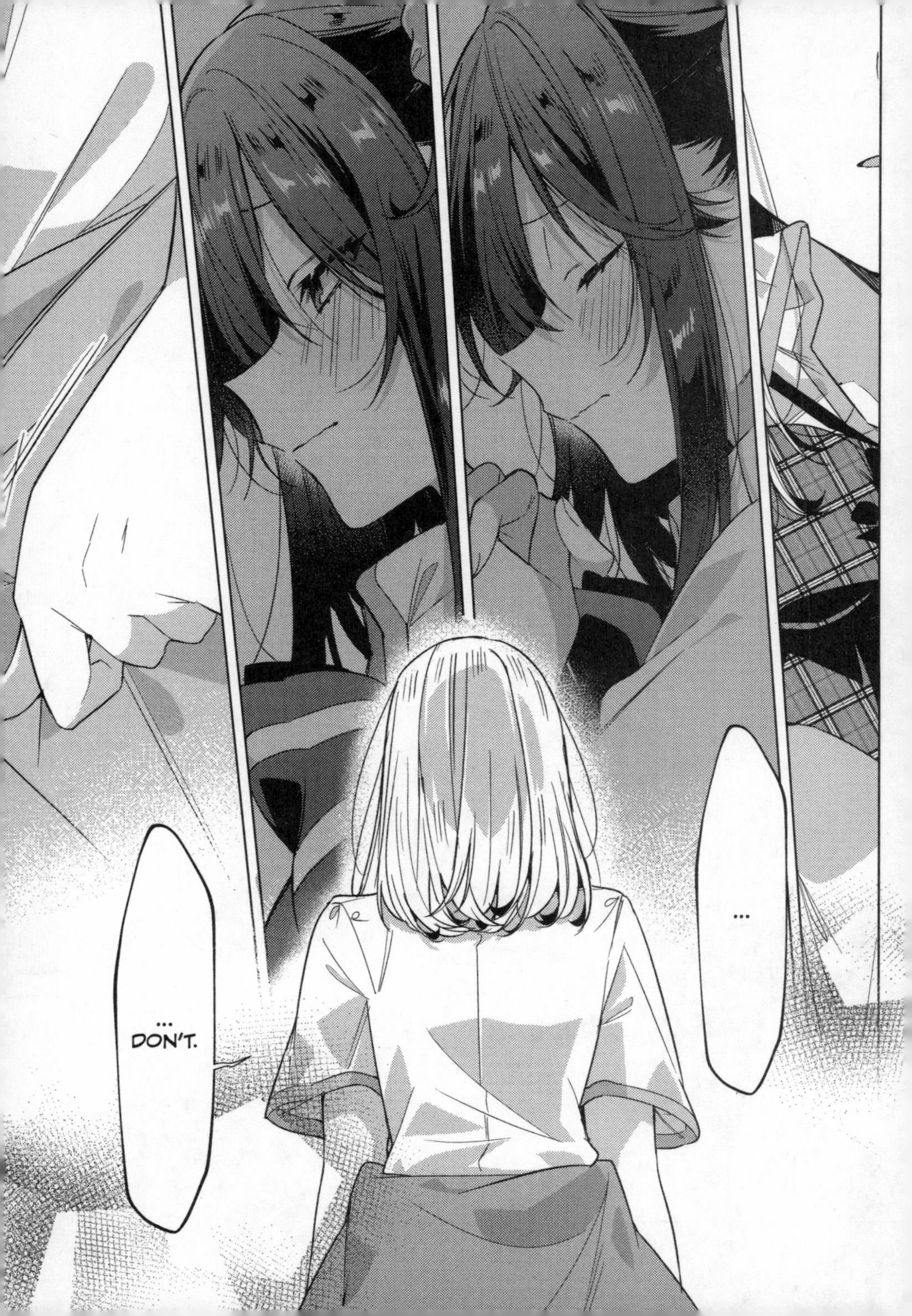
...
... DON'T.

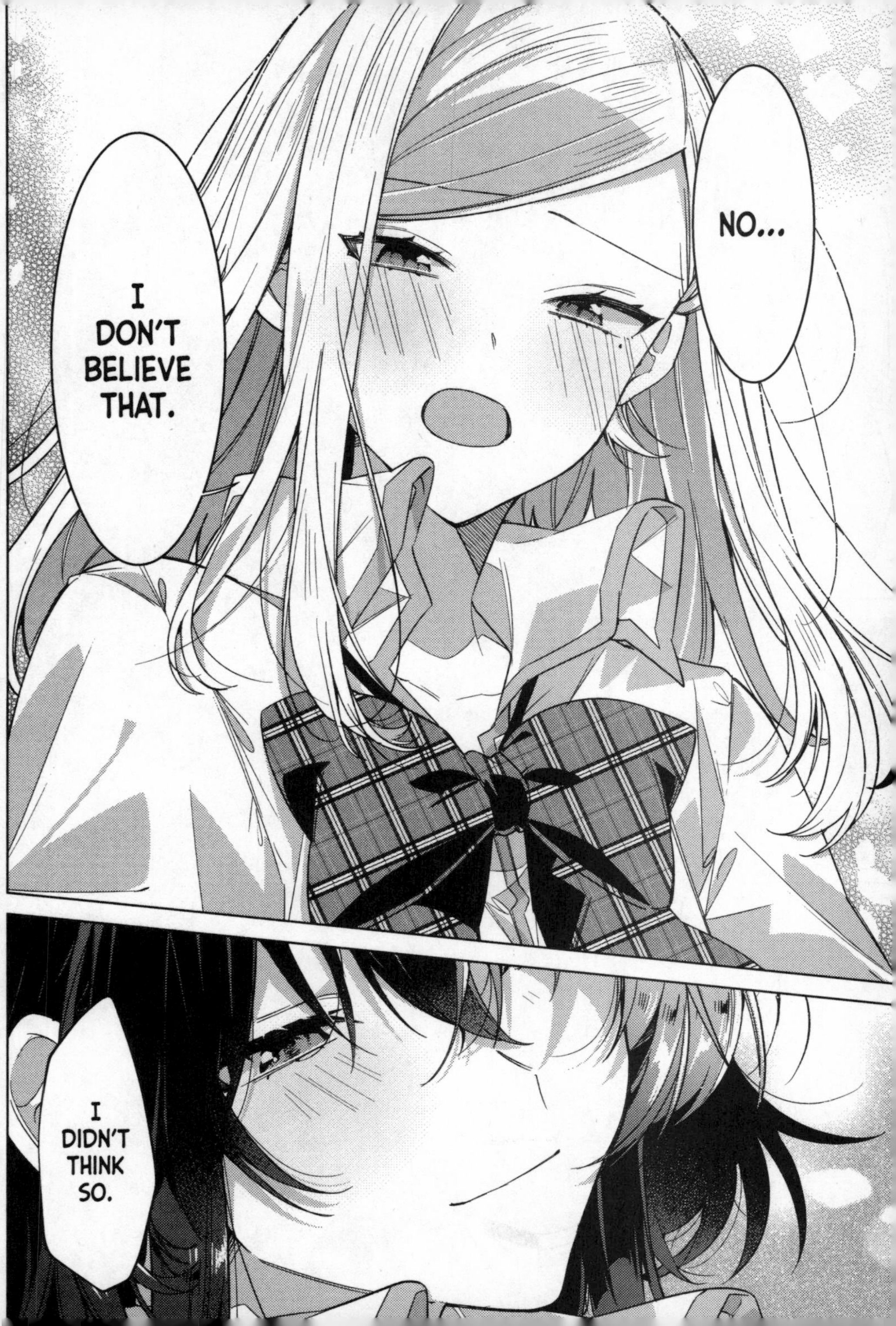
NO...
I DON'T BELIEVE THAT.
I DIDN'T THINK SO.

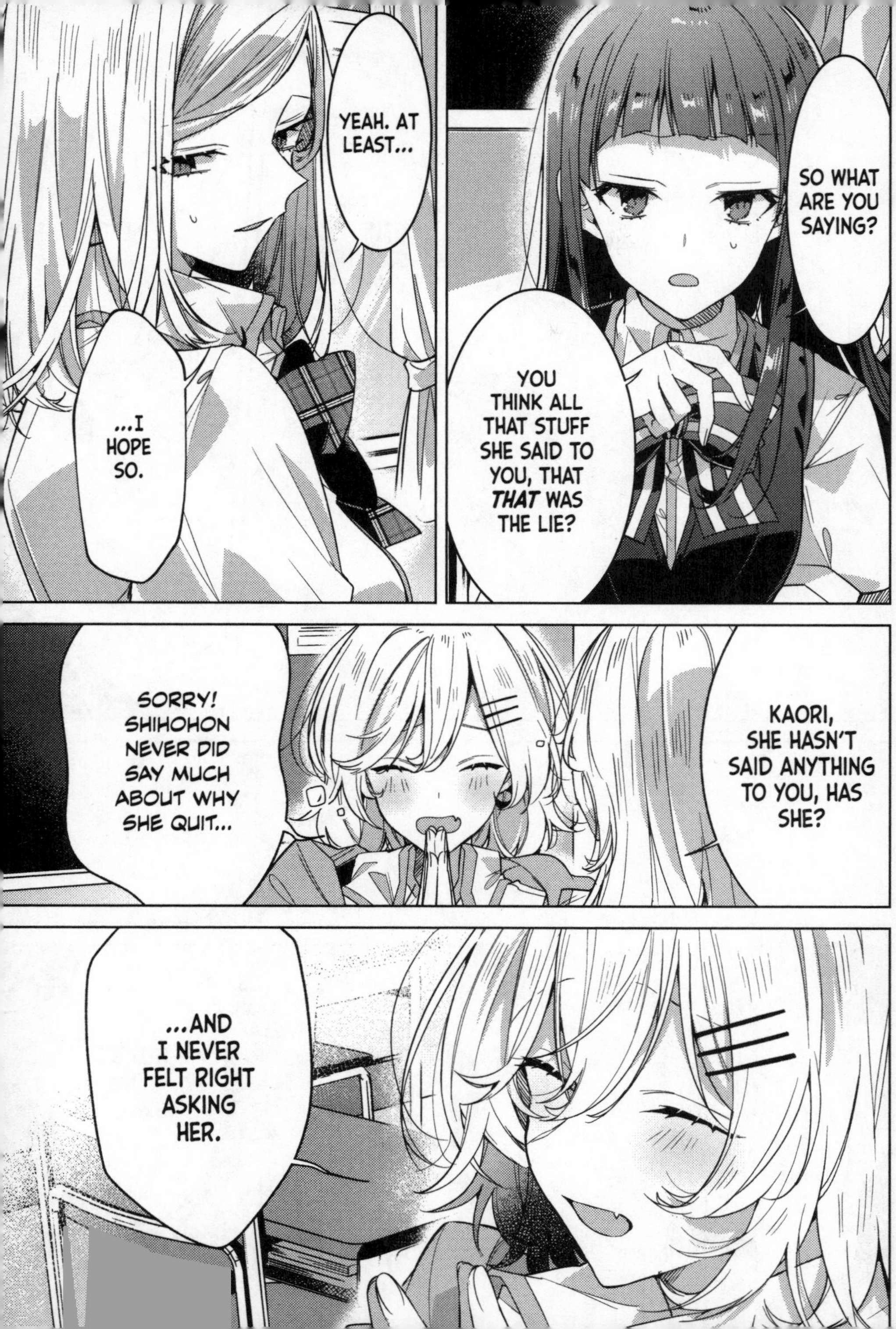
SO WHAT ARE YOU SAYING?
YOU THINK ALL THAT STUFF SHE SAID TO YOU, THAT *THAT* WAS THE LIE?
YEAH. AT LEAST...
...I HOPE SO.
KAORI, SHE HASN'T SAID ANYTHING TO YOU, HAS SHE?
SORRY! SHIHOHON NEVER DID SAY MUCH ABOUT WHY SHE QUIT...
...AND I NEVER FELT RIGHT ASKING HER.

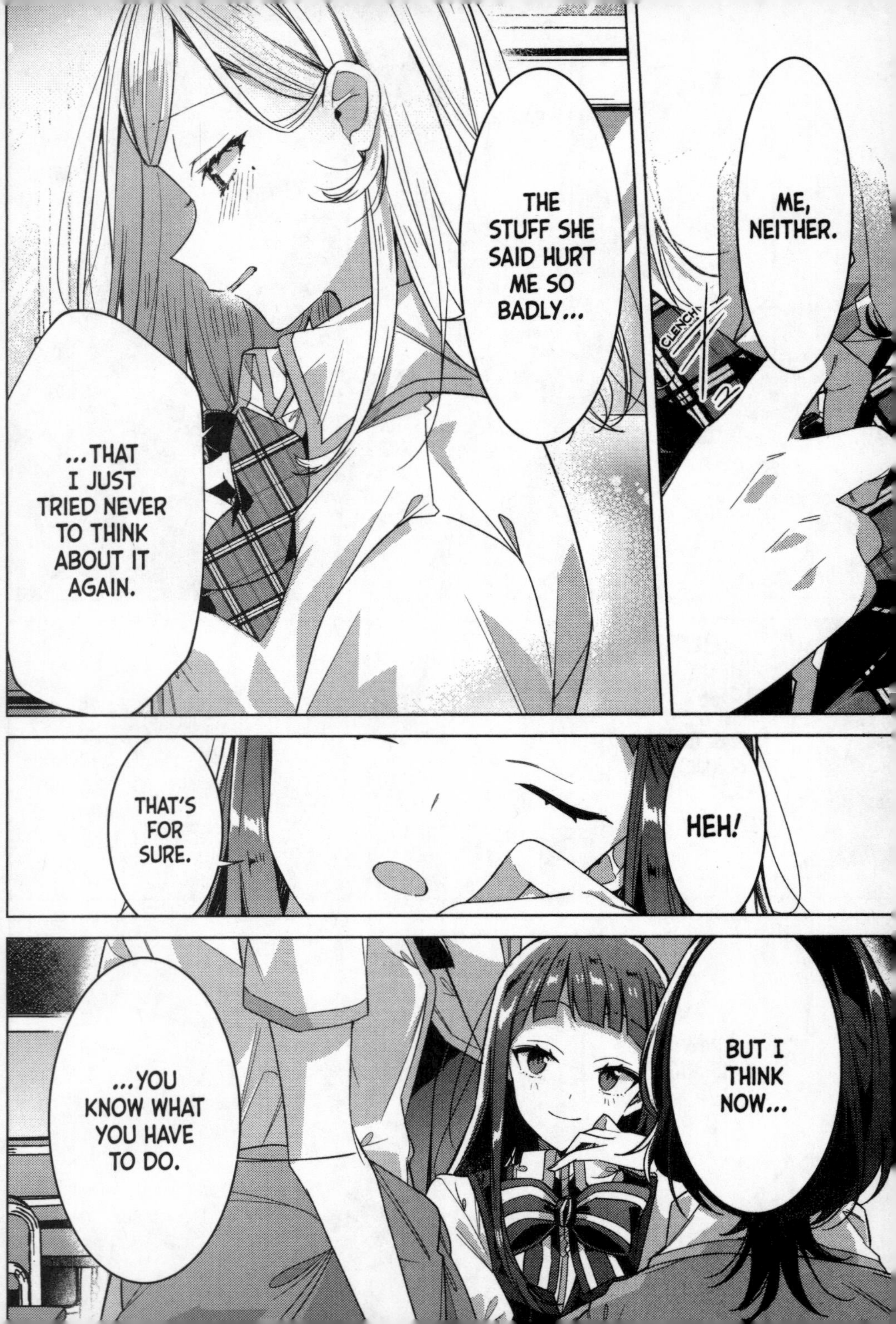
ME, NEITHER.
CLENCH
THE STUFF SHE SAID HURT ME SO BADLY...
...THAT I JUST TRIED NEVER TO THINK ABOUT IT AGAIN.
HEH!
THAT'S FOR SURE.
BUT I THINK NOW...
...YOU KNOW WHAT YOU HAVE TO DO.

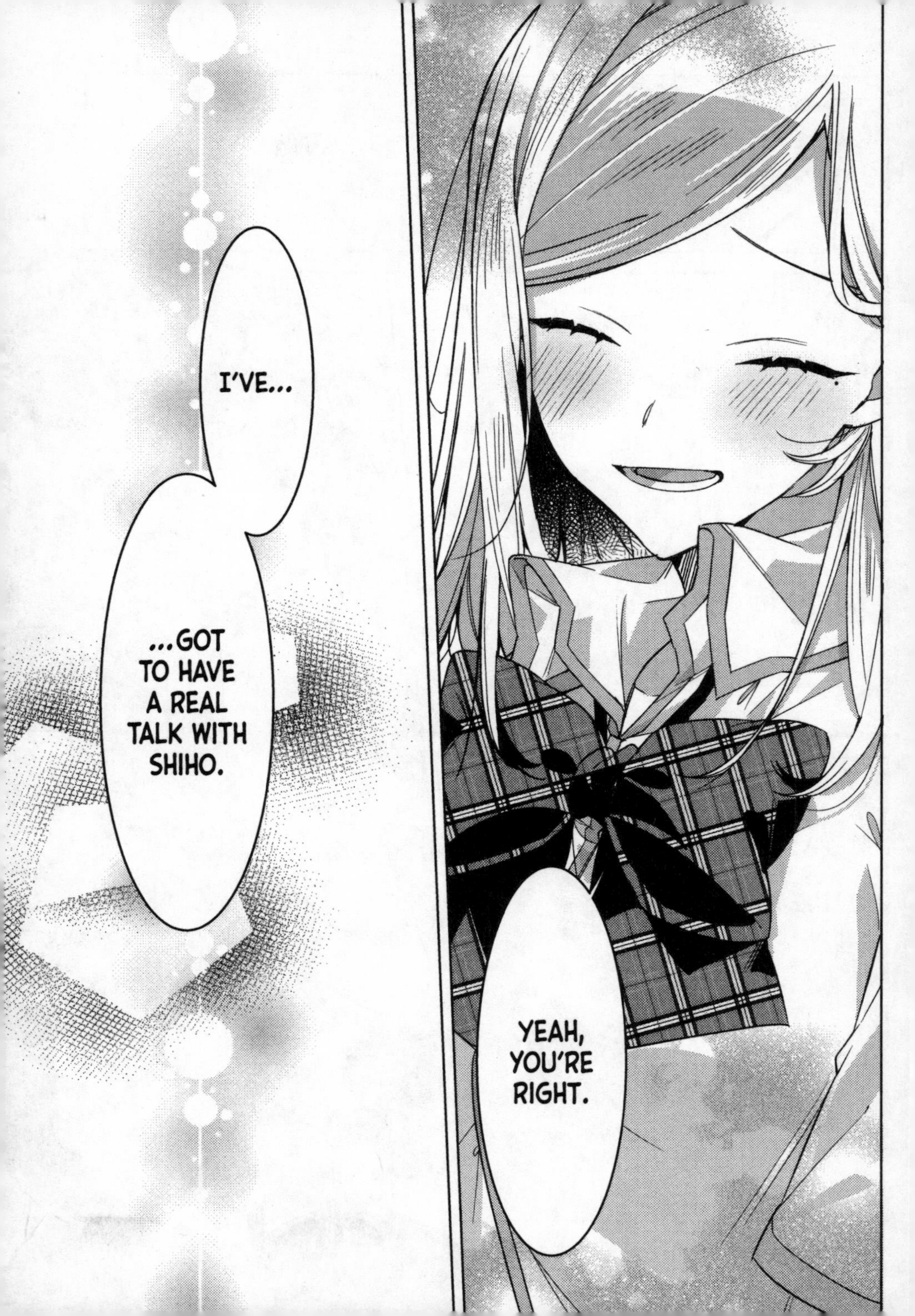
YEAH, YOU'RE RIGHT.
I'VE...
...GOT TO HAVE A REAL TALK WITH SHIHO.

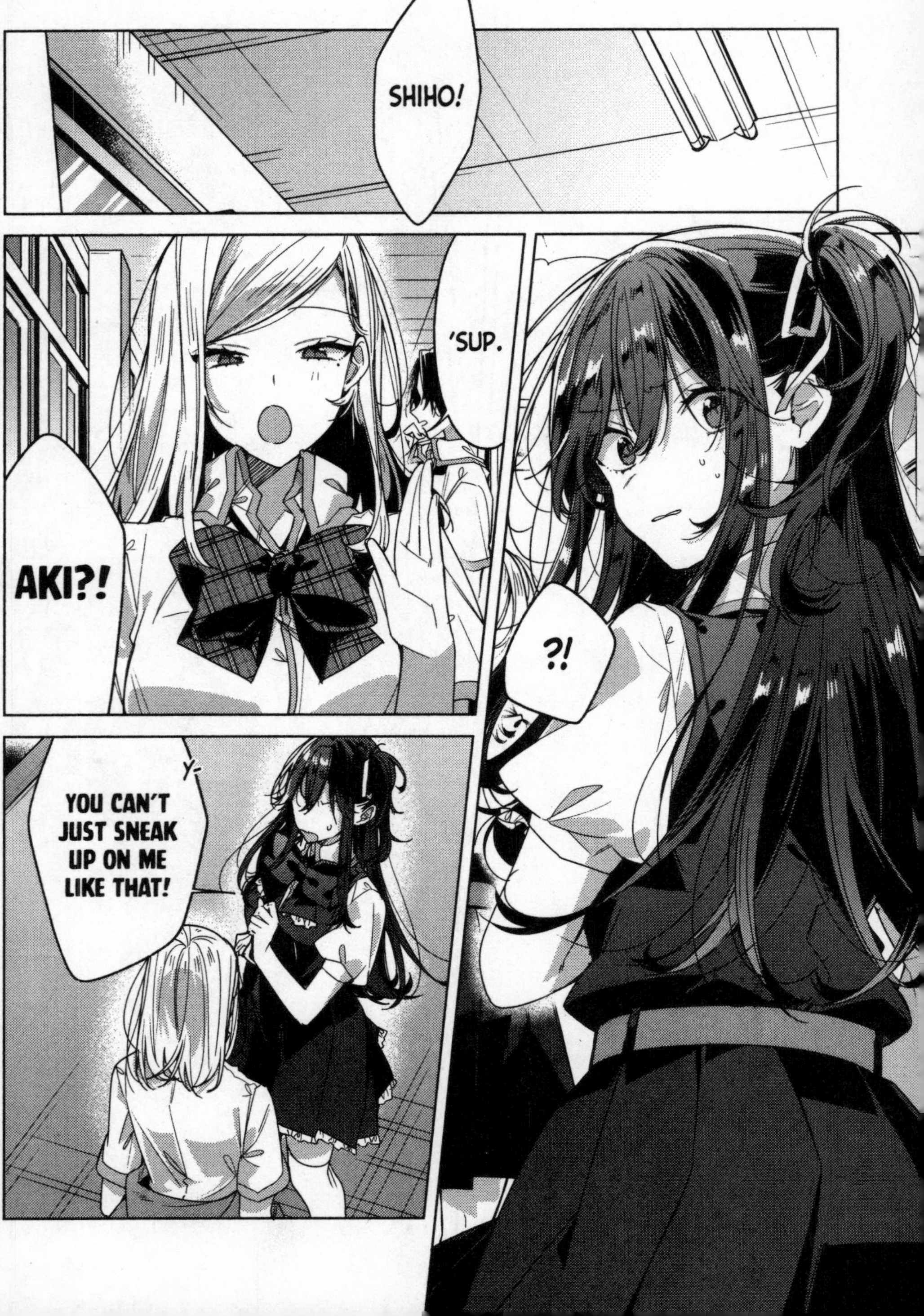
SHIHO!
?!
'SUP.
AKI?!
Y-
YOU CAN'T JUST SNEAK UP ON ME LIKE THAT!

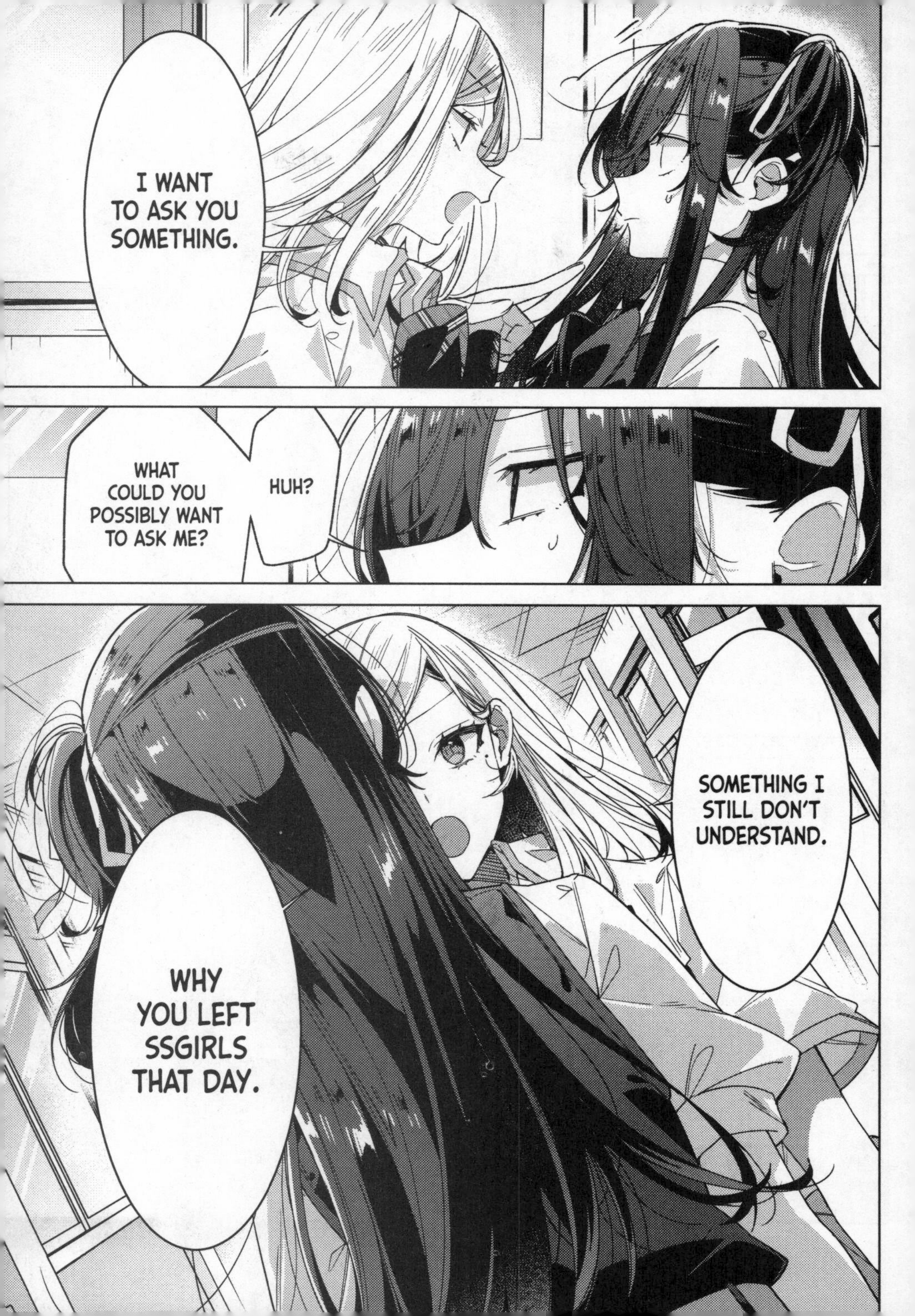
I WANT TO ASK YOU SOMETHING.
HUH?
WHAT COULD YOU POSSIBLY WANT TO ASK ME?
SOMETHING I STILL DON'T UNDERSTAND.
WHY YOU LEFT SSGIRLS THAT DAY.

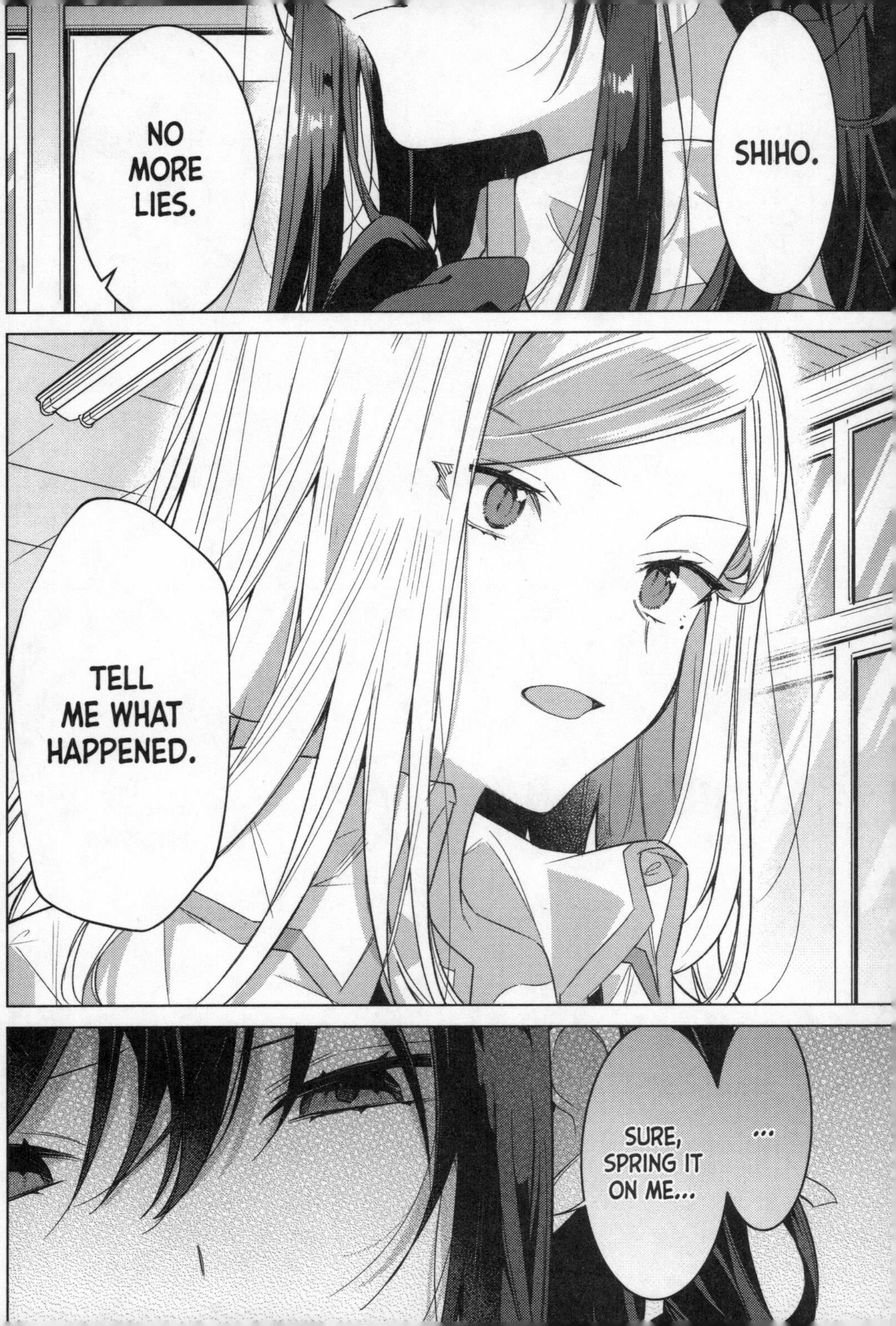
SHIHO.
NO MORE LIES.
TELL ME WHAT HAPPENED.
...
SURE, SPRING IT ON ME...

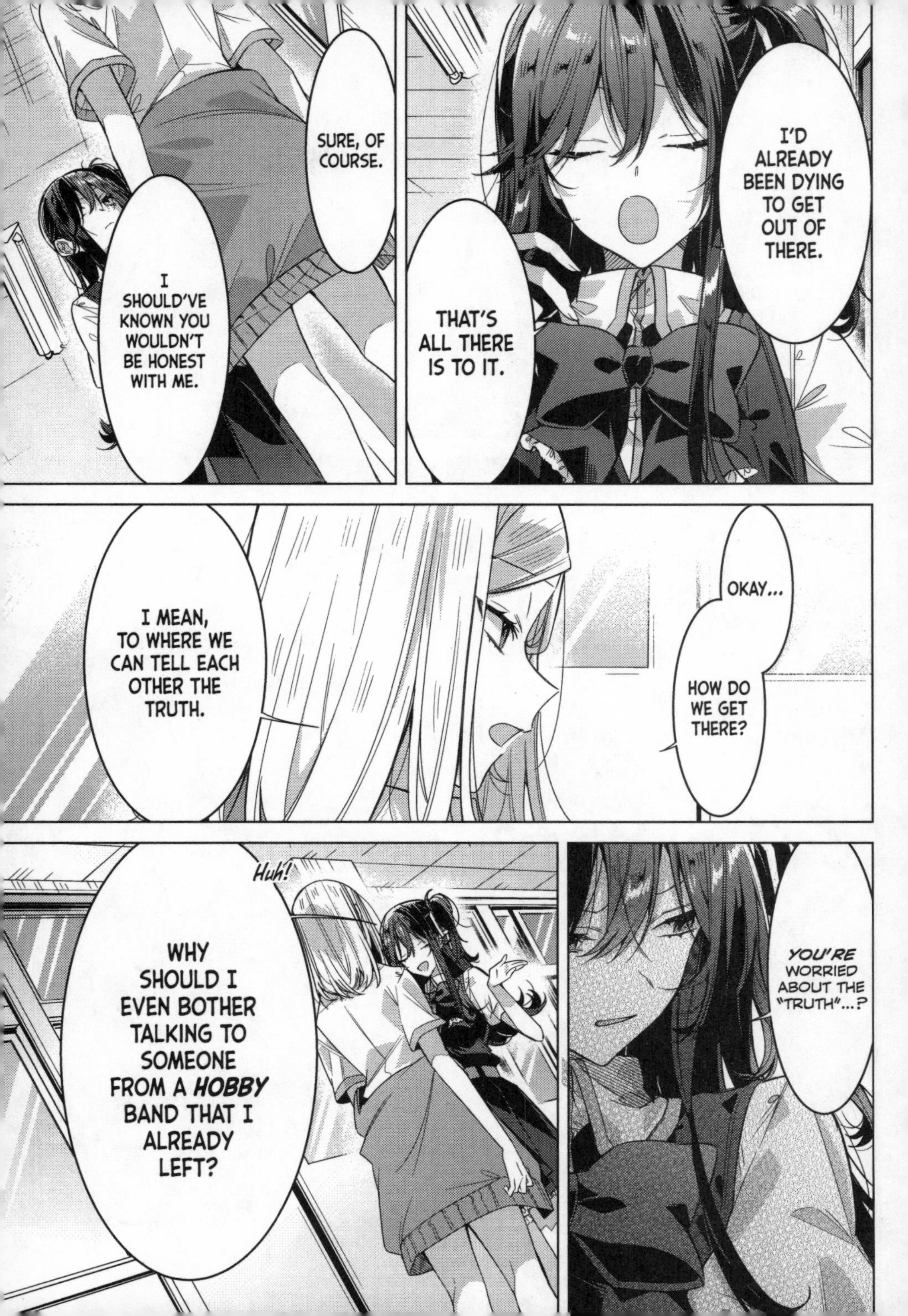
I'D ALREADY BEEN DYING TO GET OUT OF THERE.
THAT'S ALL THERE IS TO IT.
SURE, OF COURSE.
I SHOULD'VE KNOWN YOU WOULDN'T BE HONEST WITH ME.
OKAY...
HOW DO WE GET THERE?
I MEAN, TO WHERE WE CAN TELL EACH OTHER THE TRUTH.
YOU'RE WORRIED ABOUT THE "TRUTH"...?
Huh!
WHY SHOULD I EVEN BOTHER TALKING TO SOMEONE FROM A ***HOBBY*** BAND THAT I ALREADY LEFT?

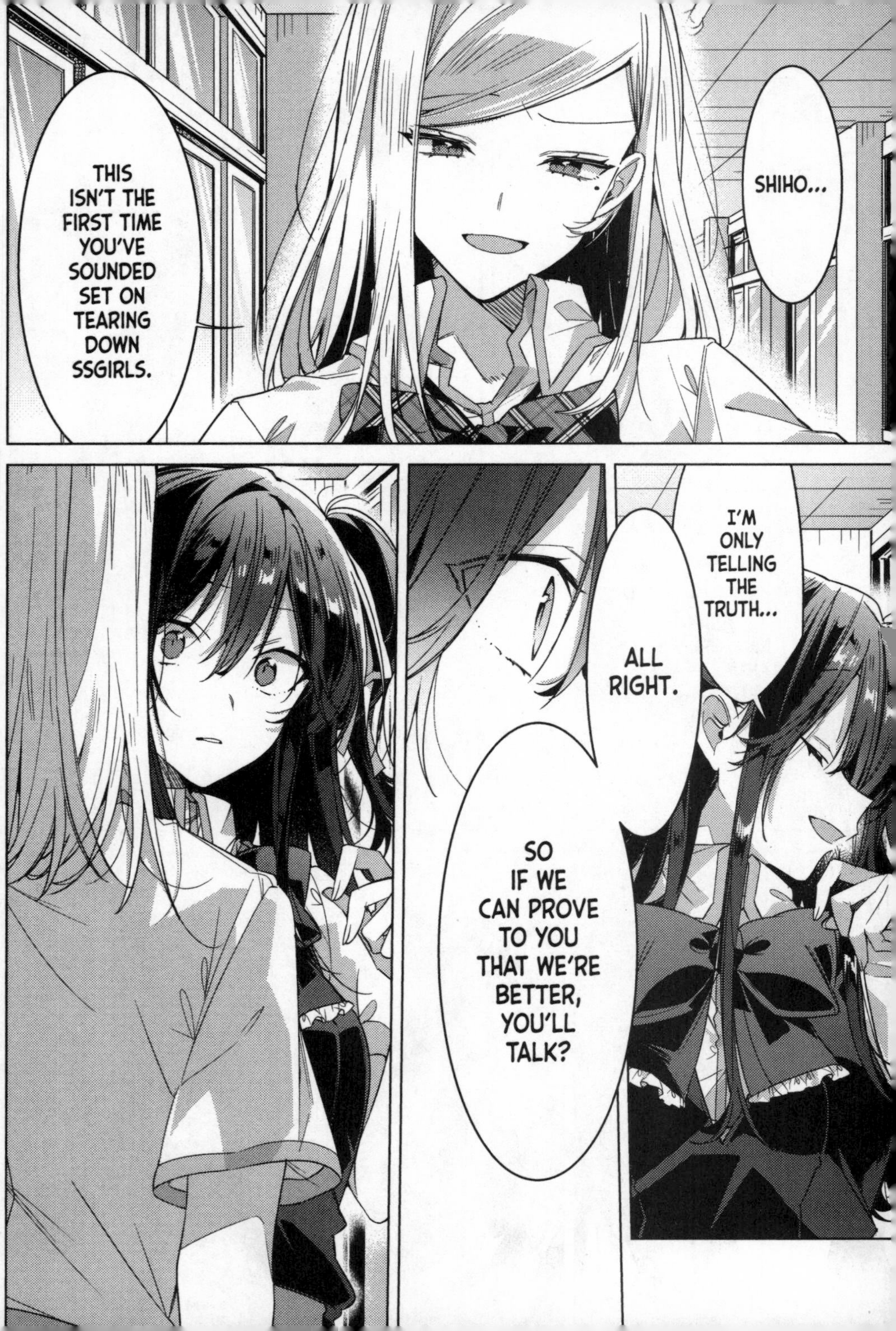
SHIHO...
THIS ISN'T THE FIRST TIME YOU'VE SOUNDED SET ON TEARING DOWN SSGIRLS.
I'M ONLY TELLING THE TRUTH...
ALL RIGHT.
SO IF WE CAN PROVE TO YOU THAT WE'RE BETTER, YOU'LL TALK?

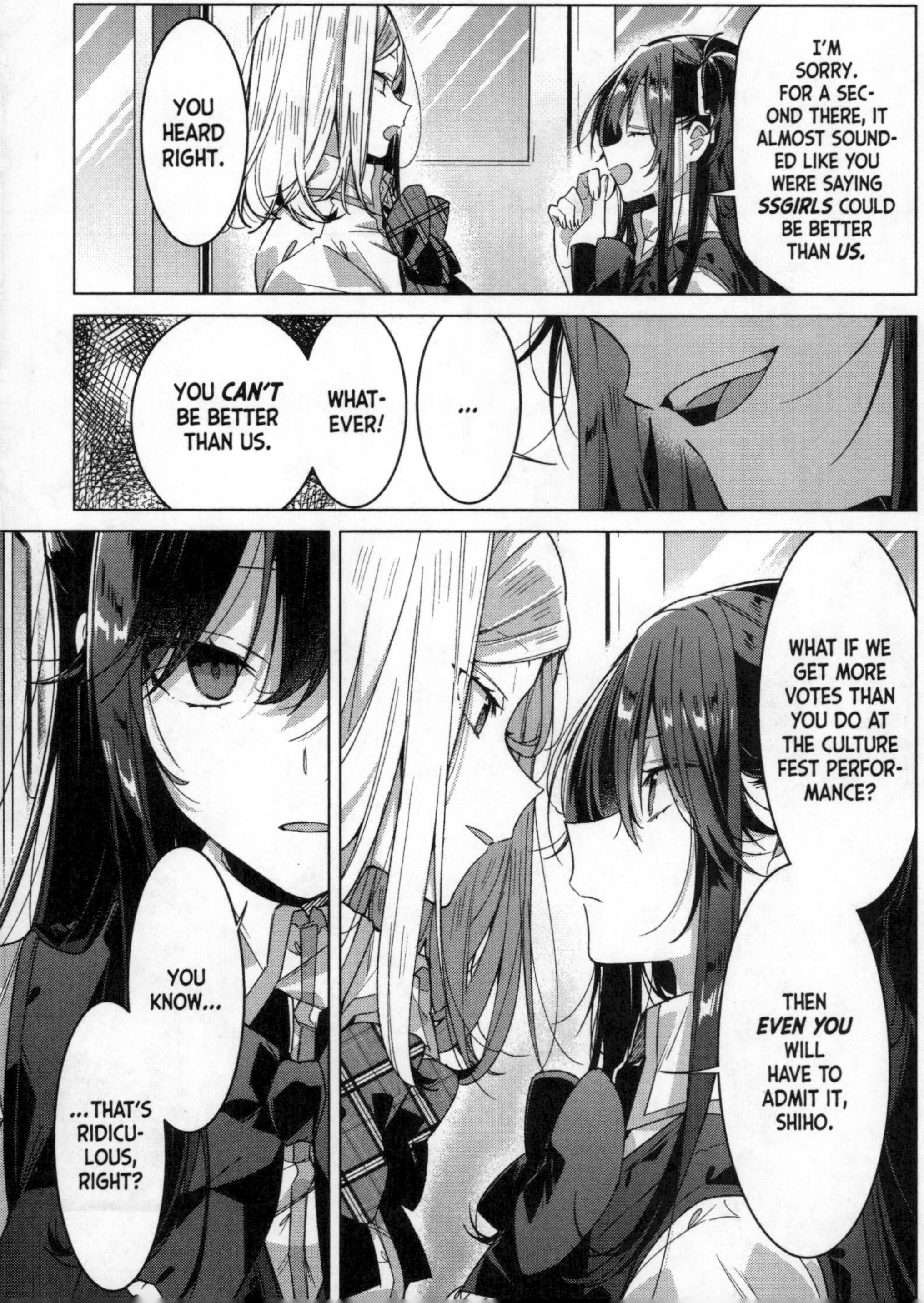
I'M SORRY. FOR A SEC-OND THERE, IT ALMOST SOUND-ED LIKE YOU WERE SAYING *SSGIRLS* COULD BE BETTER THAN *US.*
YOU HEARD RIGHT.
...
WHAT-EVER!
YOU *CAN'T* BE BETTER THAN US.
WHAT IF WE GET MORE VOTES THAN YOU DO AT THE CULTURE FEST PERFOR-MANCE?
THEN *EVEN YOU* WILL HAVE TO ADMIT IT, SHIHO.
YOU KNOW...
...THAT'S RIDICU-LOUS, RIGHT?

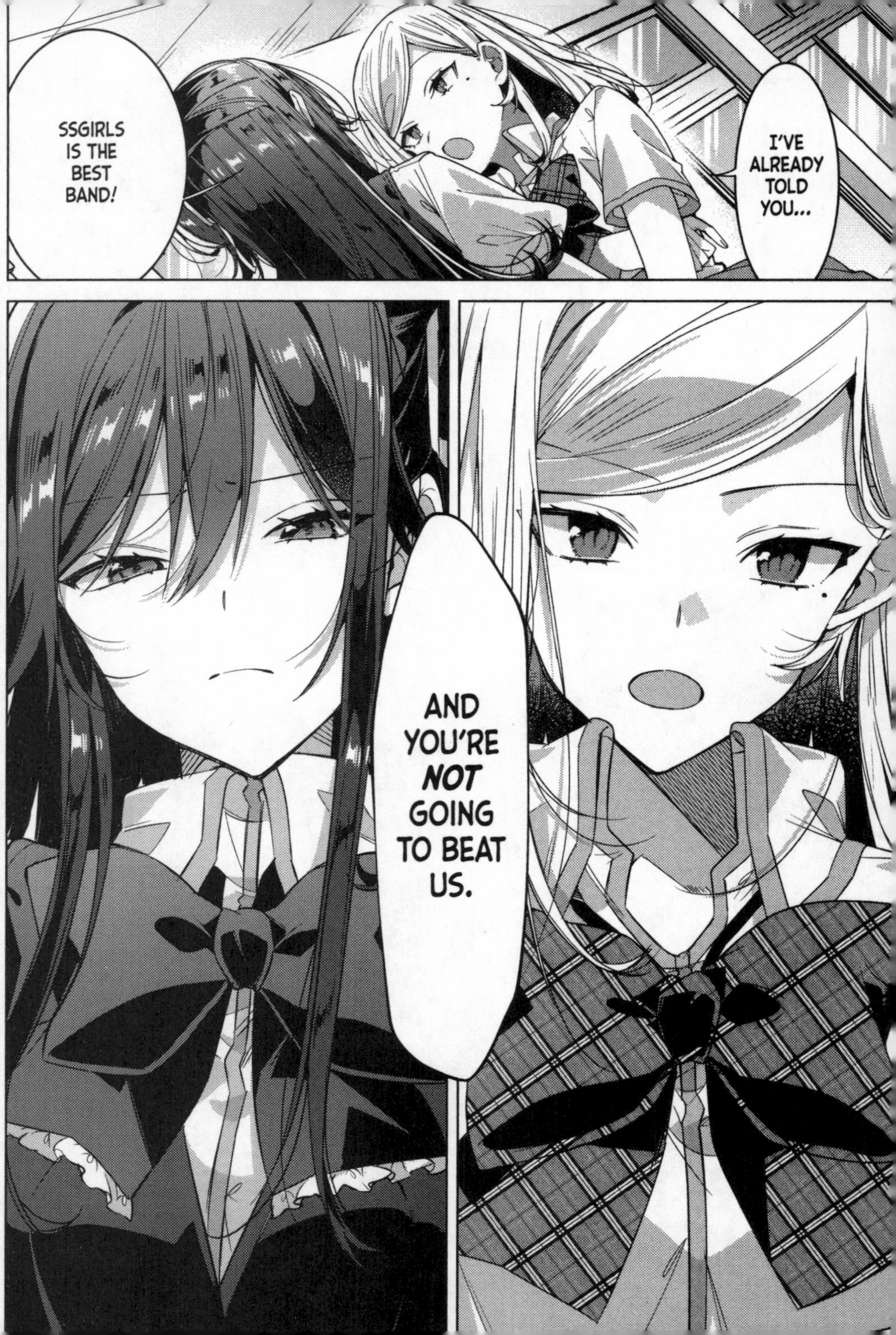
I'VE ALREADY TOLD YOU...
SSGIRLS IS THE BEST BAND!
AND YOU'RE *NOT* GOING TO BEAT US.

Whisper Me
A Love Song
Eku
Takeshima

Whisper Me
A Love Song
Eku
Takeshima

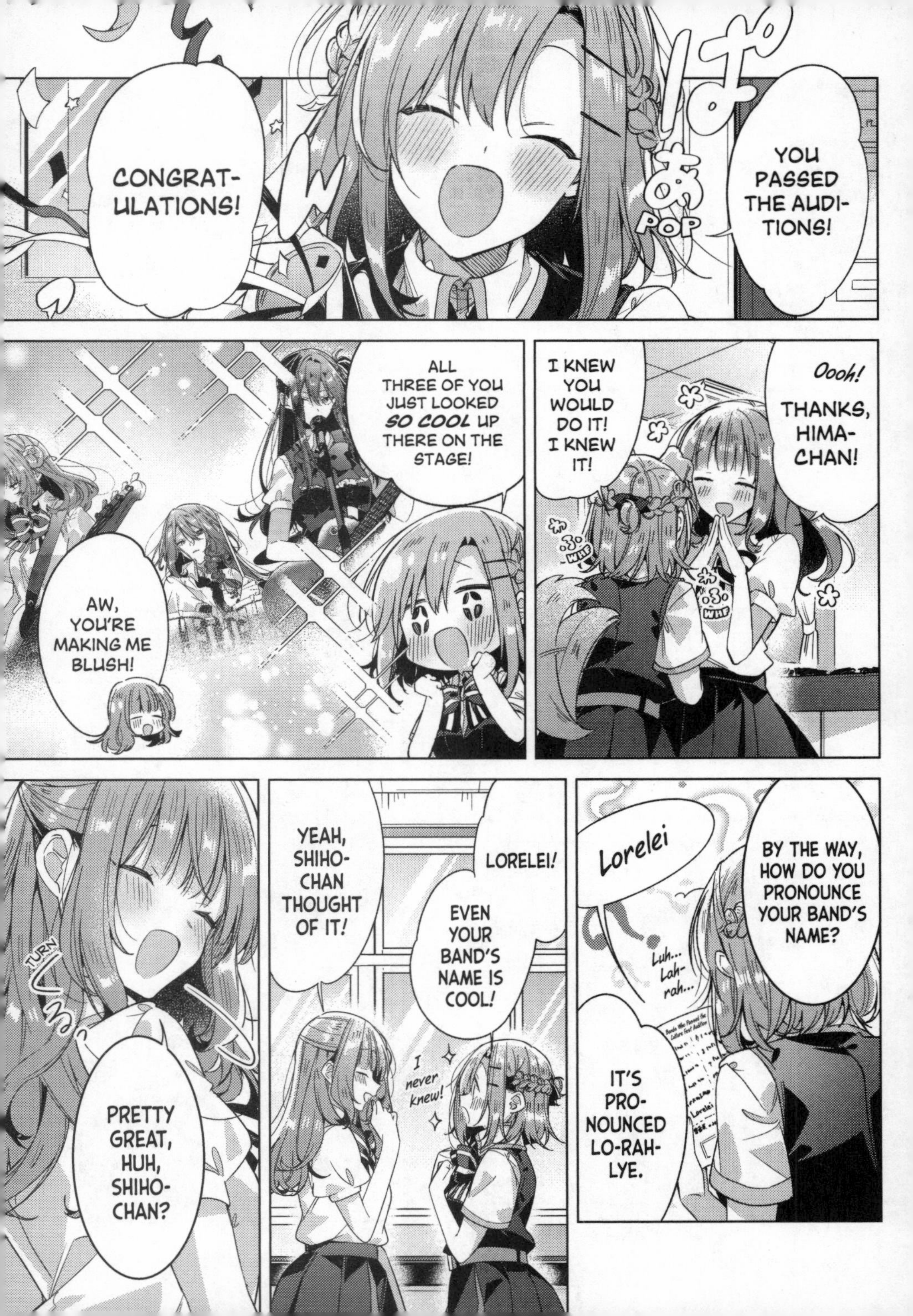
YOU PASSED THE AUDITIONS!
POP
CONGRATULATIONS!
Oooh!
THANKS, HIMA-CHAN!
I KNEW YOU WOULD DO IT! I KNEW IT!
WHF
WHF
ALL THREE OF YOU JUST LOOKED ***SO COOL*** UP THERE ON THE STAGE!
AW, YOU'RE MAKING ME BLUSH!
BY THE WAY, HOW DO YOU PRONOUNCE YOUR BAND'S NAME?
Lorelei
Luh... Lah-rah...
IT'S PRONOUNCED LO-RAH-LYE.
LORELEI*!*
EVEN YOUR BAND'S NAME IS COOL!
YEAH, SHIHO-CHAN THOUGHT OF IT*!*
I never knew!
TURN
PRETTY GREAT, HUH, SHIHO-CHAN?

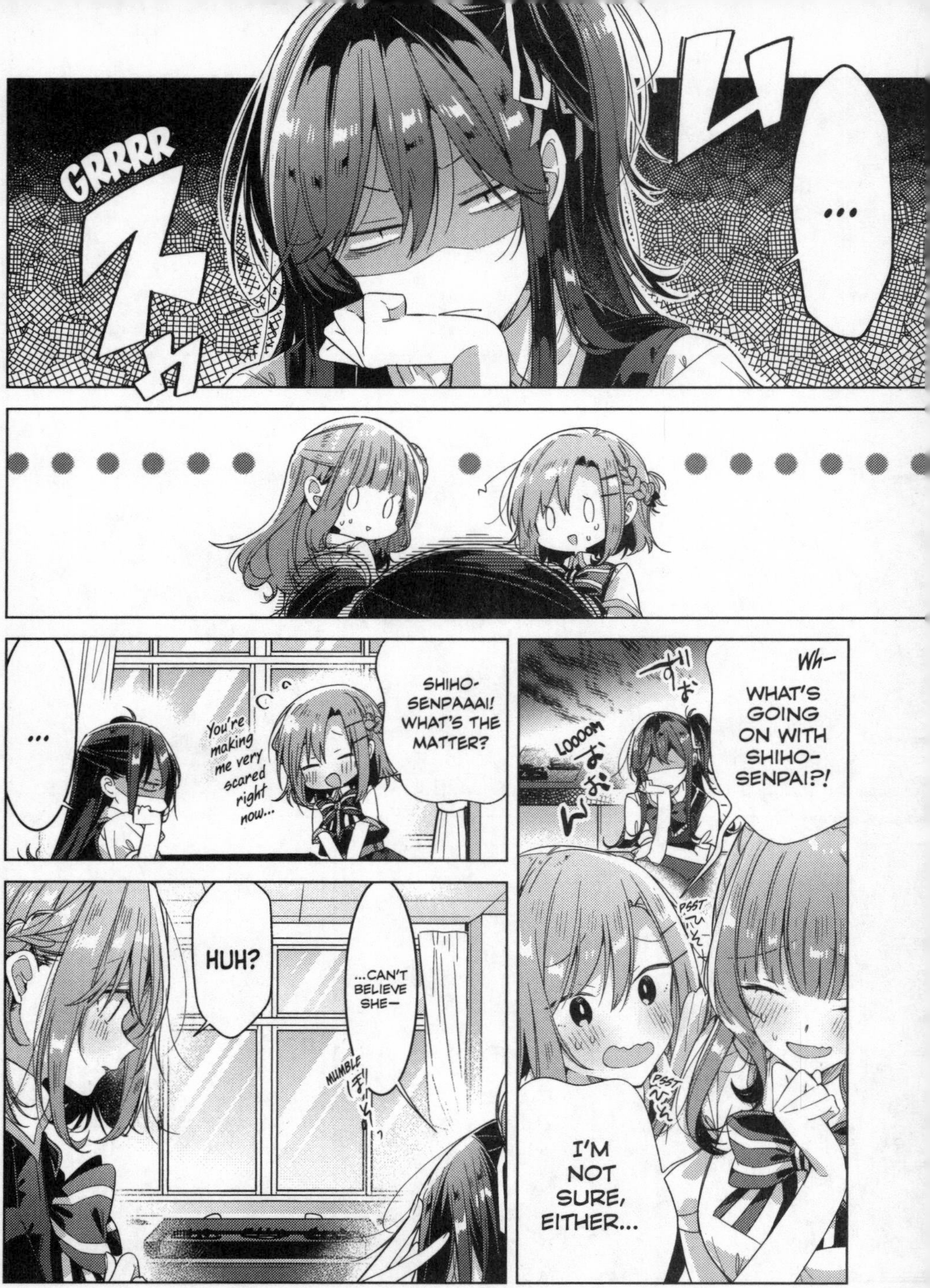
...
GRRRR
Wh— WHAT'S GOING ON WITH SHIHO-SENPAI?!
LOOOOM
SHIHO-SENPAAAI! WHAT'S THE MATTER?
You're making me very scared right now...
...
PSST
PSST
I'M NOT SURE, EITHER...
...CAN'T BELIEVE SHE—
MUMBLE
HUH?

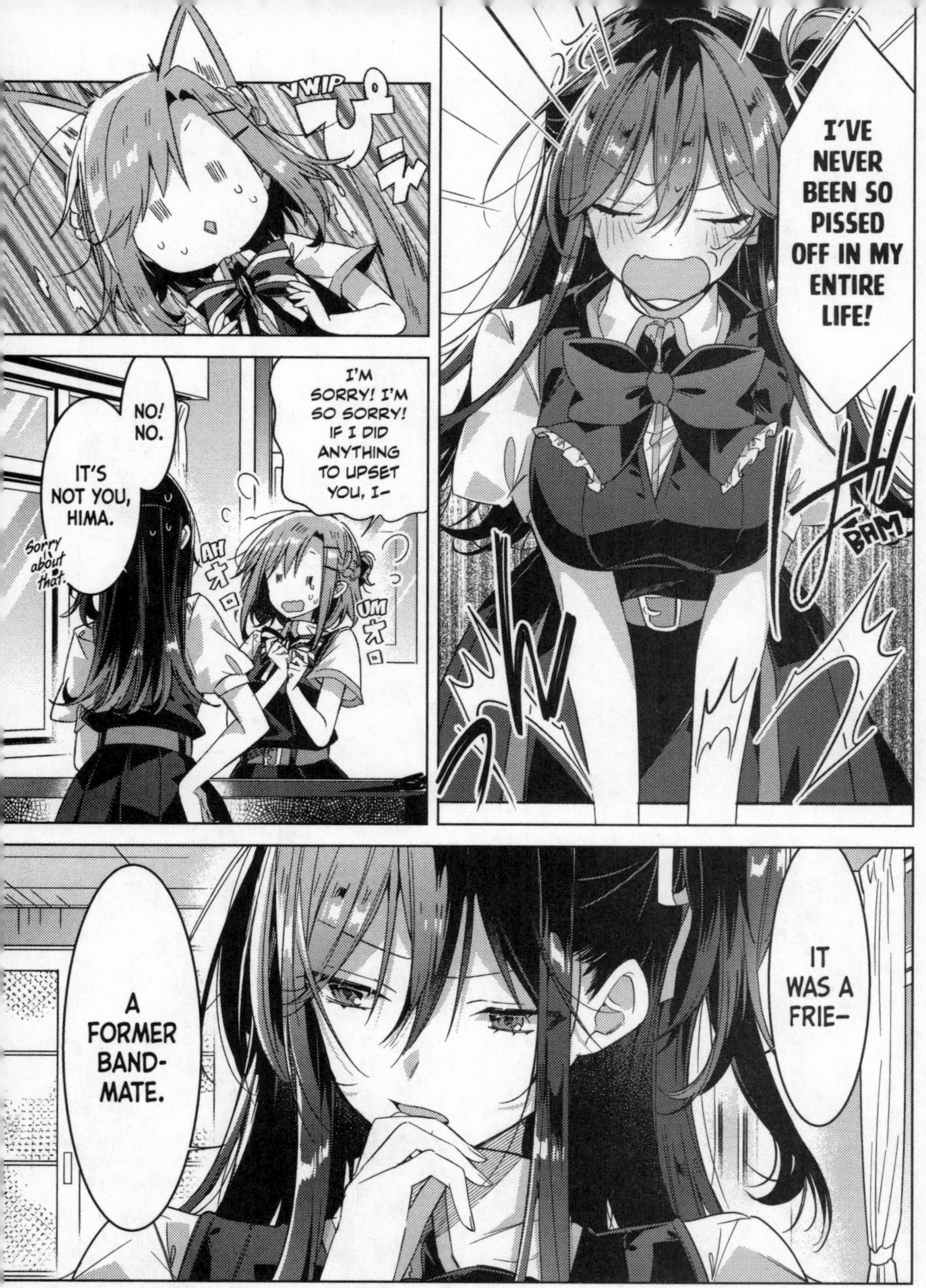
I'VE NEVER BEEN SO PISSED OFF IN MY ENTIRE LIFE!
BAM
VWIP
I'M SORRY! I'M SO SORRY! IF I DID ANYTHING TO UPSET YOU, I—
NO! NO.
IT'S NOT YOU, HIMA.
Sorry about that.
AH
UM
IT WAS A FRIE—
A FORMER BAND-MATE.

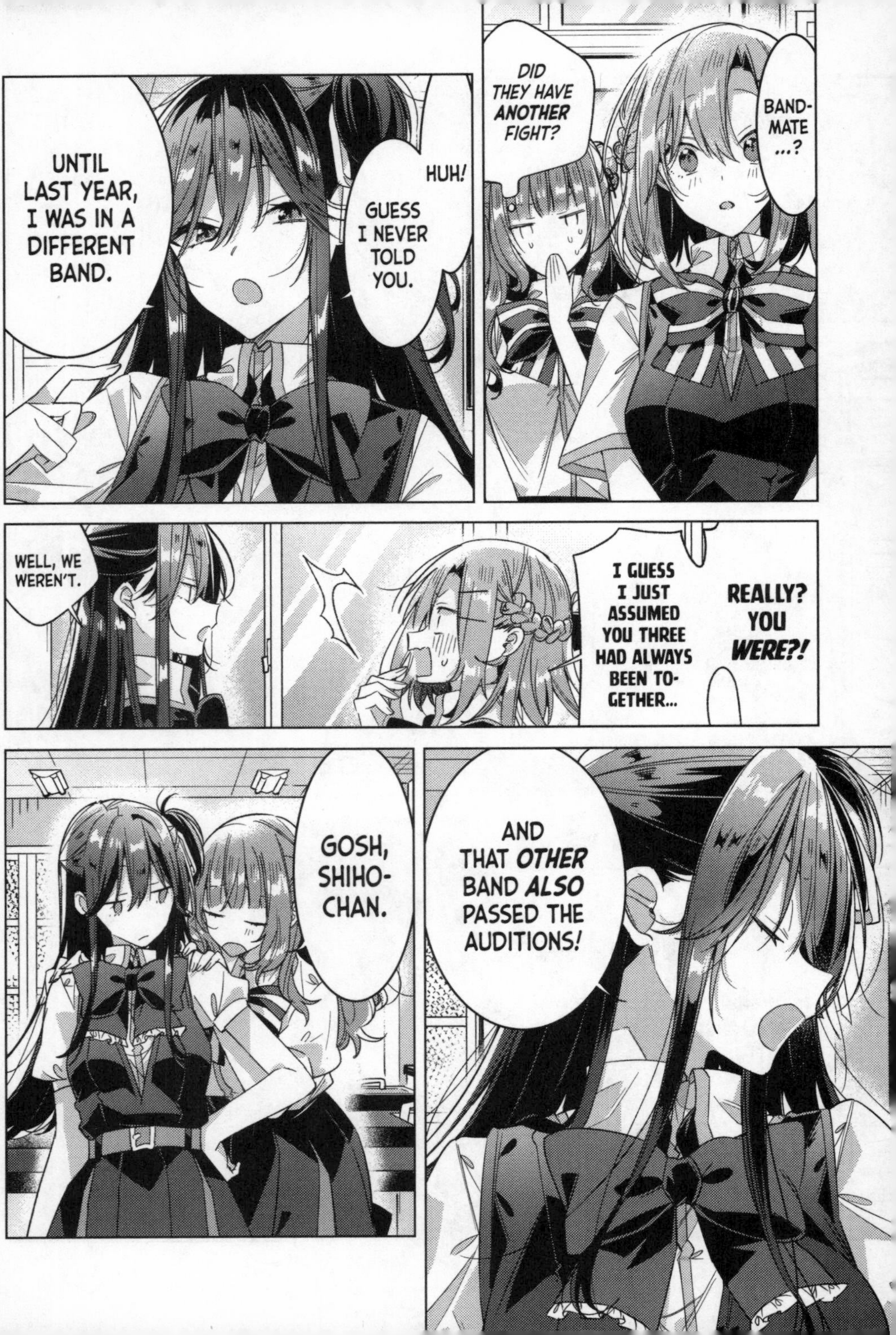
BAND-MATE ...?
DID THEY HAVE ANOTHER FIGHT?
HUH!
GUESS I NEVER TOLD YOU.
UNTIL LAST YEAR, I WAS IN A DIFFERENT BAND.
REALLY? YOU WERE?!
I GUESS I JUST ASSUMED YOU THREE HAD ALWAYS BEEN TOGETHER...
WELL, WE WEREN'T.
AND THAT OTHER BAND ALSO PASSED THE AUDITIONS!
GOSH, SHIHO-CHAN.

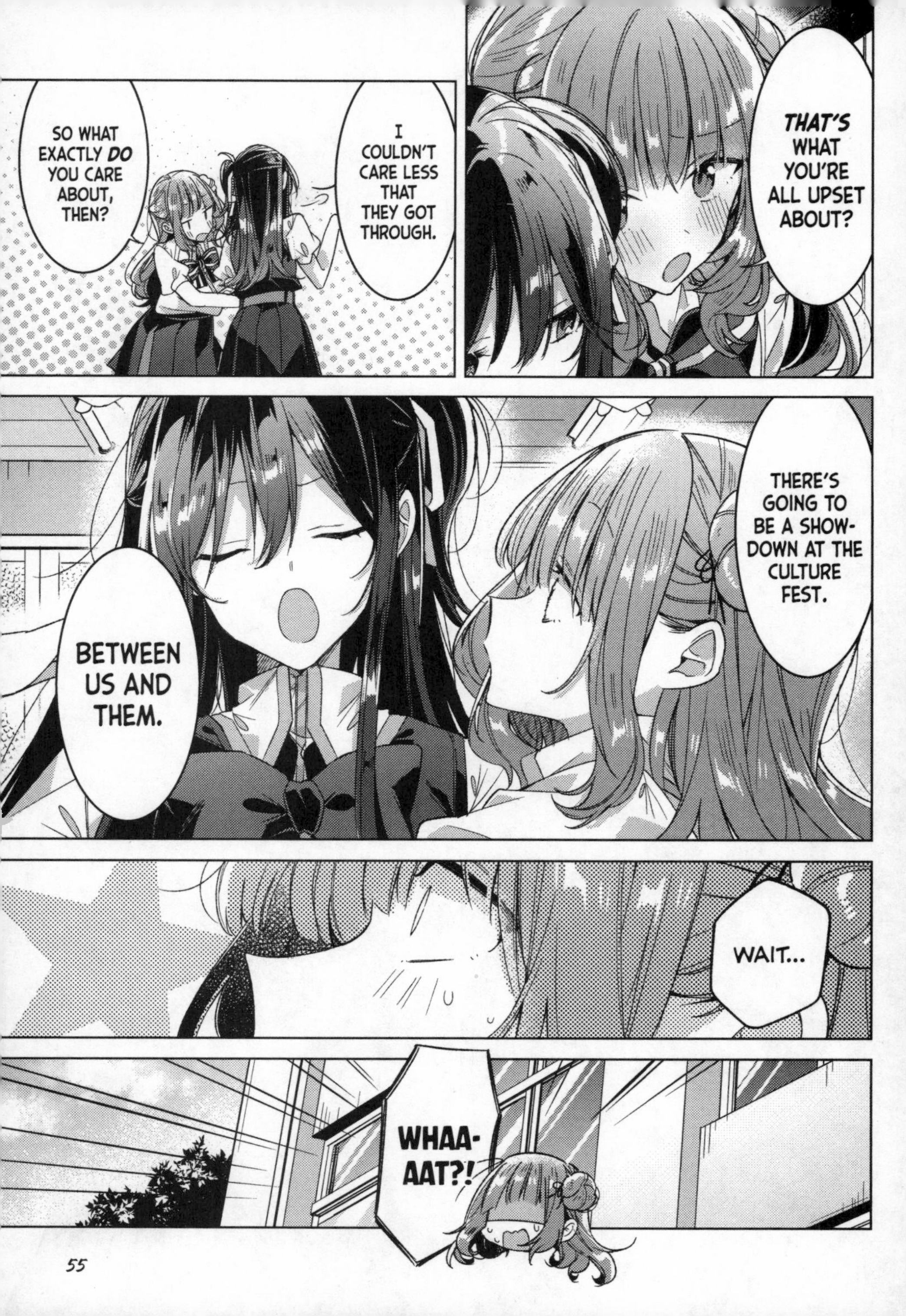
THAT'S WHAT YOU'RE ALL UPSET ABOUT?
I COULDN'T CARE LESS THAT THEY GOT THROUGH.
SO WHAT EXACTLY DO YOU CARE ABOUT, THEN?
THERE'S GOING TO BE A SHOW-DOWN AT THE CULTURE FEST.
BETWEEN US AND THEM.
WAIT...
WHAA-AAT?!

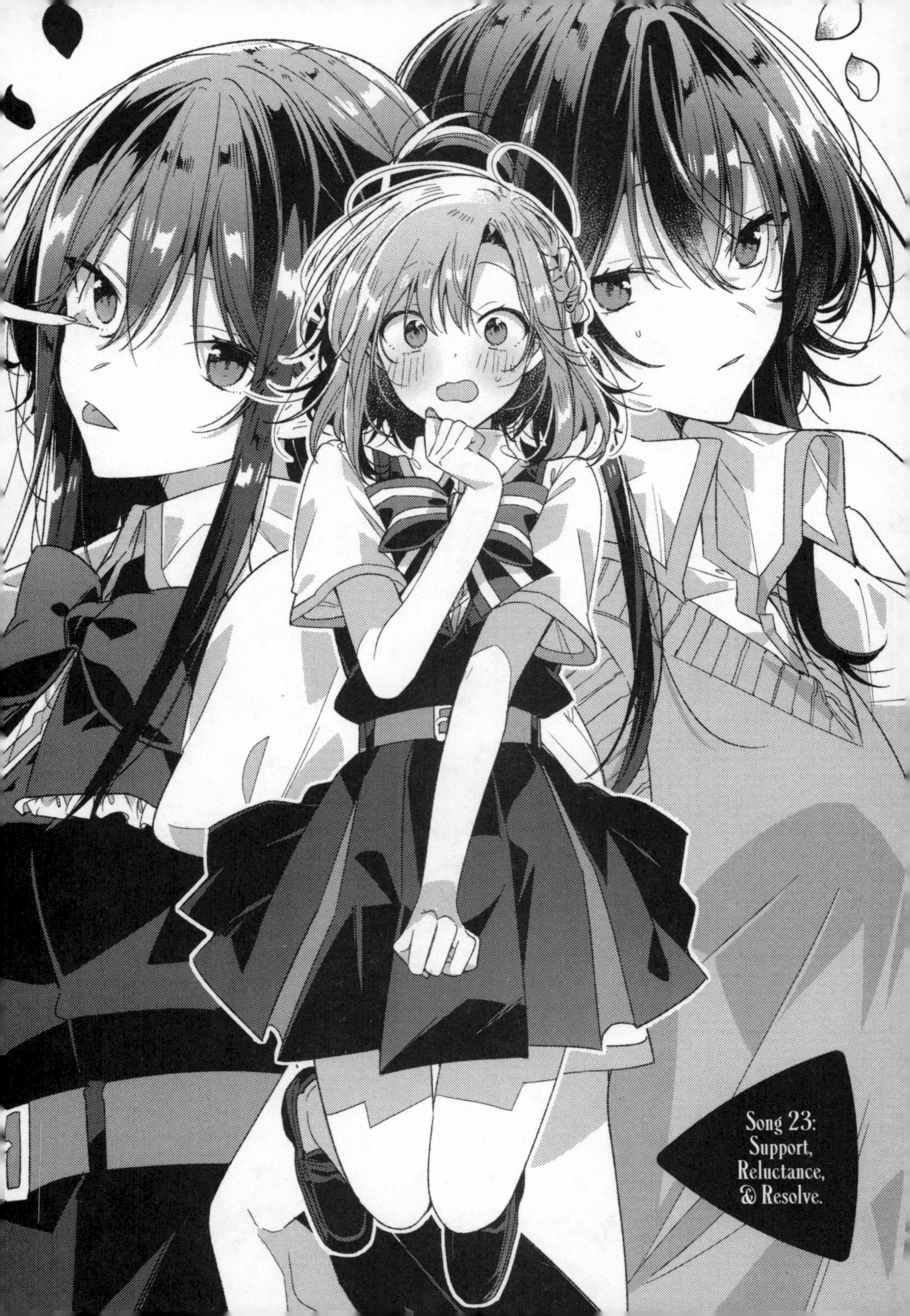
Song 23:
Support,
Reluctance,
& Resolve.

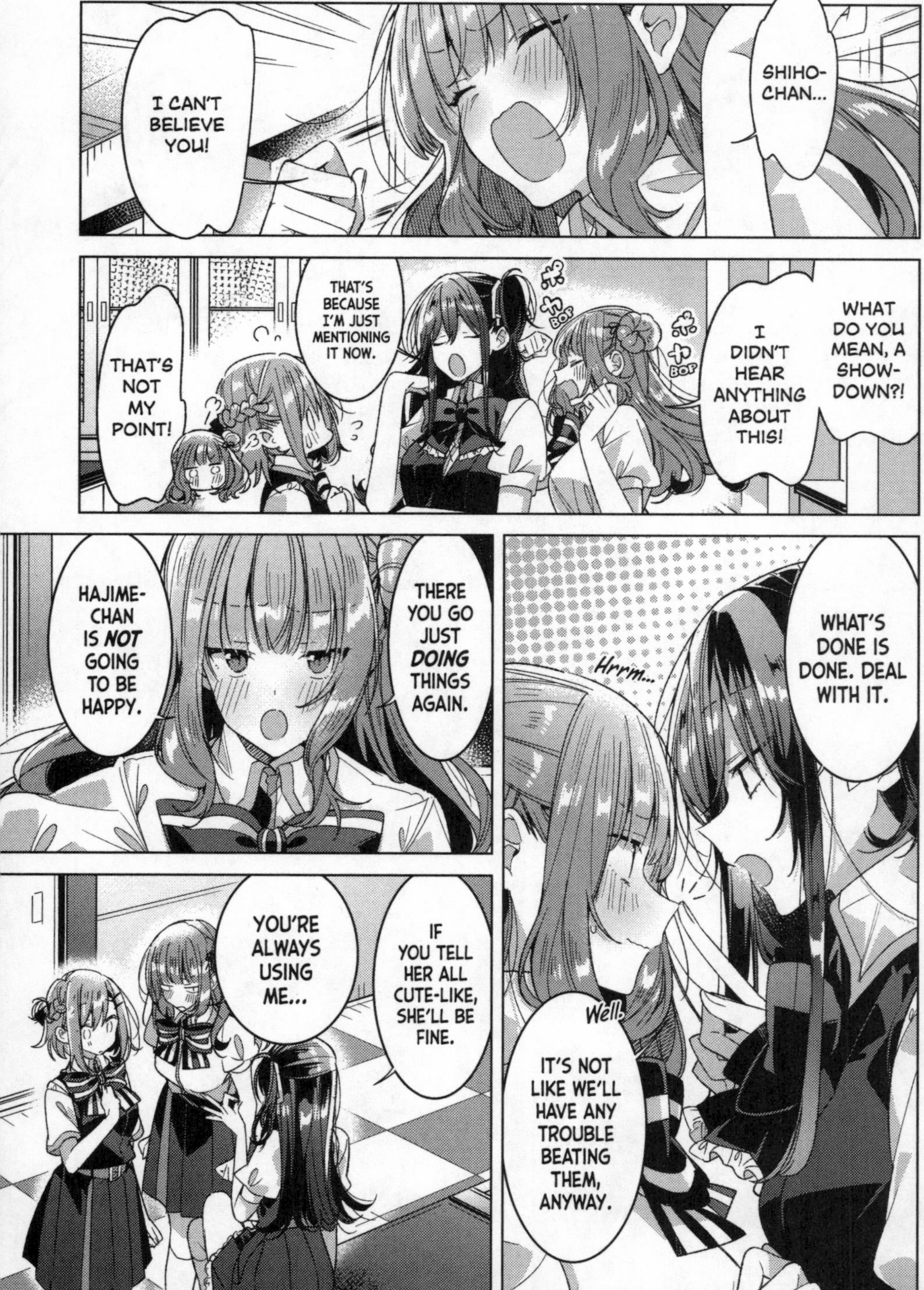
SHIHO-CHAN...
I CAN'T BELIEVE YOU!
WHAT DO YOU MEAN, A SHOW-DOWN?!
I DIDN'T HEAR ANYTHING ABOUT THIS!
BOP
BOP
THAT'S BECAUSE I'M JUST MENTIONING IT NOW.
THAT'S NOT MY POINT!
WHAT'S DONE IS DONE. DEAL WITH IT.
Hrrm...
Well
IT'S NOT LIKE WE'LL HAVE ANY TROUBLE BEATING THEM, ANYWAY.
THERE YOU GO JUST *DOING* THINGS AGAIN.
HAJIME-CHAN IS *NOT* GOING TO BE HAPPY.
IF YOU TELL HER ALL CUTE-LIKE, SHE'LL BE FINE.
YOU'RE ALWAYS USING ME...

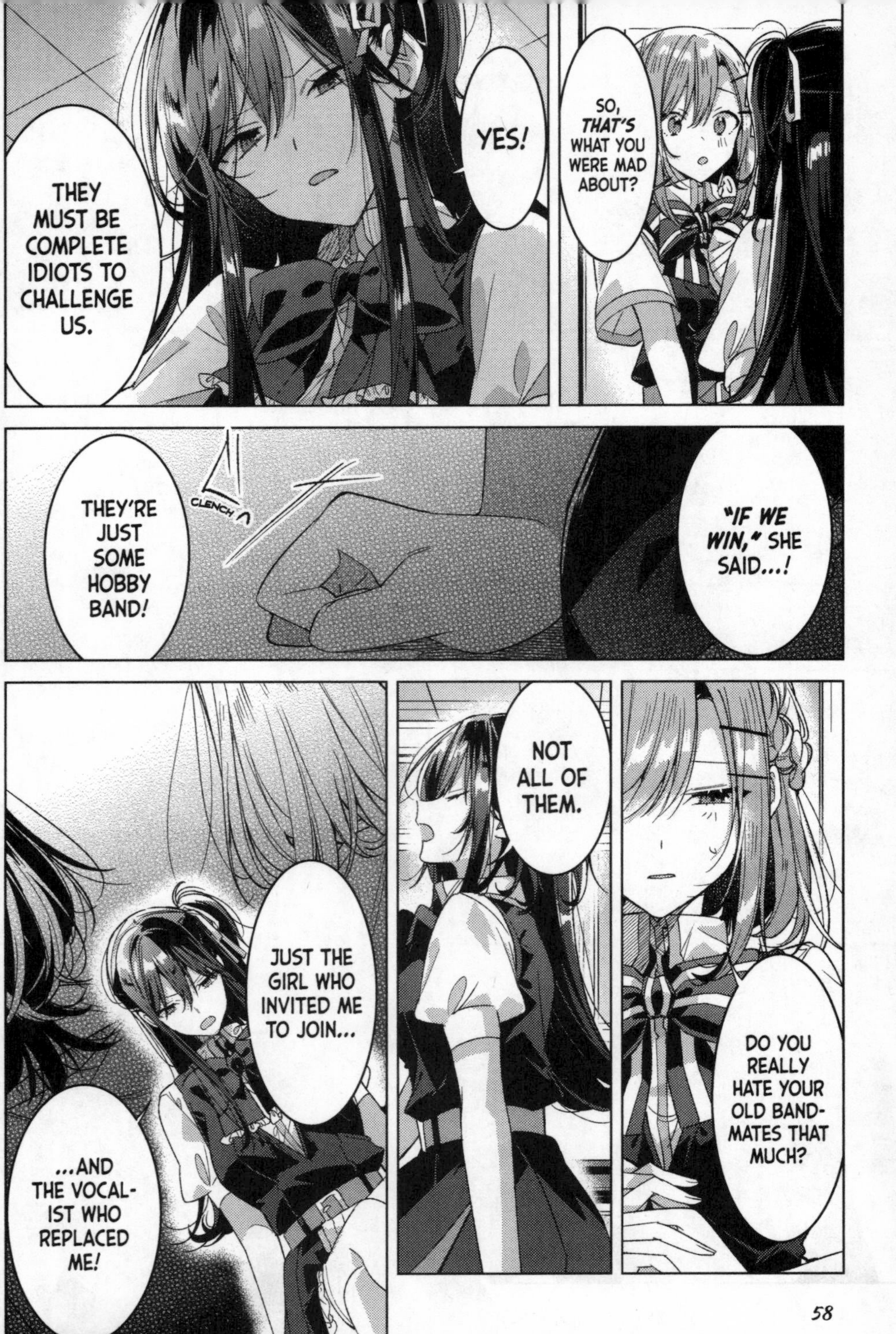
SO, *THAT'S* WHAT YOU WERE MAD ABOUT?
YES!
THEY MUST BE COMPLETE IDIOTS TO CHALLENGE US.
"IF WE WIN," SHE SAID...!
CLENCH
THEY'RE JUST SOME HOBBY BAND!
DO YOU REALLY HATE YOUR OLD BAND-MATES THAT MUCH?
NOT ALL OF THEM.
JUST THE GIRL WHO INVITED ME TO JOIN...
...AND THE VOCAL-IST WHO REPLACED ME!

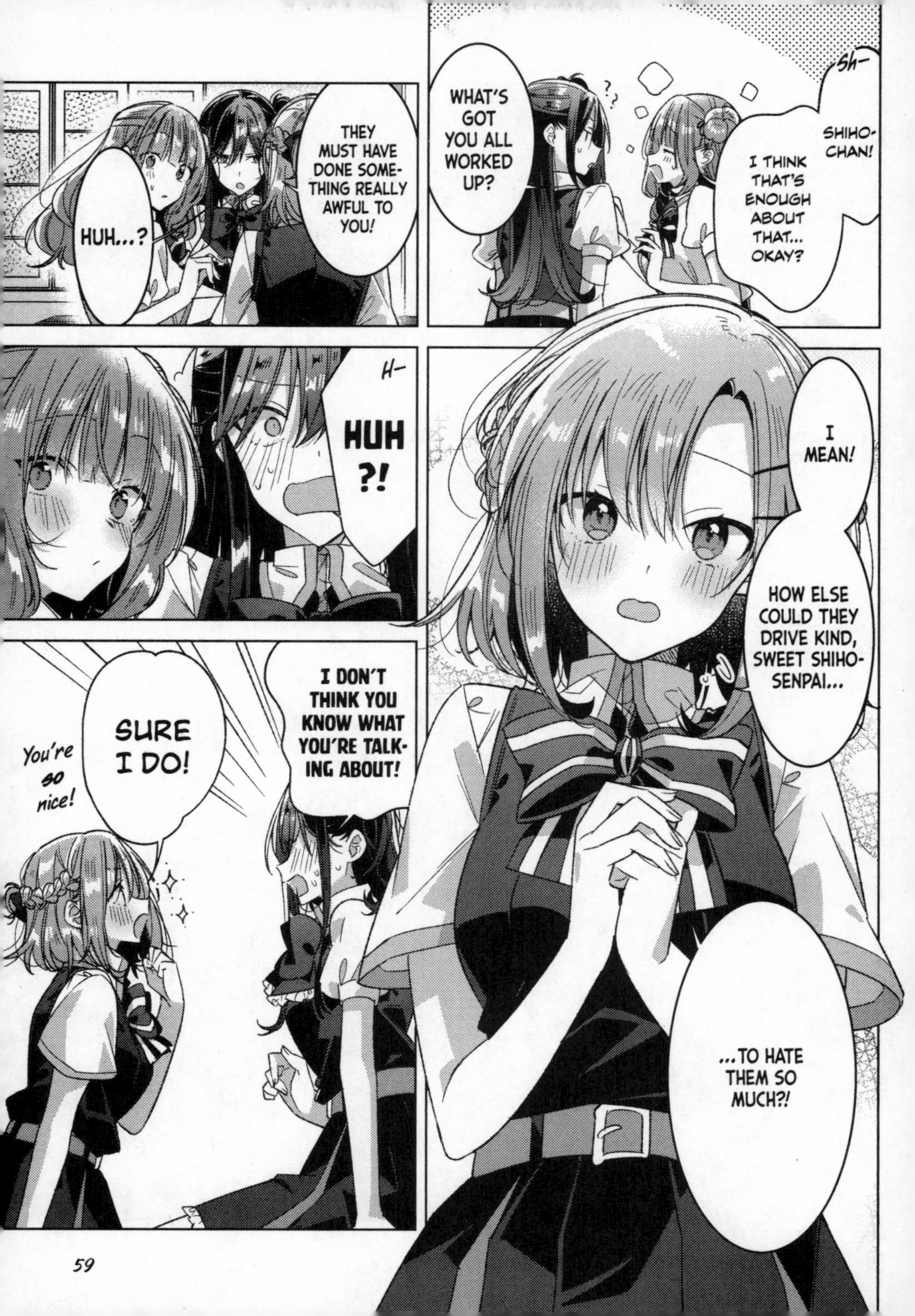
Sh—
SHIHO-CHAN! I THINK THAT'S ENOUGH ABOUT THAT... OKAY?
WHAT'S GOT YOU ALL WORKED UP?
THEY MUST HAVE DONE SOME-THING REALLY AWFUL TO YOU!
HUH...?
I MEAN!
HOW ELSE COULD THEY DRIVE KIND, SWEET SHIHO-SENPAI...
...TO HATE THEM SO MUCH?!
H—
HUH ?!
I DON'T THINK YOU KNOW WHAT YOU'RE TALK-ING ABOUT!
SURE I DO!
You're so nice!

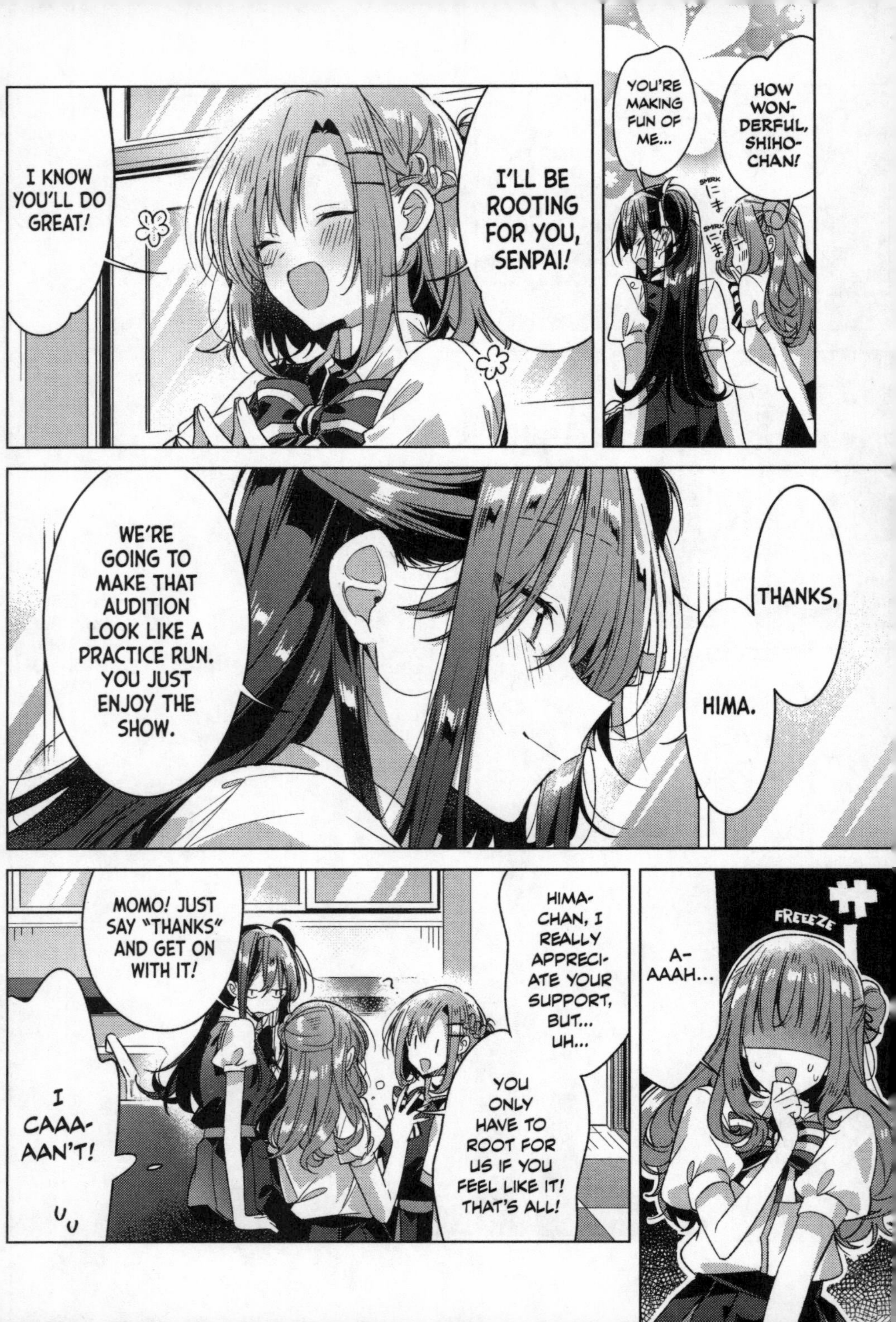
HOW WON-DERFUL, SHIHO-CHAN!
YOU'RE MAKING FUN OF ME...
SMIRK にま
SMIRK にま
I'LL BE ROOTING FOR YOU, SENPAI!
I KNOW YOU'LL DO GREAT!
THANKS,
HIMA.
WE'RE GOING TO MAKE THAT AUDITION LOOK LIKE A PRACTICE RUN. YOU JUST ENJOY THE SHOW.
FREEEZE
A-AAAH...
HIMA-CHAN, I REALLY APPRECI-ATE YOUR SUPPORT, BUT... UH...
YOU ONLY HAVE TO ROOT FOR US IF YOU FEEL LIKE IT! THAT'S ALL!
MOMO! JUST SAY "THANKS" AND GET ON WITH IT!
I CAAA-AAN'T!

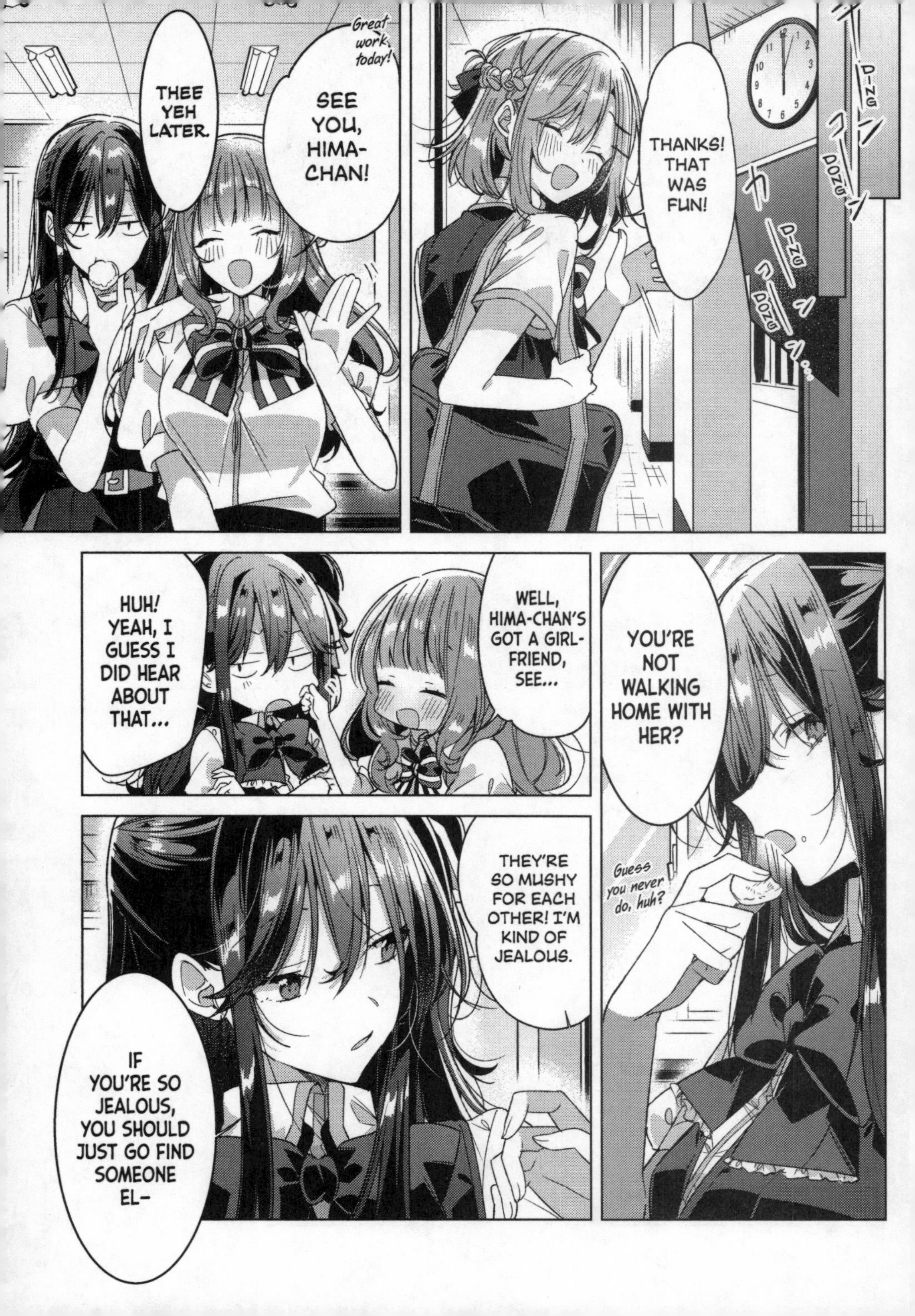
DING DONG
DING DONG
THANKS! THAT WAS FUN!
Great work today!
SEE YOU, HIMA-CHAN!
THEE YEH LATER.
YOU'RE NOT WALKING HOME WITH HER?
Guess you never do, huh?
WELL, HIMA-CHAN'S GOT A GIRL-FRIEND, SEE...
HUH! YEAH, I GUESS I DID HEAR ABOUT THAT...
THEY'RE SO MUSHY FOR EACH OTHER! I'M KIND OF JEALOUS.
IF YOU'RE SO JEALOUS, YOU SHOULD JUST GO FIND SOMEONE EL-

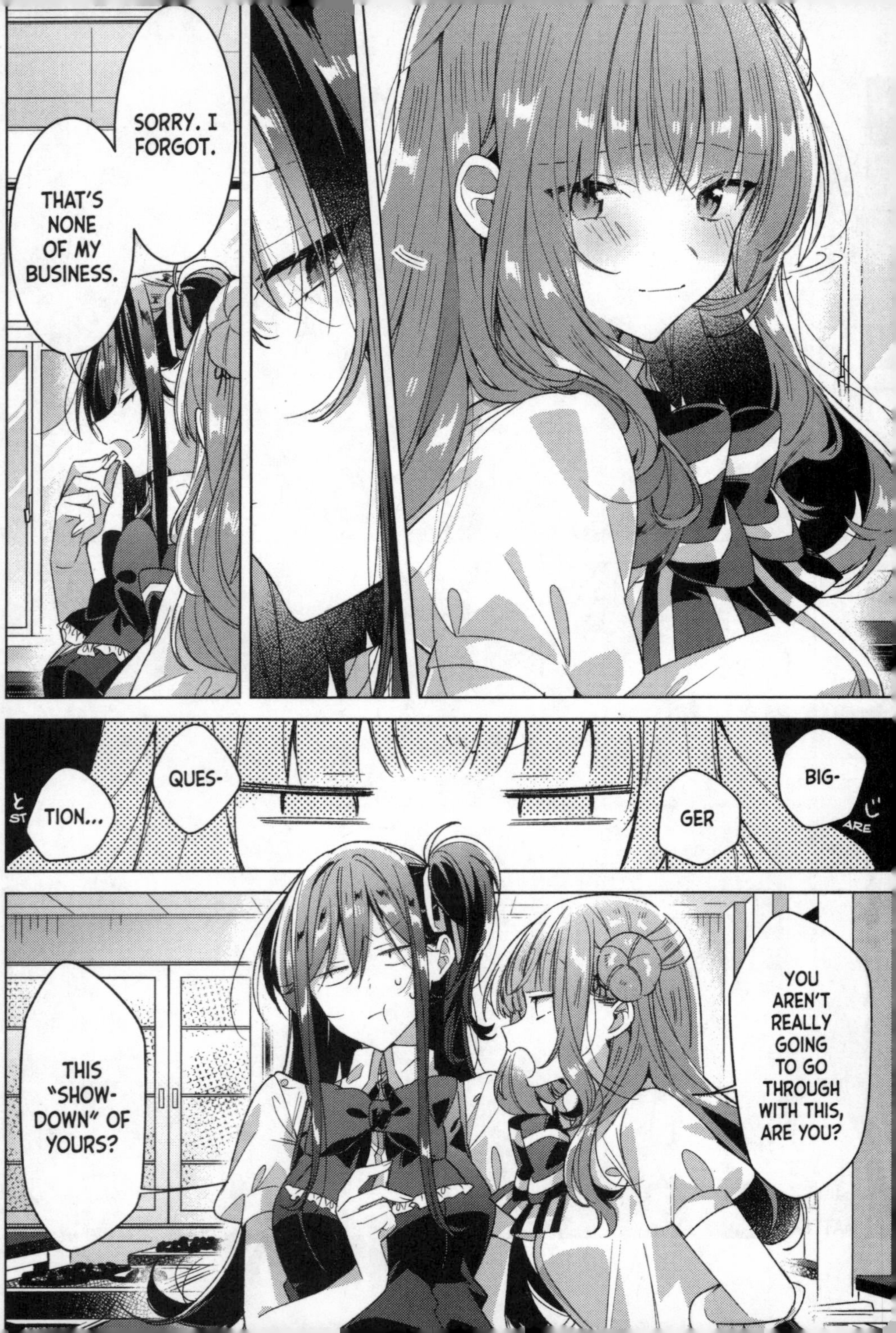
SORRY. I FORGOT.
THAT'S NONE OF MY BUSINESS.
じ
ARE
BIG-
GER
QUES-
TION...
と
ST
YOU AREN'T REALLY GOING TO GO THROUGH WITH THIS, ARE YOU?
THIS "SHOW-DOWN" OF YOURS?

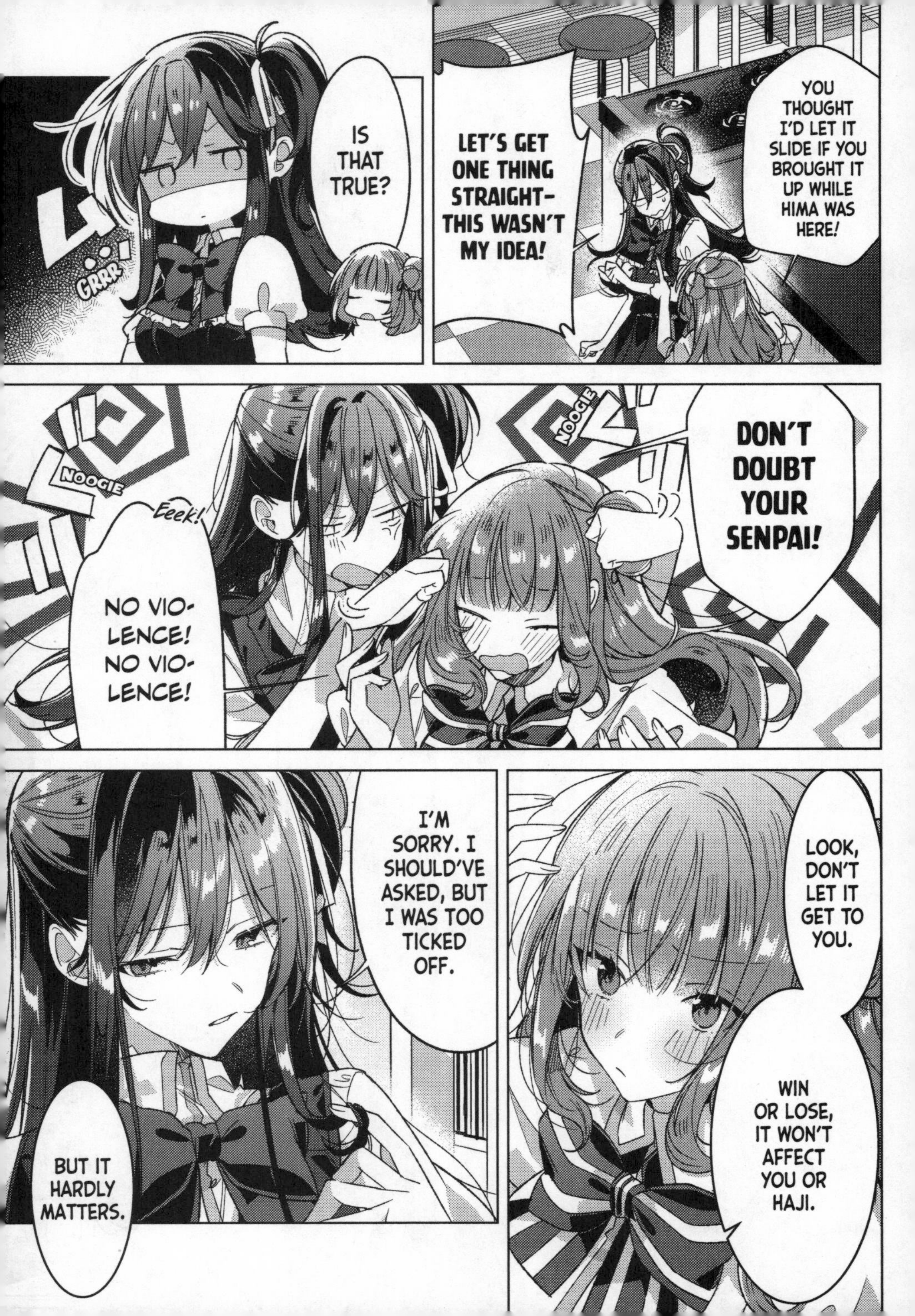

YOU THOUGHT I'D LET IT SLIDE IF YOU BROUGHT IT UP WHILE HIMA WAS HERE!
LET'S GET ONE THING STRAIGHT— THIS WASN'T MY IDEA!
IS THAT TRUE?
GRRR
DON'T DOUBT YOUR SENPAI!
NOOGIE
NOOGIE
Eeek!
NO VIO- LENCE! NO VIO- LENCE!
LOOK, DON'T LET IT GET TO YOU.
WIN OR LOSE, IT WON'T AFFECT YOU OR HAJI.
I'M SORRY. I SHOULD'VE ASKED, BUT I WAS TOO TICKED OFF.
BUT IT HARDLY MATTERS.

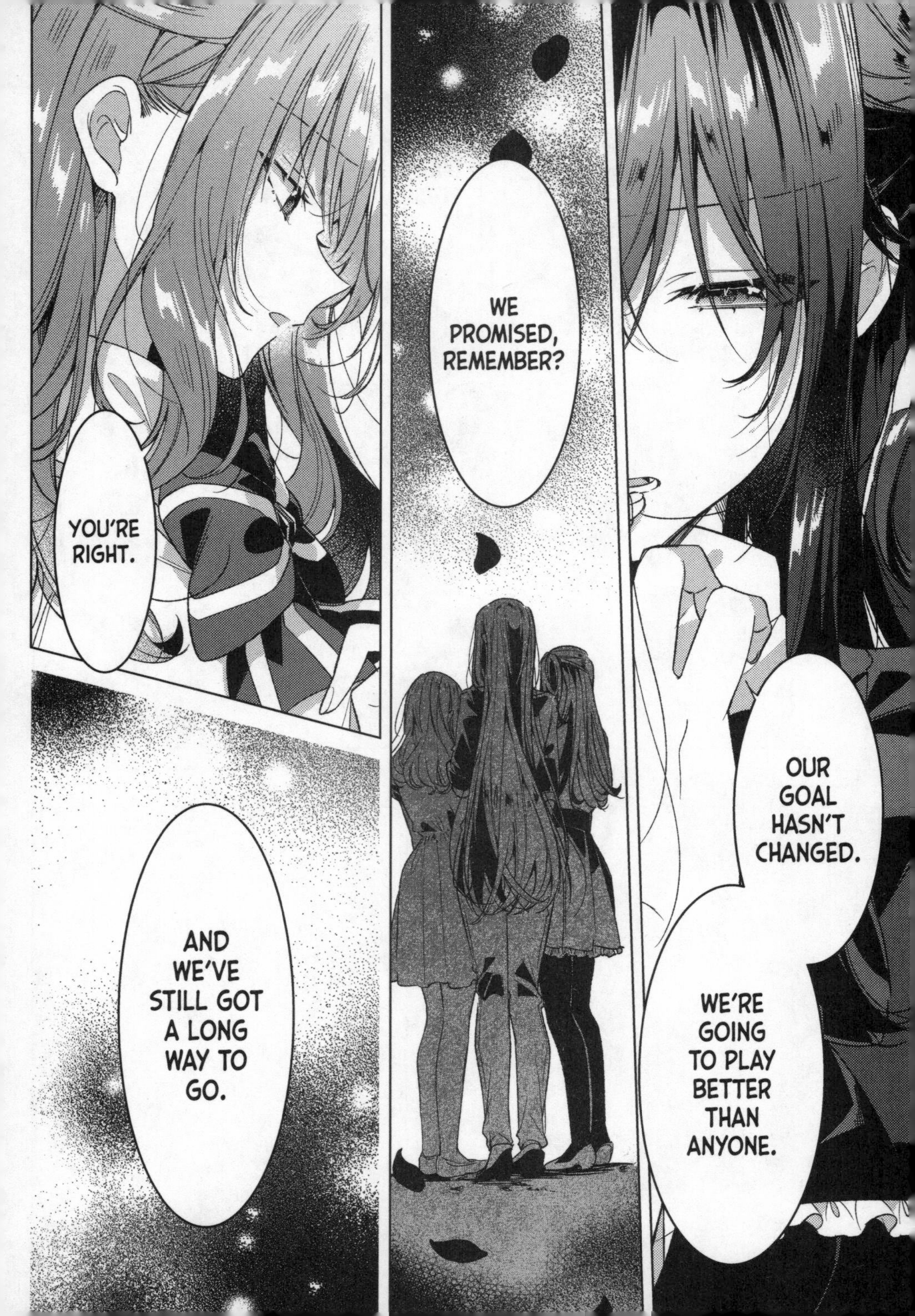
OUR GOAL HASN'T CHANGED.
WE'RE GOING TO PLAY BETTER THAN ANYONE.
WE PROMISED, REMEMBER?
YOU'RE RIGHT.
AND WE'VE STILL GOT A LONG WAY TO GO.

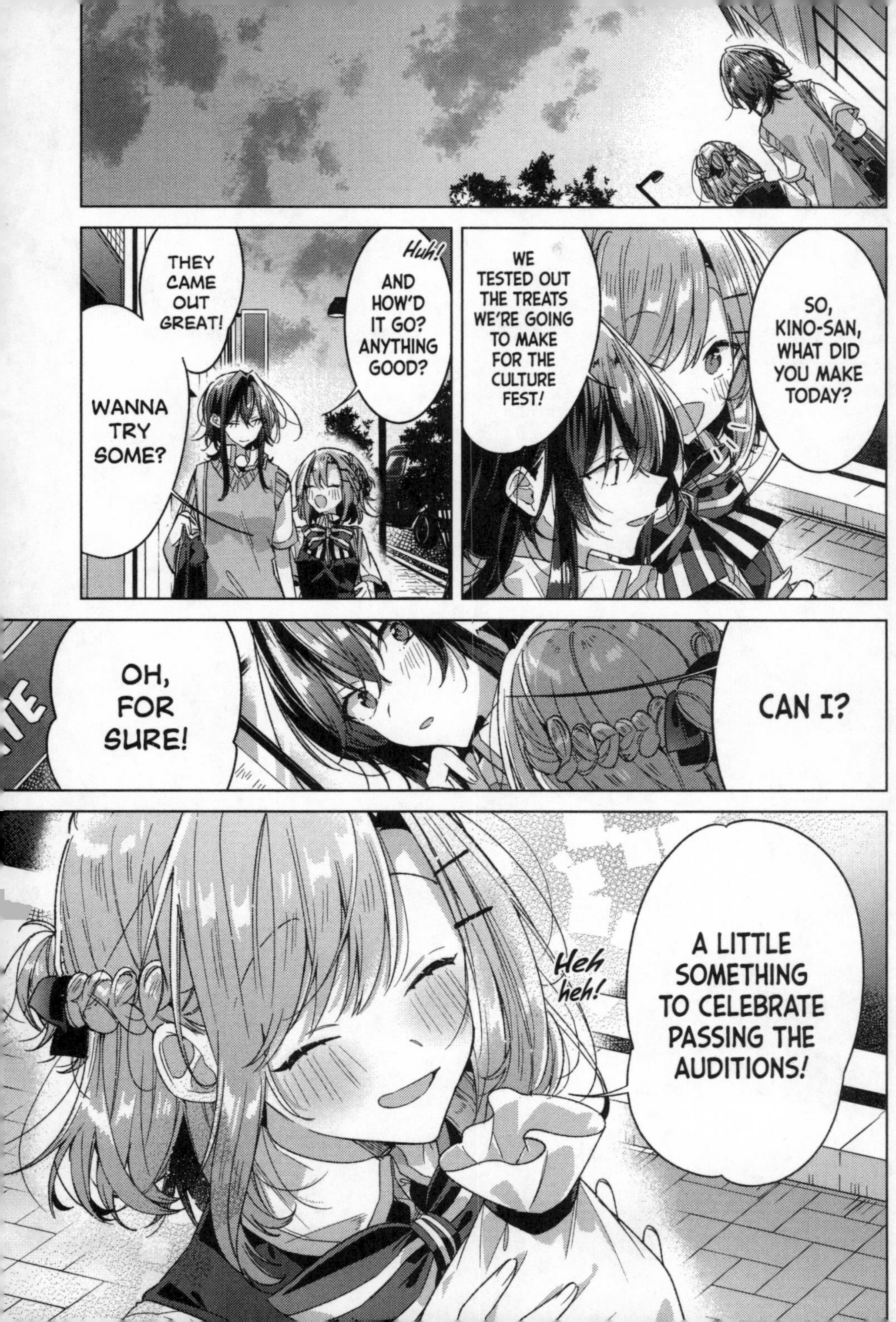
SO, KINO-SAN, WHAT DID YOU MAKE TODAY?
WE TESTED OUT THE TREATS WE'RE GOING TO MAKE FOR THE CULTURE FEST!
Huh!
AND HOW'D IT GO? ANYTHING GOOD?
THEY CAME OUT GREAT!
WANNA TRY SOME?
CAN I?
OH, FOR SURE!
A LITTLE SOMETHING TO CELEBRATE PASSING THE AUDITIONS!
Heh heh!

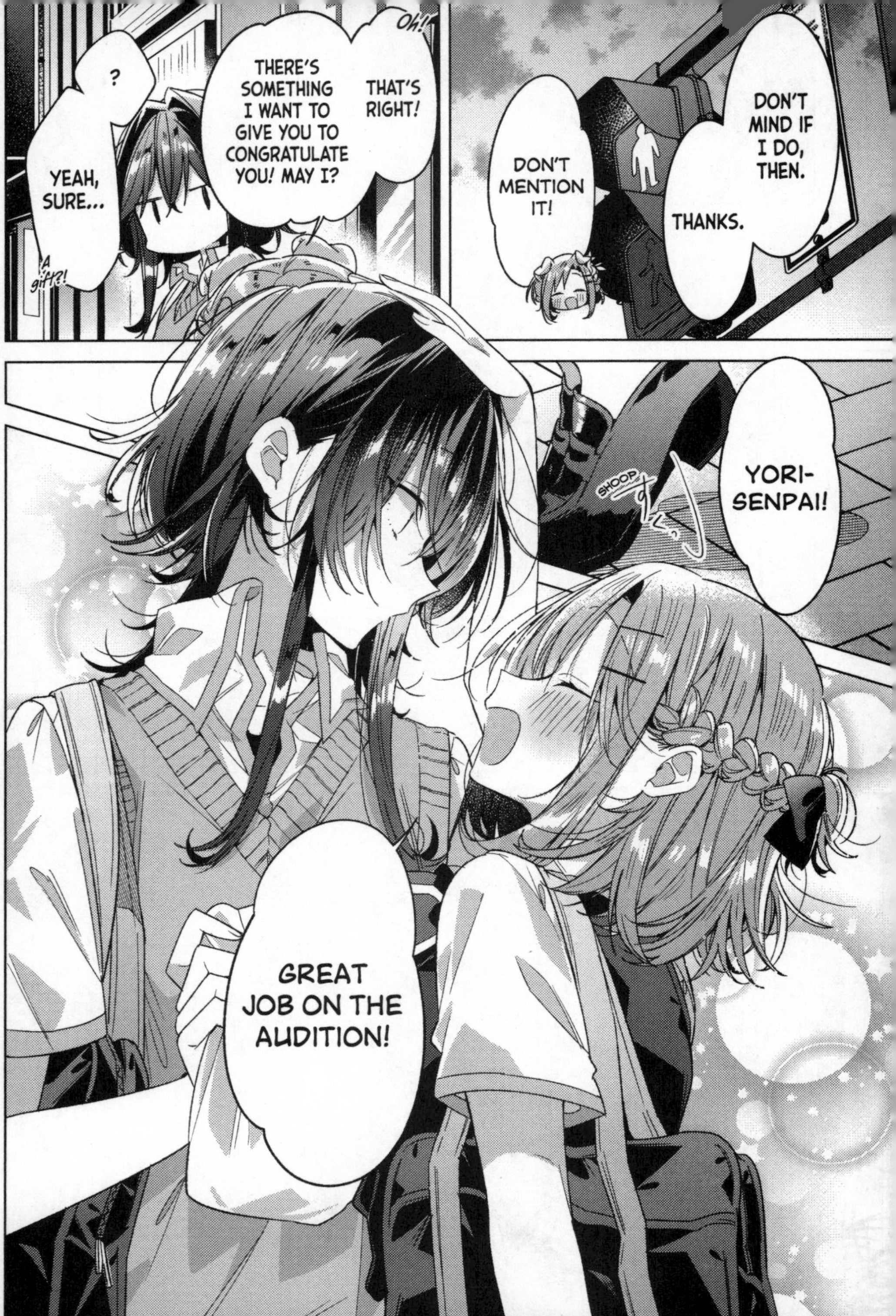
DON'T MIND IF I DO, THEN.
THANKS.
DON'T MENTION IT!
Oh!
THAT'S RIGHT!
THERE'S SOMETHING I WANT TO GIVE YOU TO CONGRATULATE YOU! MAY I?
?
YEAH, SURE...
A gift!?
YORI-SENPAI!
SHOOP
GREAT JOB ON THE AUDITION!

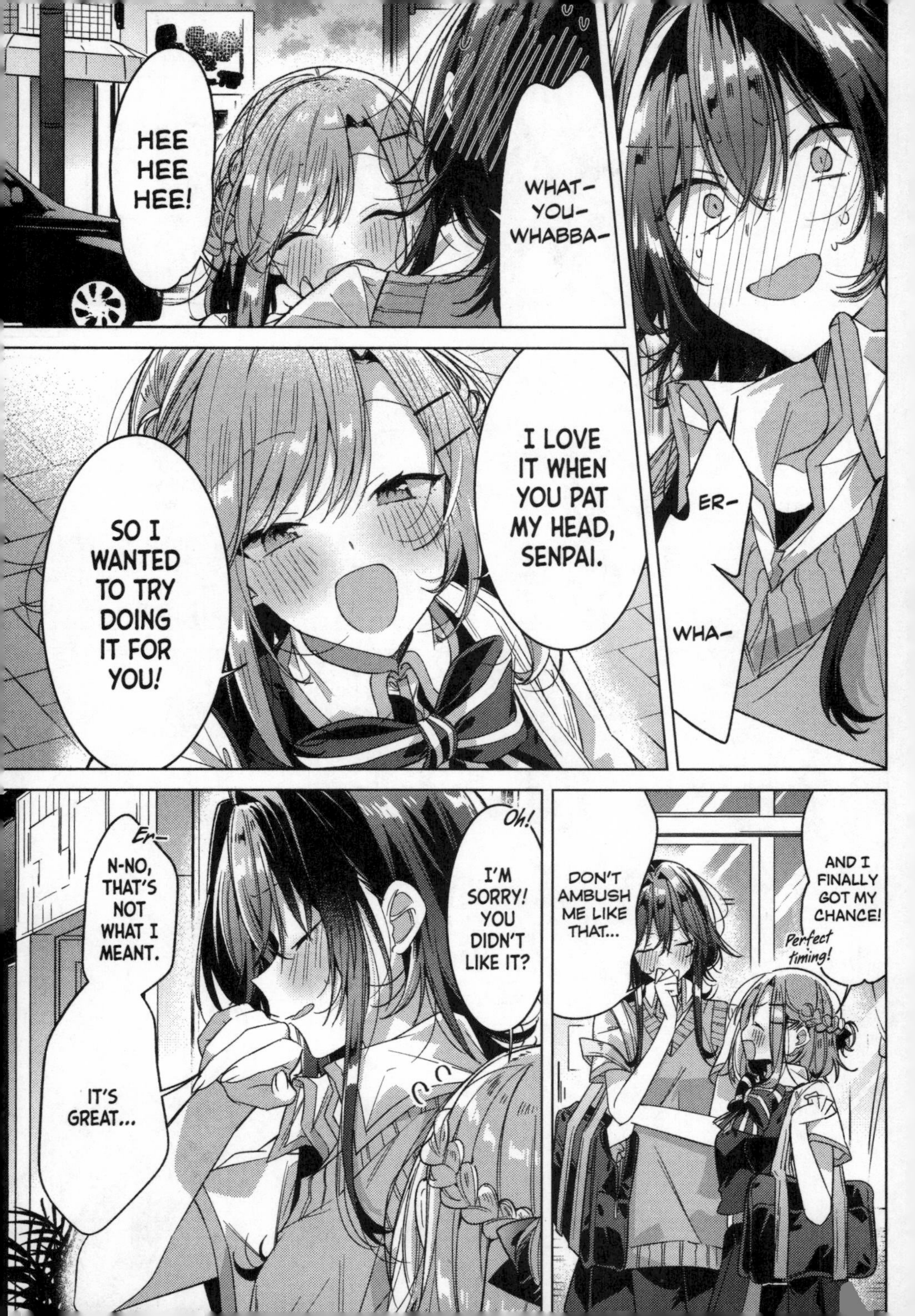
WHAT- YOU- WHABBA-
ER-
WHA-
HEE HEE HEE!
I LOVE IT WHEN YOU PAT MY HEAD, SENPAI.
SO I WANTED TO TRY DOING IT FOR YOU!
AND I FINALLY GOT MY CHANCE!
Perfect timing!
DON'T AMBUSH ME LIKE THAT...
Oh!
I'M SORRY! YOU DIDN'T LIKE IT?
Er—
N-NO, THAT'S NOT WHAT I MEANT.
IT'S GREAT...

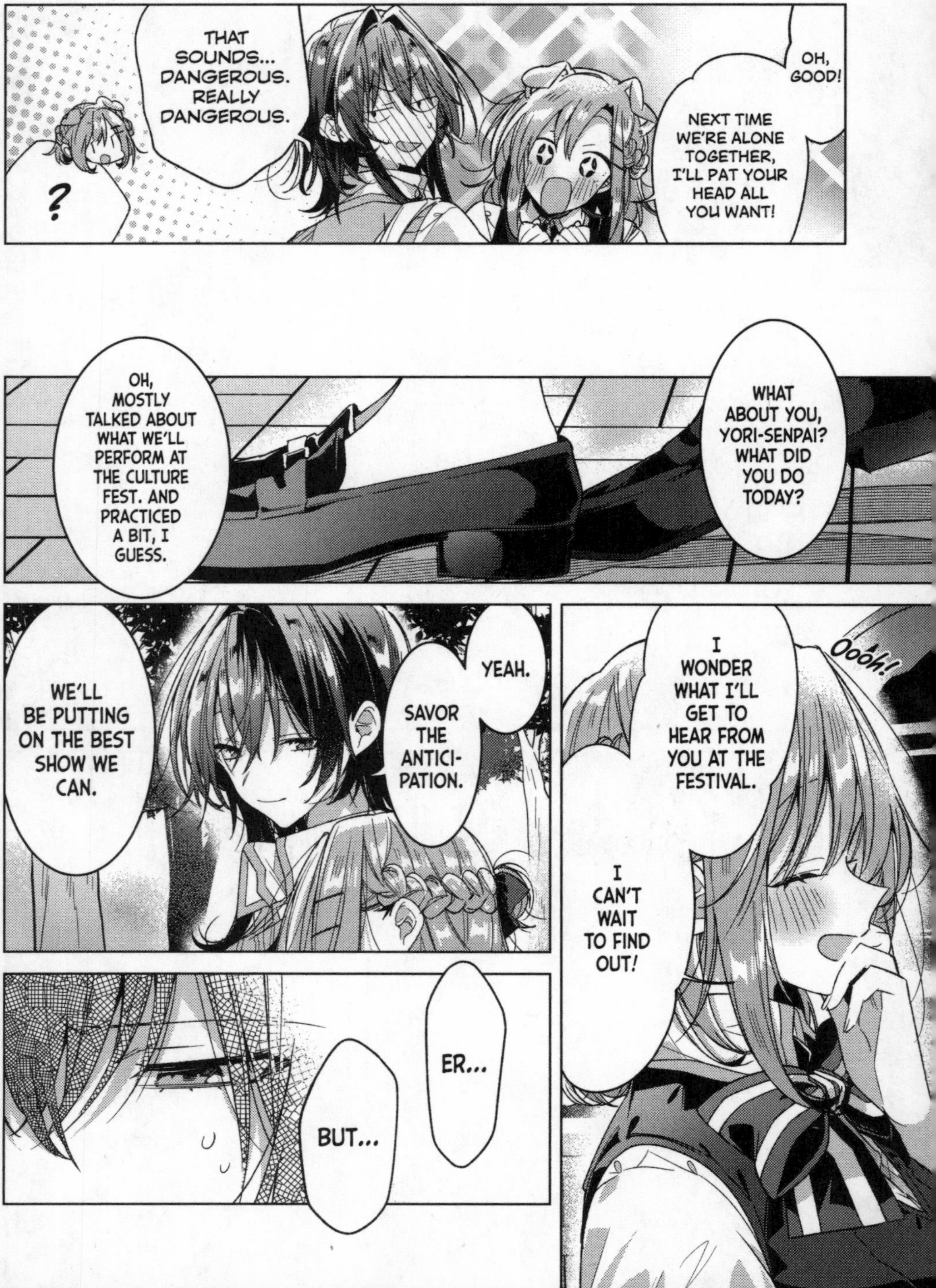
OH, GOOD!
NEXT TIME WE'RE ALONE TOGETHER, I'LL PAT YOUR HEAD ALL YOU WANT!
THAT SOUNDS... DANGEROUS. REALLY DANGEROUS.
?
WHAT ABOUT YOU, YORI-SENPAI? WHAT DID YOU DO TODAY?
OH, MOSTLY TALKED ABOUT WHAT WE'LL PERFORM AT THE CULTURE FEST. AND PRACTICED A BIT, I GUESS.
Oooh!
I WONDER WHAT I'LL GET TO HEAR FROM YOU AT THE FESTIVAL.
I CAN'T WAIT TO FIND OUT!
YEAH.
SAVOR THE ANTICI-PATION.
WE'LL BE PUTTING ON THE BEST SHOW WE CAN.
ER...
BUT...

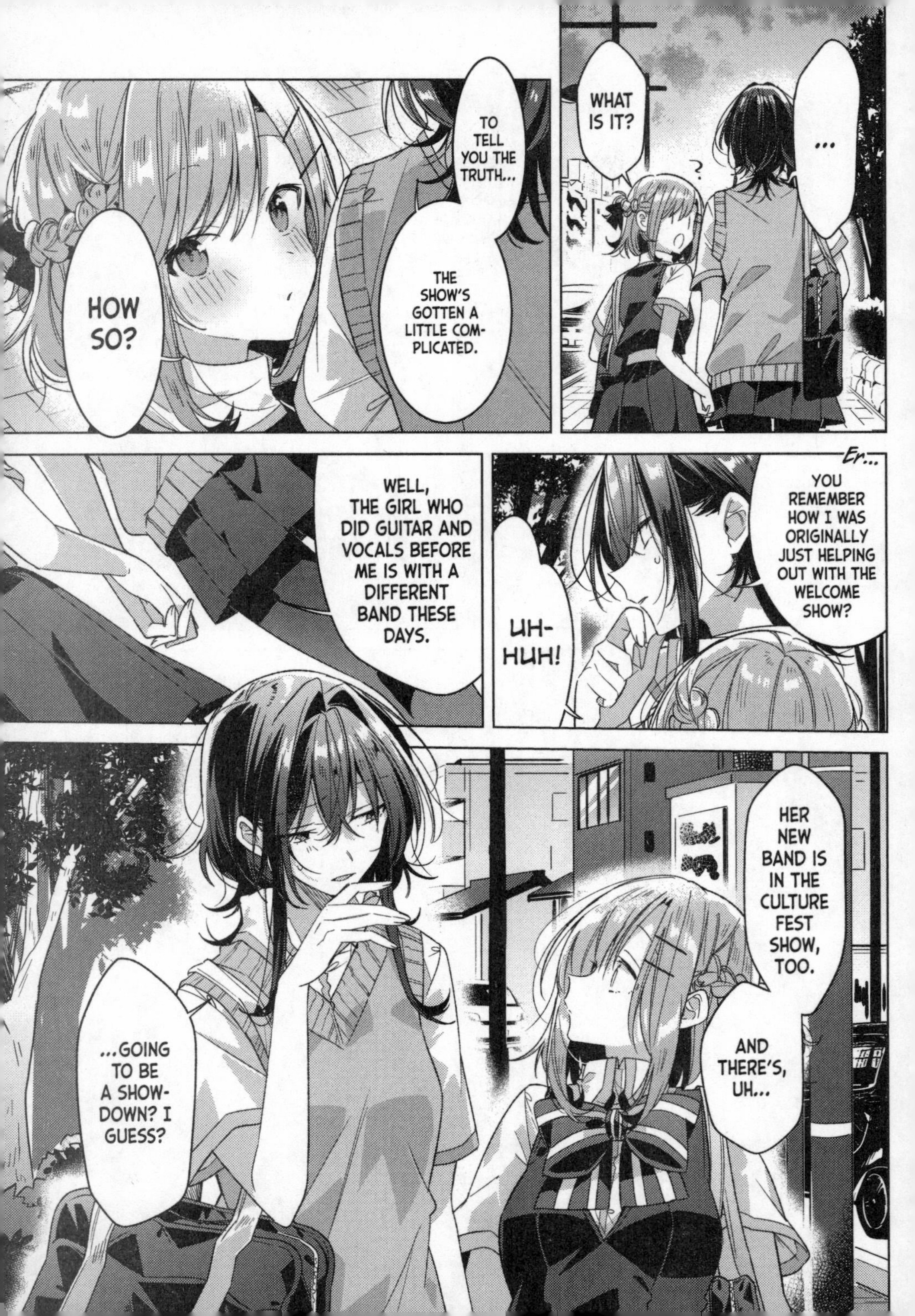
...
WHAT IS IT?
TO TELL YOU THE TRUTH...
THE SHOW'S GOTTEN A LITTLE COMPLICATED.
HOW SO?
Er...
YOU REMEMBER HOW I WAS ORIGINALLY JUST HELPING OUT WITH THE WELCOME SHOW?
UH-HUH!
WELL, THE GIRL WHO DID GUITAR AND VOCALS BEFORE ME IS WITH A DIFFERENT BAND THESE DAYS.
HER NEW BAND IS IN THE CULTURE FEST SHOW, TOO.
AND THERE'S, UH...
...GOING TO BE A SHOW-DOWN? I GUESS?

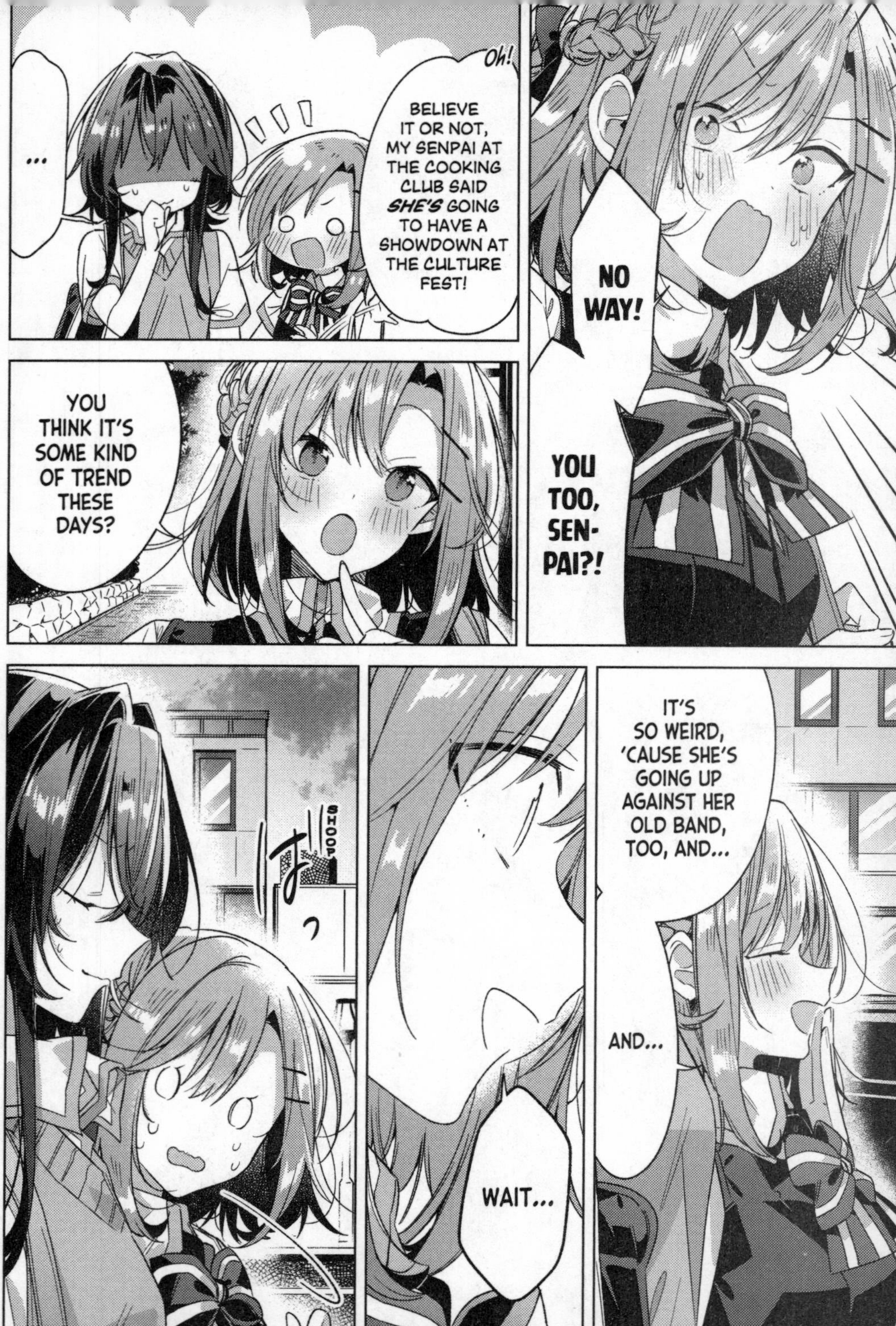
NO WAY!
YOU TOO, SEN-PAI?!
Oh!
BELIEVE IT OR NOT, MY SENPAI AT THE COOKING CLUB SAID *SHE'S* GOING TO HAVE A SHOWDOWN AT THE CULTURE FEST!
...
YOU THINK IT'S SOME KIND OF TREND THESE DAYS?
IT'S SO WEIRD, 'CAUSE SHE'S GOING UP AGAINST HER OLD BAND, TOO, AND...
AND...
WAIT...
SHOOP

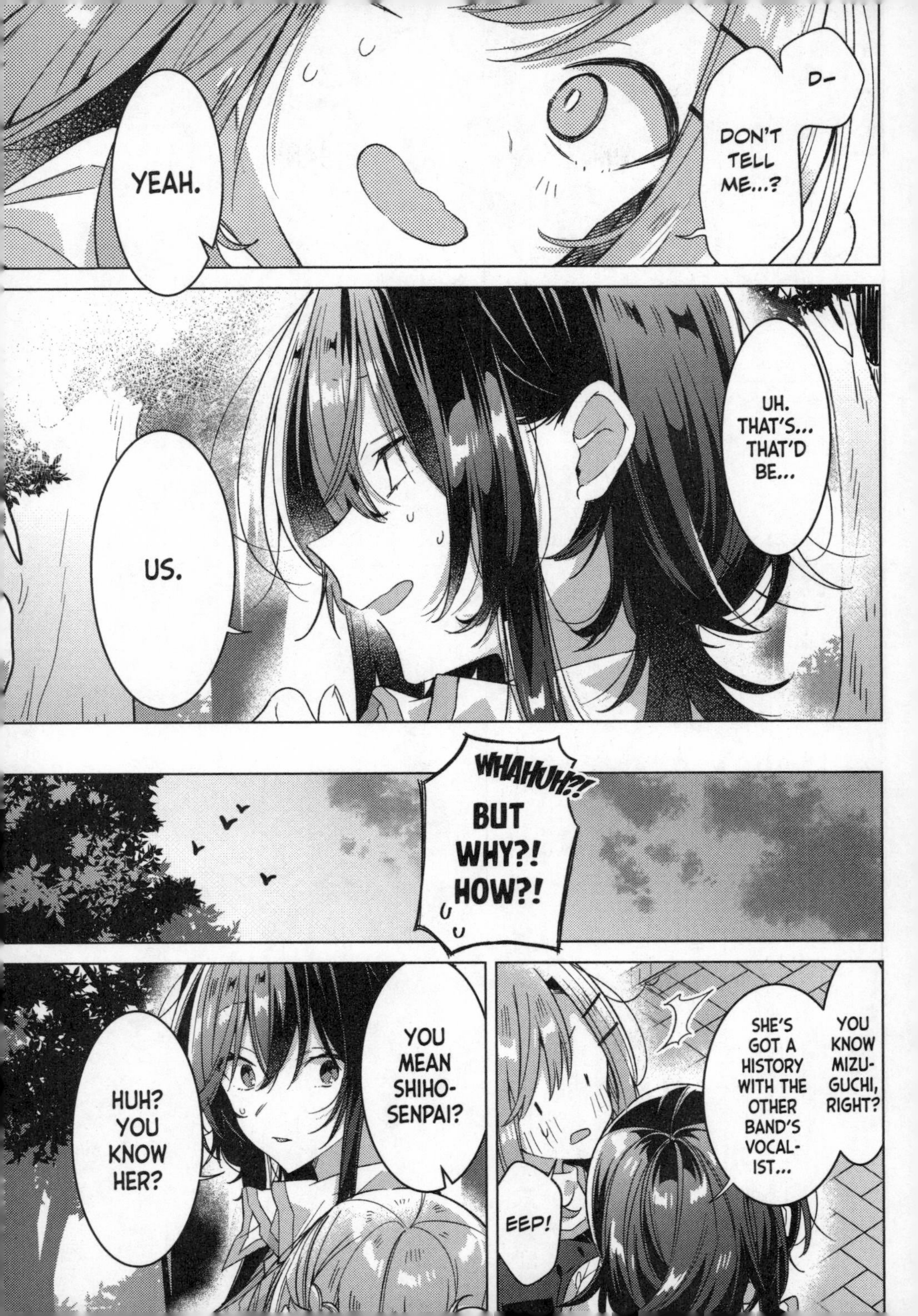
D– DON'T TELL ME...?
YEAH.
UH. THAT'S... THAT'D BE...
US.
WHAHUH?!
BUT WHY?! HOW?!
YOU KNOW MIZU-GUCHI, RIGHT?
SHE'S GOT A HISTORY WITH THE OTHER BAND'S VOCAL-IST...
EEP!
YOU MEAN SHIHO-SENPAI?
HUH? YOU KNOW HER?

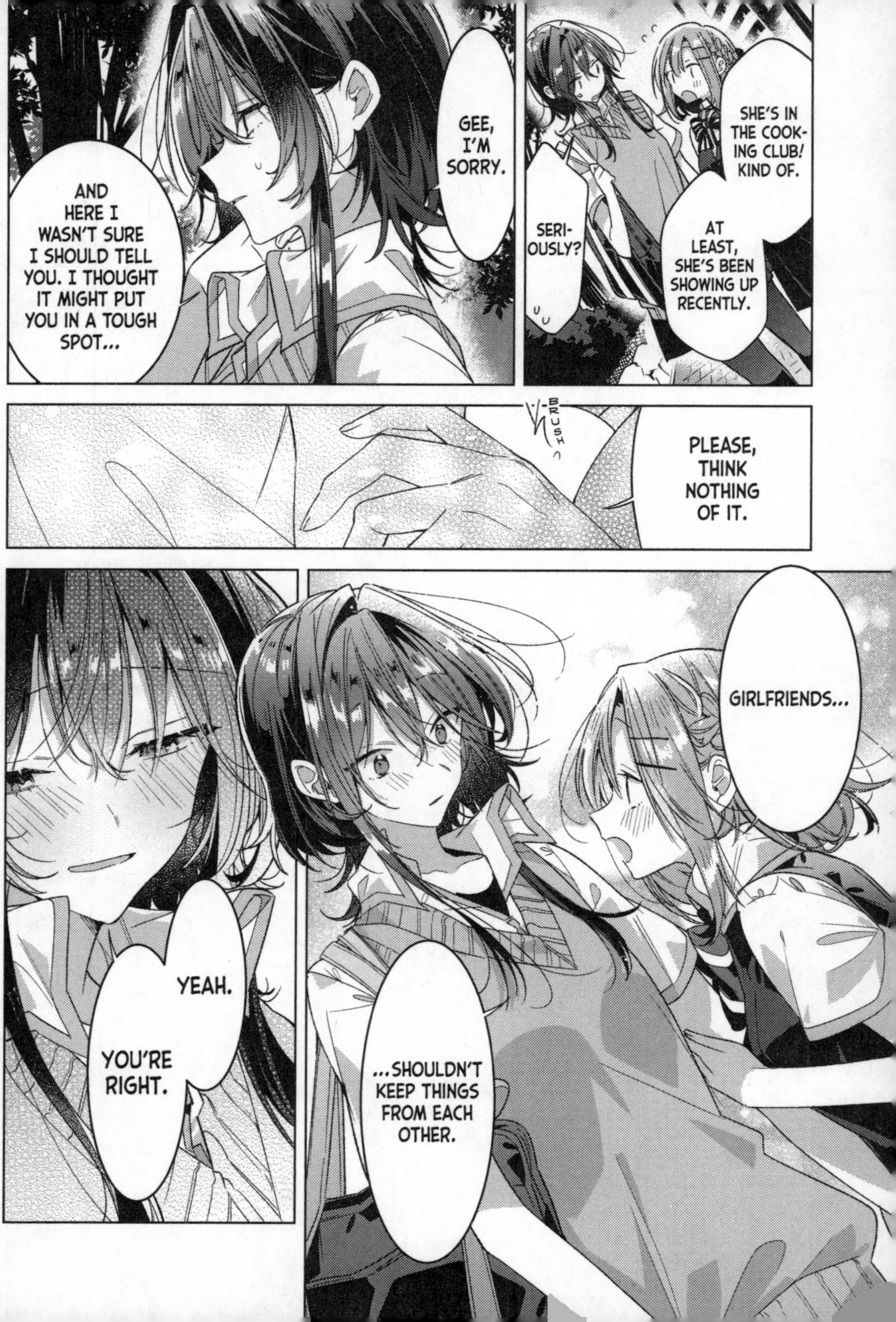
SHE'S IN THE COOKING CLUB! KIND OF.
SERIOUSLY?
AT LEAST, SHE'S BEEN SHOWING UP RECENTLY.
GEE, I'M SORRY.
AND HERE I WASN'T SURE I SHOULD TELL YOU. I THOUGHT IT MIGHT PUT YOU IN A TOUGH SPOT...
BRUSH
PLEASE, THINK NOTHING OF IT.
GIRLFRIENDS...
...SHOULDN'T KEEP THINGS FROM EACH OTHER.
YEAH.
YOU'RE RIGHT.

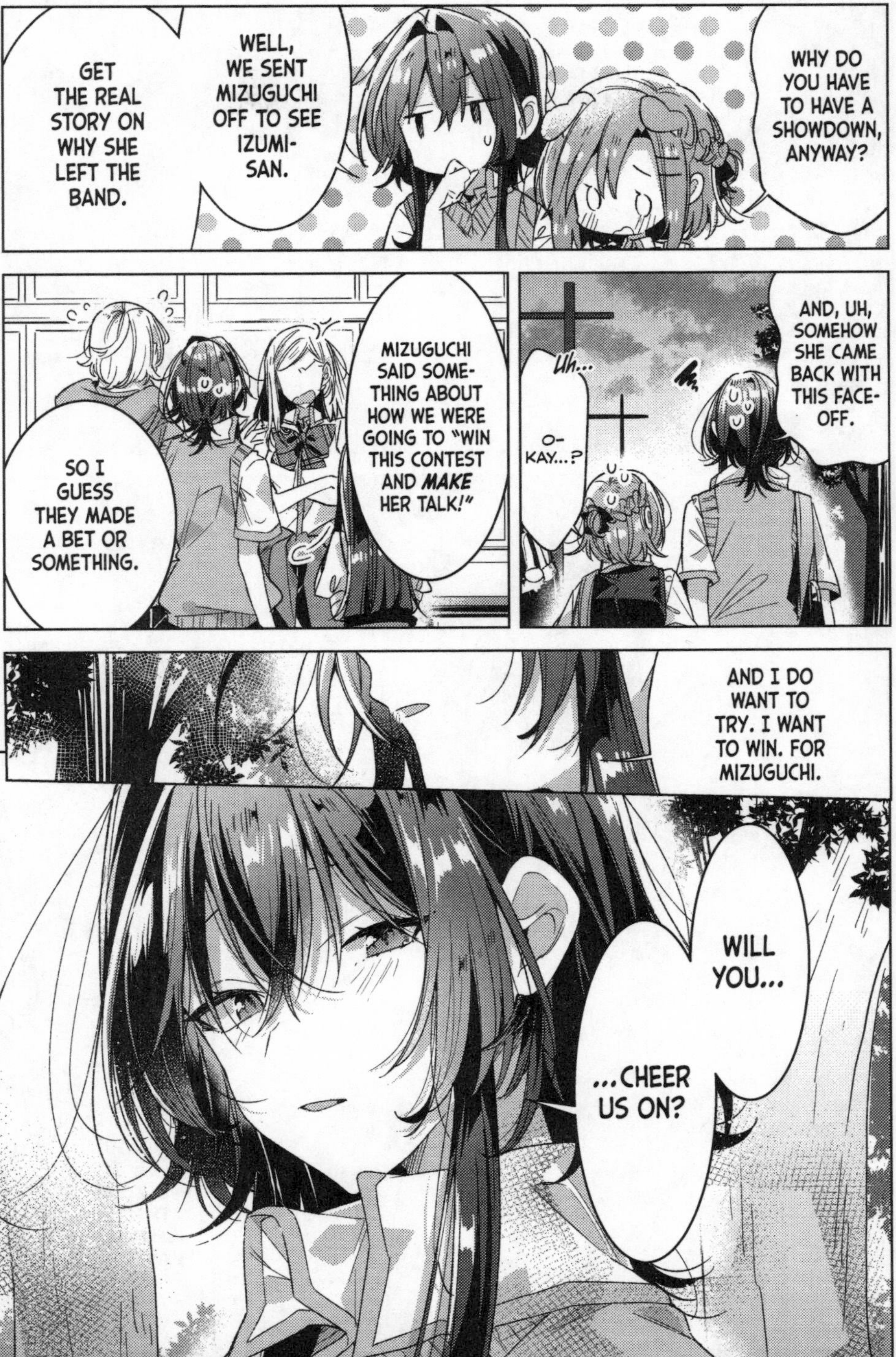
WHY DO YOU HAVE TO HAVE A SHOWDOWN, ANYWAY?
WELL, WE SENT MIZUGUCHI OFF TO SEE IZUMI-SAN.
GET THE REAL STORY ON WHY SHE LEFT THE BAND.
AND, UH, SOMEHOW SHE CAME BACK WITH THIS FACE-OFF.
UH...
O-KAY...?
MIZUGUCHI SAID SOME-THING ABOUT HOW WE WERE GOING TO "WIN THIS CONTEST AND *MAKE* HER TALK!"
SO I GUESS THEY MADE A BET OR SOMETHING.
AND I DO WANT TO TRY. I WANT TO WIN. FOR MIZUGUCHI.
WILL YOU...
...CHEER US ON?

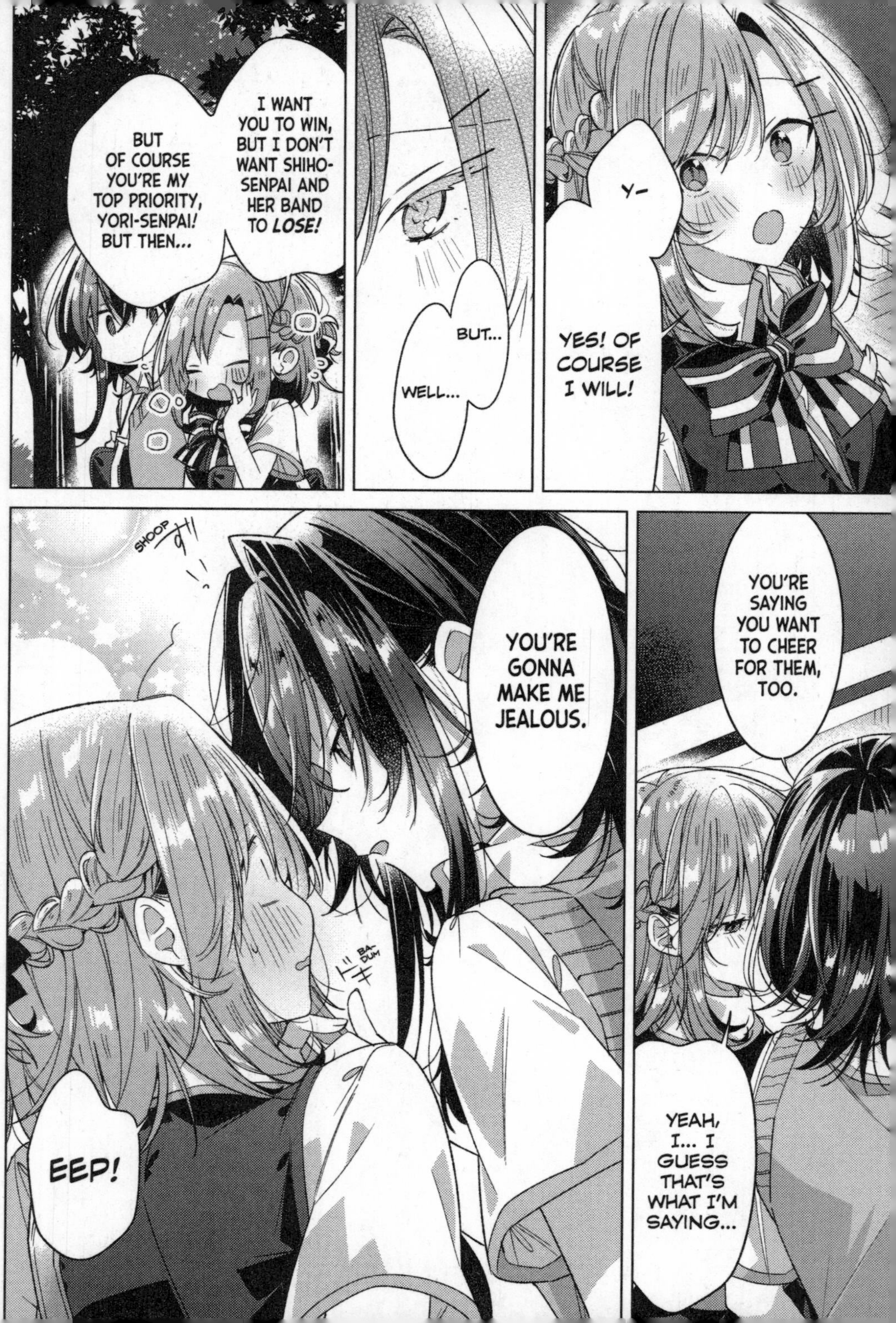
Y-
YES! OF COURSE I WILL!
BUT...
WELL...
I WANT YOU TO WIN, BUT I DON'T WANT SHIHO-SENPAI AND HER BAND TO *LOSE!*
BUT OF COURSE YOU'RE MY TOP PRIORITY, YORI-SENPAI! BUT THEN...
YOU'RE SAYING YOU WANT TO CHEER FOR THEM, TOO.
YEAH, I... I GUESS THAT'S WHAT I'M SAYING...
SHOOP
YOU'RE GONNA MAKE ME JEALOUS.
BA-DUM
EEP!

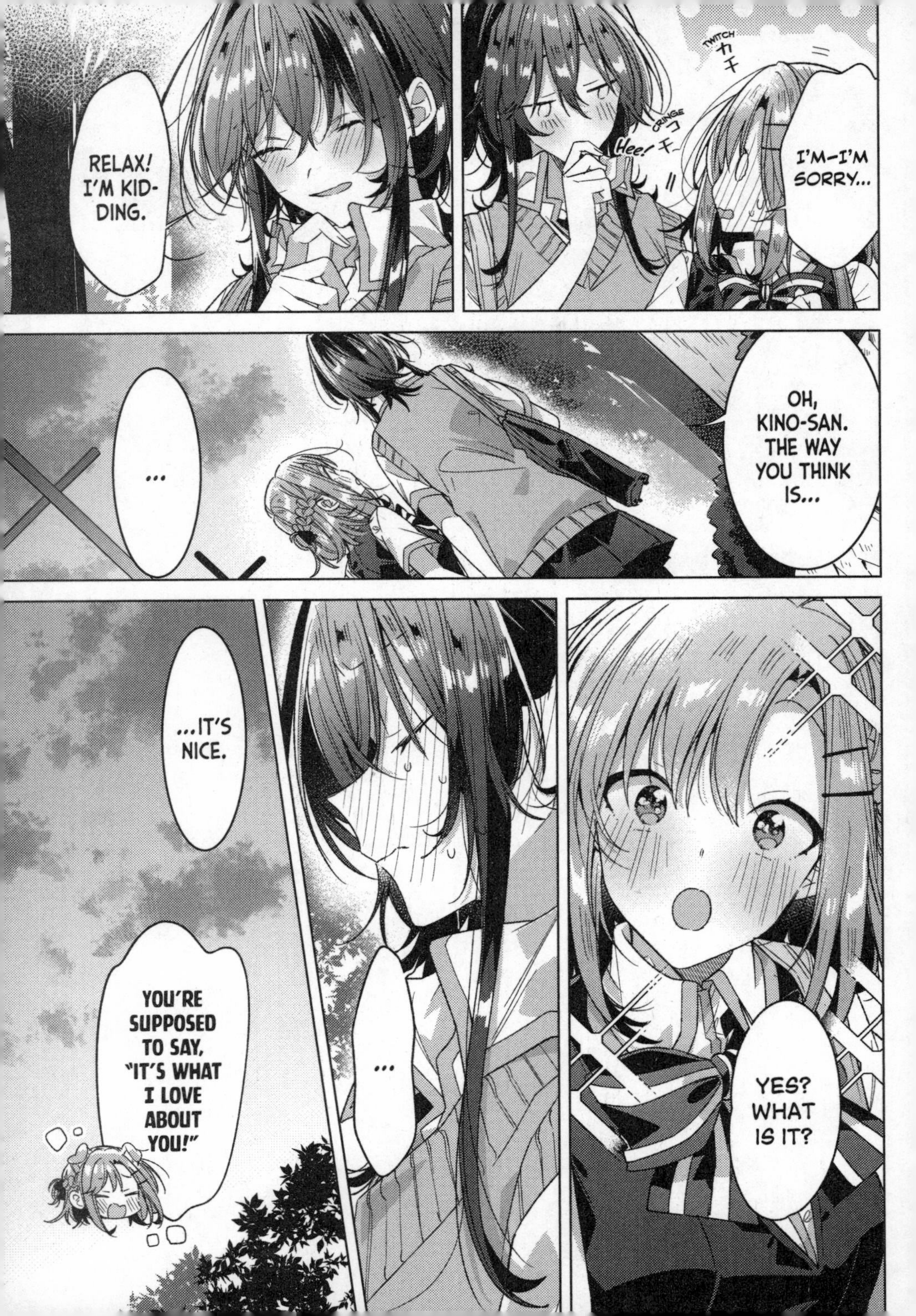
TWITCH
カチ
CRINGE
コチ
Hee!
I'M—I'M SORRY...
RELAX! I'M KID-DING.
OH, KINO-SAN. THE WAY YOU THINK IS...
...
YES? WHAT IS IT?
...
...IT'S NICE.
YOU'RE SUPPOSED TO SAY, "IT'S WHAT I LOVE ABOUT YOU!"

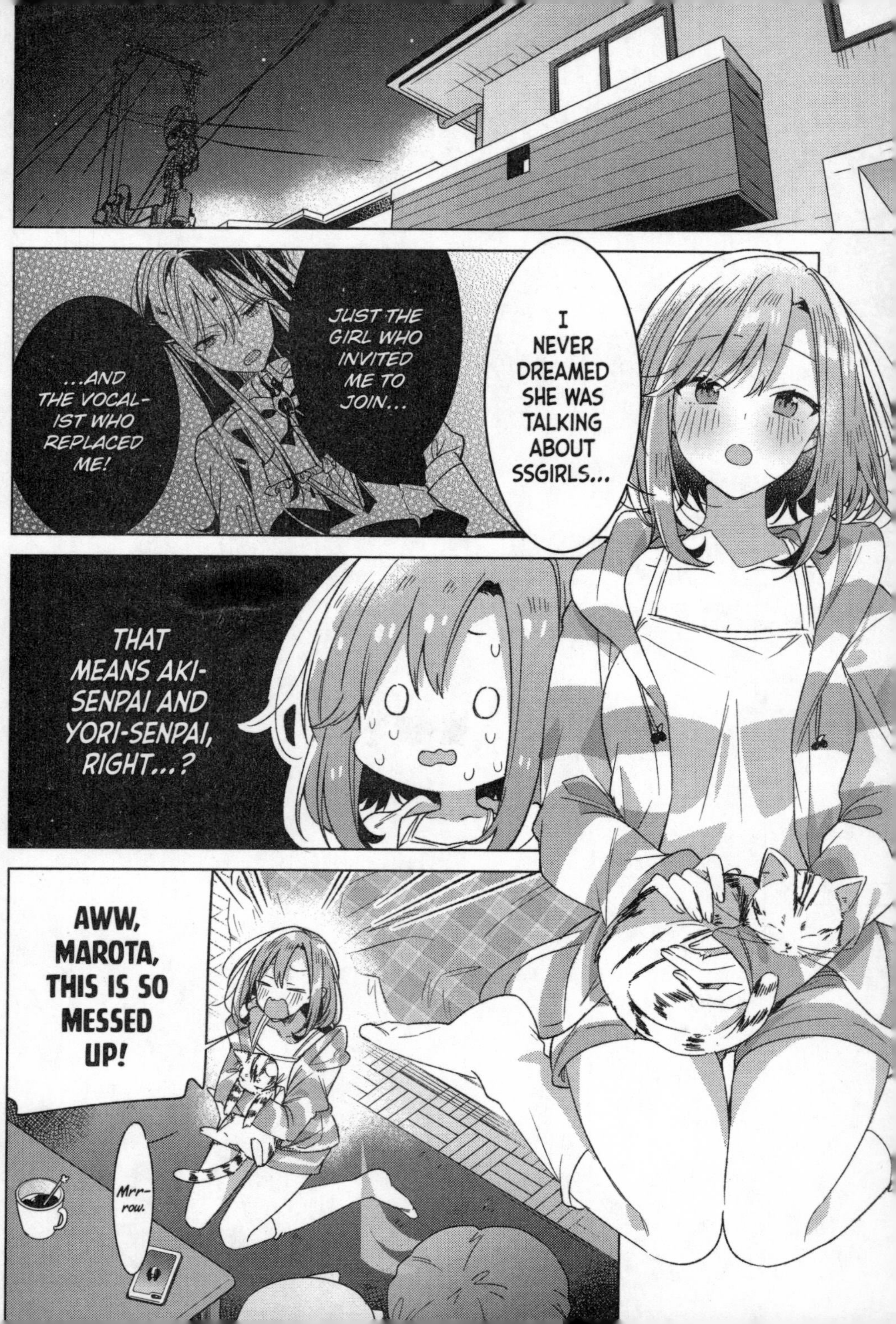
I NEVER DREAMED SHE WAS TALKING ABOUT SSGIRLS...
JUST THE GIRL WHO INVITED ME TO JOIN...
...AND THE VOCAL-IST WHO REPLACED ME!
THAT MEANS AKI-SENPAI AND YORI-SENPAI, RIGHT...?
AWW, MAROTA, THIS IS SO MESSED UP!
Mrr-row.

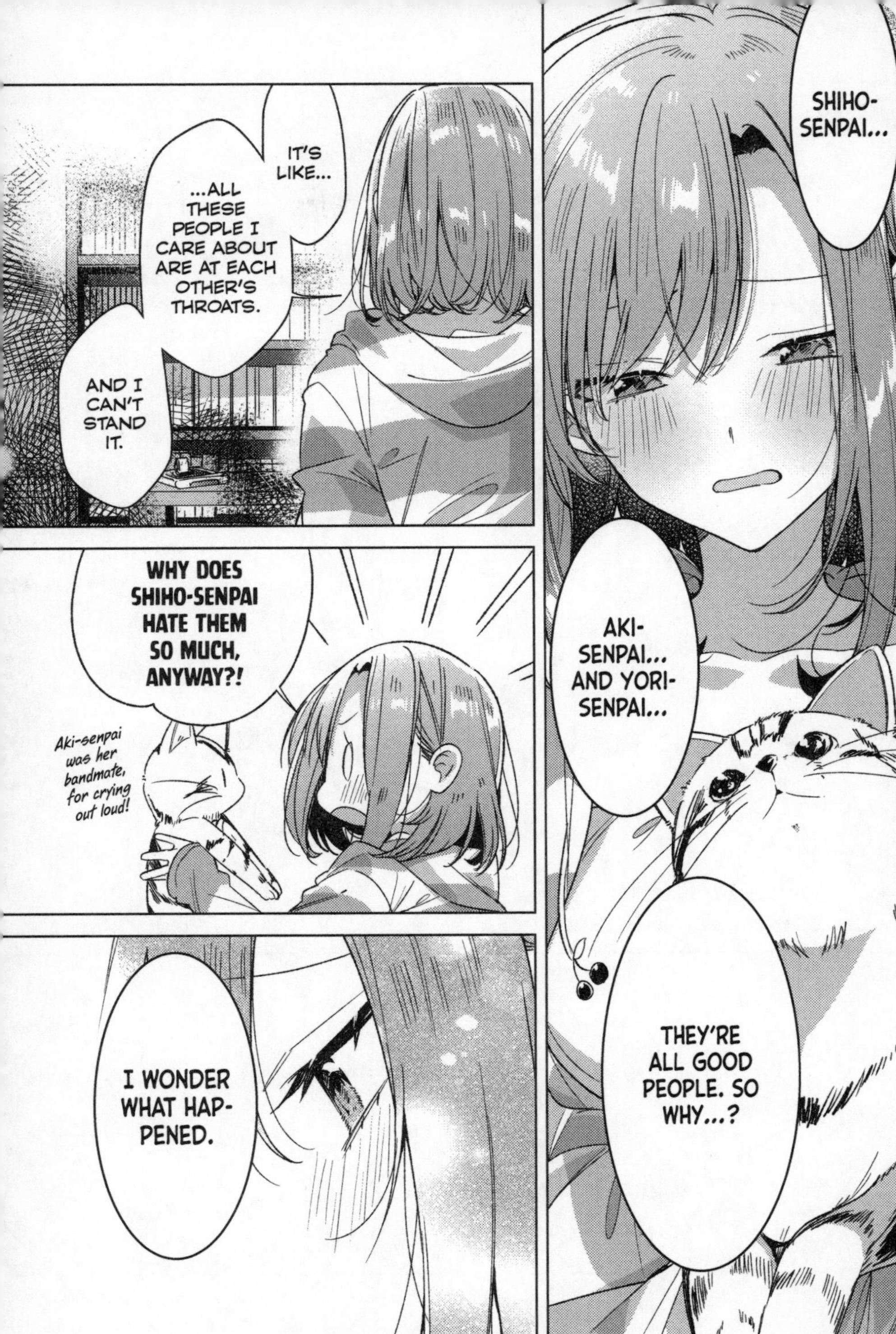
SHIHO-SENPAI...
AKI-SENPAI... AND YORI-SENPAI...
THEY'RE ALL GOOD PEOPLE. SO WHY...?
IT'S LIKE...
...ALL THESE PEOPLE I CARE ABOUT ARE AT EACH OTHER'S THROATS.
AND I CAN'T STAND IT.
WHY DOES SHIHO-SENPAI HATE THEM SO MUCH, ANYWAY?!
Aki-senpai was her bandmate, for crying out loud!
I WONDER WHAT HAP-PENED.

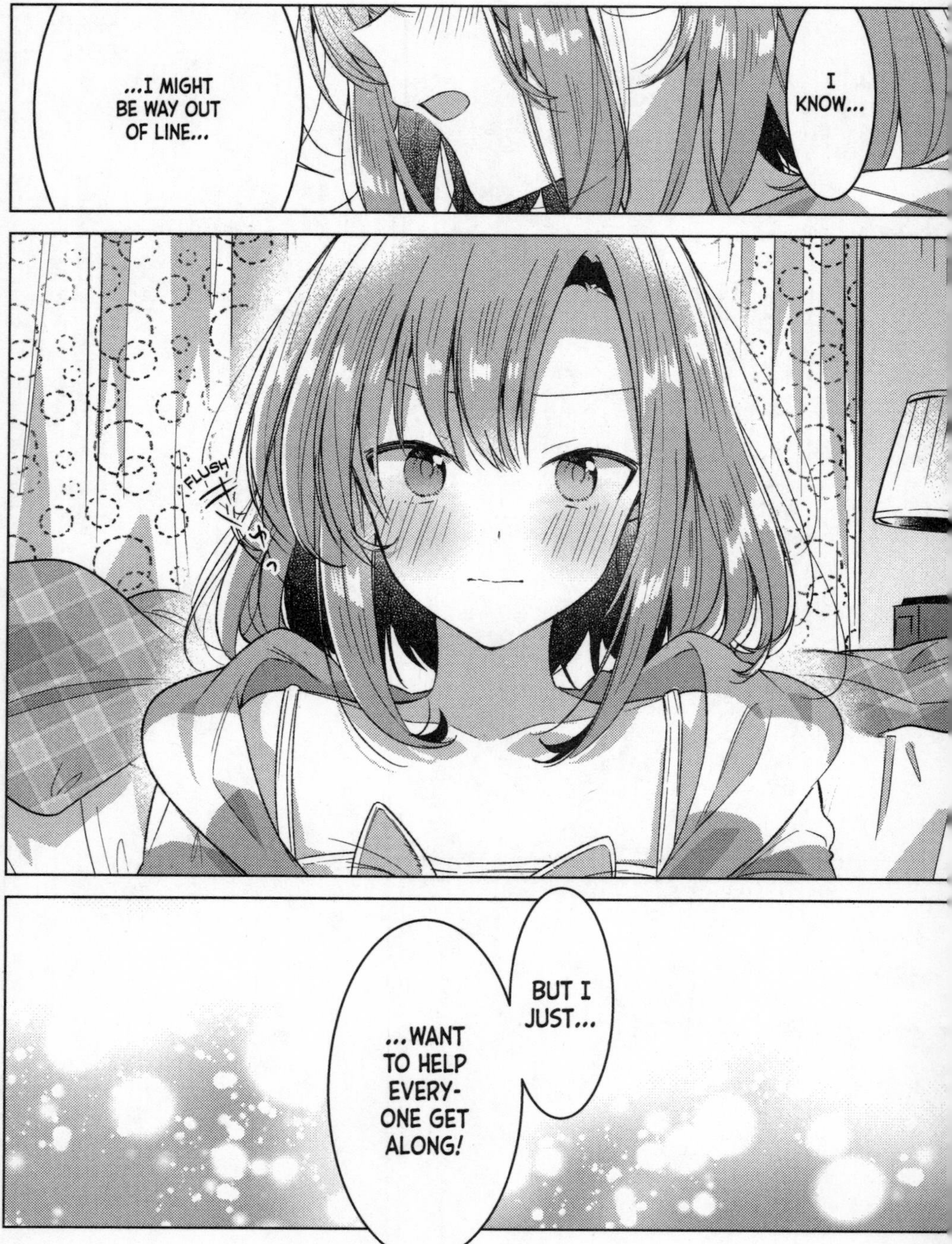
I KNOW...
...I MIGHT BE WAY OUT OF LINE...
FLUSH
BUT I JUST...
...WANT TO HELP EVERY-ONE GET ALONG!

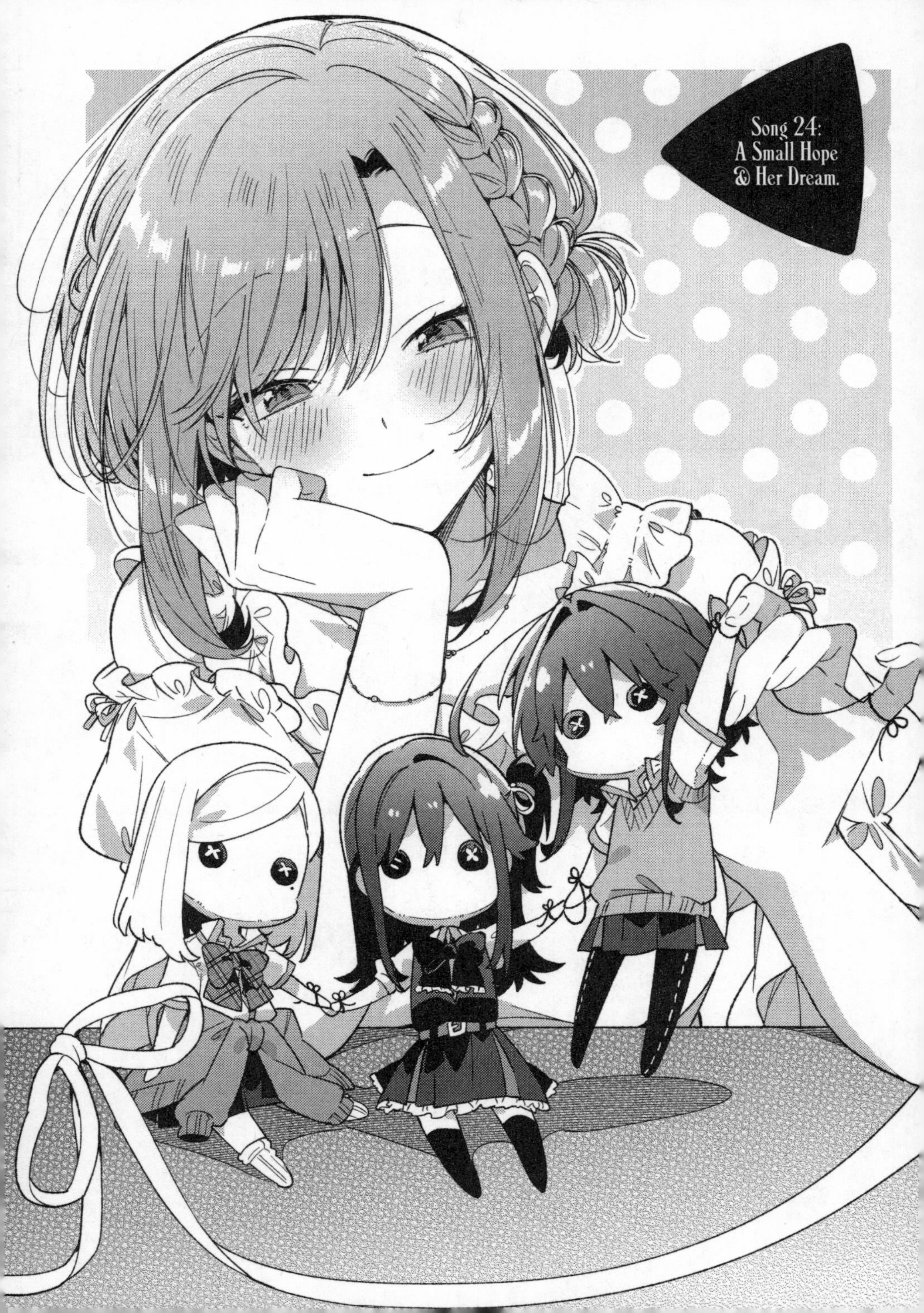
Song 24:
A Small Hope
& Her Dream.

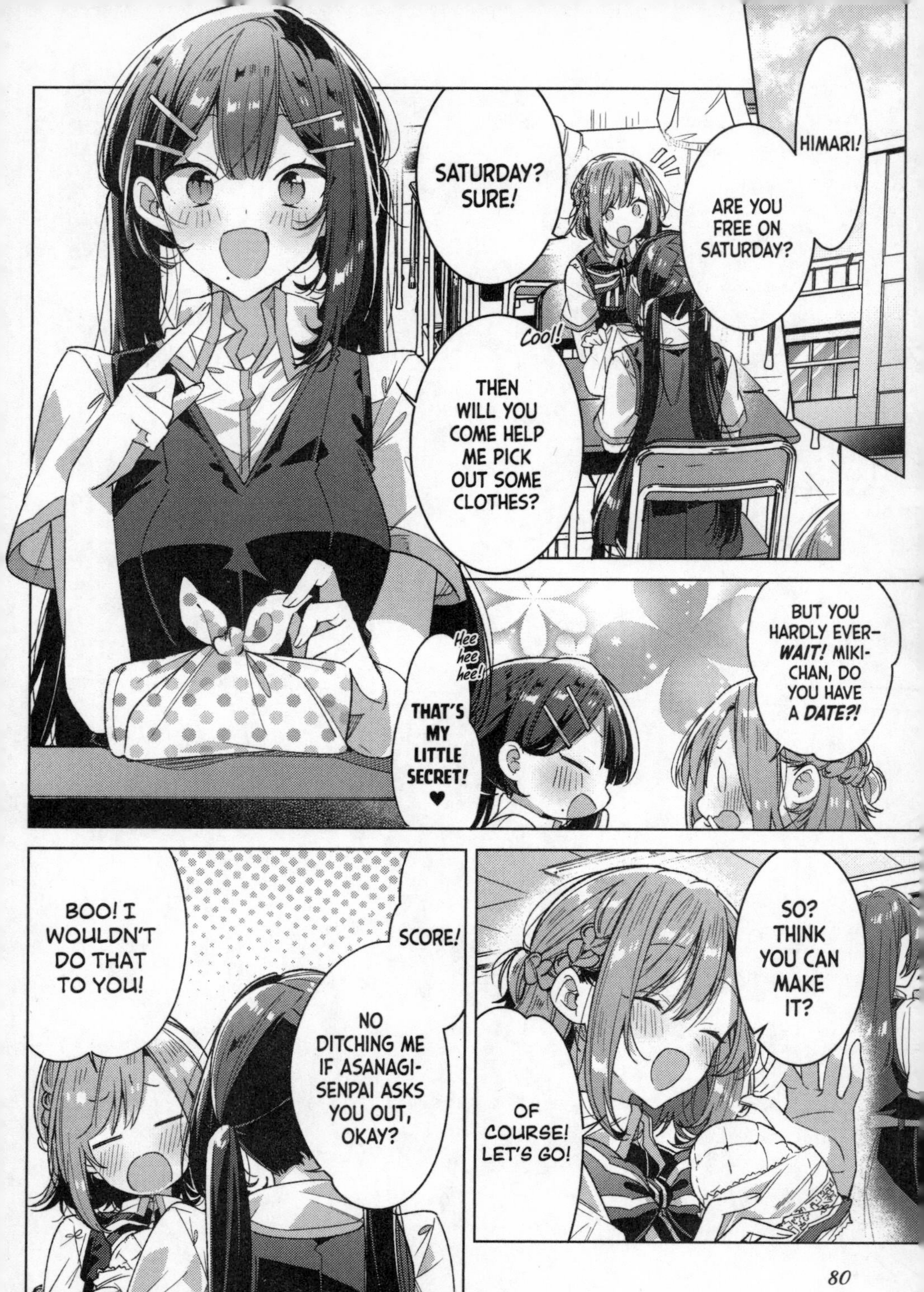
HIMARI!
ARE YOU FREE ON SATURDAY?
SATURDAY? SURE!
Cool!
THEN WILL YOU COME HELP ME PICK OUT SOME CLOTHES?
BUT YOU HARDLY EVER— WAIT! MIKI-CHAN, DO YOU HAVE A DATE?!
Hee hee hee!
THAT'S MY LITTLE SECRET! ♥
SO? THINK YOU CAN MAKE IT?
OF COURSE! LET'S GO!
SCORE!
NO DITCHING ME IF ASANAGI-SENPAI ASKS YOU OUT, OKAY?
BOO! I WOULDN'T DO THAT TO YOU!

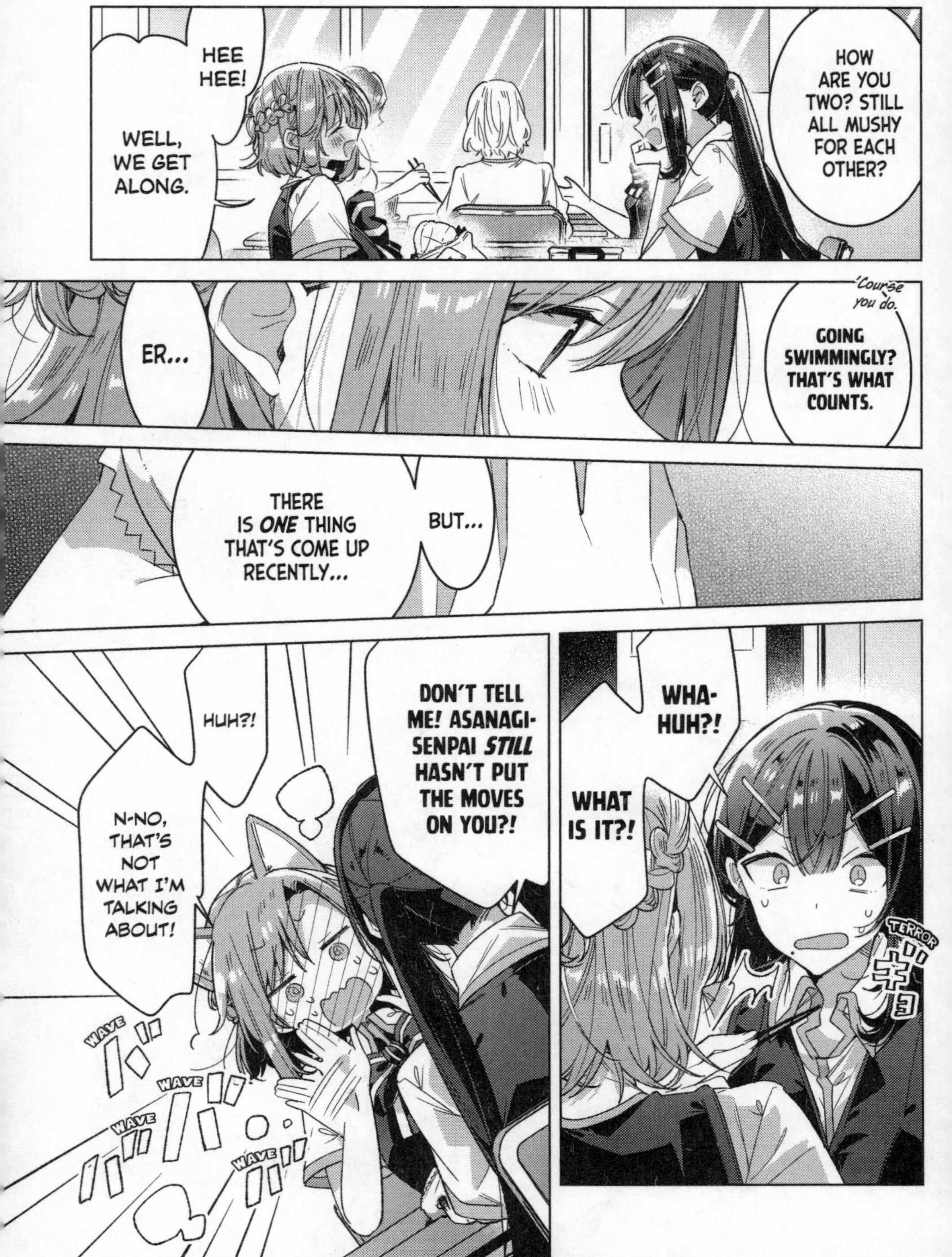
HOW ARE YOU TWO? STILL ALL MUSHY FOR EACH OTHER?
HEE HEE!
WELL, WE GET ALONG.
'Course you do.
GOING SWIMMINGLY? THAT'S WHAT COUNTS.
ER...
BUT...
THERE IS ONE THING THAT'S COME UP RECENTLY...
WHA- HUH?!
WHAT IS IT?!
TERROR
DON'T TELL ME! ASANAGI-SENPAI STILL HASN'T PUT THE MOVES ON YOU?!
HUH?!
N-NO, THAT'S NOT WHAT I'M TALKING ABOUT!
WAVE
WAVE
WAVE
WAVE

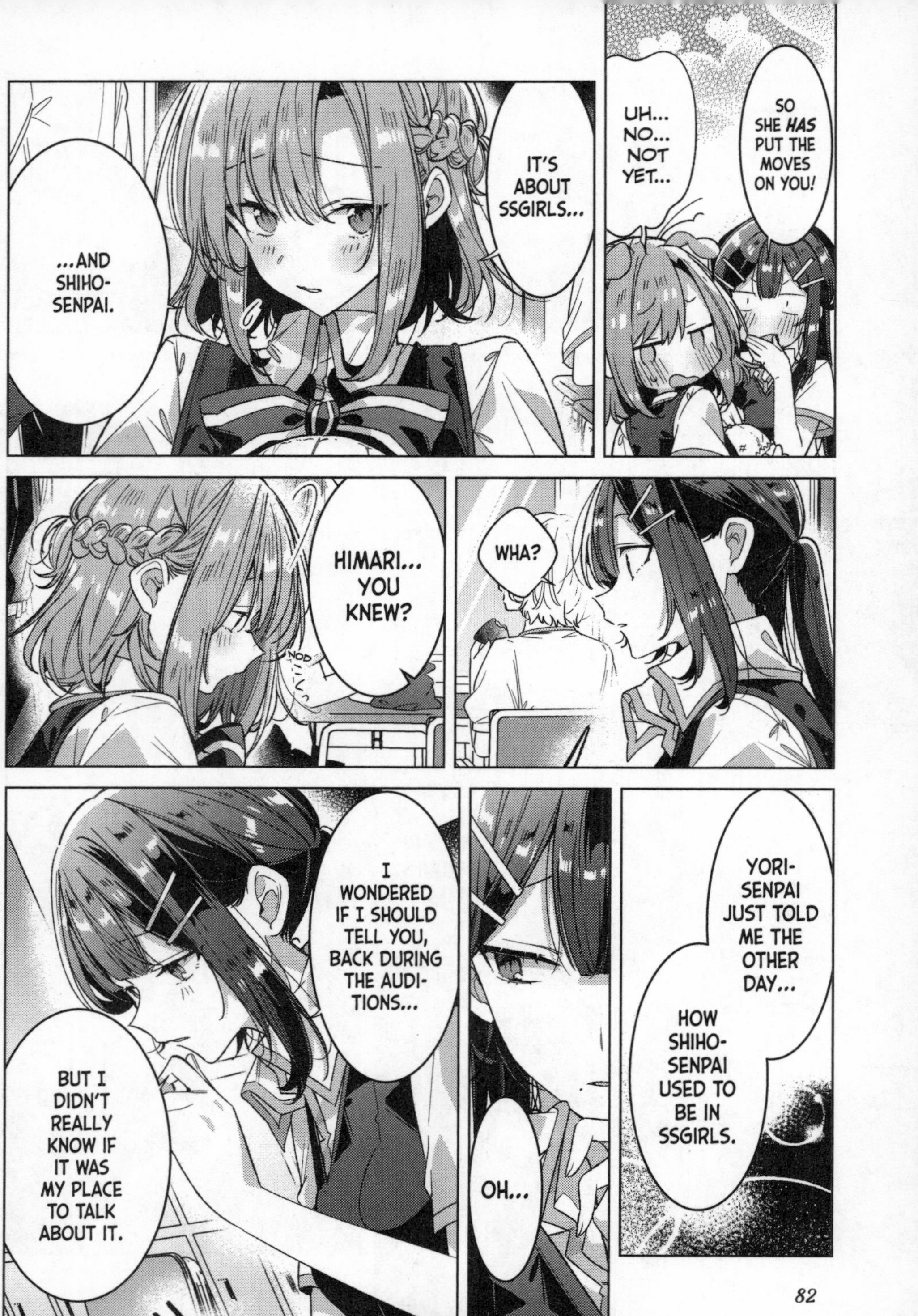
SO SHE *HAS* PUT THE MOVES ON YOU!
UH... NO... NOT YET...
IT'S ABOUT SSGIRLS...
...AND SHIHO-SENPAI.
WHA?
HIMARI... YOU KNEW?
NOD
YORI-SENPAI JUST TOLD ME THE OTHER DAY...
HOW SHIHO-SENPAI USED TO BE IN SSGIRLS.
OH...
I WONDERED IF I SHOULD TELL YOU, BACK DURING THE AUDITIONS...
BUT I DIDN'T REALLY KNOW IF IT WAS MY PLACE TO TALK ABOUT IT.

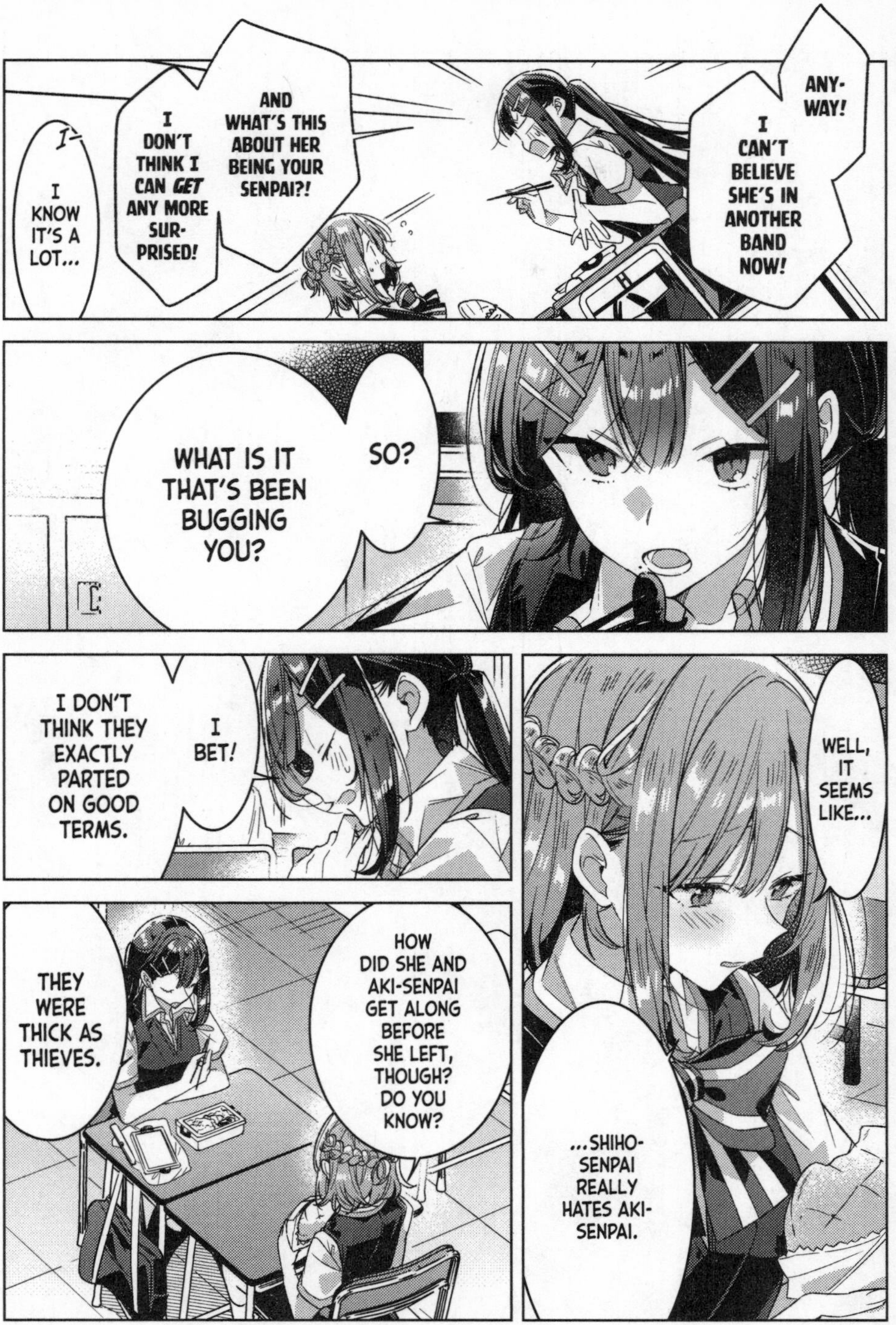
ANY-WAY!
I CAN'T BELIEVE SHE'S IN ANOTHER BAND NOW!
AND WHAT'S THIS ABOUT HER BEING YOUR SENPAI?!
I DON'T THINK I CAN *GET* ANY MORE SUR-PRISED!
I—
I KNOW IT'S A LOT...
SO?
WHAT IS IT THAT'S BEEN BUGGING YOU?
WELL, IT SEEMS LIKE...
...SHIHO-SENPAI REALLY HATES AKI-SENPAI.
I BET!
I DON'T THINK THEY EXACTLY PARTED ON GOOD TERMS.
HOW DID SHE AND AKI-SENPAI GET ALONG BEFORE SHE LEFT, THOUGH? DO YOU KNOW?
THEY WERE THICK AS THIEVES.

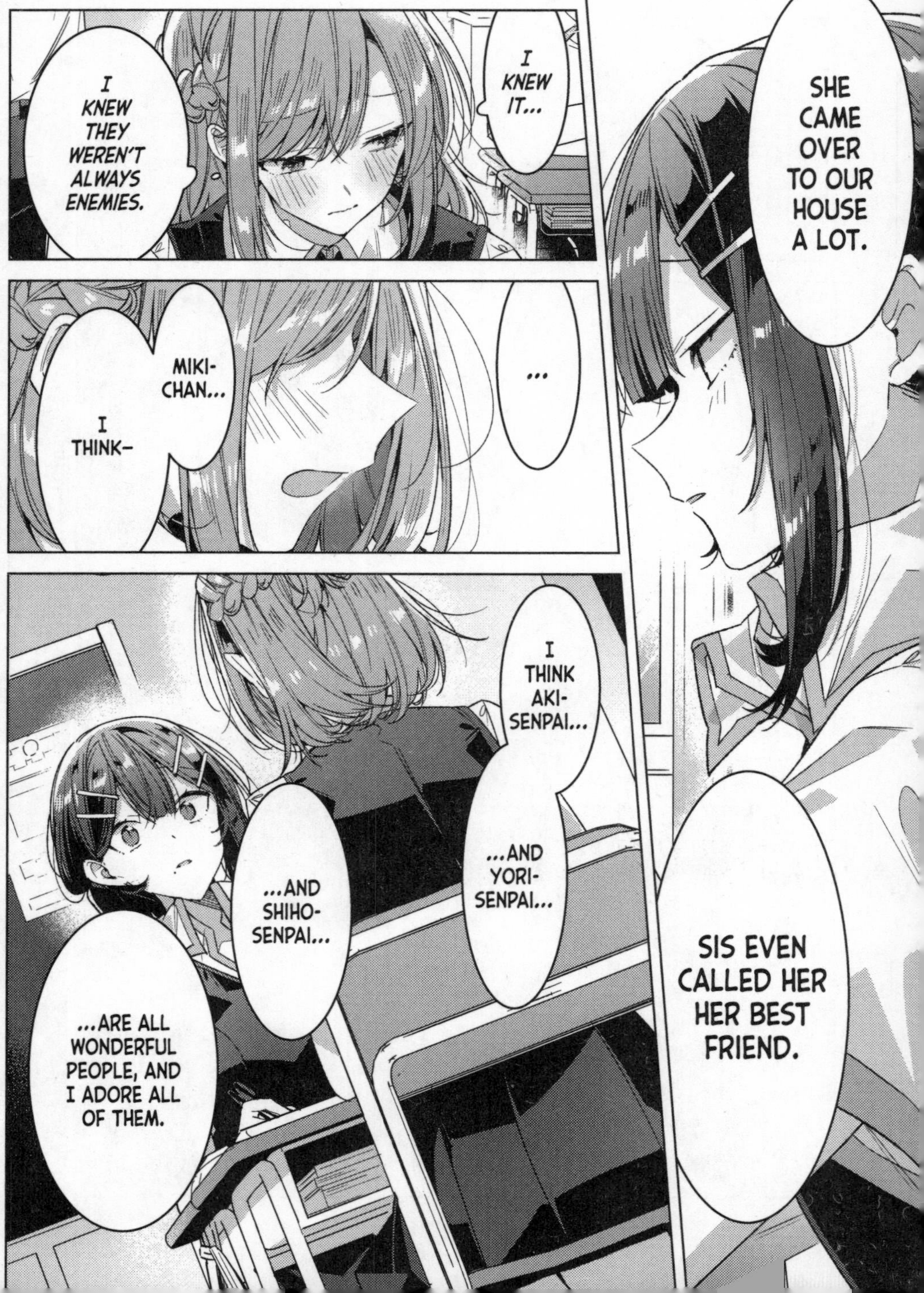
SHE CAME OVER TO OUR HOUSE A LOT.
SIS EVEN CALLED HER HER BEST FRIEND.
I KNEW IT...
I KNEW THEY WEREN'T ALWAYS ENEMIES.
...
MIKI-CHAN...
I THINK—
I THINK AKI-SENPAI...
...AND YORI-SENPAI...
...AND SHIHO-SENPAI...
...ARE ALL WONDERFUL PEOPLE, AND I ADORE ALL OF THEM.

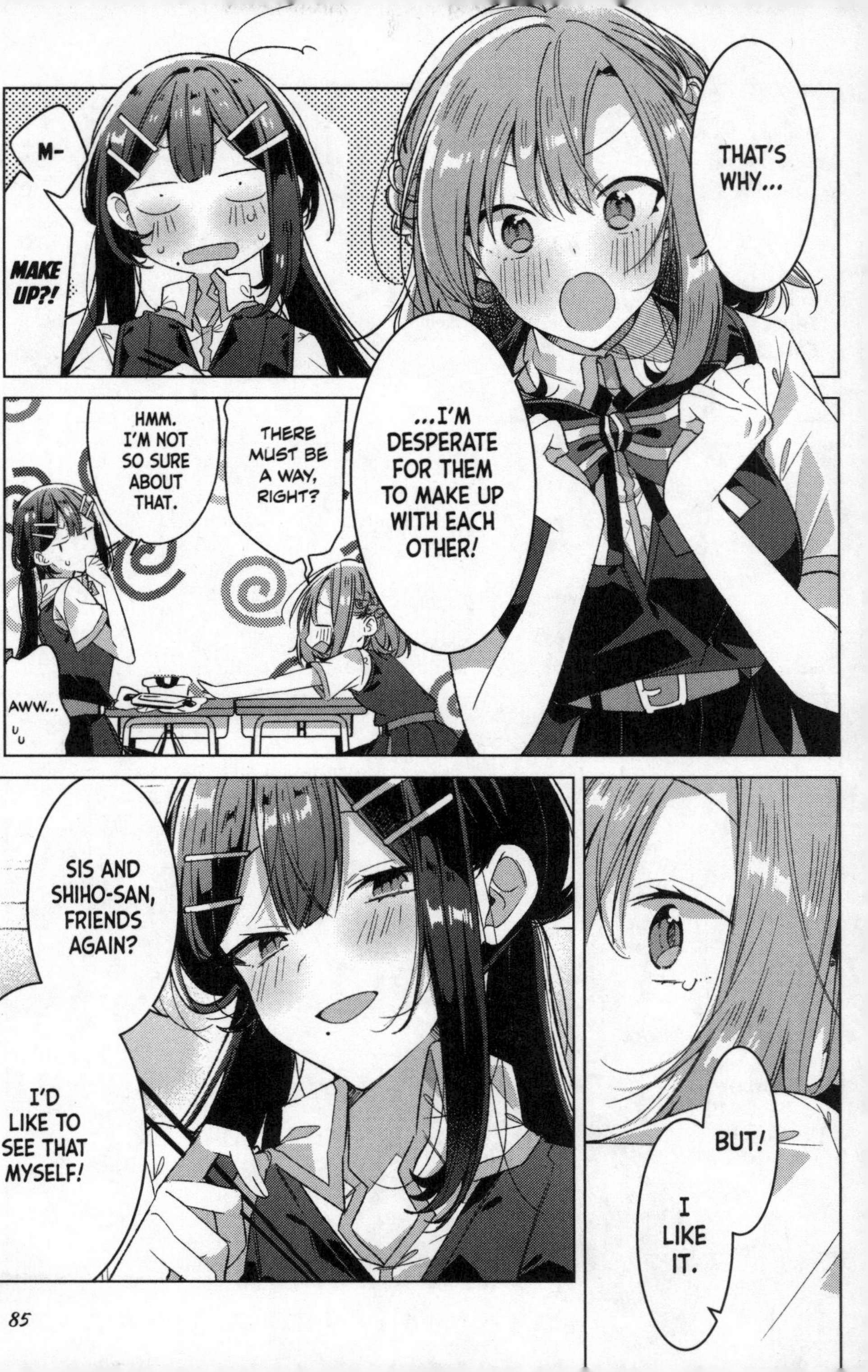
THAT'S WHY...
...I'M DESPERATE FOR THEM TO MAKE UP WITH EACH OTHER!
M-
MAKE UP?!
THERE MUST BE A WAY, RIGHT?
HMM. I'M NOT SO SURE ABOUT THAT.
AWW...
UU
BUT!
I LIKE IT.
SIS AND SHIHO-SAN, FRIENDS AGAIN?
I'D LIKE TO SEE THAT MYSELF!

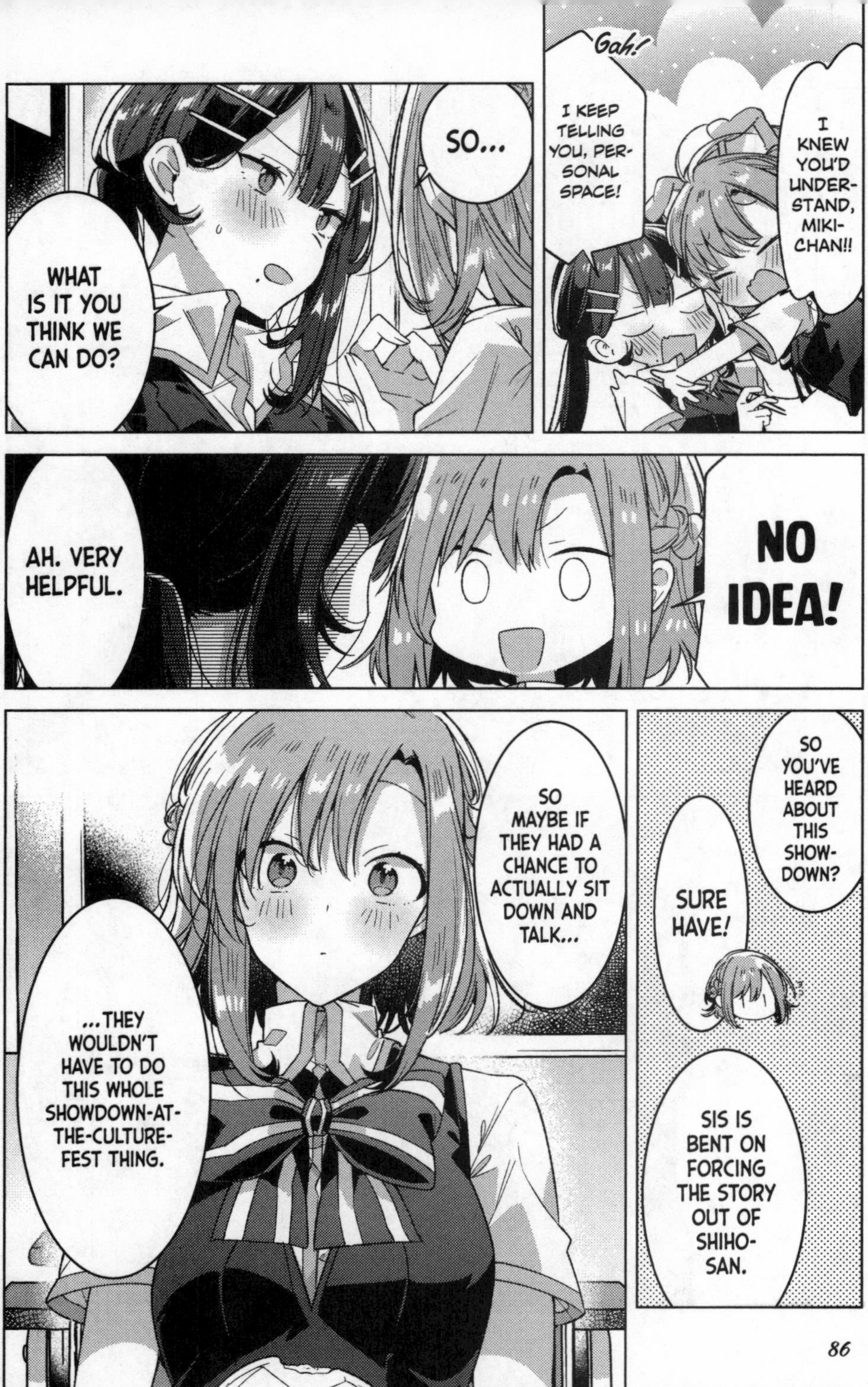
I KNEW YOU'D UNDERSTAND, MIKI-CHAN!!
Gah!
I KEEP TELLING YOU, PERSONAL SPACE!
SO...
WHAT IS IT YOU THINK WE CAN DO?
NO IDEA!
AH. VERY HELPFUL.
SO YOU'VE HEARD ABOUT THIS SHOWDOWN?
SURE HAVE!
SIS IS BENT ON FORCING THE STORY OUT OF SHIHO-SAN.
SO MAYBE IF THEY HAD A CHANCE TO ACTUALLY SIT DOWN AND TALK...
...THEY WOULDN'T HAVE TO DO THIS WHOLE SHOWDOWN-AT-THE-CULTURE-FEST THING.

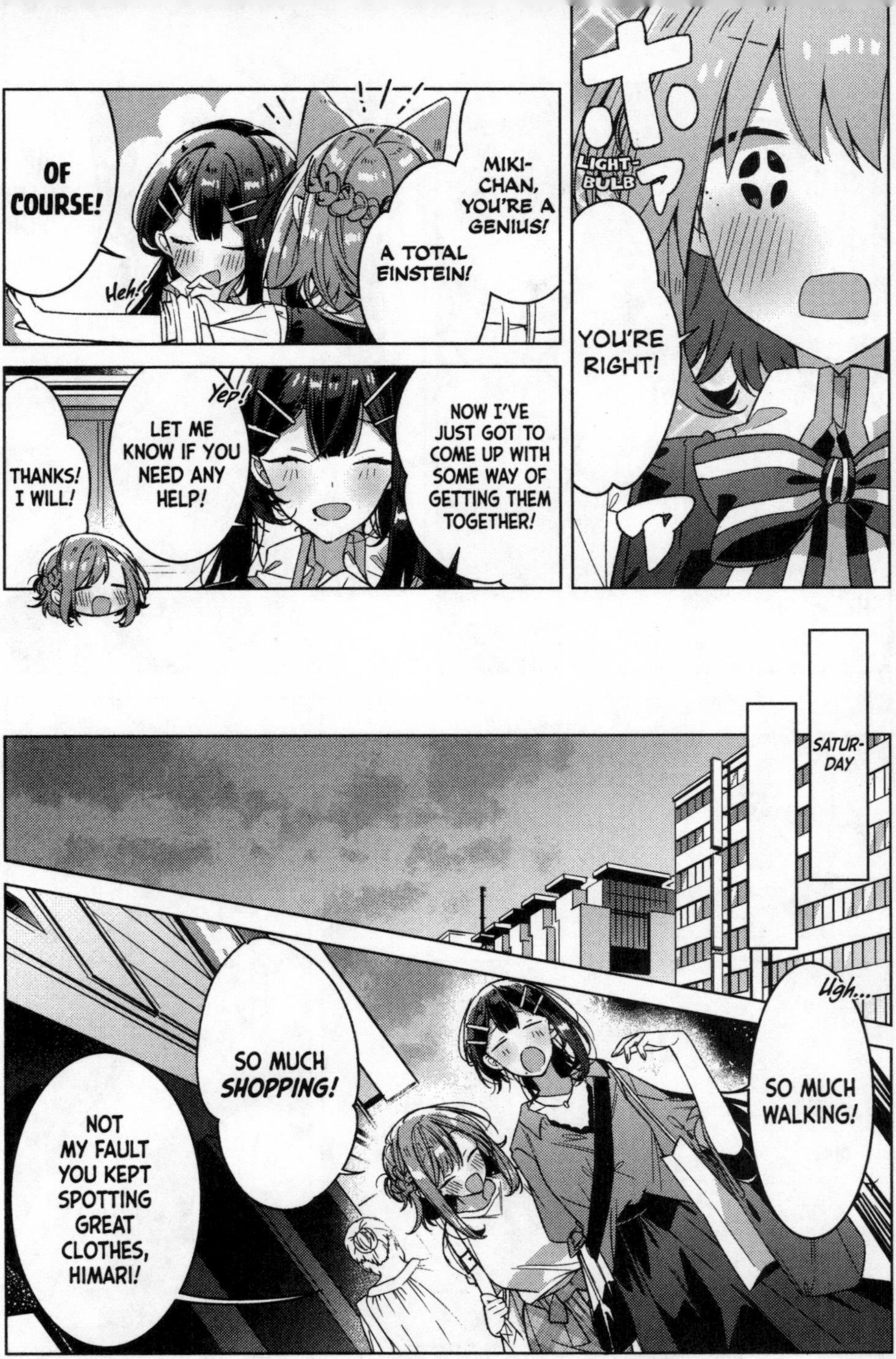
LIGHT-BULB
YOU'RE RIGHT!
MIKI-CHAN, YOU'RE A GENIUS!
A TOTAL EINSTEIN!
Heh!
OF COURSE!
NOW I'VE JUST GOT TO COME UP WITH SOME WAY OF GETTING THEM TOGETHER!
Yep!
LET ME KNOW IF YOU NEED ANY HELP!
THANKS! I WILL!
SATURDAY
Ugh...
SO MUCH WALKING!
SO MUCH SHOPPING!
NOT MY FAULT YOU KEPT SPOTTING GREAT CLOTHES, HIMARI!

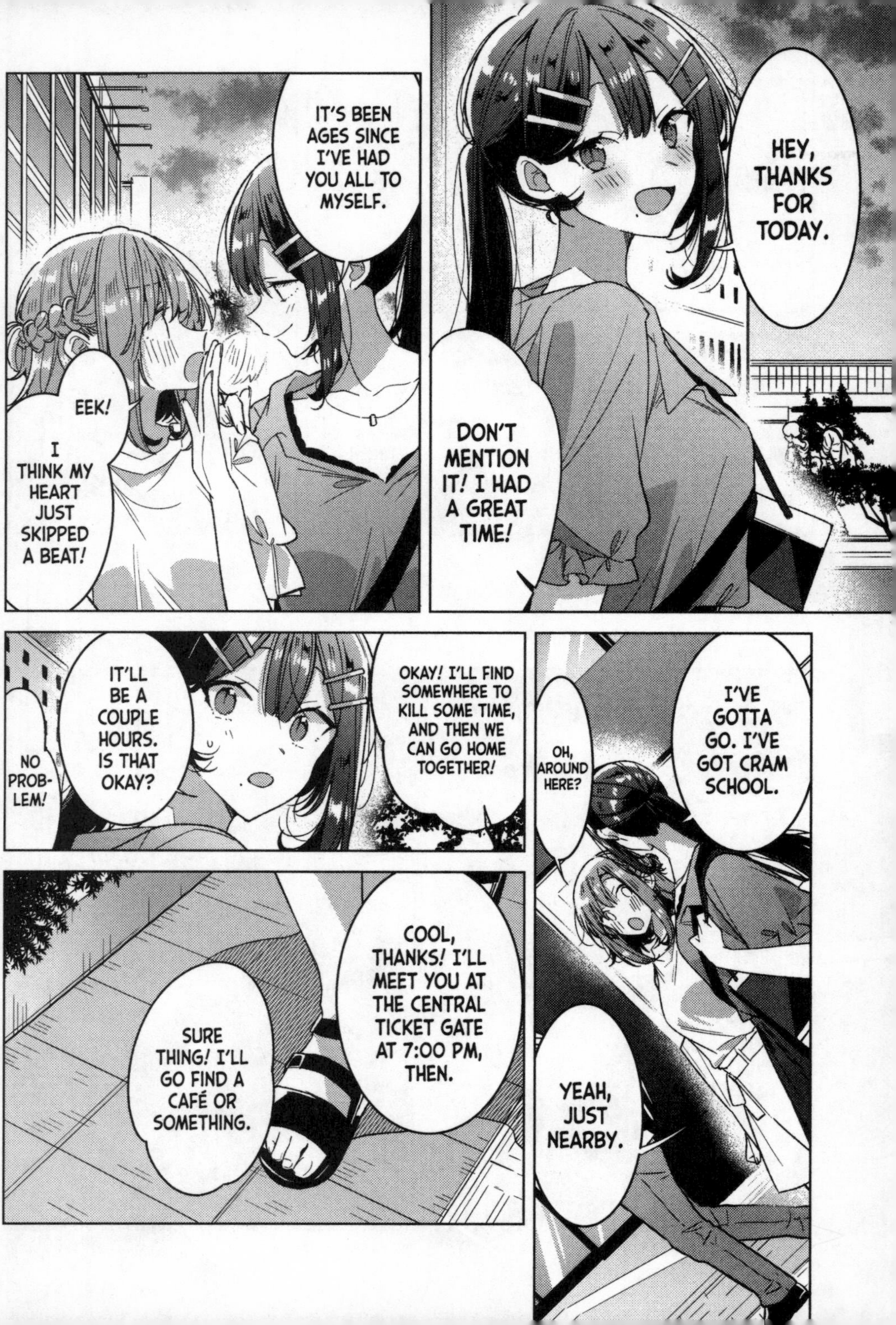
HEY, THANKS FOR TODAY.
DON'T MENTION IT! I HAD A GREAT TIME!
IT'S BEEN AGES SINCE I'VE HAD YOU ALL TO MYSELF.
EEK!
I THINK MY HEART JUST SKIPPED A BEAT!
I'VE GOTTA GO. I'VE GOT CRAM SCHOOL.
OH, AROUND HERE?
YEAH, JUST NEARBY.
OKAY! I'LL FIND SOMEWHERE TO KILL SOME TIME, AND THEN WE CAN GO HOME TOGETHER!
IT'LL BE A COUPLE HOURS. IS THAT OKAY?
NO PROB-LEM!
COOL, THANKS! I'LL MEET YOU AT THE CENTRAL TICKET GATE AT 7:00 PM, THEN.
SURE THING! I'LL GO FIND A CAFÉ OR SOMETHING.

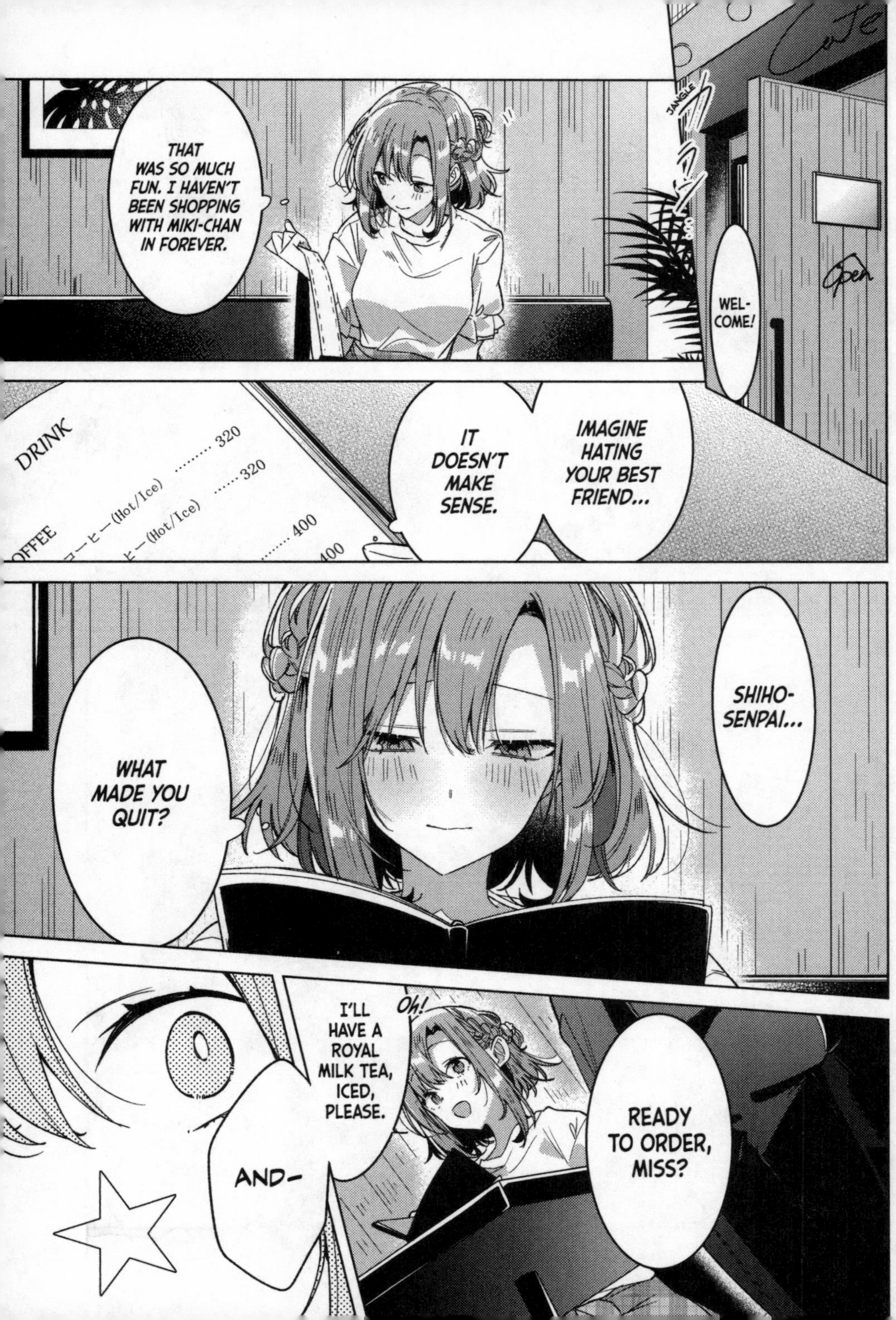
JANGLE
WELCOME!
THAT WAS SO MUCH FUN. I HAVEN'T BEEN SHOPPING WITH MIKI-CHAN IN FOREVER.
Open
IMAGINE HATING YOUR BEST FRIEND...
IT DOESN'T MAKE SENSE.
DRINK
SHIHO-SENPAI...
WHAT MADE YOU QUIT?
READY TO ORDER, MISS?
Oh!
I'LL HAVE A ROYAL MILK TEA, ICED, PLEASE.
AND—

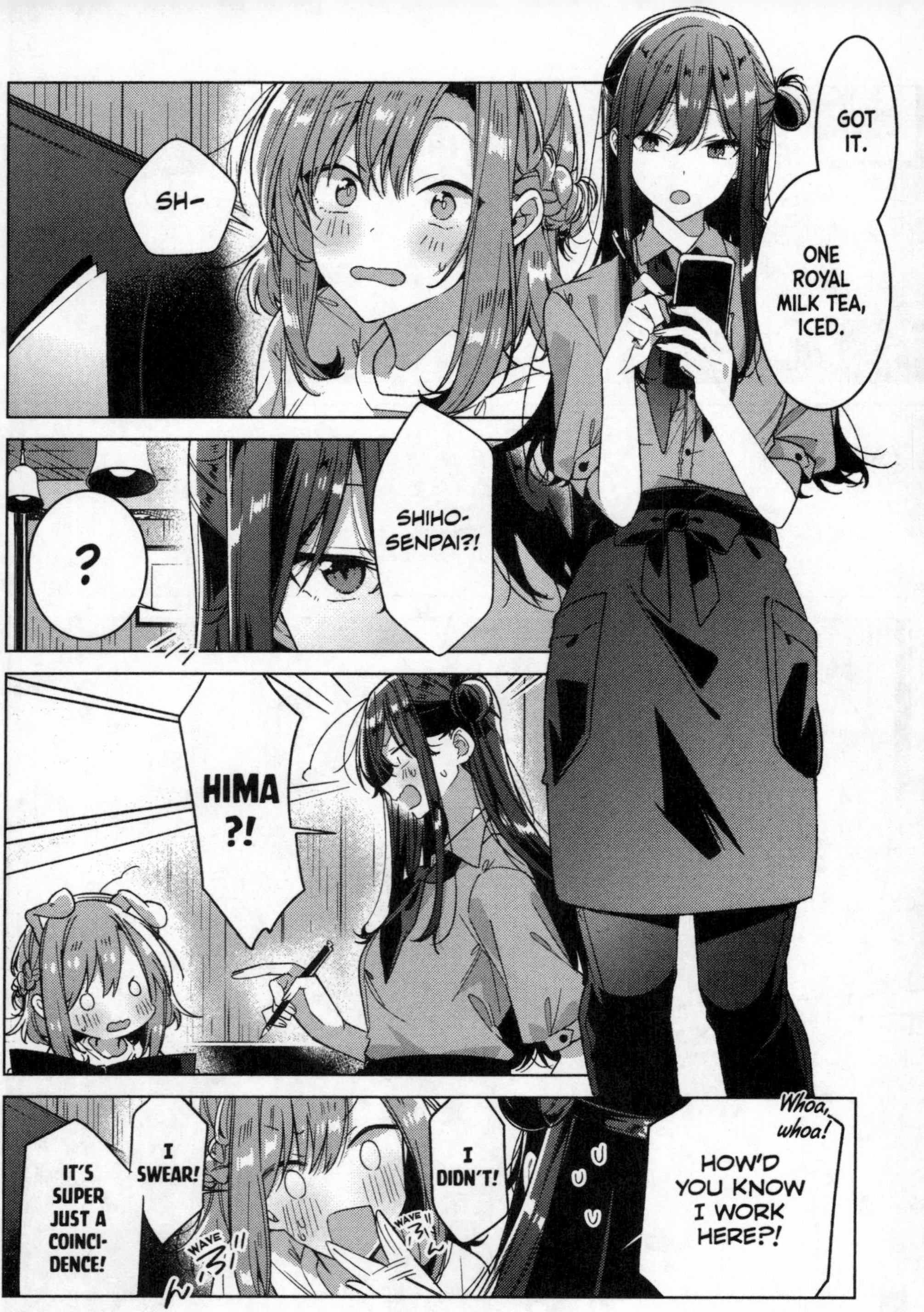
GOT IT.
ONE ROYAL MILK TEA, ICED.
SH-
SHIHO-SENPAI?!
?
HIMA?!
Whoa, whoa!
HOW'D YOU KNOW I WORK HERE?!
I DIDN'T!
WAVE
I SWEAR!
WAVE
IT'S SUPER JUST A COINCIDENCE!

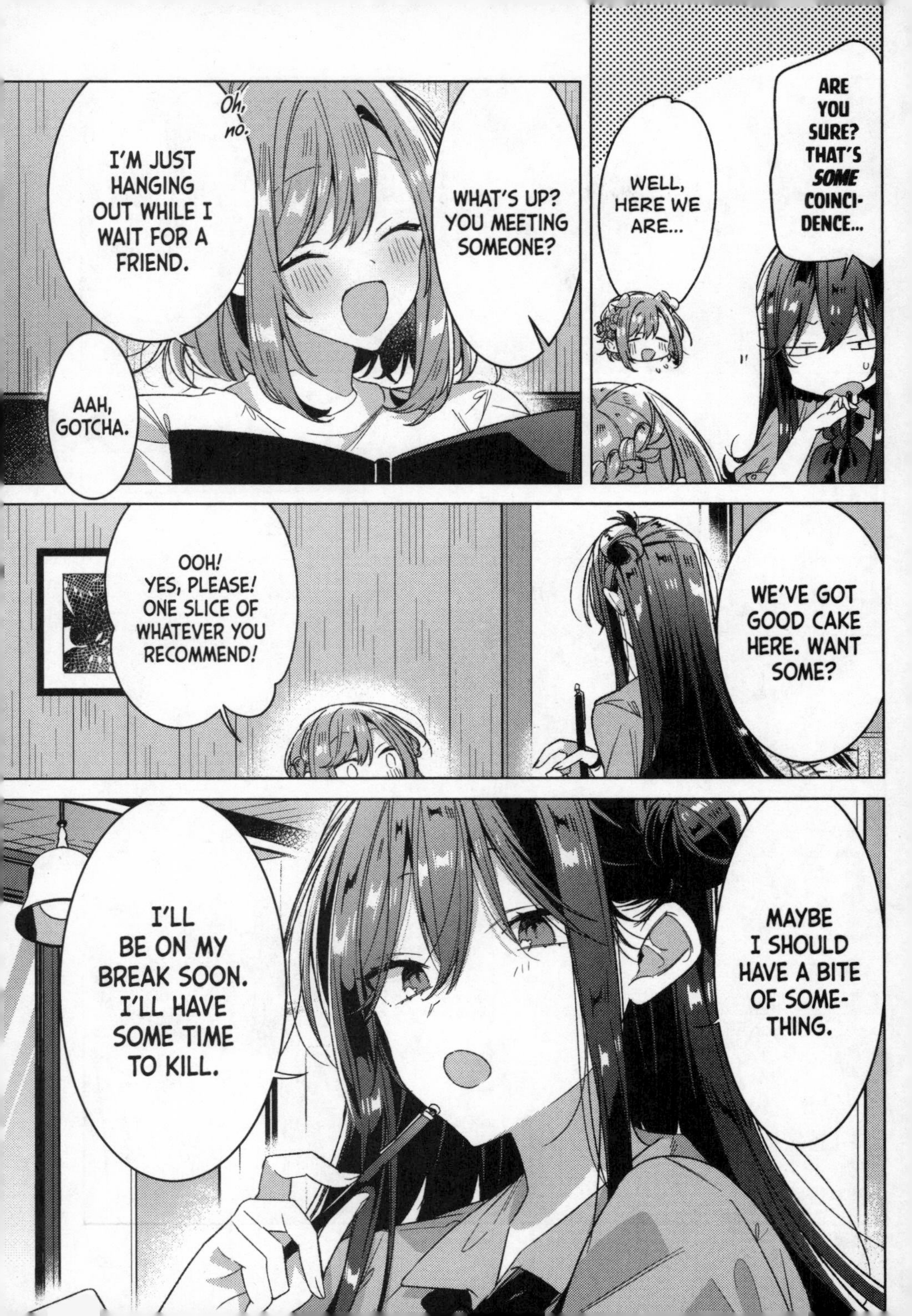
ARE YOU SURE? THAT'S *SOME* COINCIDENCE...
WELL, HERE WE ARE...
WHAT'S UP? YOU MEETING SOMEONE?
Oh, no.
I'M JUST HANGING OUT WHILE I WAIT FOR A FRIEND.
AAH, GOTCHA.
WE'VE GOT GOOD CAKE HERE. WANT SOME?
OOH! YES, PLEASE! ONE SLICE OF WHATEVER YOU RECOMMEND!
MAYBE I SHOULD HAVE A BITE OF SOMETHING.
I'LL BE ON MY BREAK SOON. I'LL HAVE SOME TIME TO KILL.

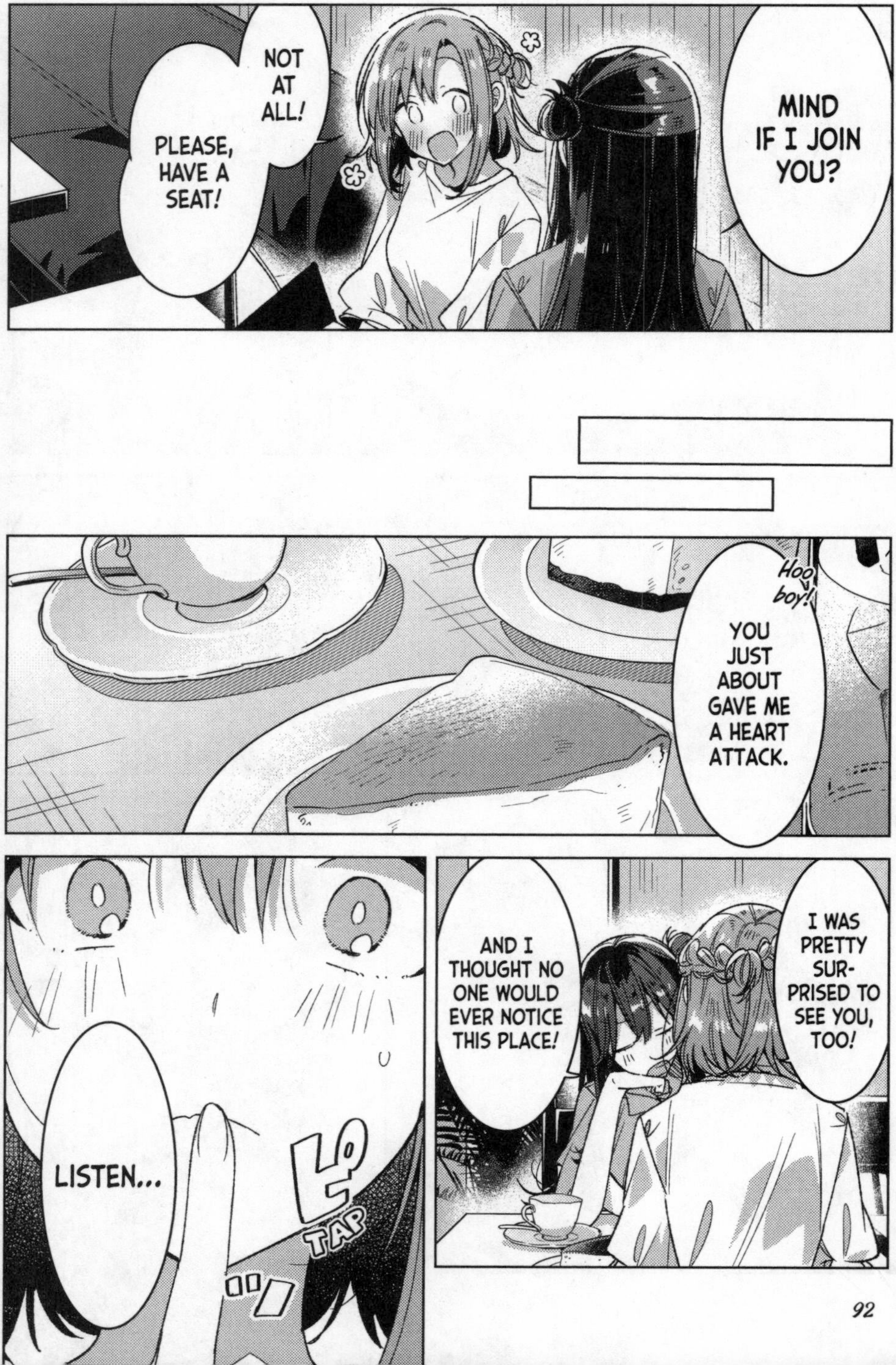
MIND IF I JOIN YOU?
NOT AT ALL!
PLEASE, HAVE A SEAT!
Hoo boy!
YOU JUST ABOUT GAVE ME A HEART ATTACK.
I WAS PRETTY SUR-PRISED TO SEE YOU, TOO!
AND I THOUGHT NO ONE WOULD EVER NOTICE THIS PLACE!
LISTEN...
TAP

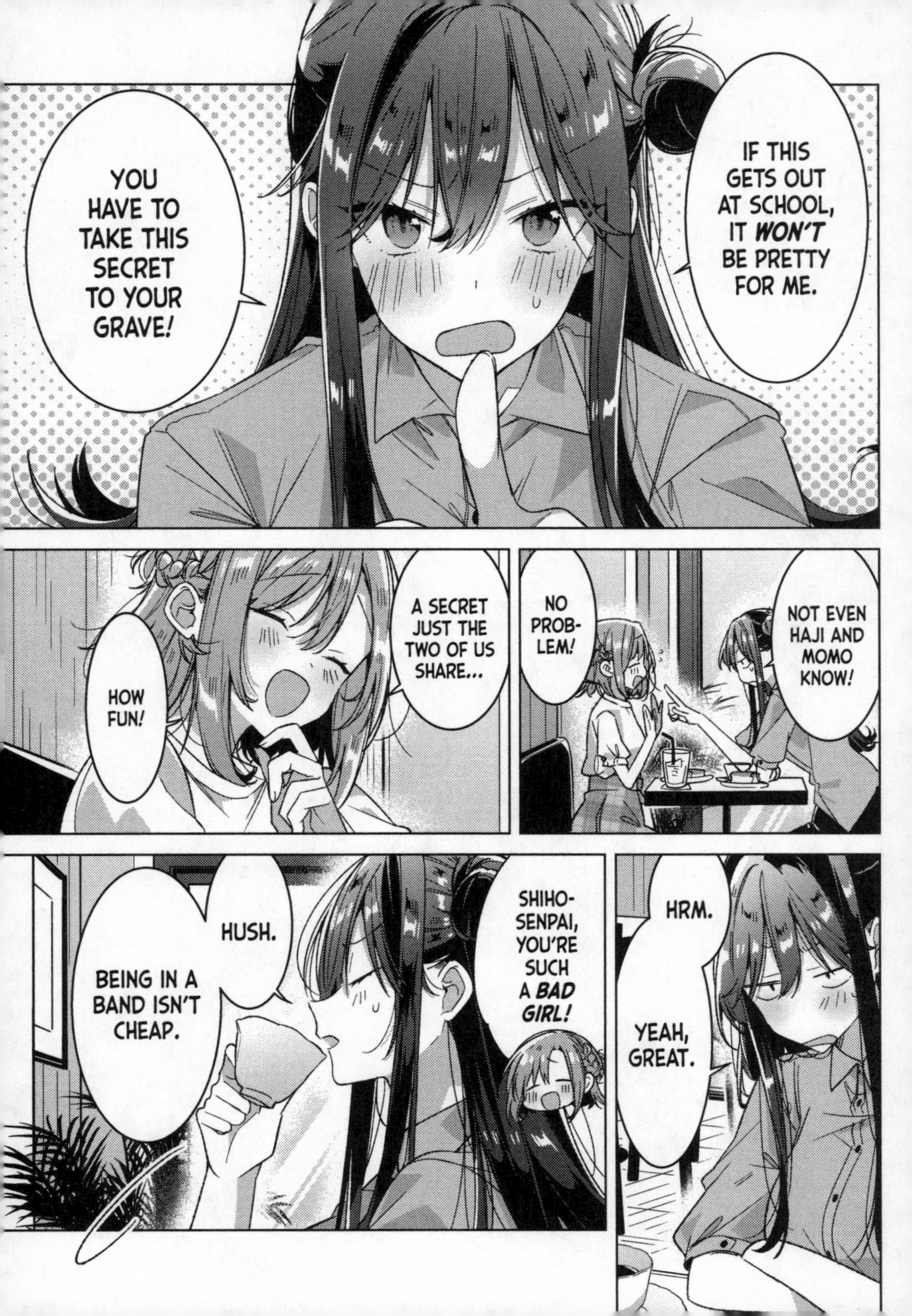
IF THIS GETS OUT AT SCHOOL, IT *WON'T* BE PRETTY FOR ME.
YOU HAVE TO TAKE THIS SECRET TO YOUR GRAVE!
NOT EVEN HAJI AND MOMO KNOW!
NO PROB-LEM!
A SECRET JUST THE TWO OF US SHARE...
HOW FUN!
HRM.
YEAH, GREAT.
SHIHO-SENPAI, YOU'RE SUCH A *BAD GIRL!*
HUSH.
BEING IN A BAND ISN'T CHEAP.

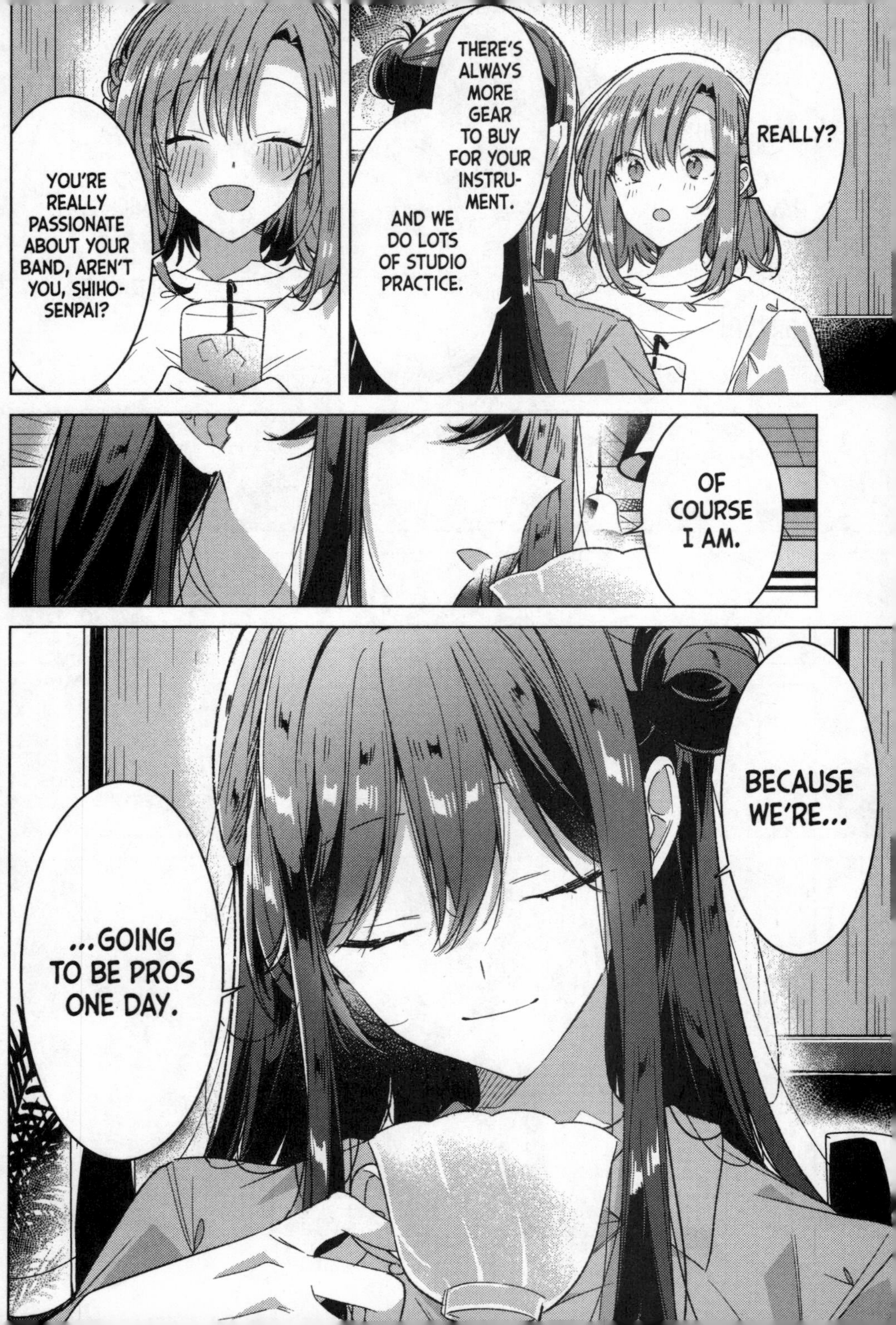
REALLY?
THERE'S ALWAYS MORE GEAR TO BUY FOR YOUR INSTRU- MENT.
AND WE DO LOTS OF STUDIO PRACTICE.
YOU'RE REALLY PASSIONATE ABOUT YOUR BAND, AREN'T YOU, SHIHO-SENPAI?
OF COURSE I AM.
BECAUSE WE'RE...
...GOING TO BE PROS ONE DAY.

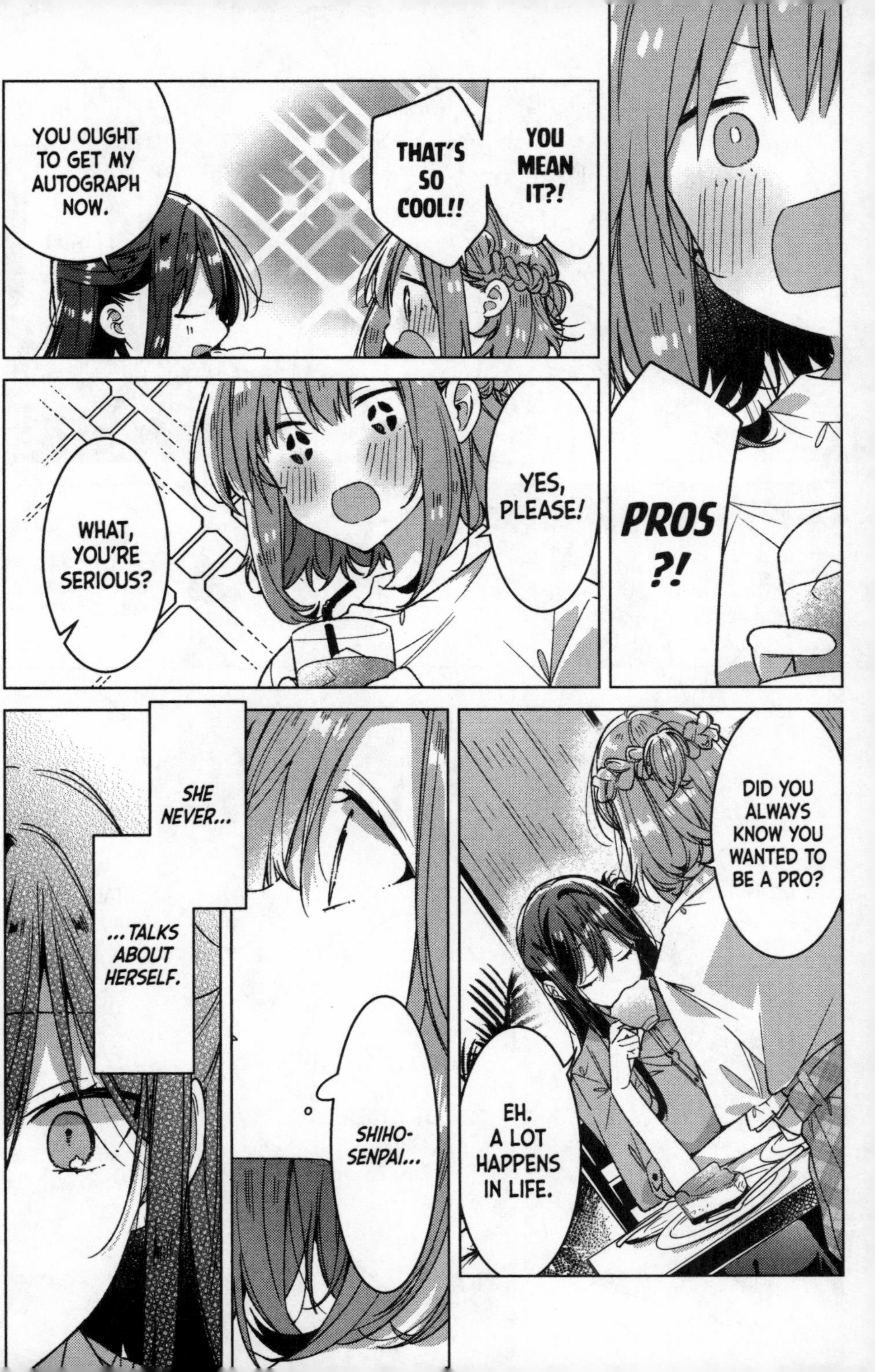
PROS ?!
YOU MEAN IT?!
THAT'S SO COOL!!
YOU OUGHT TO GET MY AUTOGRAPH NOW.
YES, PLEASE!
WHAT, YOU'RE SERIOUS?
DID YOU ALWAYS KNOW YOU WANTED TO BE A PRO?
EH. A LOT HAPPENS IN LIFE.
SHE NEVER...
...TALKS ABOUT HERSELF.
SHIHO-SENPAI...

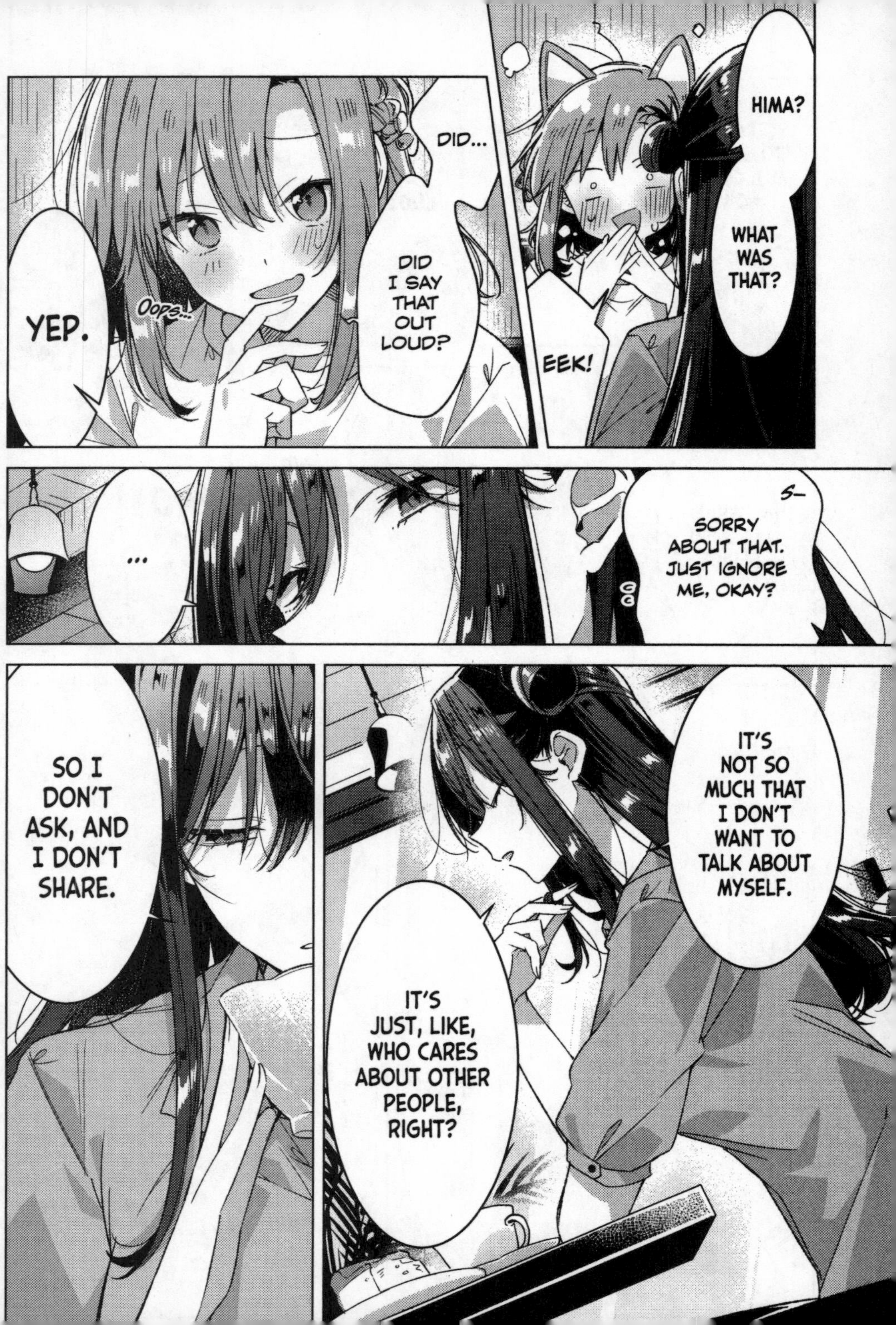
HIMA?
WHAT WAS THAT?
EEK!
DID...
DID I SAY THAT OUT LOUD?
Oops...
YEP.
S— SORRY ABOUT THAT. JUST IGNORE ME, OKAY?
...
IT'S NOT SO MUCH THAT I DON'T WANT TO TALK ABOUT MYSELF.
IT'S JUST, LIKE, WHO CARES ABOUT OTHER PEOPLE, RIGHT?
SO I DON'T ASK, AND I DON'T SHARE.

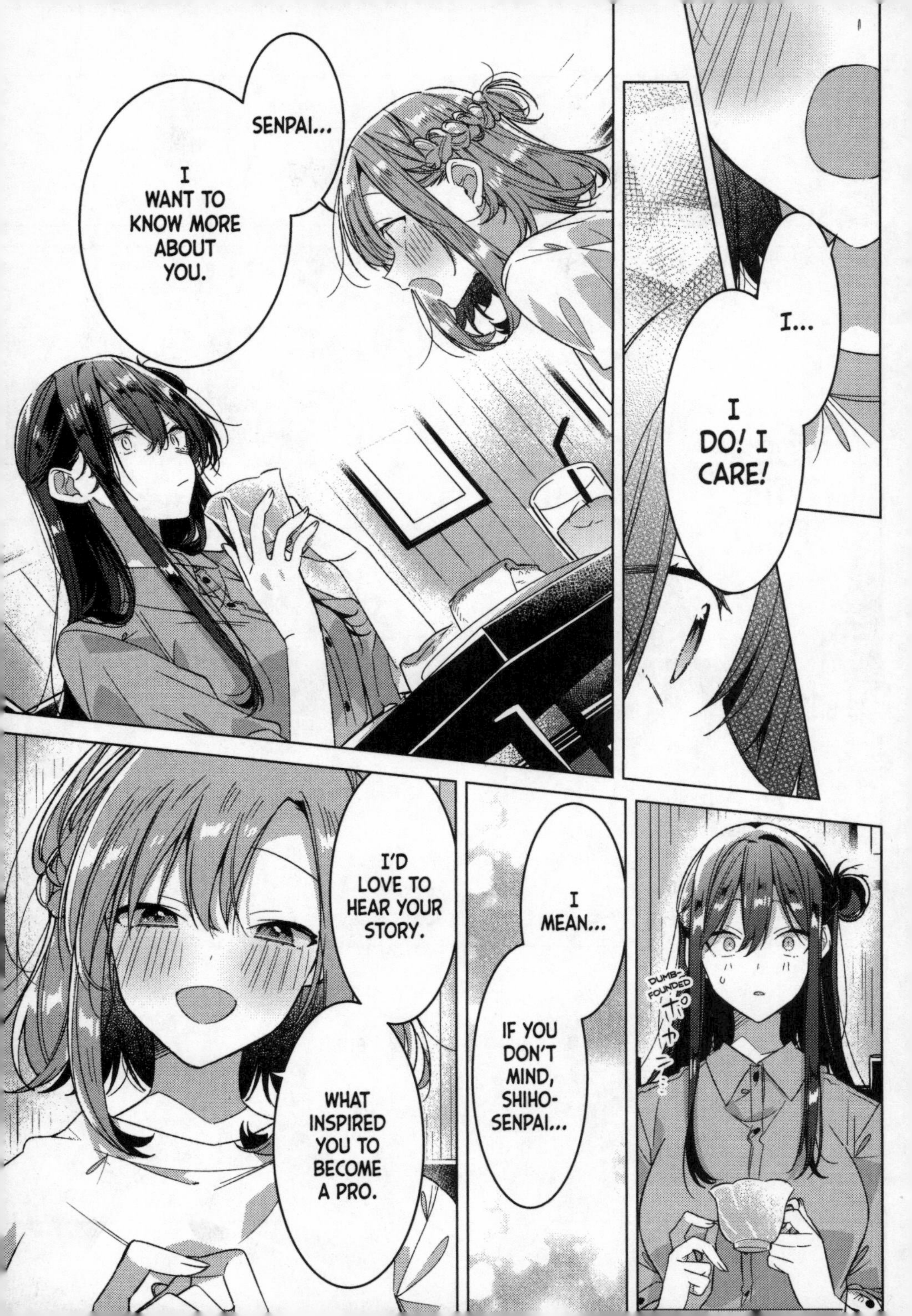
I...
I DO! I CARE!
SENPAI...
I WANT TO KNOW MORE ABOUT YOU.
DUMB-FOUNDED
I MEAN...
IF YOU DON'T MIND, SHIHO-SENPAI...
I'D LOVE TO HEAR YOUR STORY.
WHAT INSPIRED YOU TO BECOME A PRO.

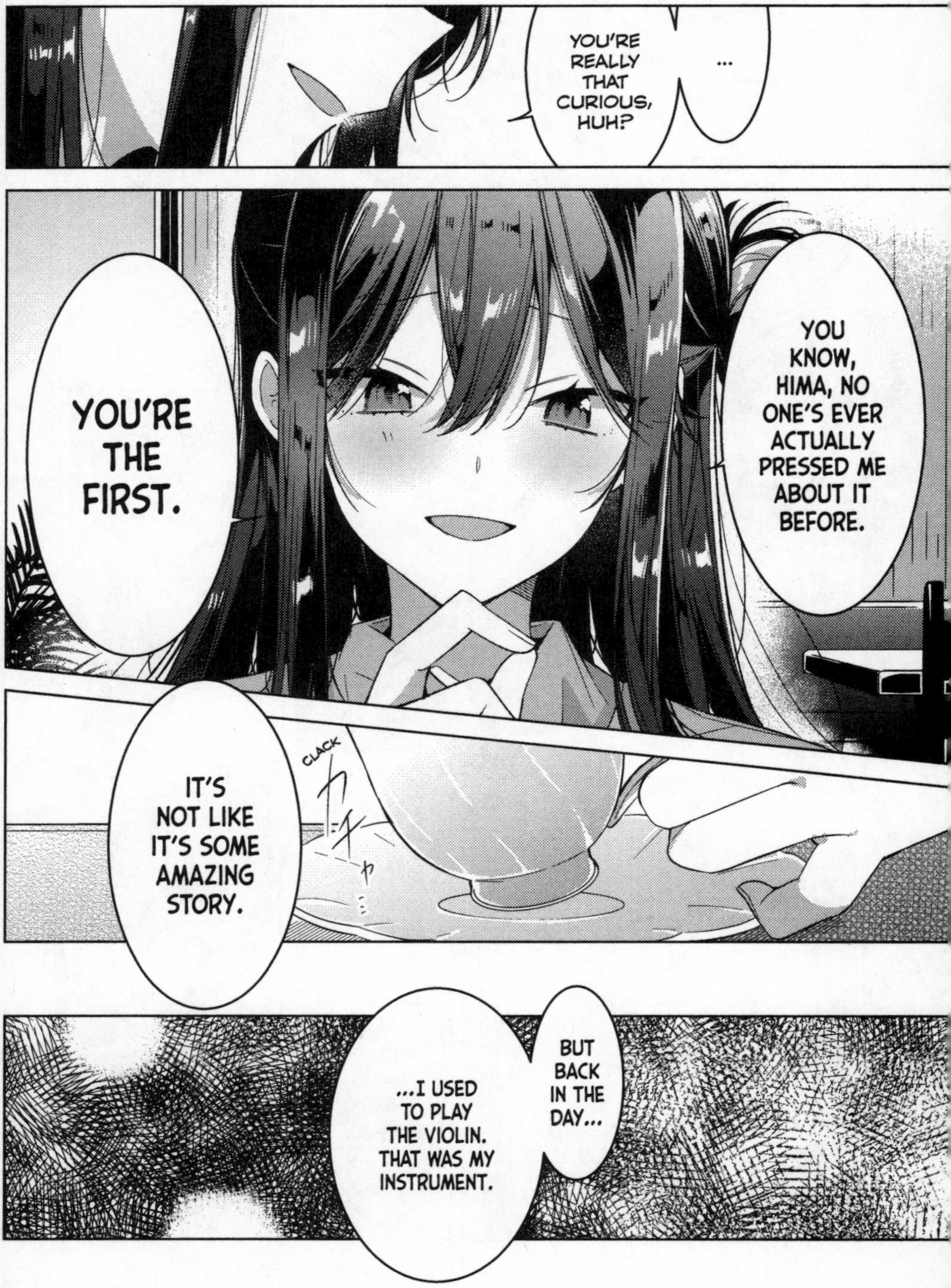
...
YOU'RE REALLY THAT CURIOUS, HUH?
YOU KNOW, HIMA, NO ONE'S EVER ACTUALLY PRESSED ME ABOUT IT BEFORE.
YOU'RE THE FIRST.
CLACK
IT'S NOT LIKE IT'S SOME AMAZING STORY.
BUT BACK IN THE DAY...
...I USED TO PLAY THE VIOLIN. THAT WAS MY INSTRUMENT.

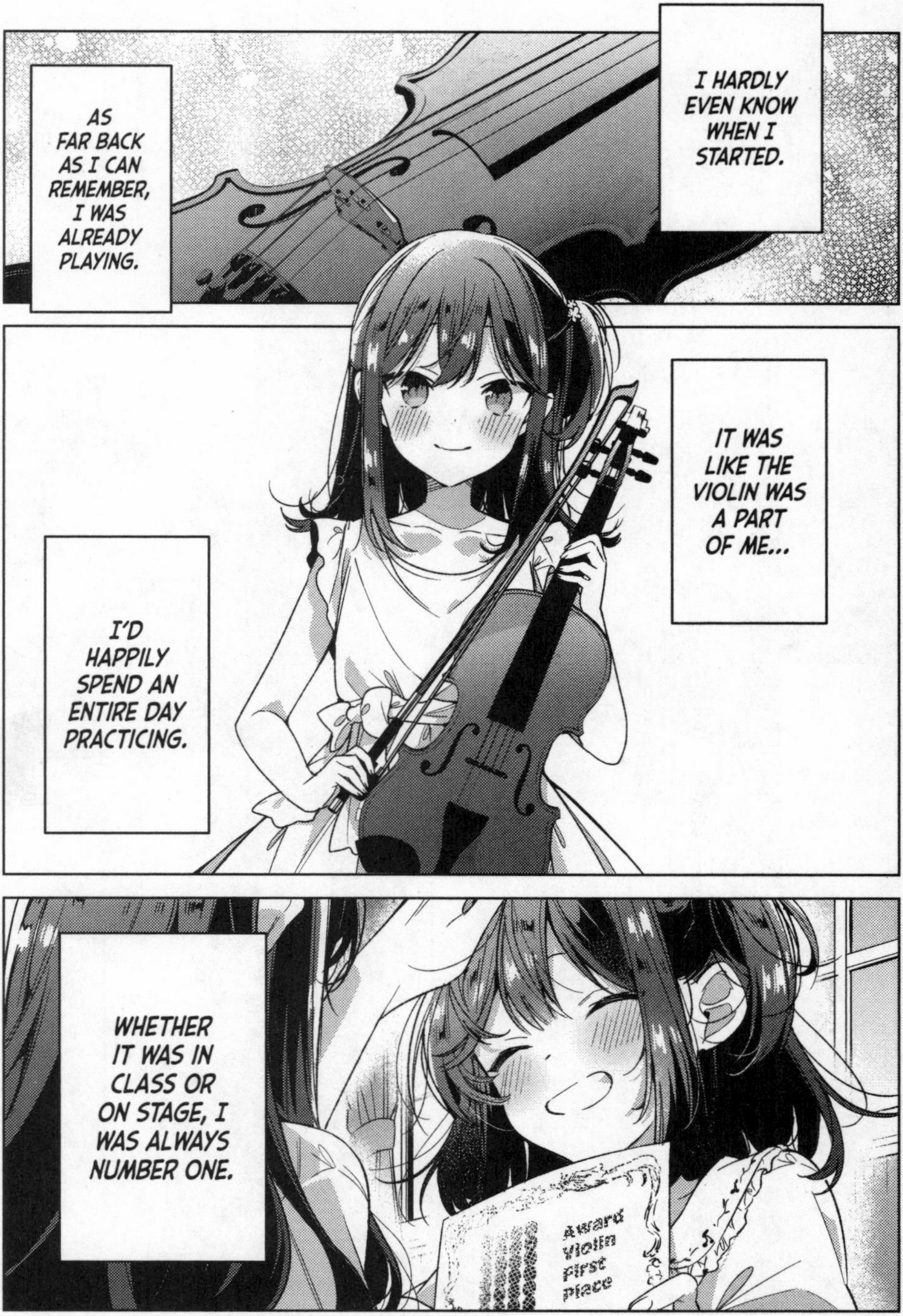
I HARDLY EVEN KNOW WHEN I STARTED.
AS FAR BACK AS I CAN REMEMBER, I WAS ALREADY PLAYING.
IT WAS LIKE THE VIOLIN WAS A PART OF ME...
I'D HAPPILY SPEND AN ENTIRE DAY PRACTICING.
WHETHER IT WAS IN CLASS OR ON STAGE, I WAS ALWAYS NUMBER ONE.
Award Violin First Place

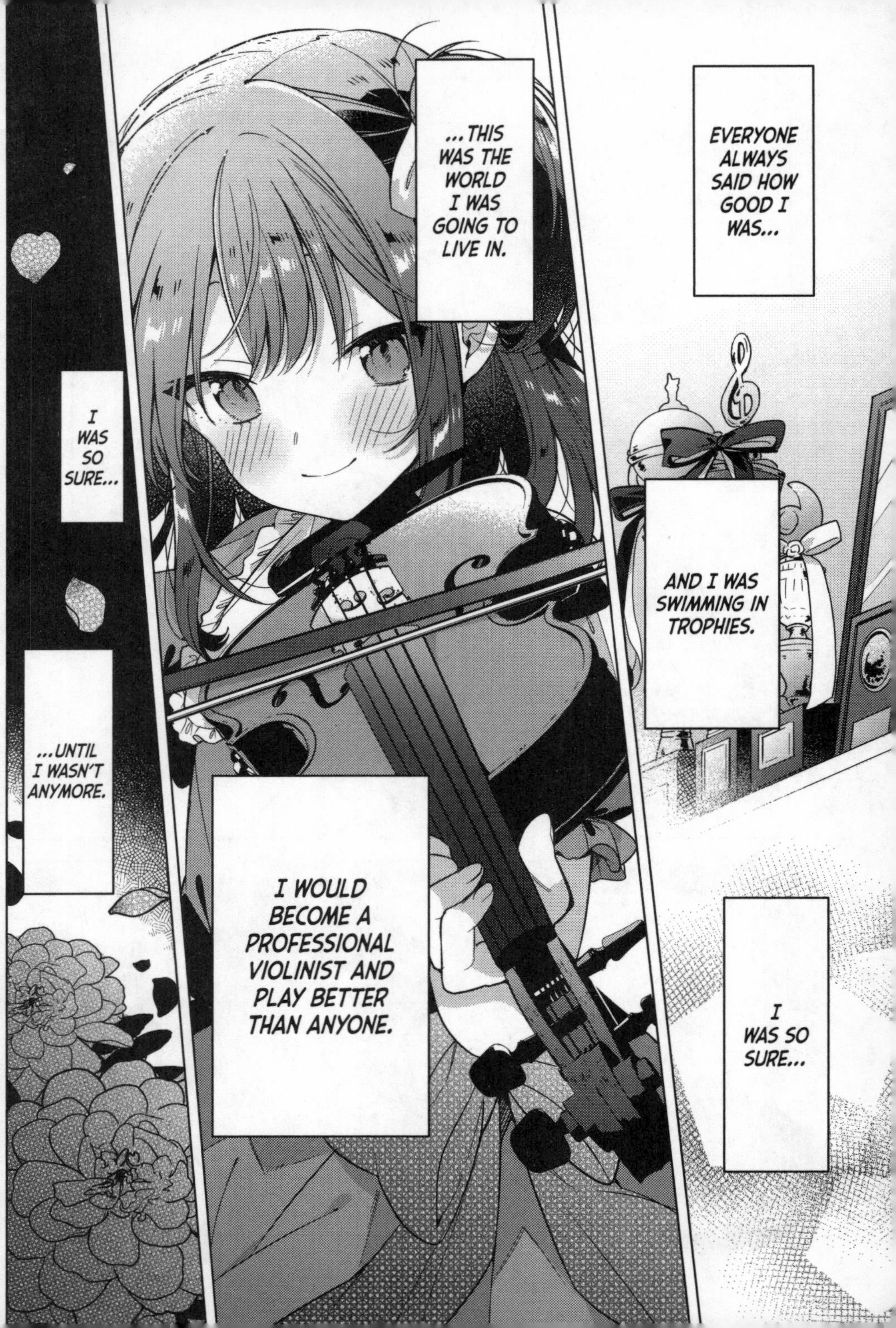
EVERYONE ALWAYS SAID HOW GOOD I WAS...
AND I WAS SWIMMING IN TROPHIES.
I WAS SO SURE...
I WOULD BECOME A PROFESSIONAL VIOLINIST AND PLAY BETTER THAN ANYONE.
...THIS WAS THE WORLD I WAS GOING TO LIVE IN.
I WAS SO SURE...
...UNTIL I WASN'T ANYMORE.

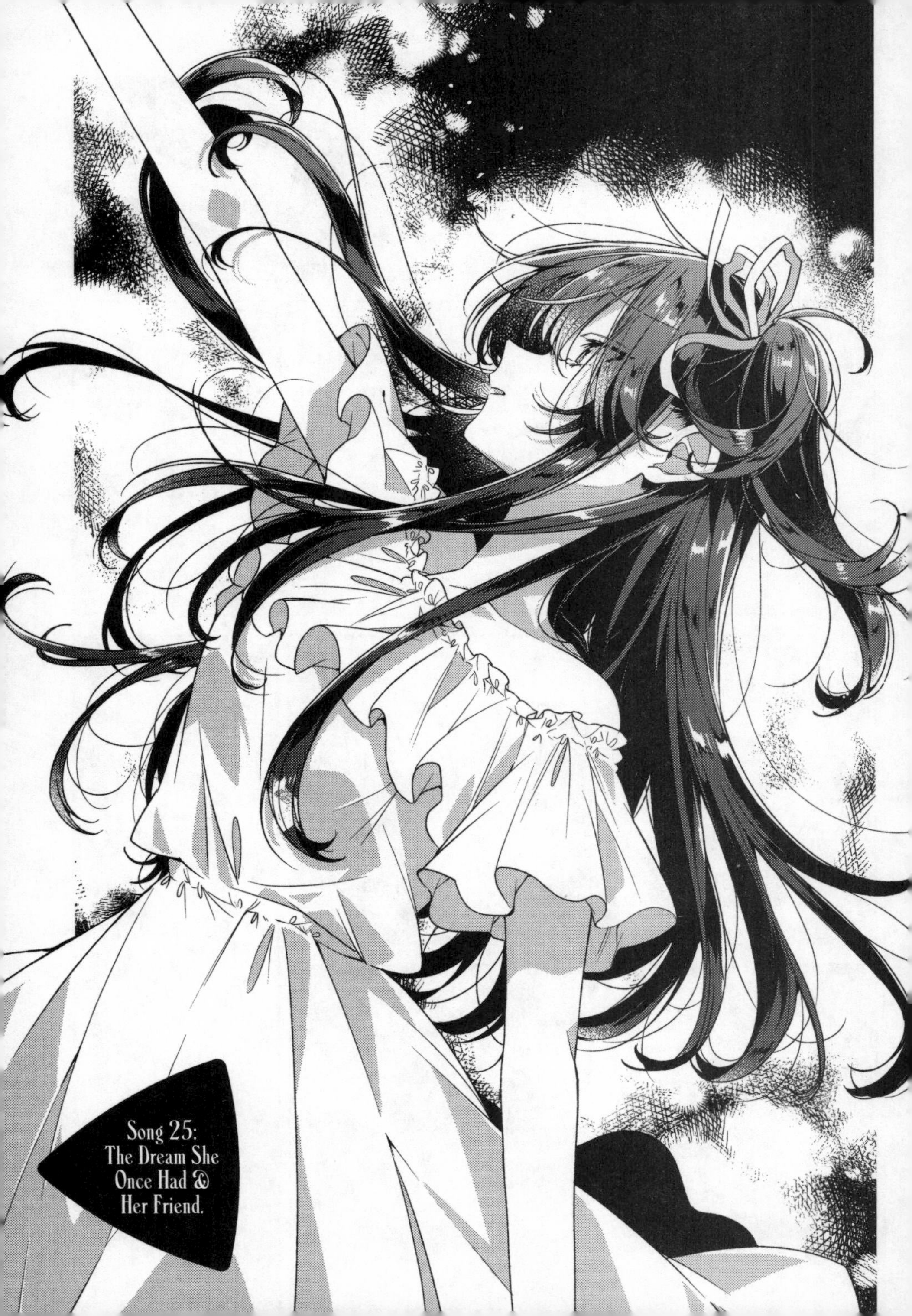
Song 25:
The Dream She Once Had & Her Friend.

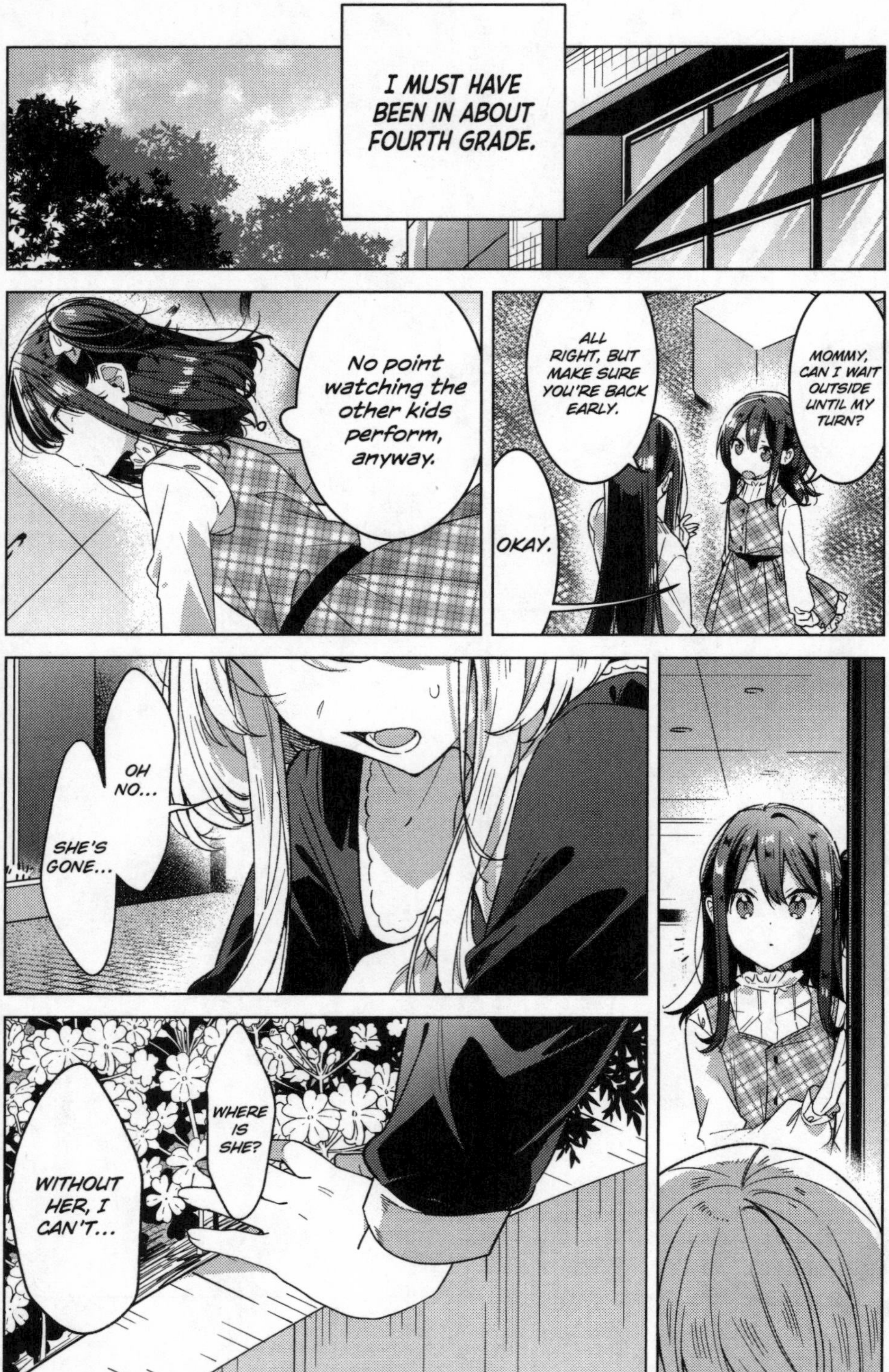
I MUST HAVE BEEN IN ABOUT FOURTH GRADE.
MOMMY, CAN I WAIT OUTSIDE UNTIL MY TURN?
ALL RIGHT, BUT MAKE SURE YOU'RE BACK EARLY.
OKAY.
No point watching the other kids perform, anyway.
OH NO...
SHE'S GONE...
WHERE IS SHE?
WITHOUT HER, I CAN'T...

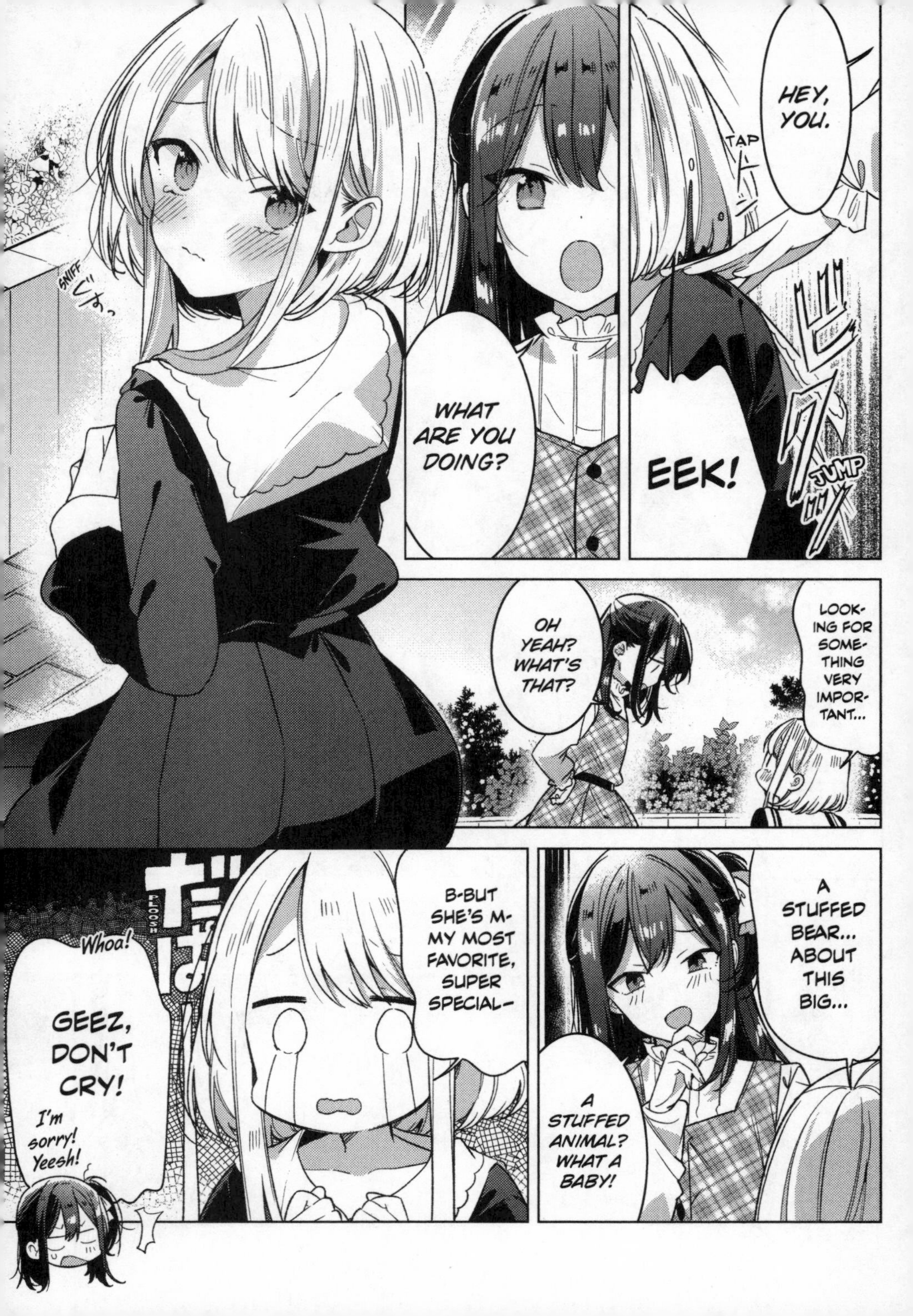
HEY, YOU.
TAP
EEK!
JUMP
WHAT ARE YOU DOING?
LOOKING FOR SOMETHING VERY IMPORTANT...
OH YEAH? WHAT'S THAT?
SNIFF
A STUFFED BEAR... ABOUT THIS BIG...
A STUFFED ANIMAL? WHAT A BABY!
B-BUT SHE'S M-MY MOST FAVORITE, SUPER SPECIAL-
PLOOSH
Whoa!
GEEZ, DON'T CRY!
I'm sorry! Yeesh!

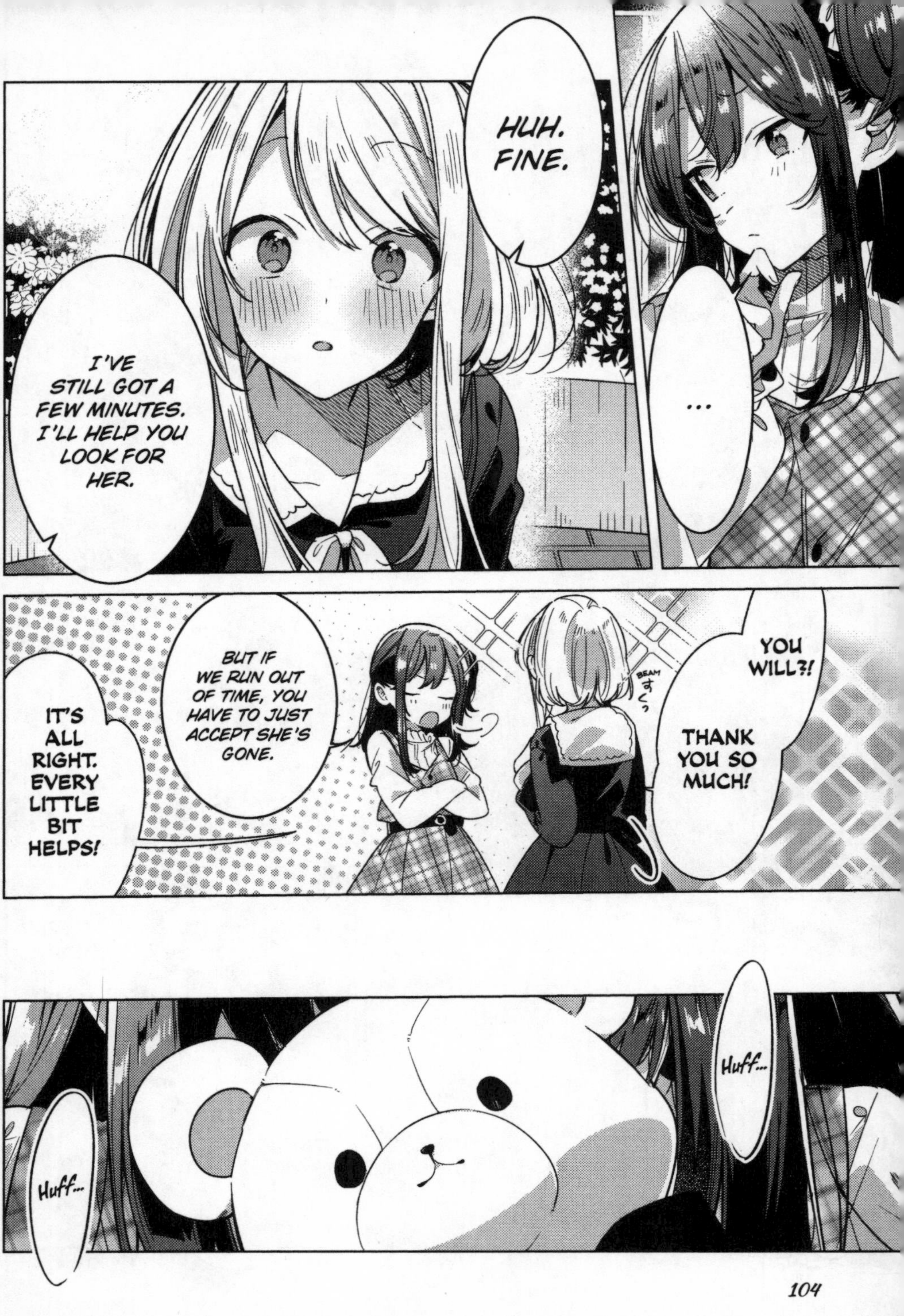
HUH. FINE.
...
I'VE STILL GOT A FEW MINUTES. I'LL HELP YOU LOOK FOR HER.
YOU WILL?!
THANK YOU SO MUCH!
BEAM
すくっ
BUT IF WE RUN OUT OF TIME, YOU HAVE TO JUST ACCEPT SHE'S GONE.
IT'S ALL RIGHT. EVERY LITTLE BIT HELPS!
Huff...
Huff...

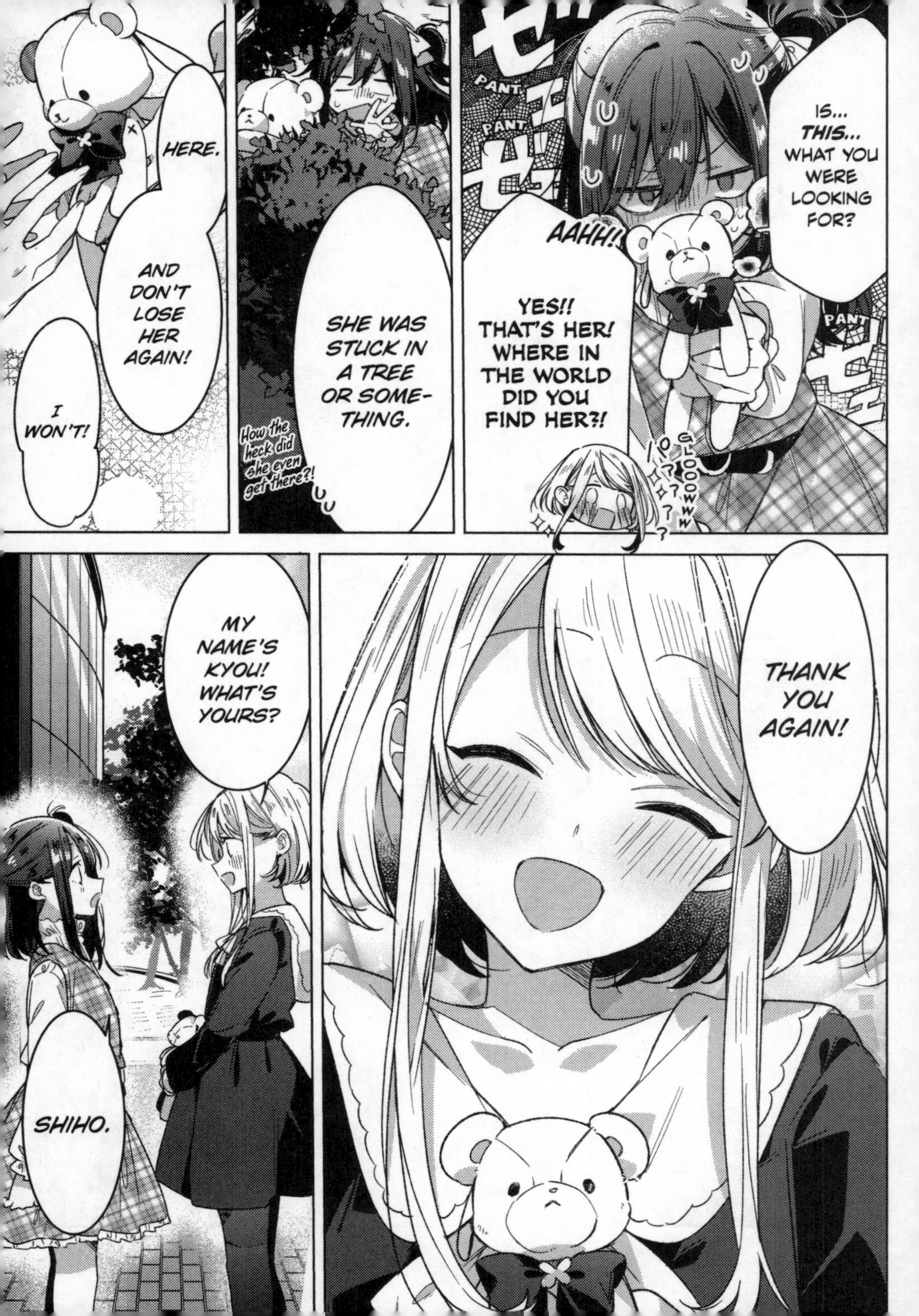
IS... THIS... WHAT YOU WERE LOOKING FOR?
PANT
PANT
AAHH!!
PANT
YES!! THAT'S HER! WHERE IN THE WORLD DID YOU FIND HER?!
GLOOOWWW
SHE WAS STUCK IN A TREE OR SOME-THING.
How the heck did she even get there?!
HERE.
AND DON'T LOSE HER AGAIN!
I WON'T!
THANK YOU AGAIN!
MY NAME'S KYOU! WHAT'S YOURS?
SHIHO.

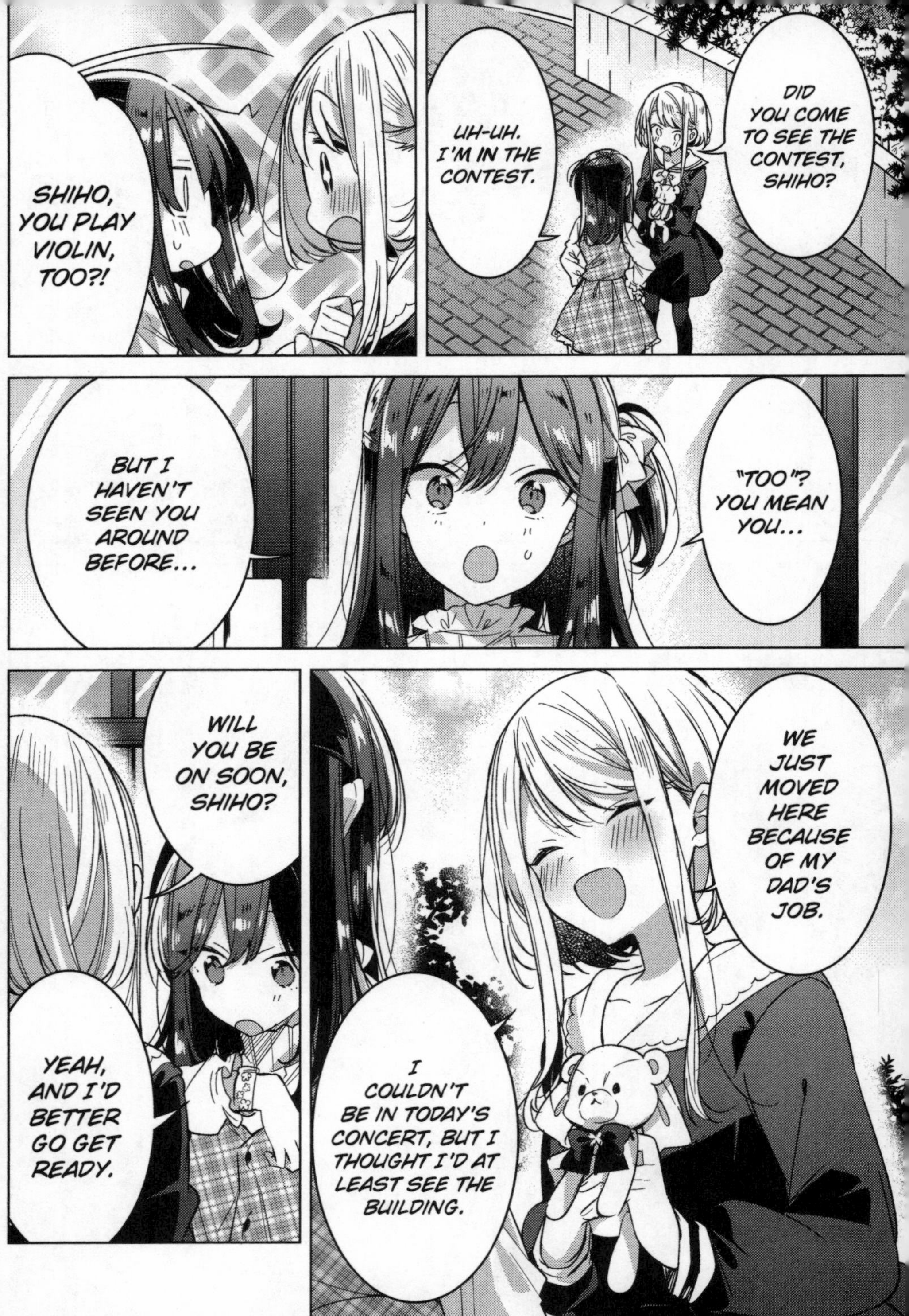
DID YOU COME TO SEE THE CONTEST, SHIHO?
UH-UH. I'M IN THE CONTEST.
SHIHO, YOU PLAY VIOLIN, TOO?!
"TOO"? YOU MEAN YOU...
BUT I HAVEN'T SEEN YOU AROUND BEFORE...
WE JUST MOVED HERE BECAUSE OF MY DAD'S JOB.
I COULDN'T BE IN TODAY'S CONCERT, BUT I THOUGHT I'D AT LEAST SEE THE BUILDING.
WILL YOU BE ON SOON, SHIHO?
YEAH, AND I'D BETTER GO GET READY.

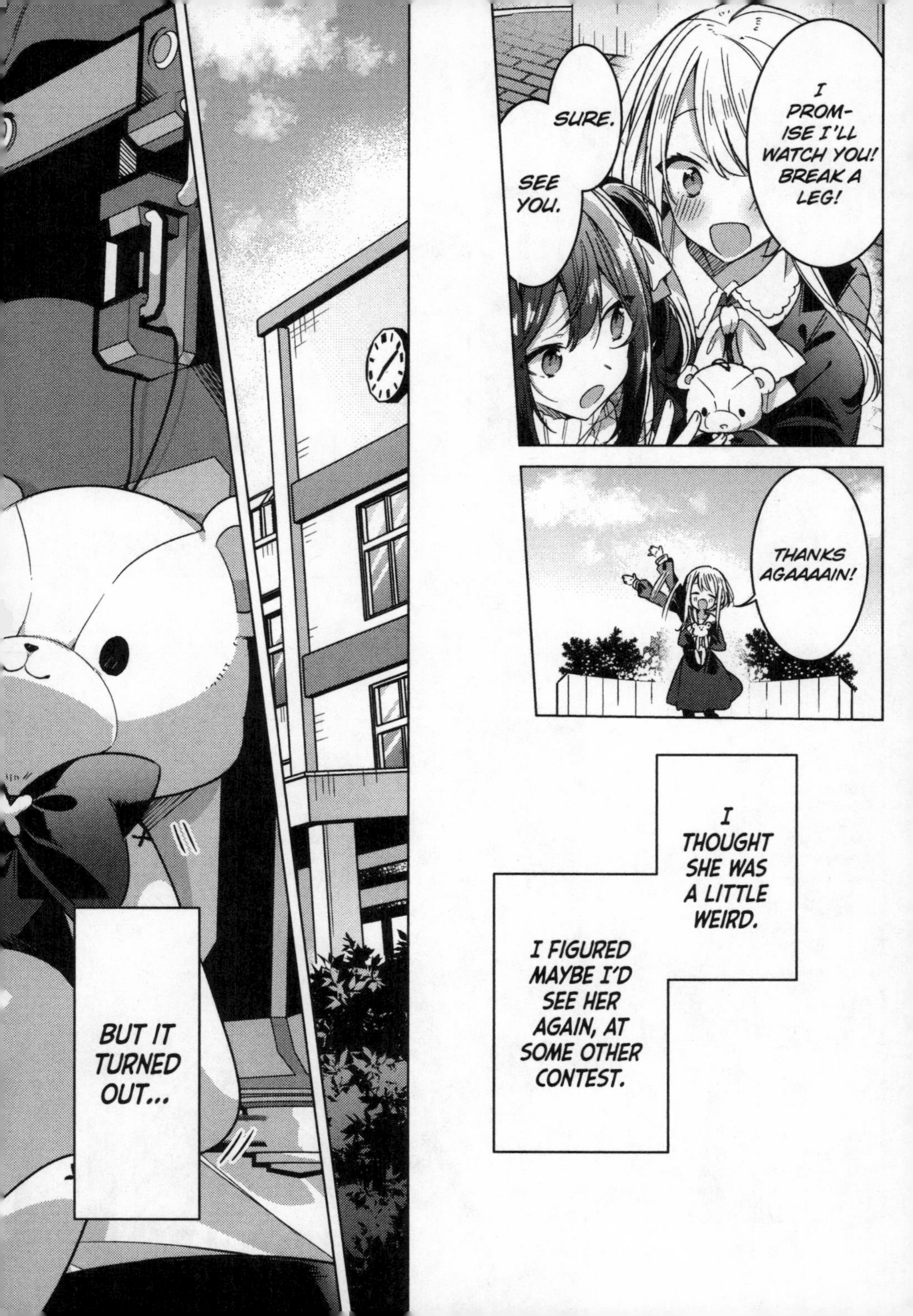
I PROMISE I'LL WATCH YOU! BREAK A LEG!
SURE.
SEE YOU.
THANKS AGAAAAIN!
I THOUGHT SHE WAS A LITTLE WEIRD.
I FIGURED MAYBE I'D SEE HER AGAIN, AT SOME OTHER CONTEST.
BUT IT TURNED OUT...

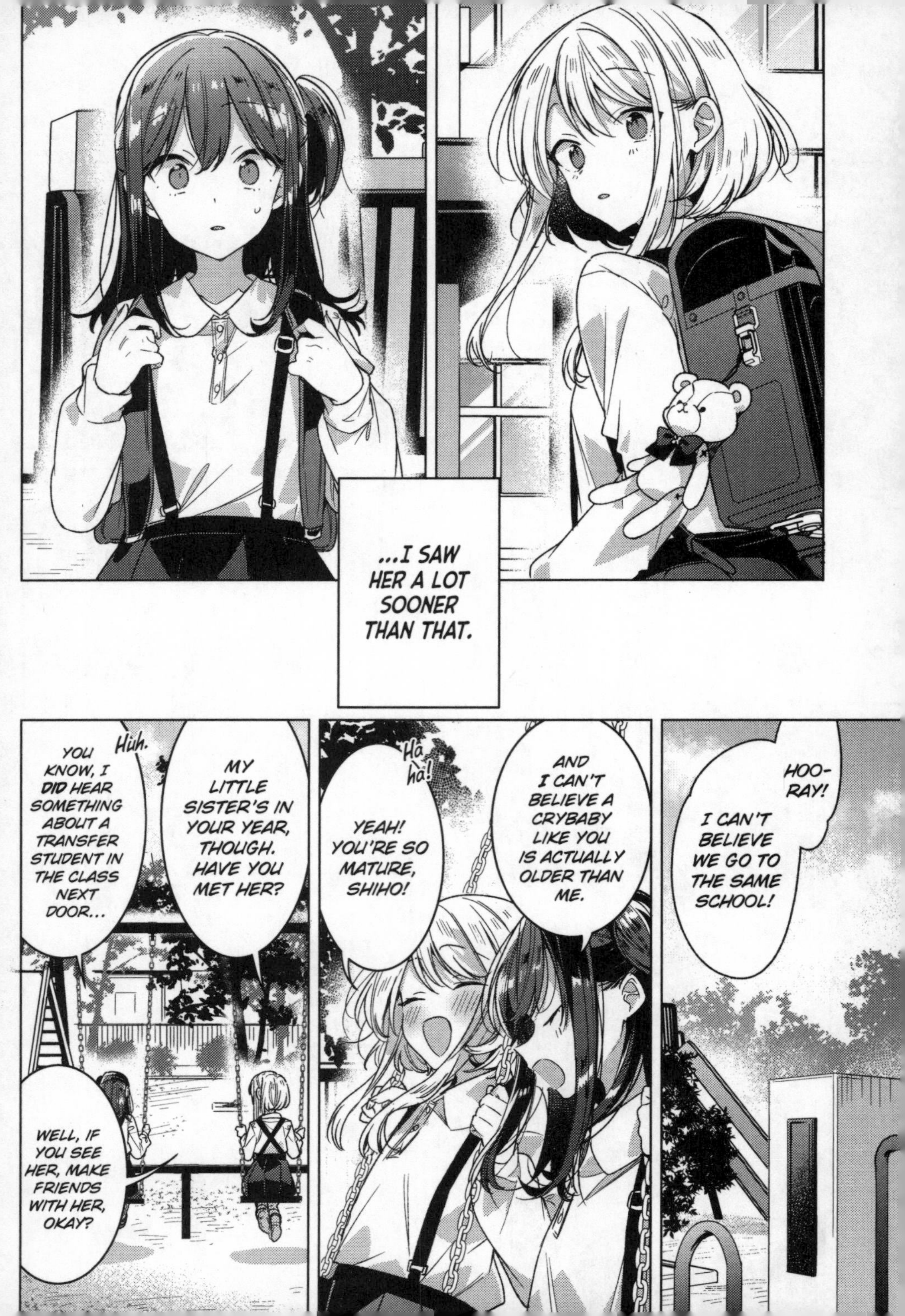
...I SAW HER A LOT SOONER THAN THAT.
HOO-RAY!
I CAN'T BELIEVE WE GO TO THE SAME SCHOOL!
AND I CAN'T BELIEVE A CRYBABY LIKE YOU IS ACTUALLY OLDER THAN ME.
Hà hà!
YEAH! YOU'RE SO MATURE, SHIHO!
MY LITTLE SISTER'S IN YOUR YEAR, THOUGH. HAVE YOU MET HER?
Hùh.
YOU KNOW, I DID HEAR SOMETHING ABOUT A TRANSFER STUDENT IN THE CLASS NEXT DOOR...
WELL, IF YOU SEE HER, MAKE FRIENDS WITH HER, OKAY?

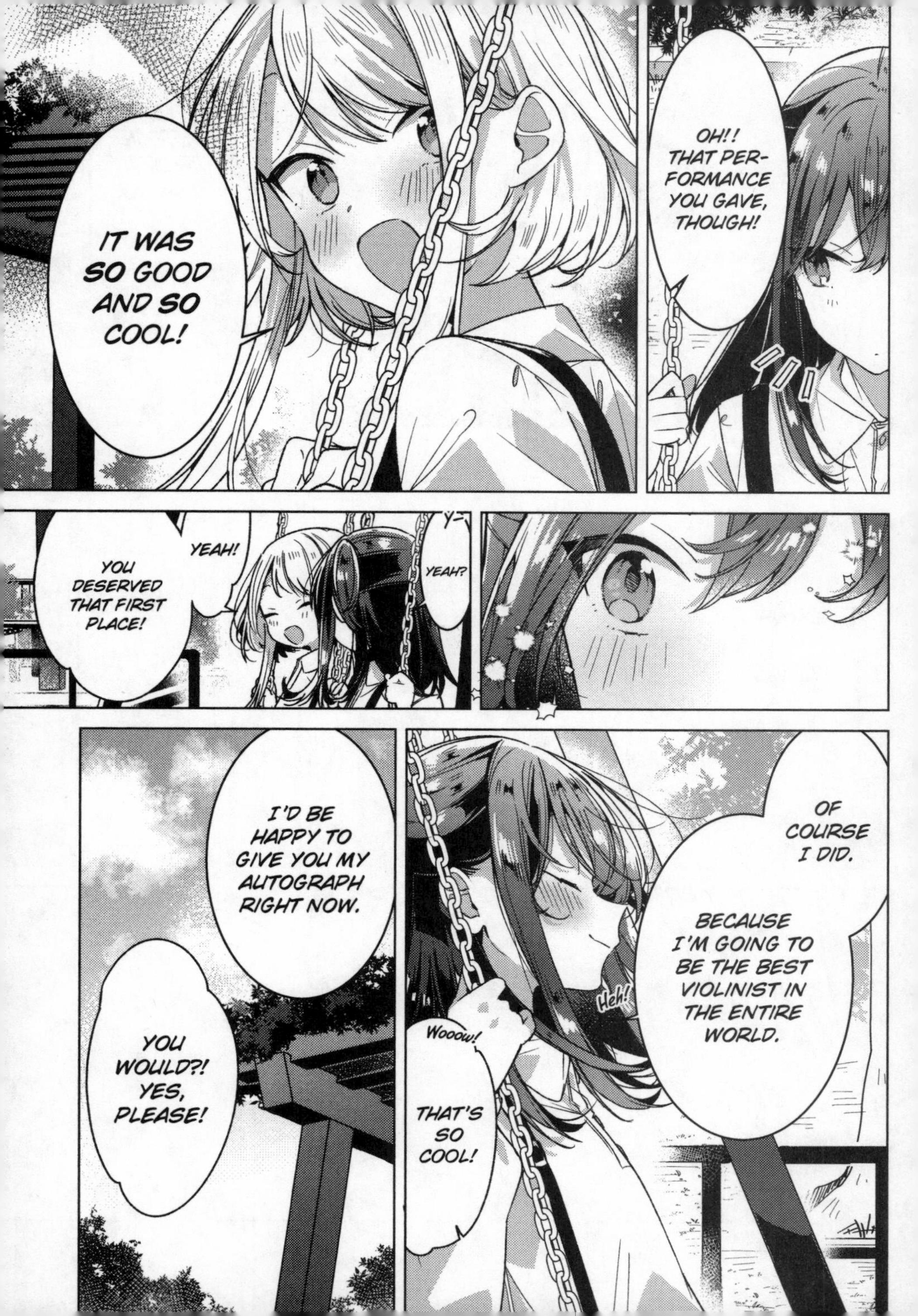
OH!! THAT PER-FORMANCE YOU GAVE, THOUGH!
IT WAS SO GOOD AND SO COOL!
YEAH?
YEAH!
YOU DESERVED THAT FIRST PLACE!
OF COURSE I DID.
BECAUSE I'M GOING TO BE THE BEST VIOLINIST IN THE ENTIRE WORLD.
Heh!
Wooow!
THAT'S SO COOL!
I'D BE HAPPY TO GIVE YOU MY AUTOGRAPH RIGHT NOW.
YOU WOULD?! YES, PLEASE!

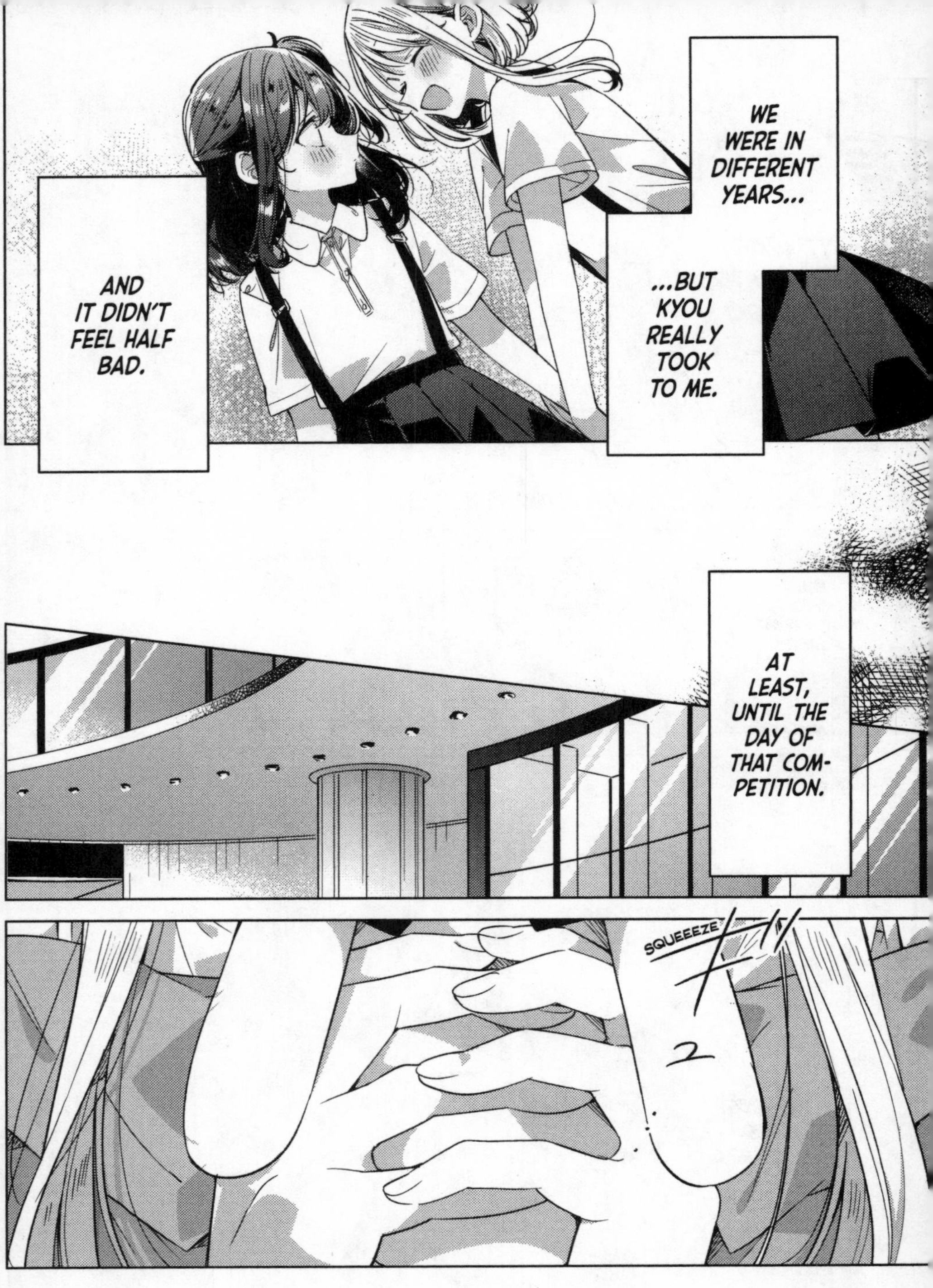
WE WERE IN DIFFERENT YEARS...
...BUT KYOU REALLY TOOK TO ME.
AND IT DIDN'T FEEL HALF BAD.
AT LEAST, UNTIL THE DAY OF THAT COM-PETITION.
SQUEEEZE

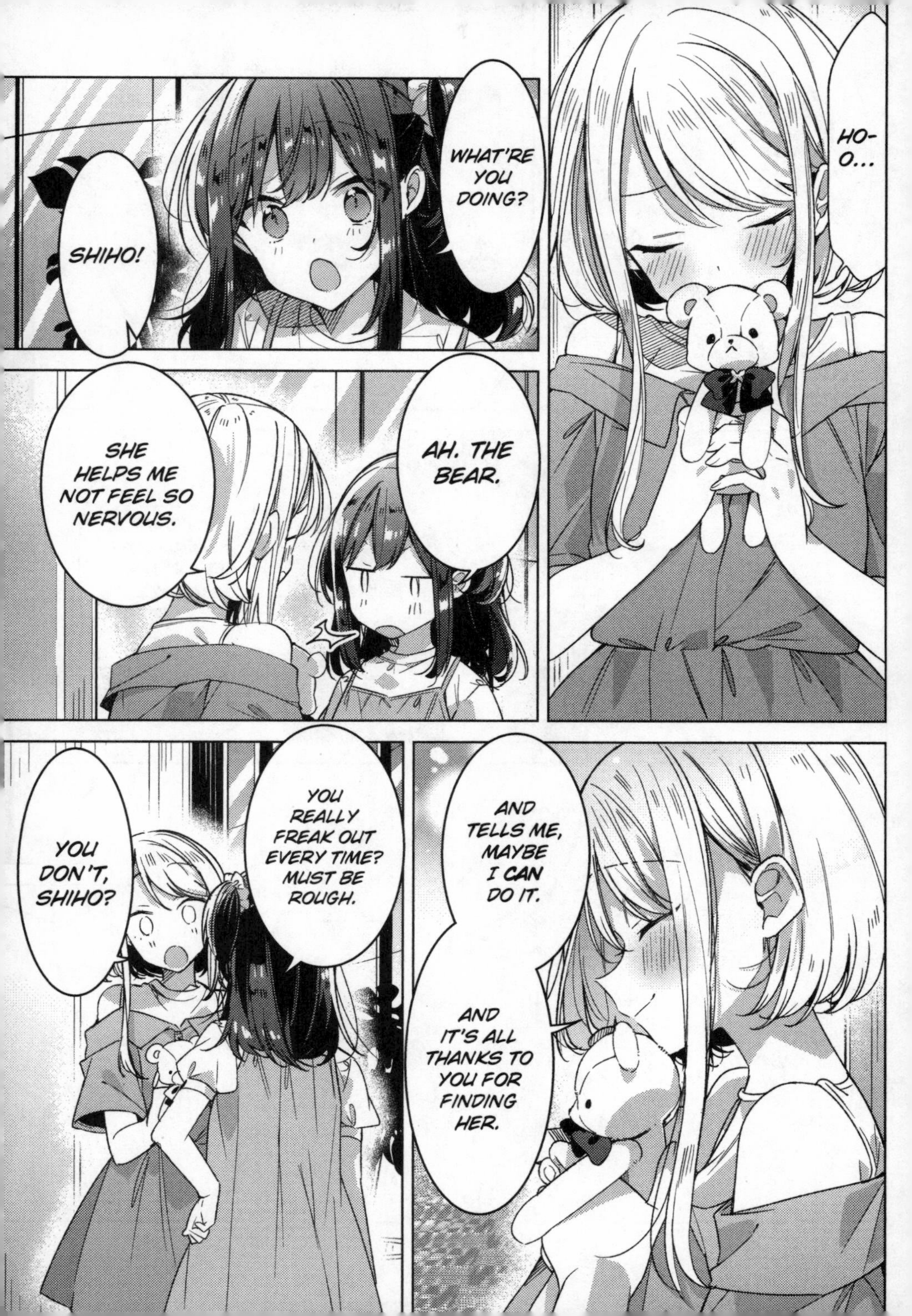
HO-O...
WHAT'RE YOU DOING?
SHIHO!
AH. THE BEAR.
SHE HELPS ME NOT FEEL SO NERVOUS.
AND TELLS ME, MAYBE I CAN DO IT.
AND IT'S ALL THANKS TO YOU FOR FINDING HER.
YOU REALLY FREAK OUT EVERY TIME? MUST BE ROUGH.
YOU DON'T, SHIHO?

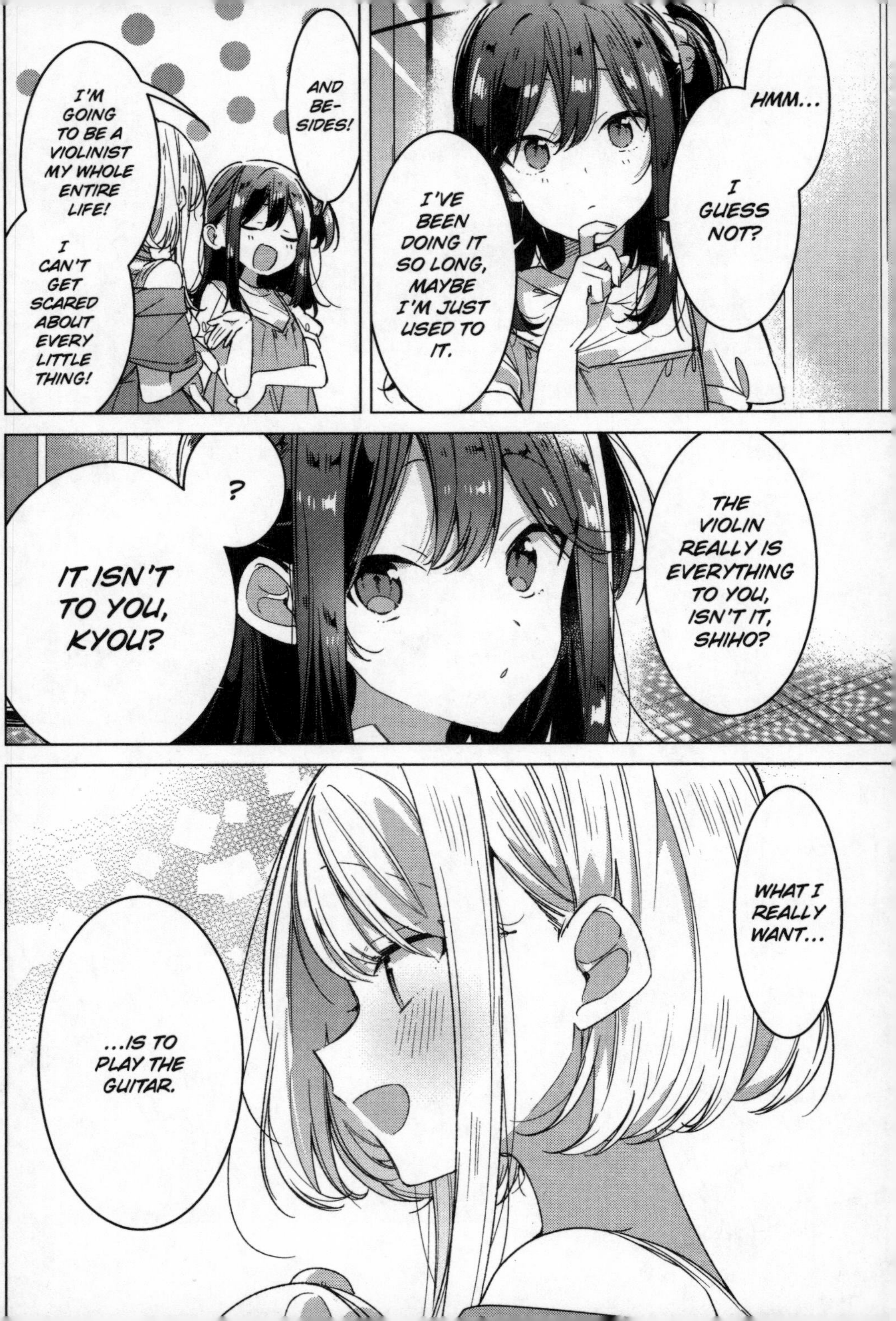
HMM... I GUESS NOT?
I'VE BEEN DOING IT SO LONG, MAYBE I'M JUST USED TO IT.
AND BE-SIDES!
I'M GOING TO BE A VIOLINIST MY WHOLE ENTIRE LIFE!
I CAN'T GET SCARED ABOUT EVERY LITTLE THING!
THE VIOLIN REALLY IS EVERYTHING TO YOU, ISN'T IT, SHIHO?
?
IT ISN'T TO YOU, KYOU?
WHAT I REALLY WANT...
...IS TO PLAY THE GUITAR.

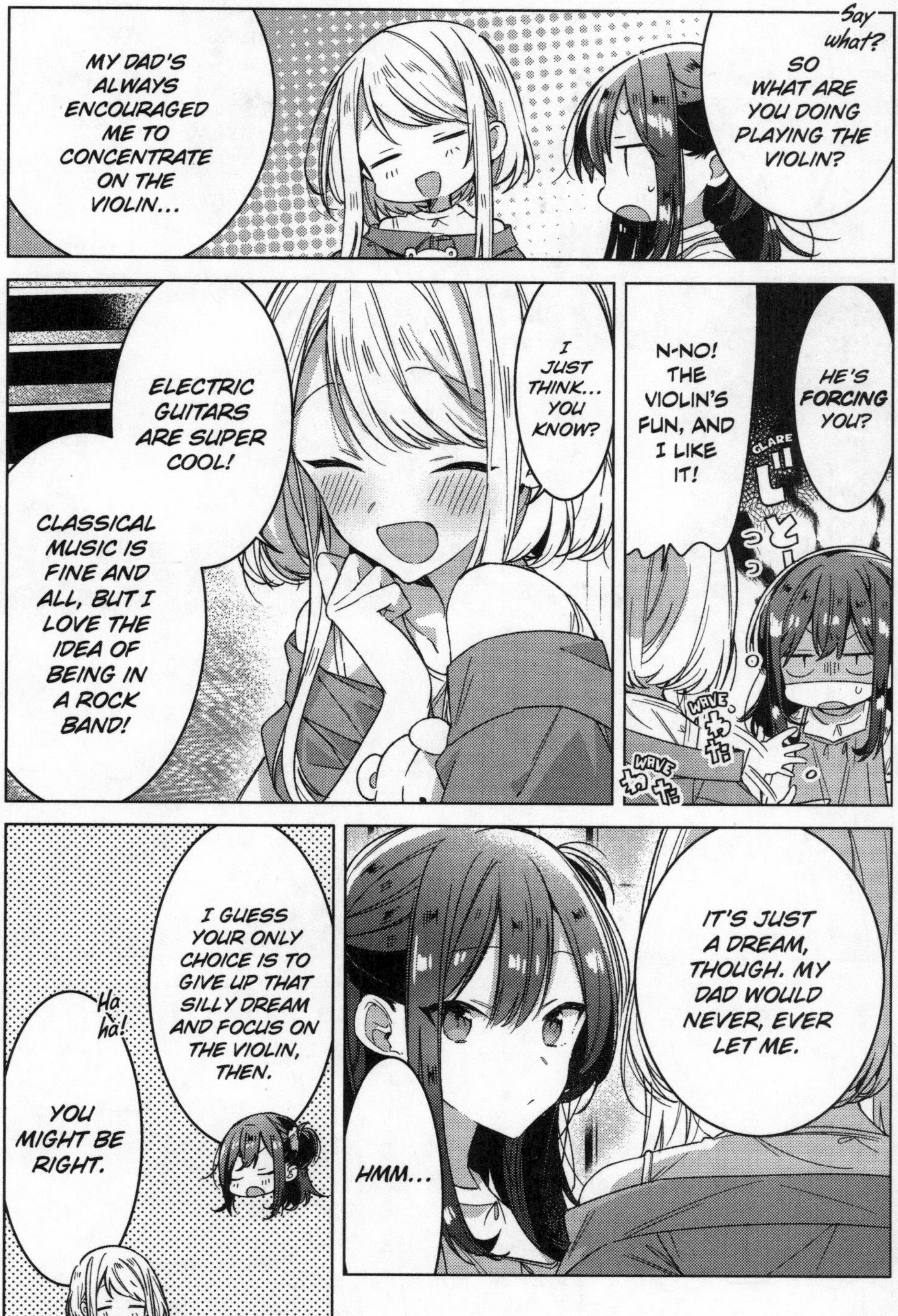

Say what?
SO WHAT ARE YOU DOING PLAYING THE VIOLIN?
MY DAD'S ALWAYS ENCOURAGED ME TO CONCENTRATE ON THE VIOLIN...
HE'S FORCING YOU?
GLARE
N-NO! THE VIOLIN'S FUN, AND I LIKE IT!
WAVE
WAVE
I JUST THINK... YOU KNOW?
ELECTRIC GUITARS ARE SUPER COOL!
CLASSICAL MUSIC IS FINE AND ALL, BUT I LOVE THE IDEA OF BEING IN A ROCK BAND!
IT'S JUST A DREAM, THOUGH. MY DAD WOULD NEVER, EVER LET ME.
HMM...
I GUESS YOUR ONLY CHOICE IS TO GIVE UP THAT SILLY DREAM AND FOCUS ON THE VIOLIN, THEN.
Ha ha!
YOU MIGHT BE RIGHT.

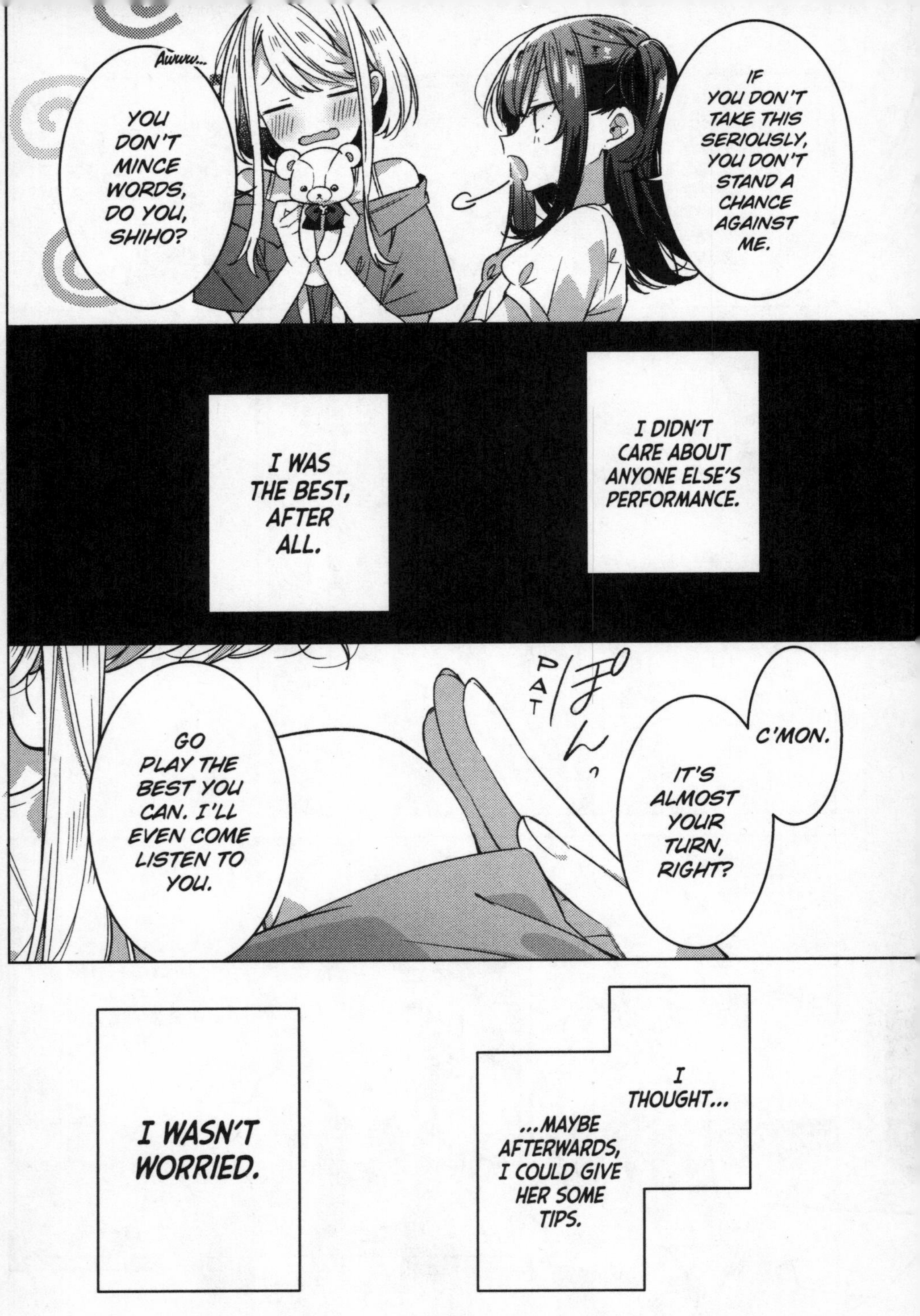
IF YOU DON'T TAKE THIS SERIOUSLY, YOU DON'T STAND A CHANCE AGAINST ME.
Auuuu...
YOU DON'T MINCE WORDS, DO YOU, SHIHO?
I DIDN'T CARE ABOUT ANYONE ELSE'S PERFORMANCE.
I WAS THE BEST, AFTER ALL.
PAT
C'MON.
IT'S ALMOST YOUR TURN, RIGHT?
GO PLAY THE BEST YOU CAN. I'LL EVEN COME LISTEN TO YOU.
I THOUGHT...
...MAYBE AFTERWARDS, I COULD GIVE HER SOME TIPS.
I WASN'T WORRIED.

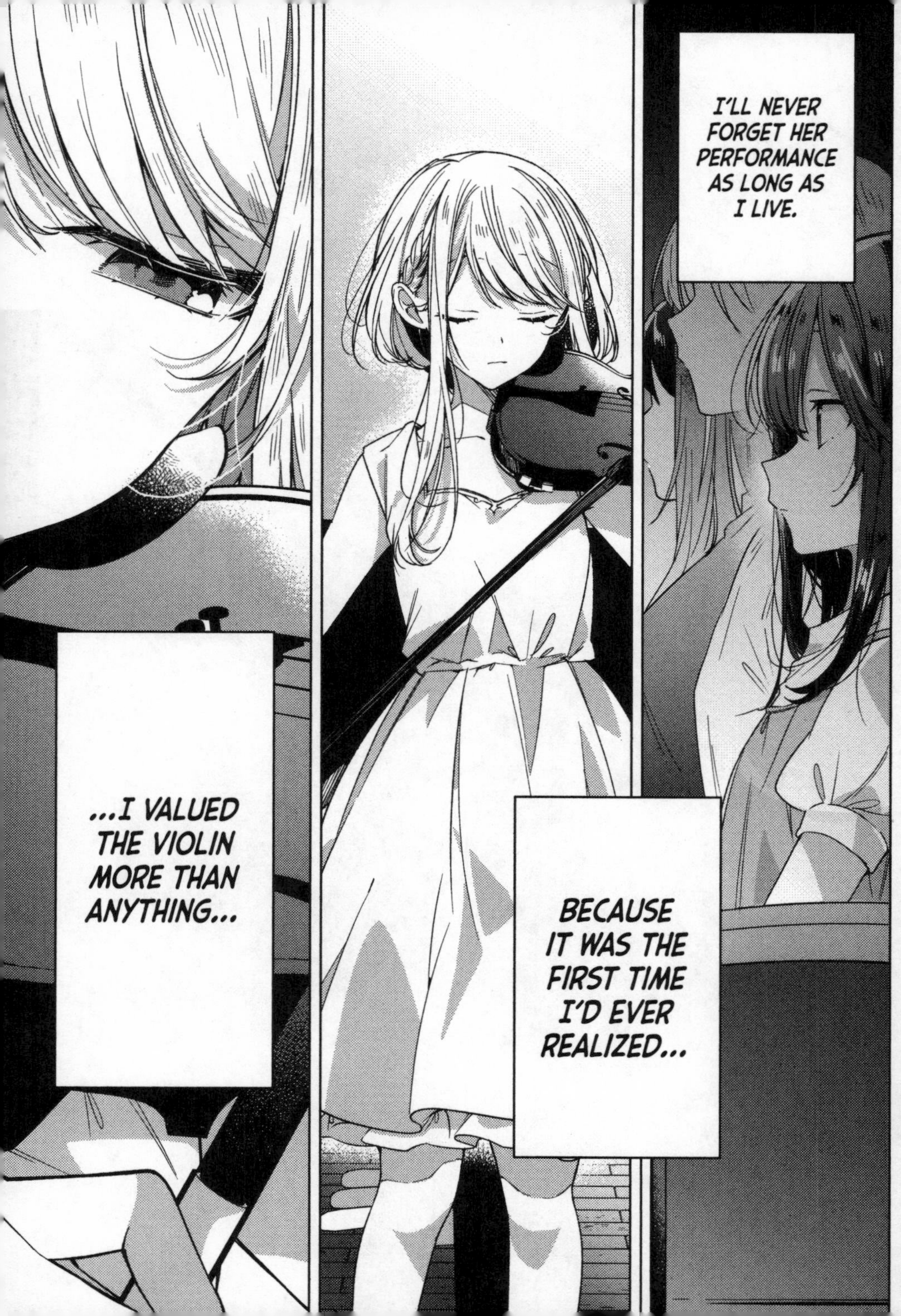
I'LL NEVER FORGET HER PERFORMANCE AS LONG AS I LIVE.
BECAUSE IT WAS THE FIRST TIME I'D EVER REALIZED...
...I VALUED THE VIOLIN MORE THAN ANYTHING...

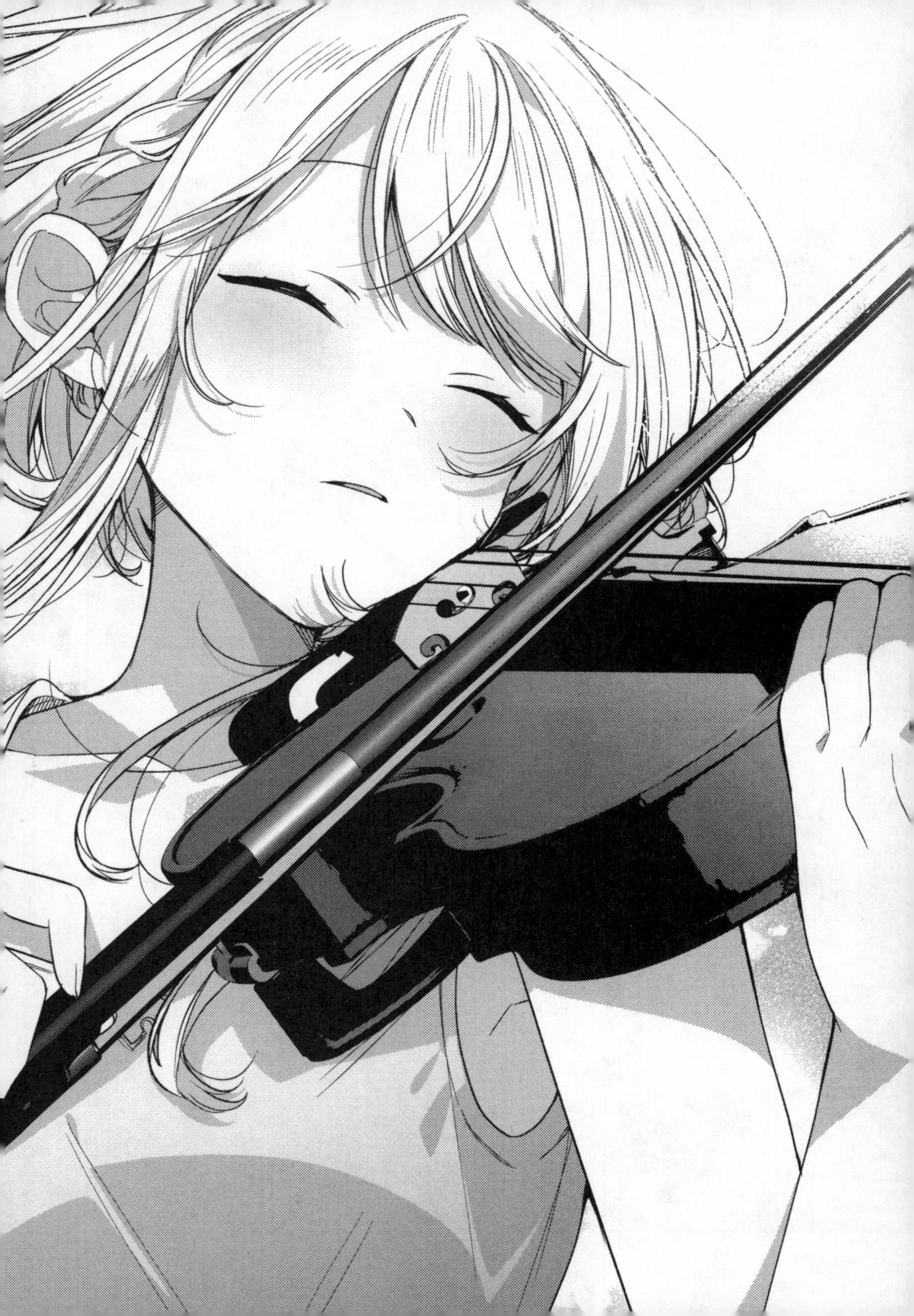

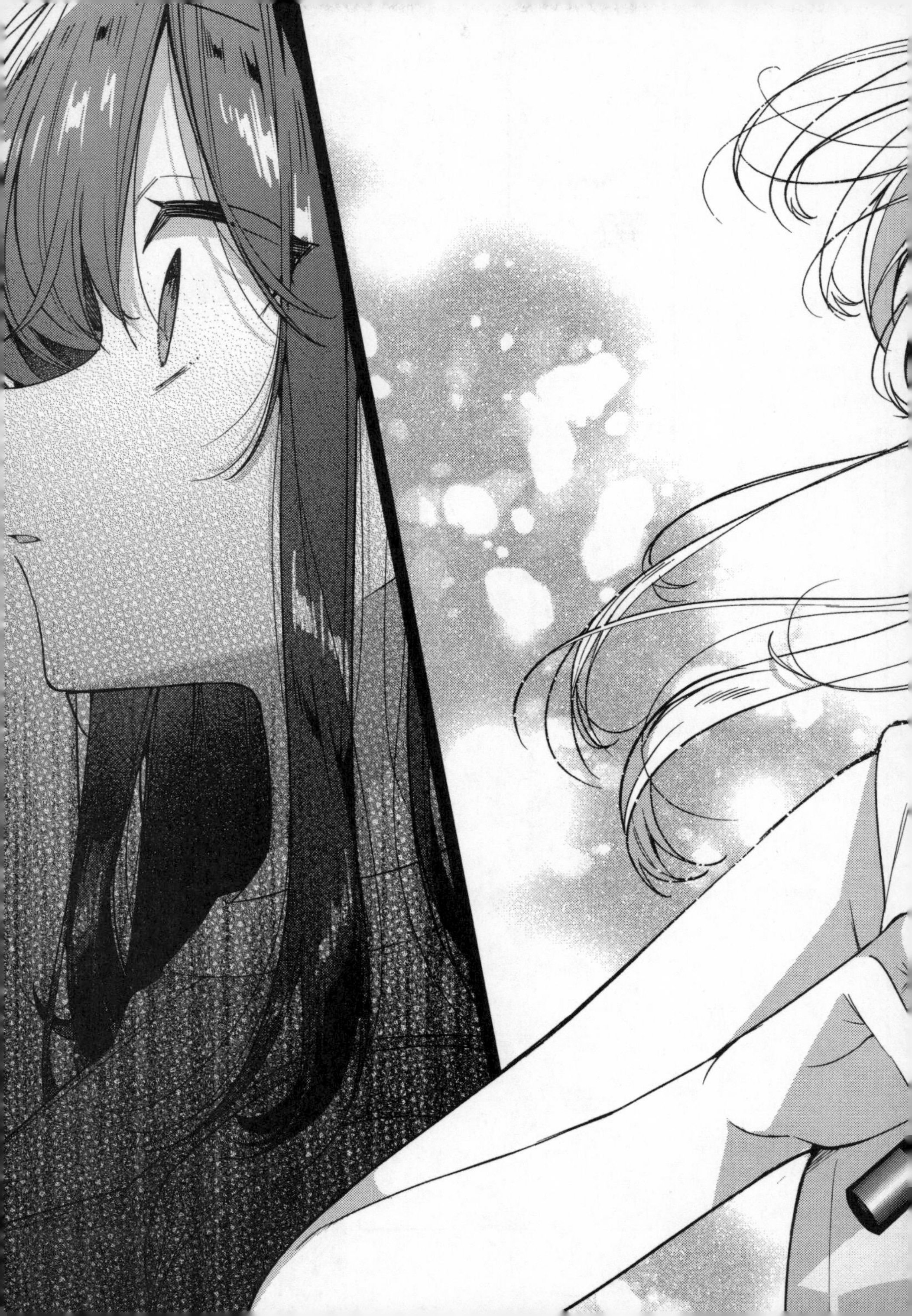

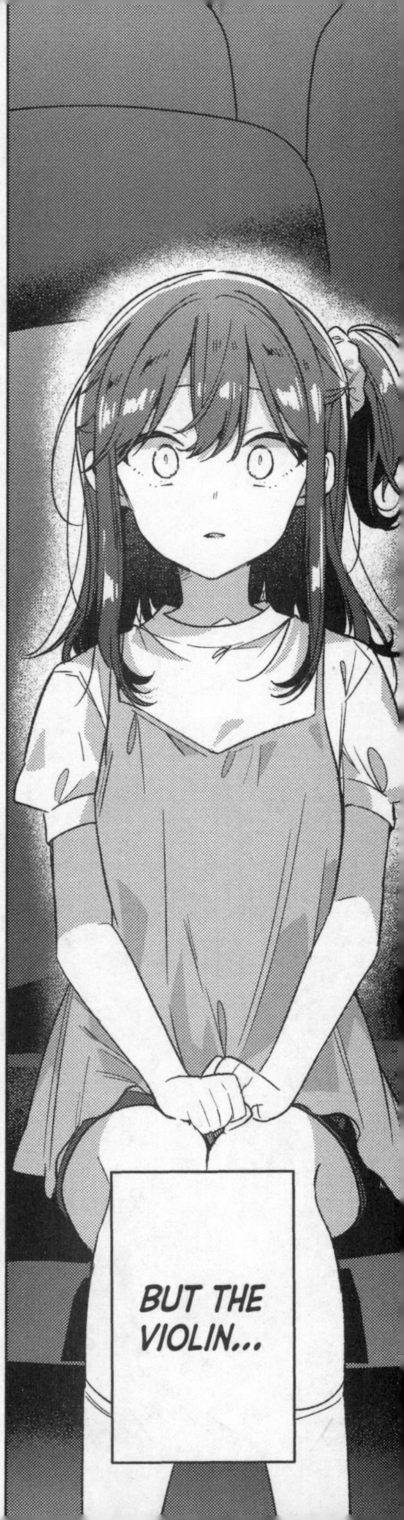
BUT THE VIOLIN...
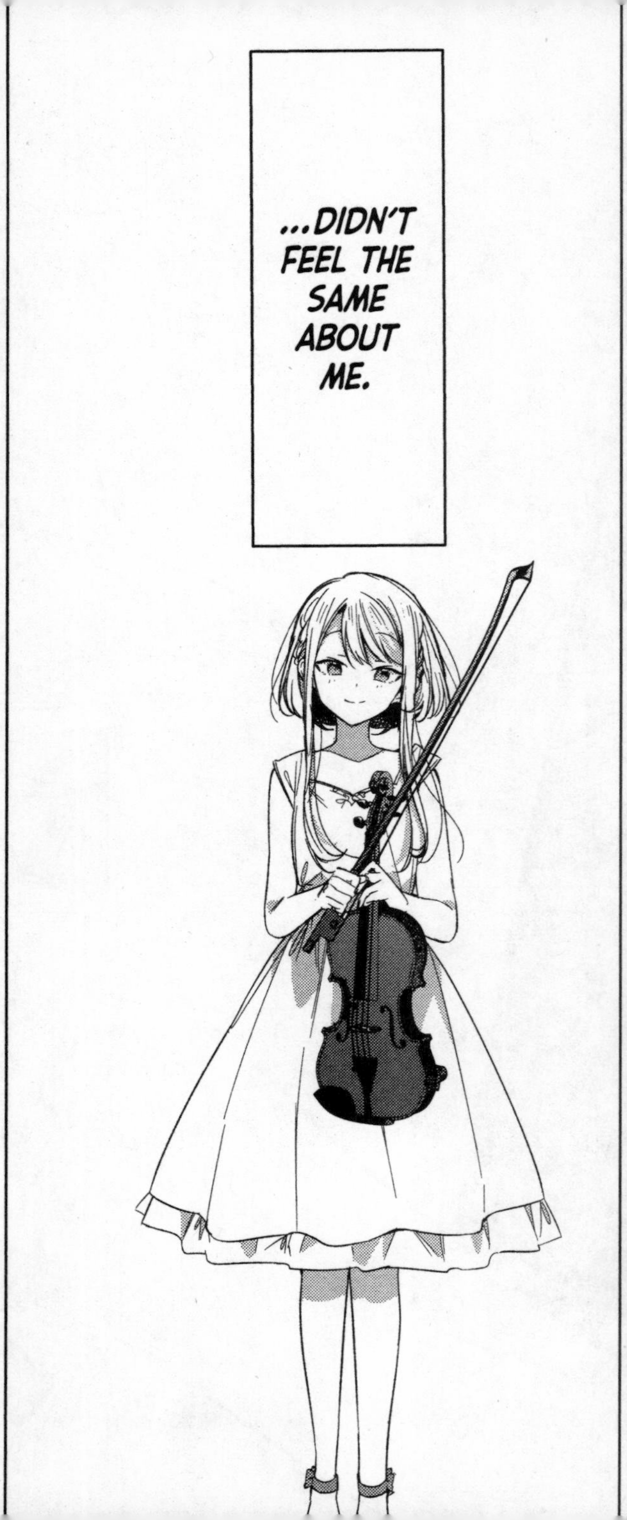
...DIDN'T FEEL THE SAME ABOUT ME.

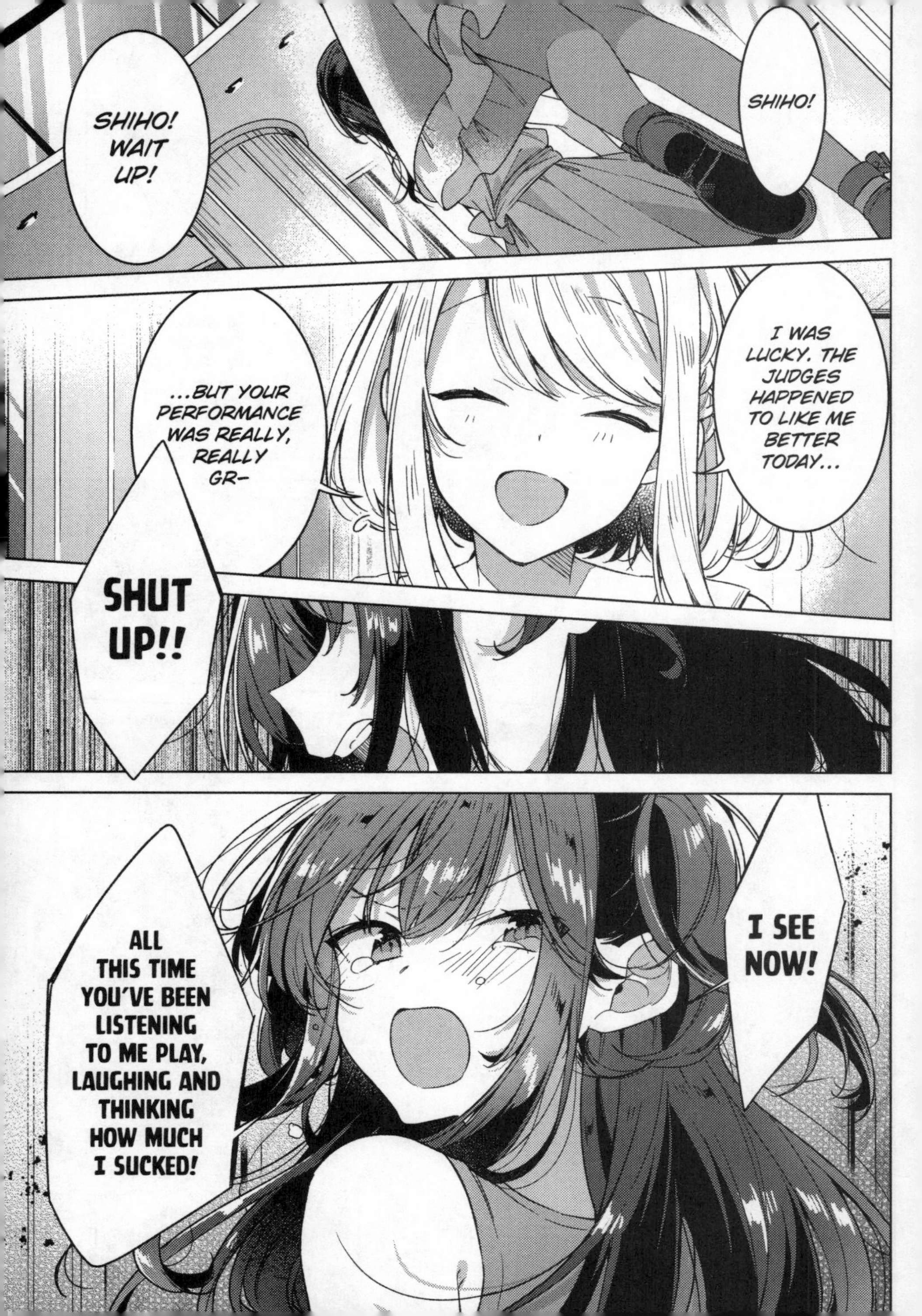
SHIHO!
SHIHO! WAIT UP!
I WAS LUCKY. THE JUDGES HAPPENED TO LIKE ME BETTER TODAY...
...BUT YOUR PERFORMANCE WAS REALLY, REALLY GR-
SHUT UP!!
I SEE NOW!
ALL THIS TIME YOU'VE BEEN LISTENING TO ME PLAY, LAUGHING AND THINKING HOW MUCH I SUCKED!

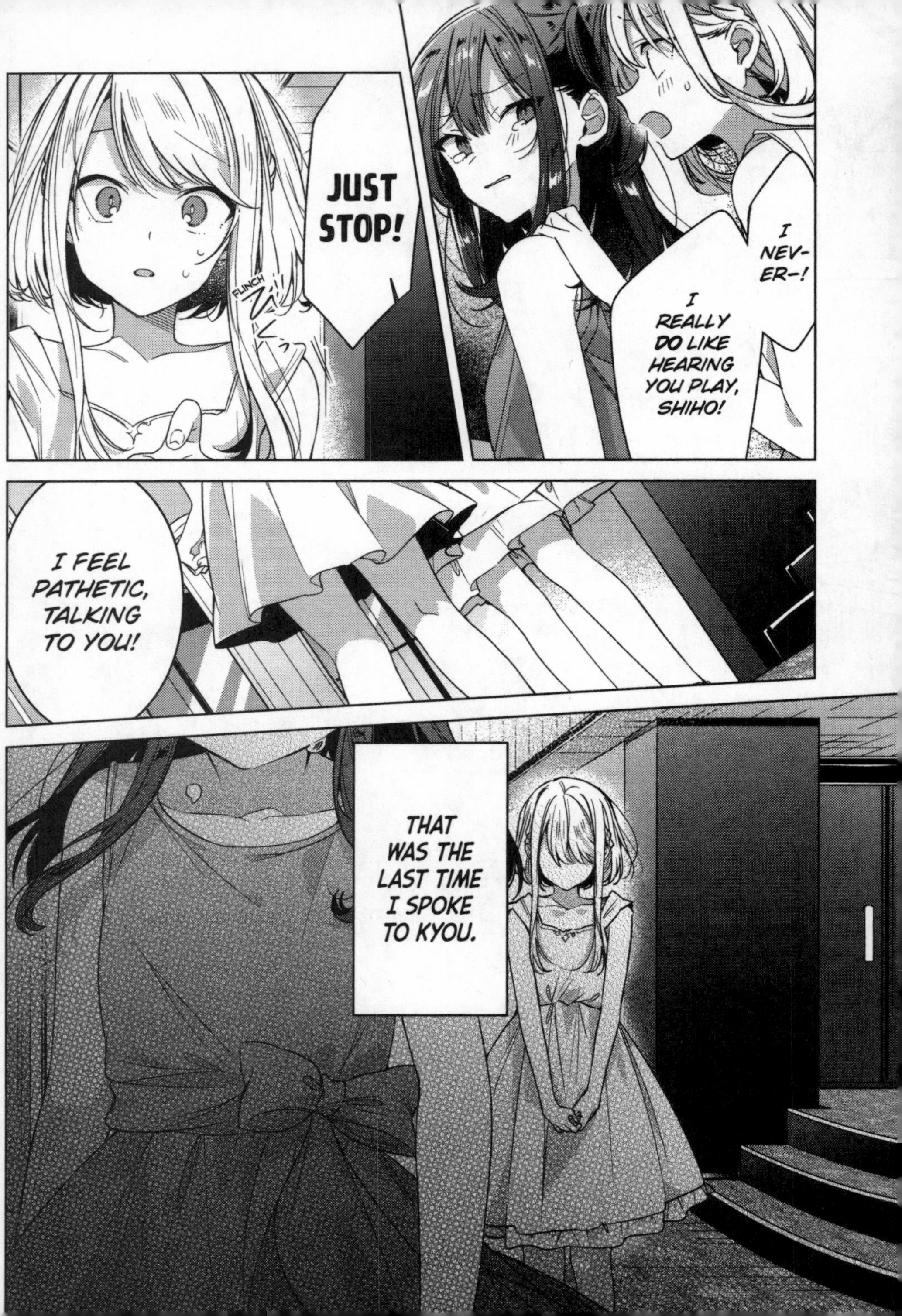
I NEV-ER-!
I REALLY DO LIKE HEARING YOU PLAY, SHIHO!
JUST STOP!
FLINCH
I FEEL PATHETIC, TALKING TO YOU!
THAT WAS THE LAST TIME I SPOKE TO KYOU.

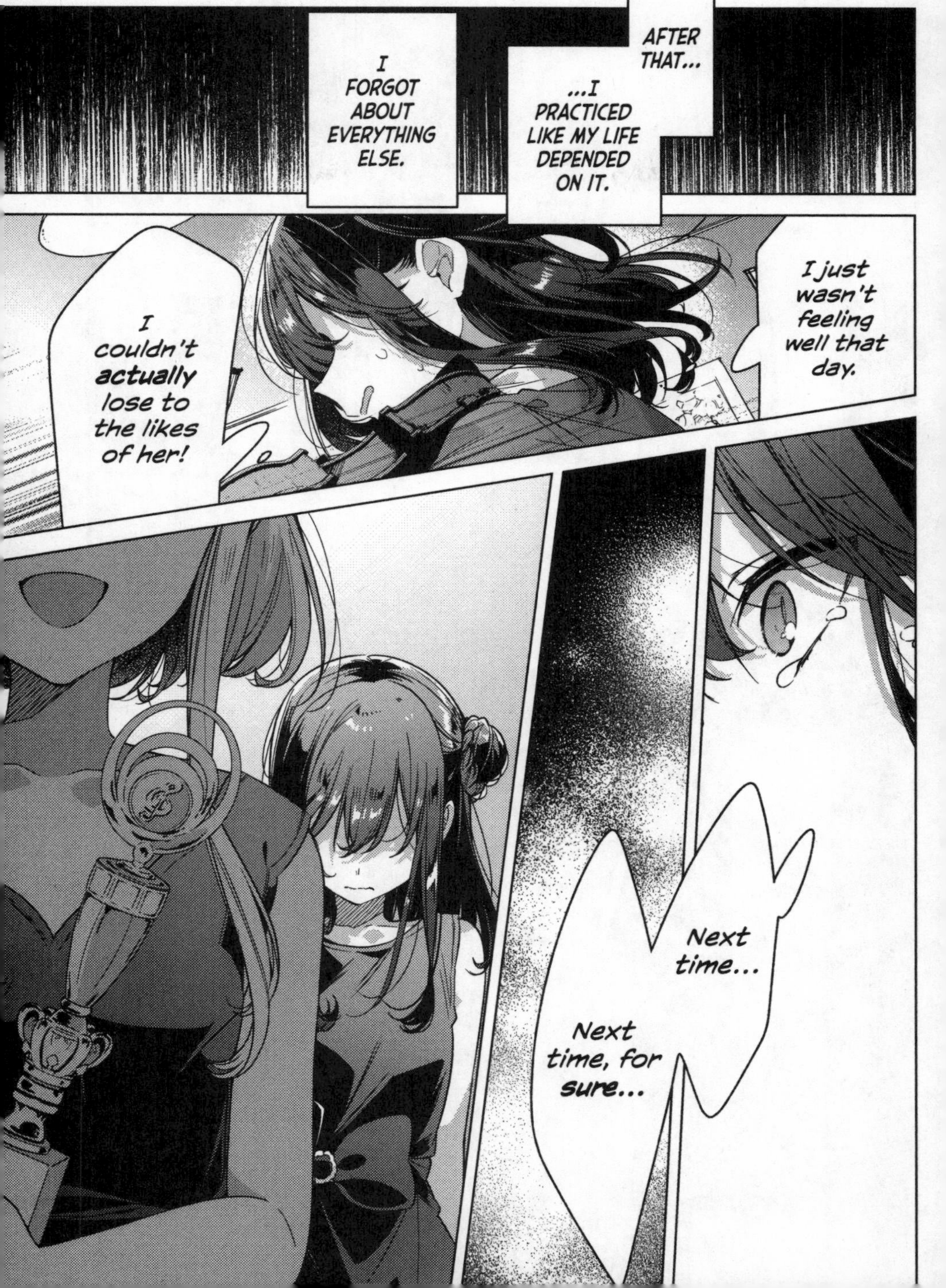
AFTER THAT...
...I PRACTICED LIKE MY LIFE DEPENDED ON IT.
I FORGOT ABOUT EVERYTHING ELSE.
I just wasn't feeling well that day.
I couldn't **actually** lose to the likes of her!
Next time...
Next time, for **sure**...

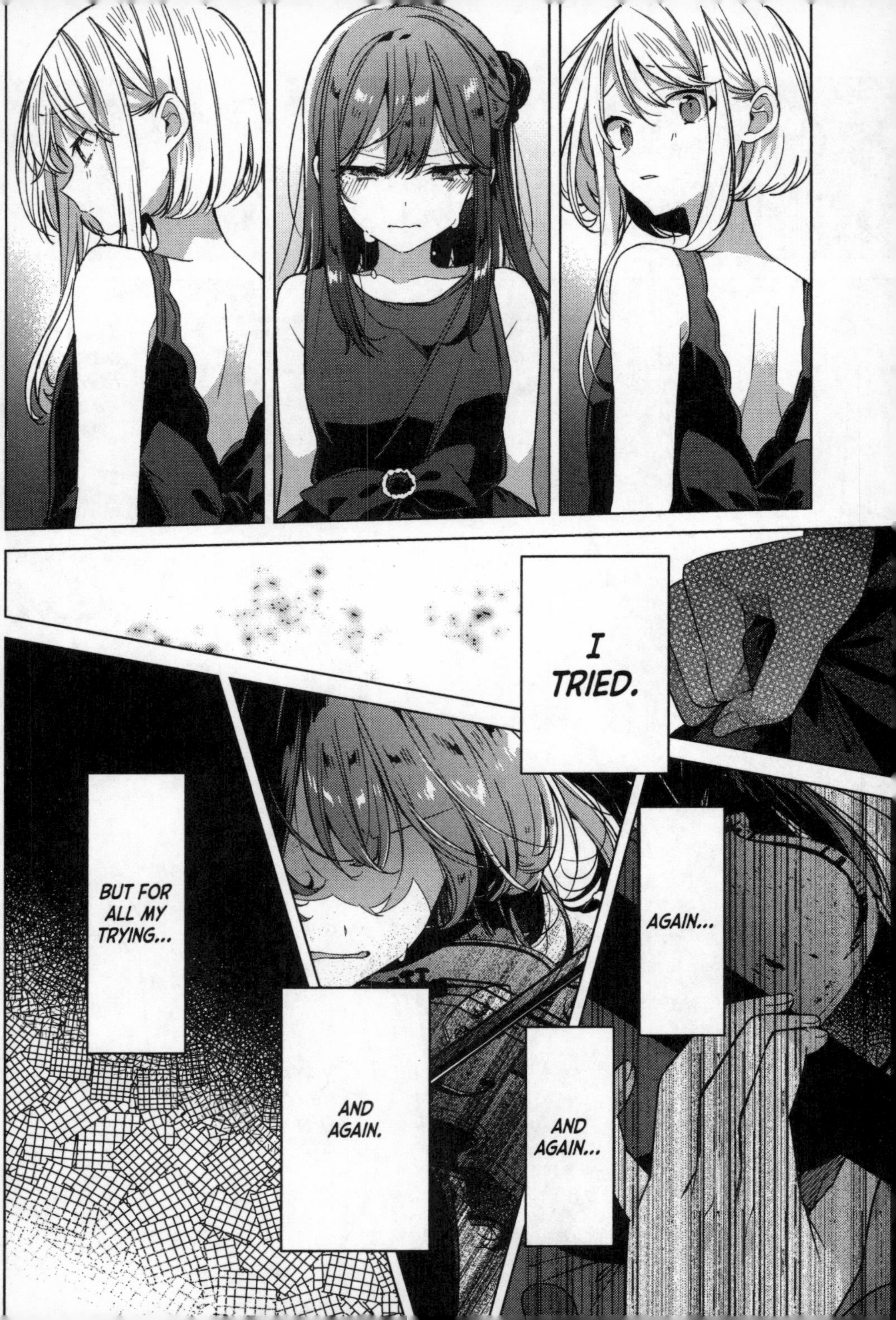
I TRIED.
AGAIN...
AND AGAIN...
AND AGAIN.
BUT FOR ALL MY TRYING...

...I
NEVER
REACHED
HER.

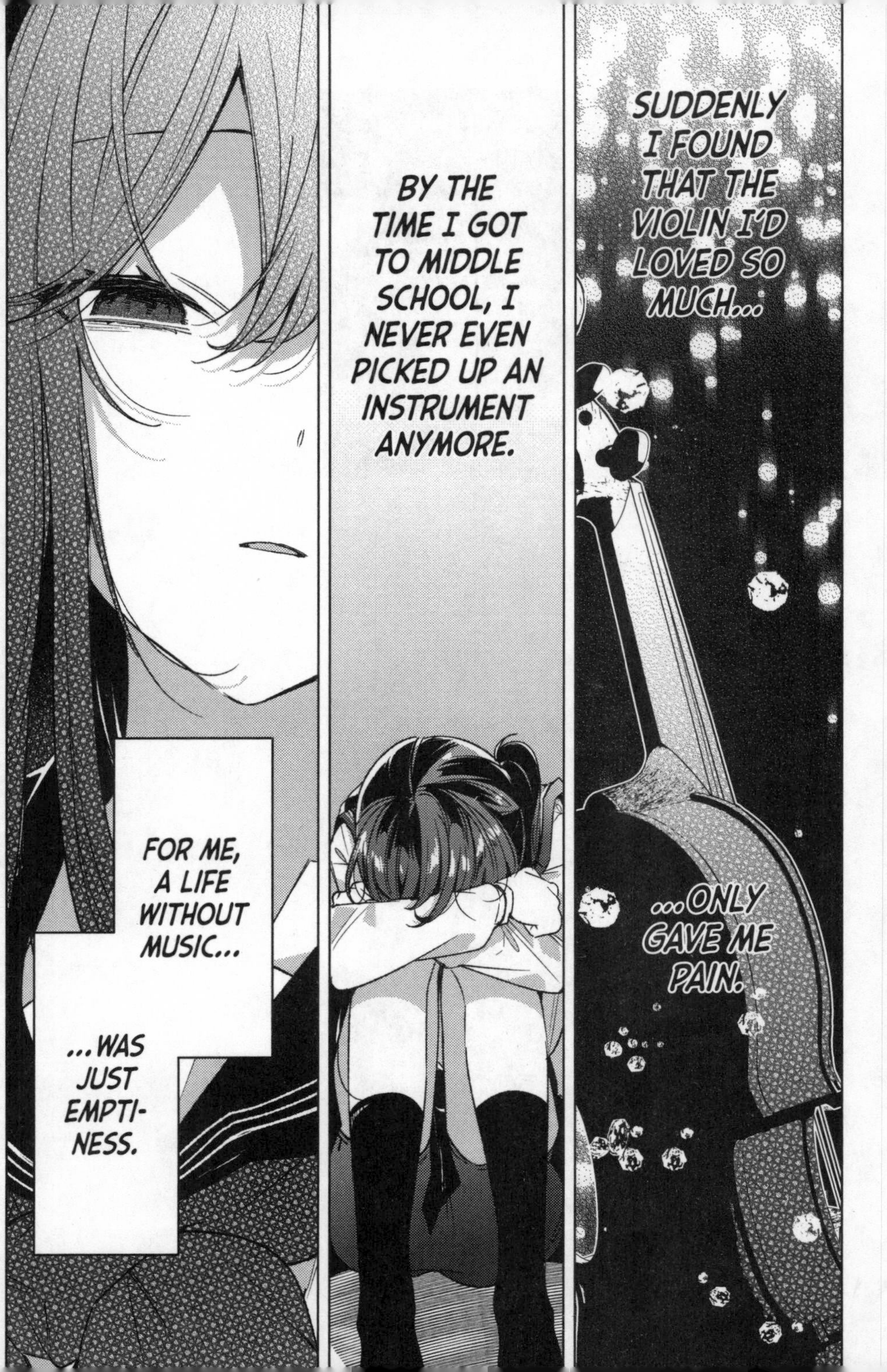
SUDDENLY I FOUND THAT THE VIOLIN I'D LOVED SO MUCH...
...ONLY GAVE ME PAIN.
BY THE TIME I GOT TO MIDDLE SCHOOL, I NEVER EVEN PICKED UP AN INSTRUMENT ANYMORE.
FOR ME, A LIFE WITHOUT MUSIC...
...WAS JUST EMPTINESS.

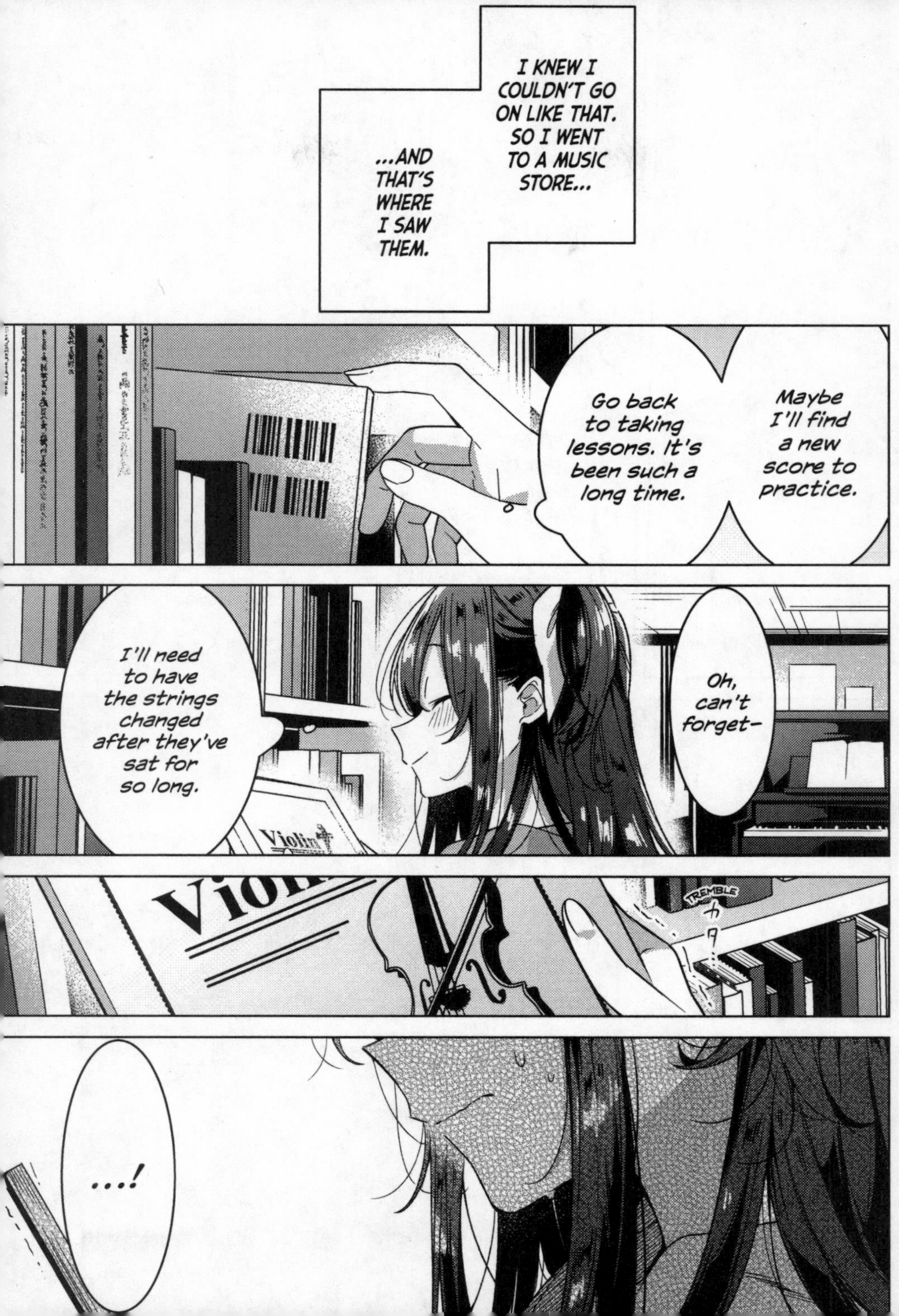
I KNEW I COULDN'T GO ON LIKE THAT. SO I WENT TO A MUSIC STORE...
...AND THAT'S WHERE I SAW THEM.
Maybe I'll find a new score to practice.
Go back to taking lessons. It's been such a long time.
Oh, can't forget-
I'll need to have the strings changed after they've sat for so long.
TREMBLE
...!

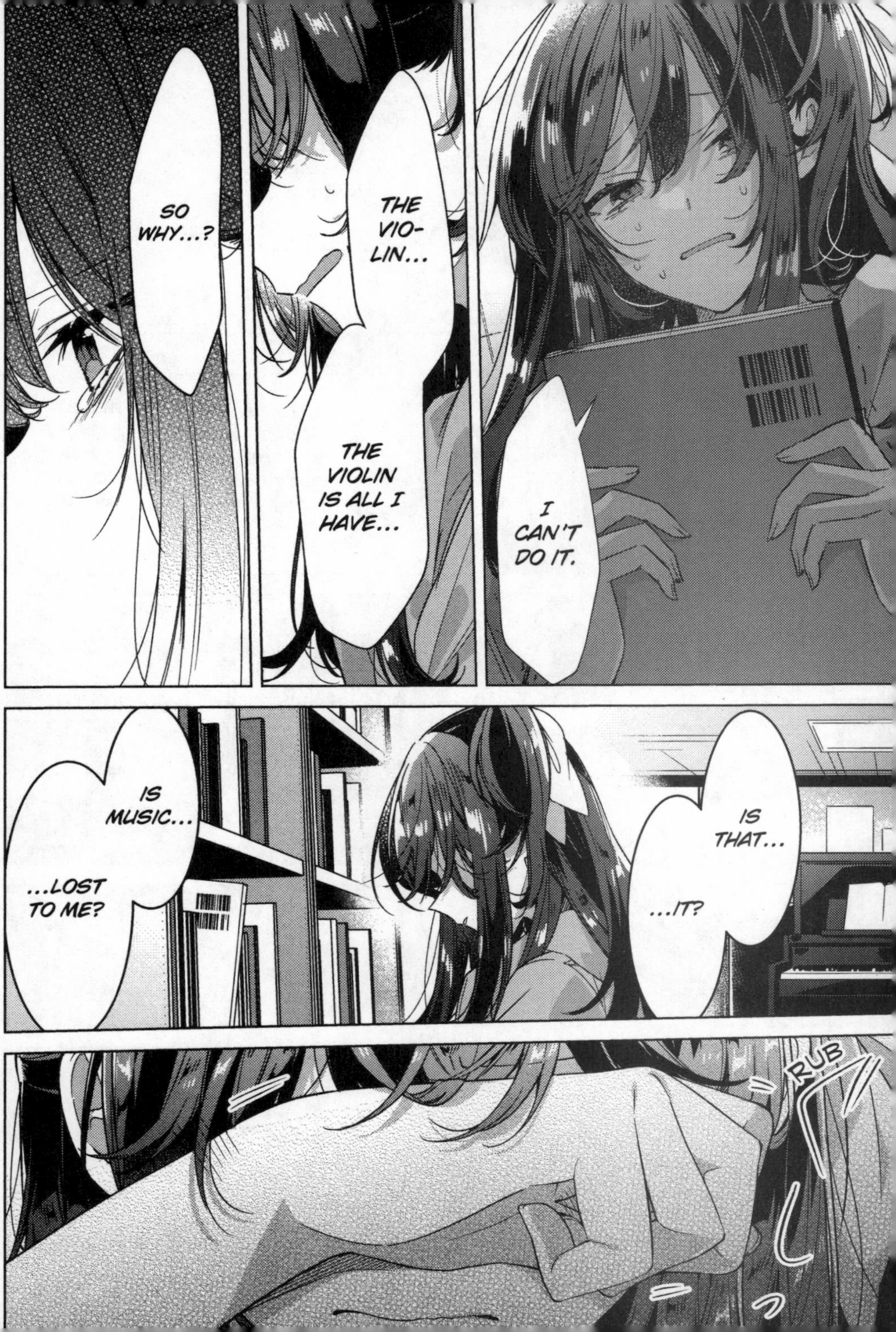
I CAN'T DO IT.
THE VIOLIN...
THE VIOLIN IS ALL I HAVE...
SO WHY...?
IS THAT...
...IT?
IS MUSIC...
...LOST TO ME?
RUB

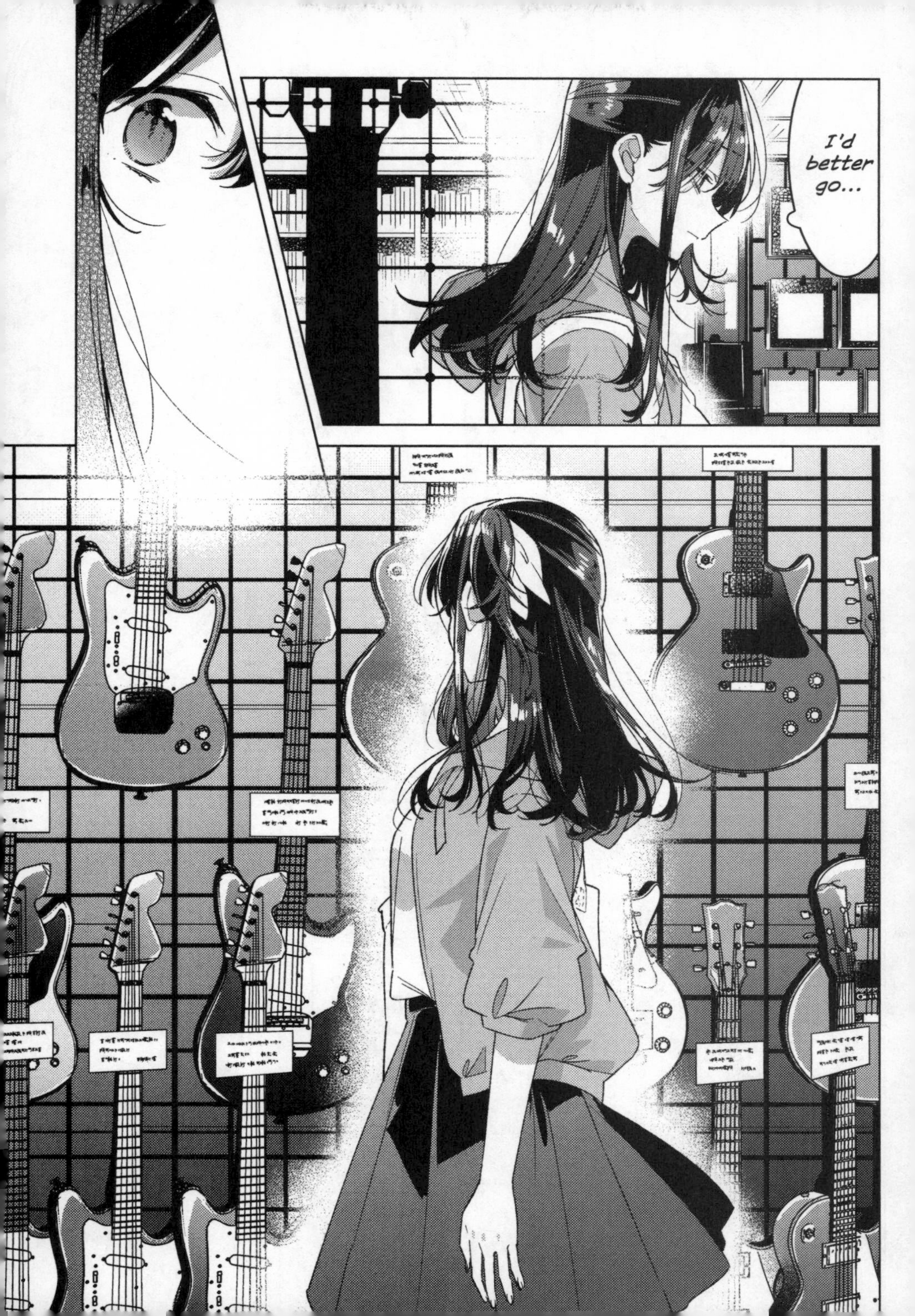
I'd better go...

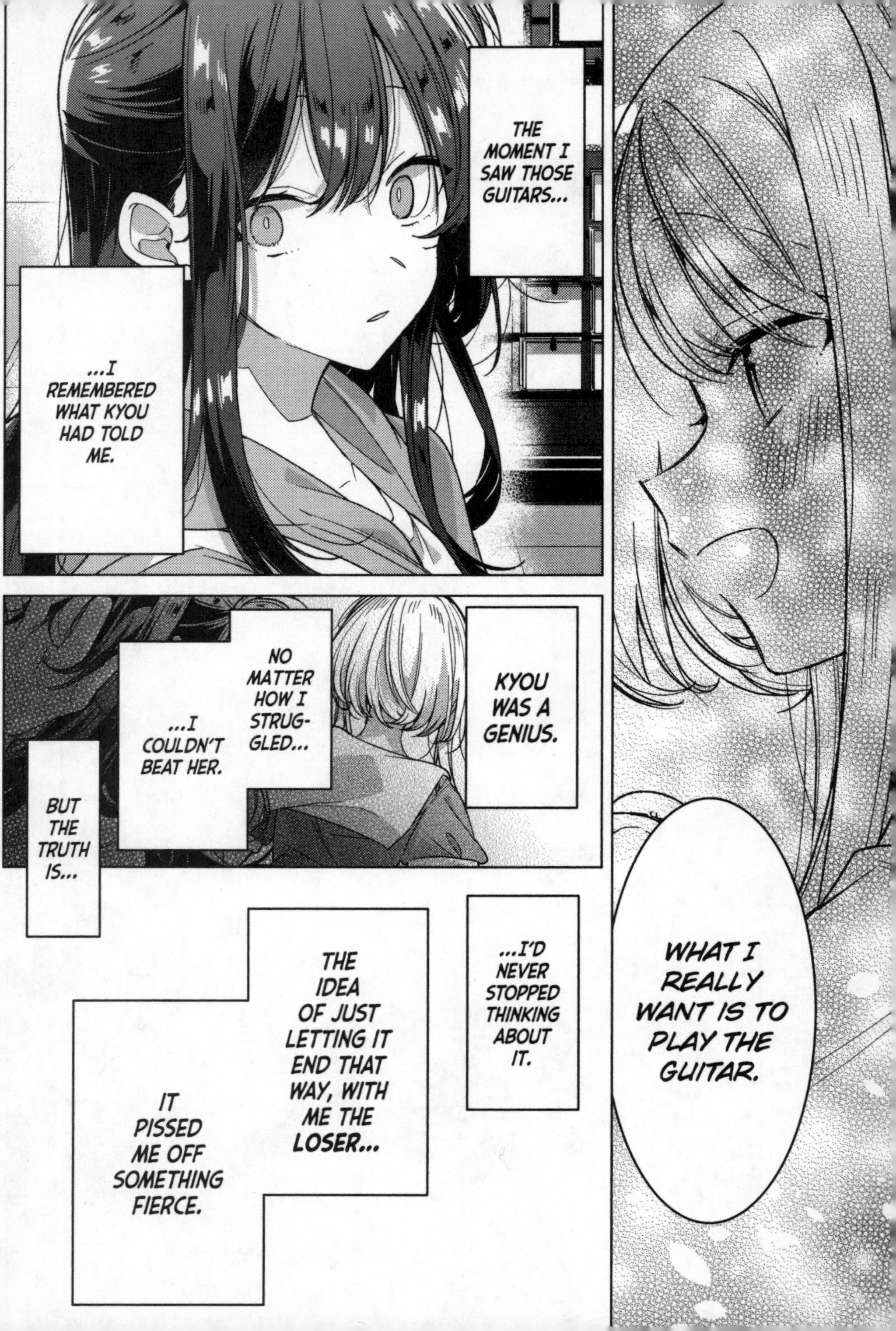
WHAT I REALLY WANT IS TO PLAY THE GUITAR.
THE MOMENT I SAW THOSE GUITARS...
...I REMEMBERED WHAT KYOU HAD TOLD ME.
KYOU WAS A GENIUS.
NO MATTER HOW I STRUG-GLED...
...I COULDN'T BEAT HER.
BUT THE TRUTH IS...
...I'D NEVER STOPPED THINKING ABOUT IT.
THE IDEA OF JUST LETTING IT END THAT WAY, WITH ME THE LOSER...
IT PISSED ME OFF SOMETHING FIERCE.

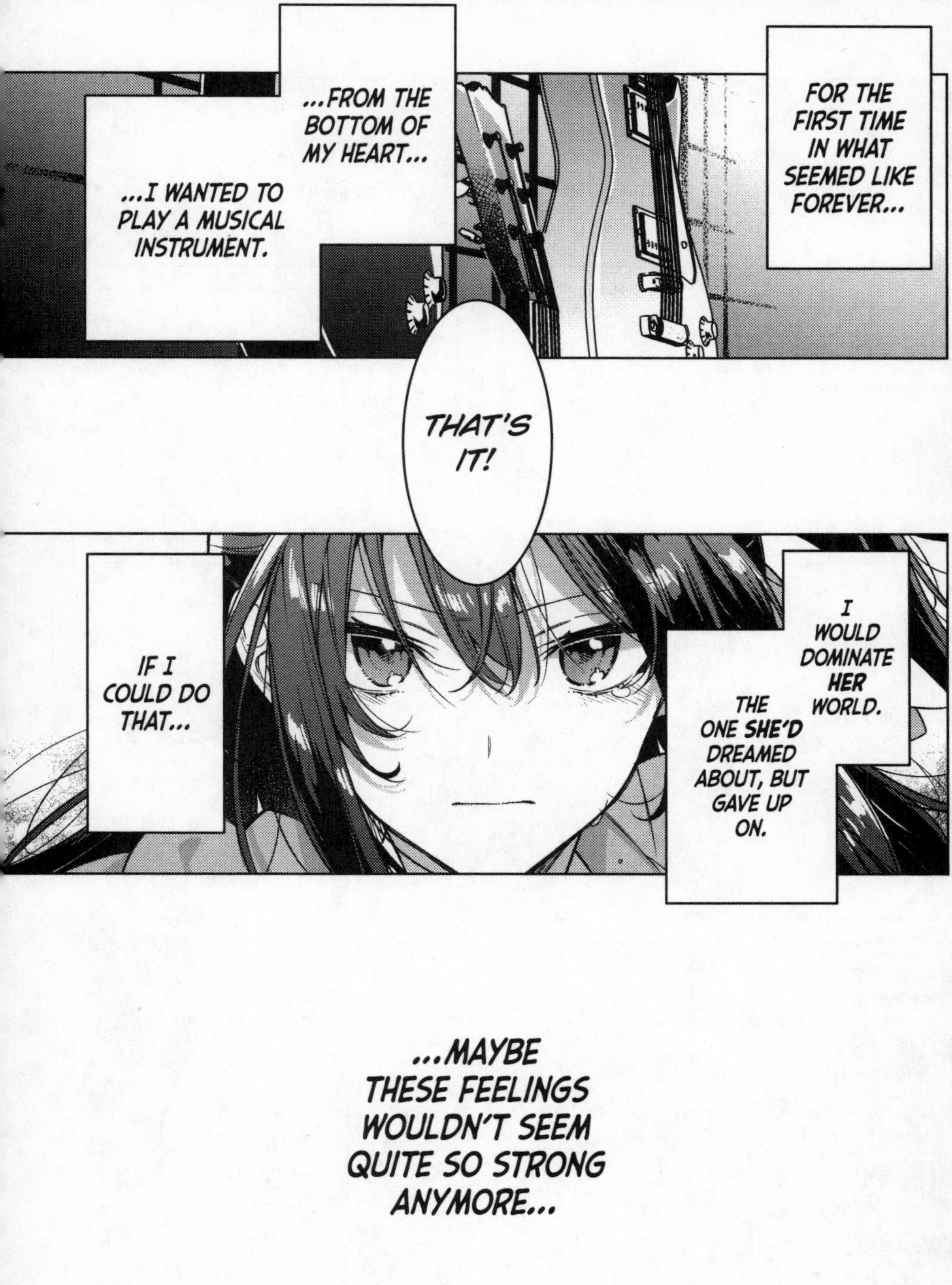
FOR THE FIRST TIME IN WHAT SEEMED LIKE FOREVER...
...FROM THE BOTTOM OF MY HEART...
...I WANTED TO PLAY A MUSICAL INSTRUMENT.
THAT'S IT!
I WOULD DOMINATE HER WORLD.
THE ONE SHE'D DREAMED ABOUT, BUT GAVE UP ON.
IF I COULD DO THAT...
...MAYBE THESE FEELINGS WOULDN'T SEEM QUITE SO STRONG ANYMORE...

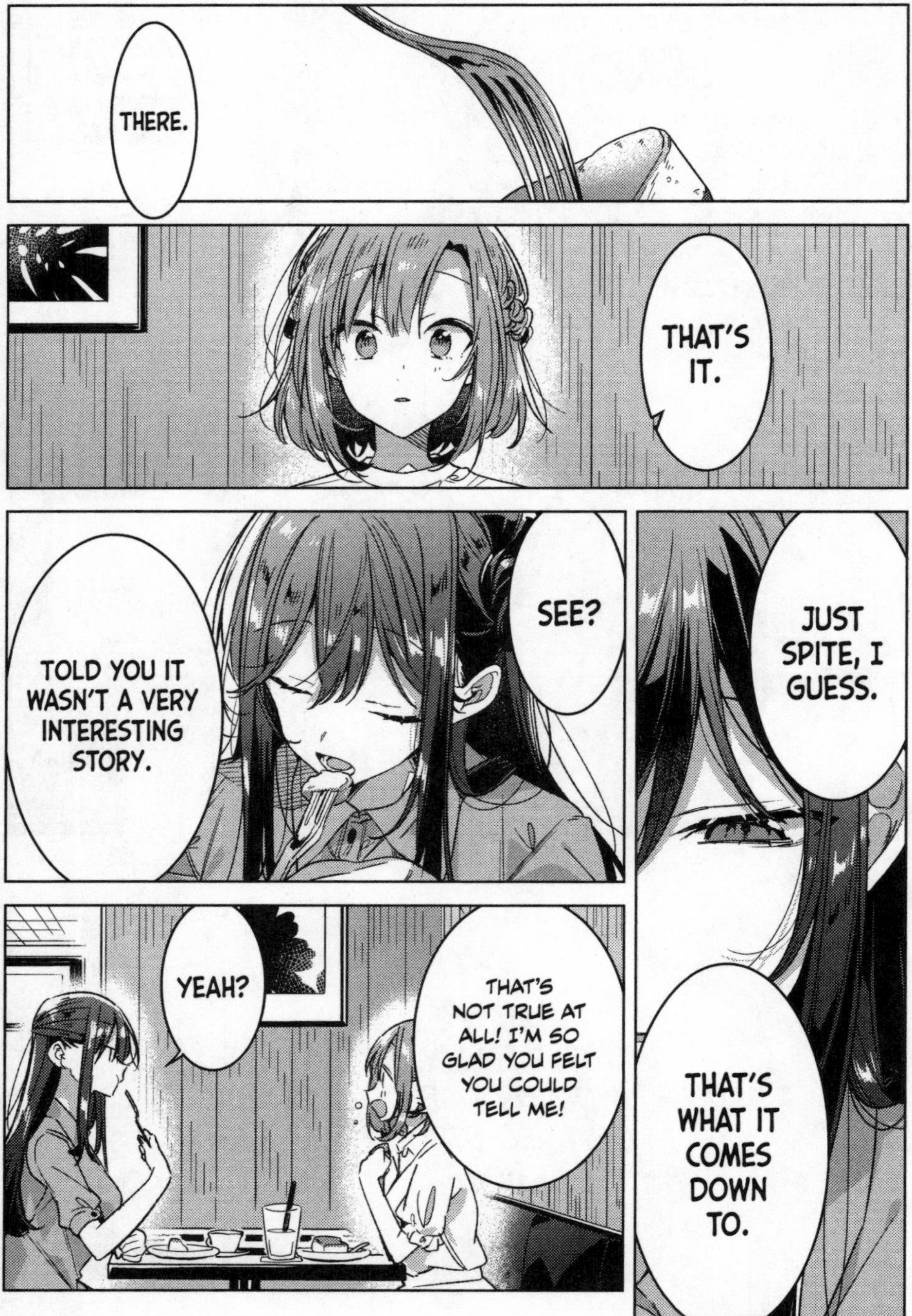
THERE.
THAT'S IT.
JUST SPITE, I GUESS.
THAT'S WHAT IT COMES DOWN TO.
SEE?
TOLD YOU IT WASN'T A VERY INTERESTING STORY.
THAT'S NOT TRUE AT ALL! I'M SO GLAD YOU FELT YOU COULD TELL ME!
YEAH?

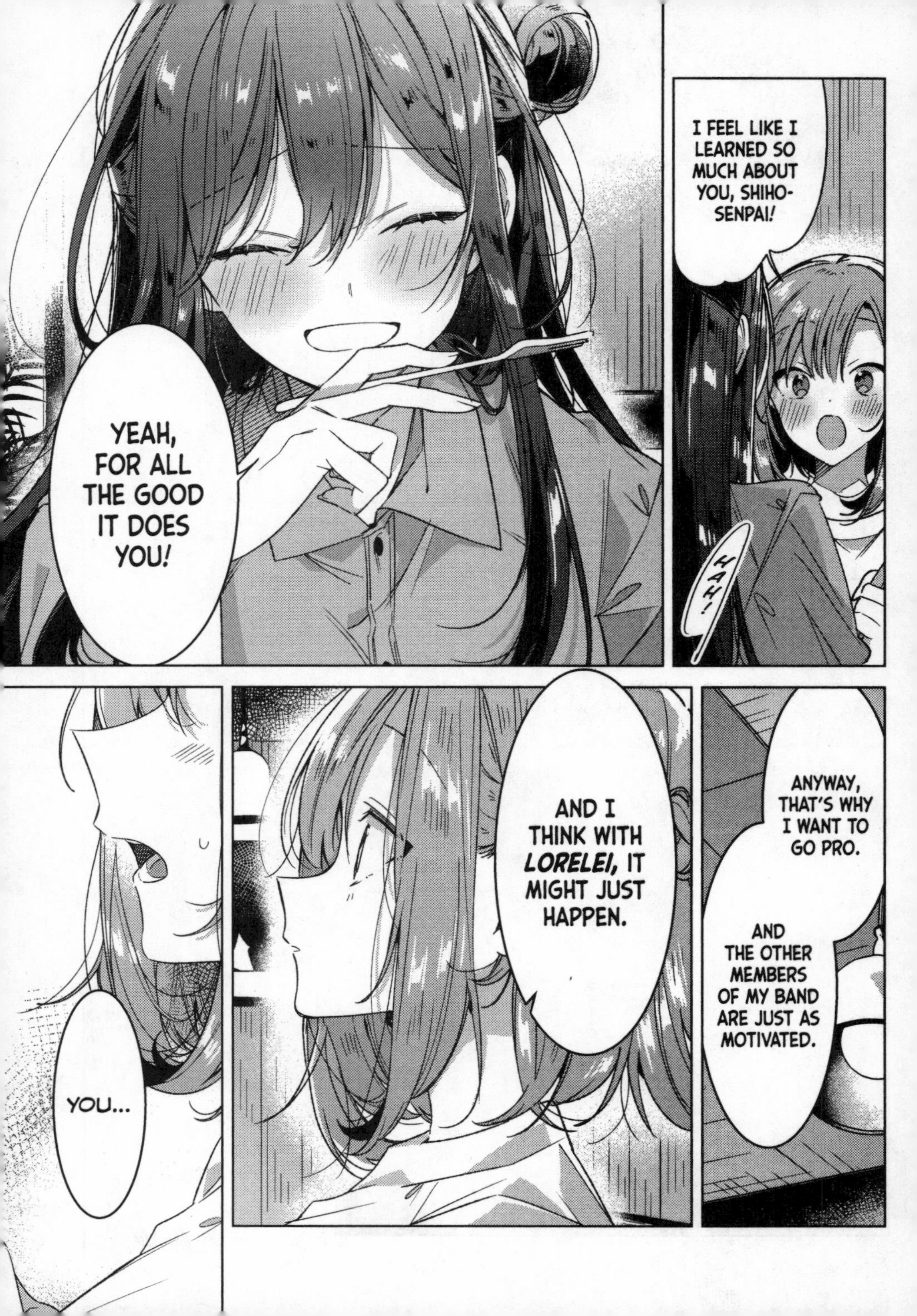
I FEEL LIKE I LEARNED SO MUCH ABOUT YOU, SHIHO-SENPAI!
HAH!
YEAH, FOR ALL THE GOOD IT DOES YOU!
ANYWAY, THAT'S WHY I WANT TO GO PRO.
AND THE OTHER MEMBERS OF MY BAND ARE JUST AS MOTIVATED.
AND I THINK WITH *LORELEI*, IT MIGHT JUST HAPPEN.
YOU...

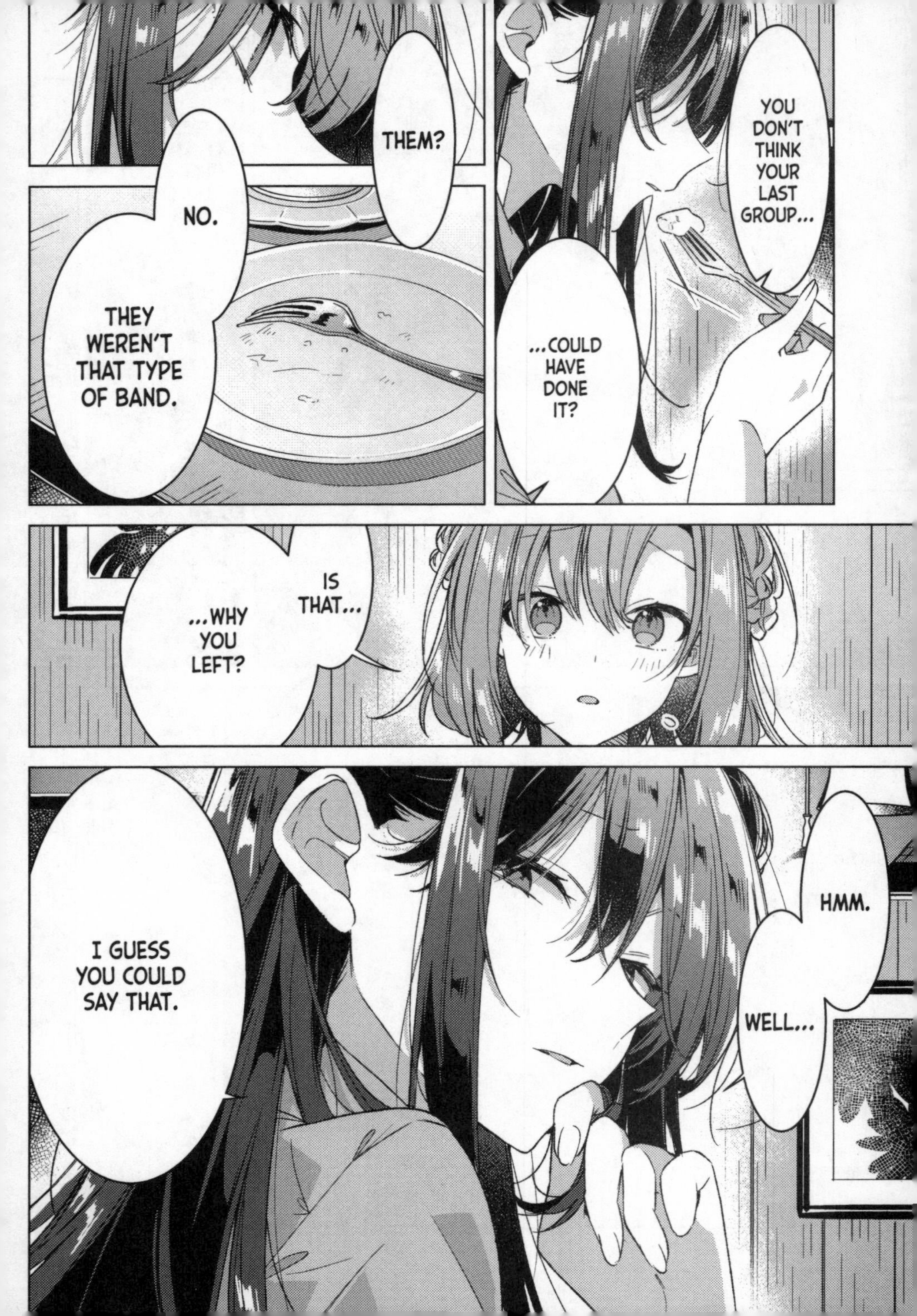
YOU DON'T THINK YOUR LAST GROUP...
...COULD HAVE DONE IT?
THEM?
NO.
THEY WEREN'T THAT TYPE OF BAND.
IS THAT...
...WHY YOU LEFT?
HMM.
WELL...
I GUESS YOU COULD SAY THAT.

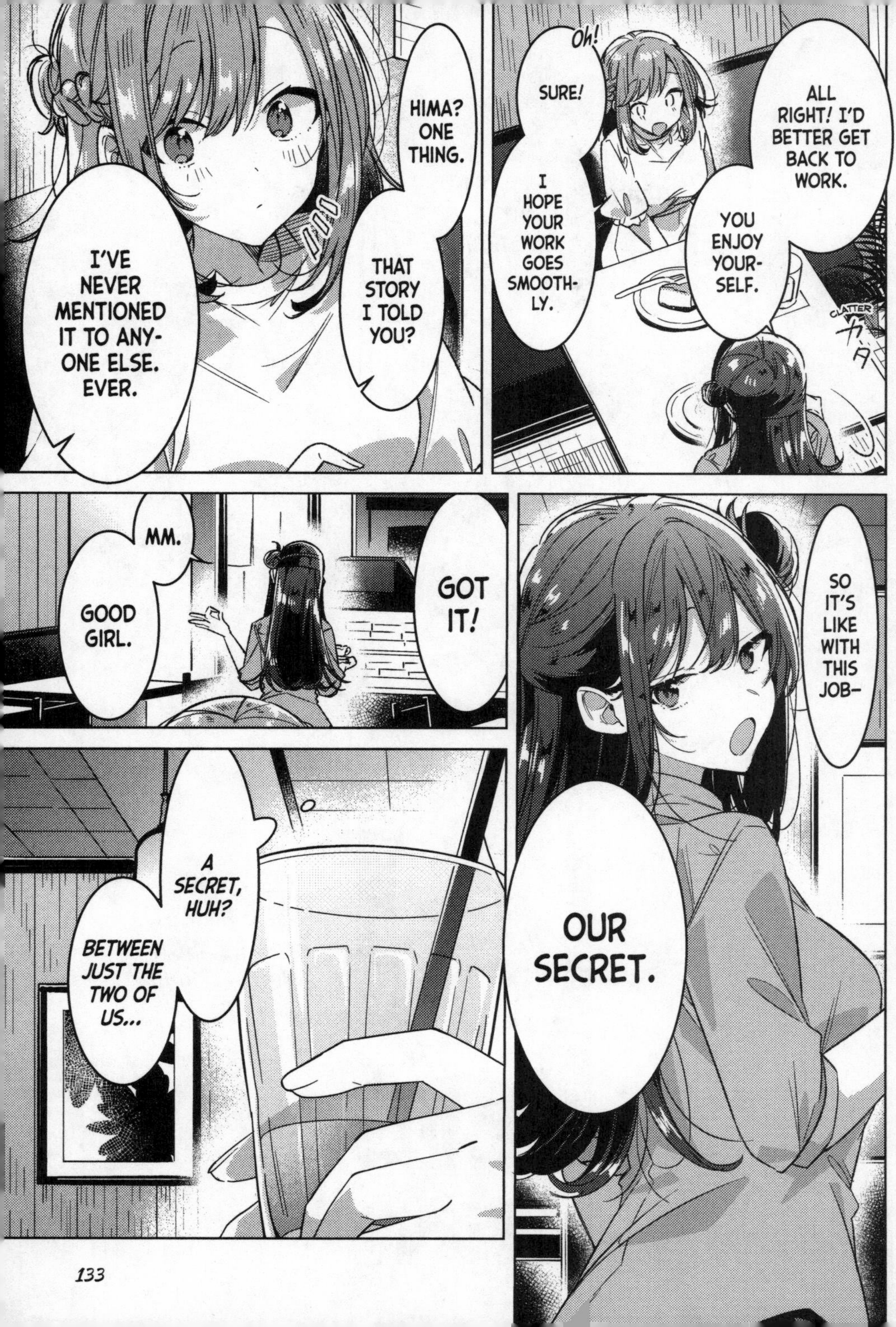
ALL RIGHT! I'D BETTER GET BACK TO WORK.
YOU ENJOY YOUR-SELF.
CLATTER
Oh!
SURE!
I HOPE YOUR WORK GOES SMOOTH-LY.
HIMA? ONE THING.
THAT STORY I TOLD YOU?
I'VE NEVER MENTIONED IT TO ANY-ONE ELSE. EVER.
SO IT'S LIKE WITH THIS JOB—
OUR SECRET.
GOT IT!
MM.
GOOD GIRL.
A SECRET, HUH?
BETWEEN JUST THE TWO OF US...

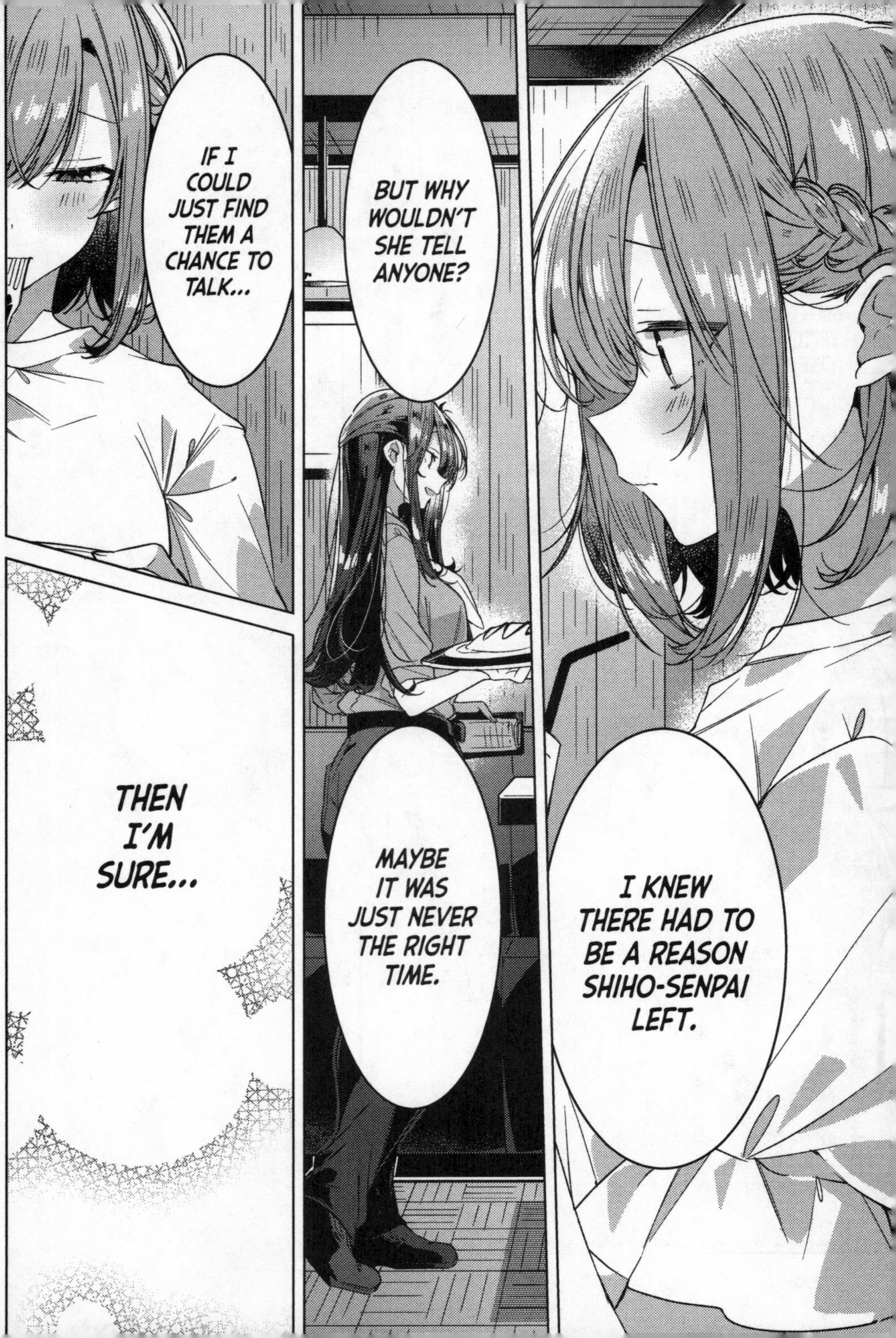
I KNEW THERE HAD TO BE A REASON SHIHO-SENPAI LEFT.
BUT WHY WOULDN'T SHE TELL ANYONE?
MAYBE IT WAS JUST NEVER THE RIGHT TIME.
IF I COULD JUST FIND THEM A CHANCE TO TALK...
THEN I'M SURE...

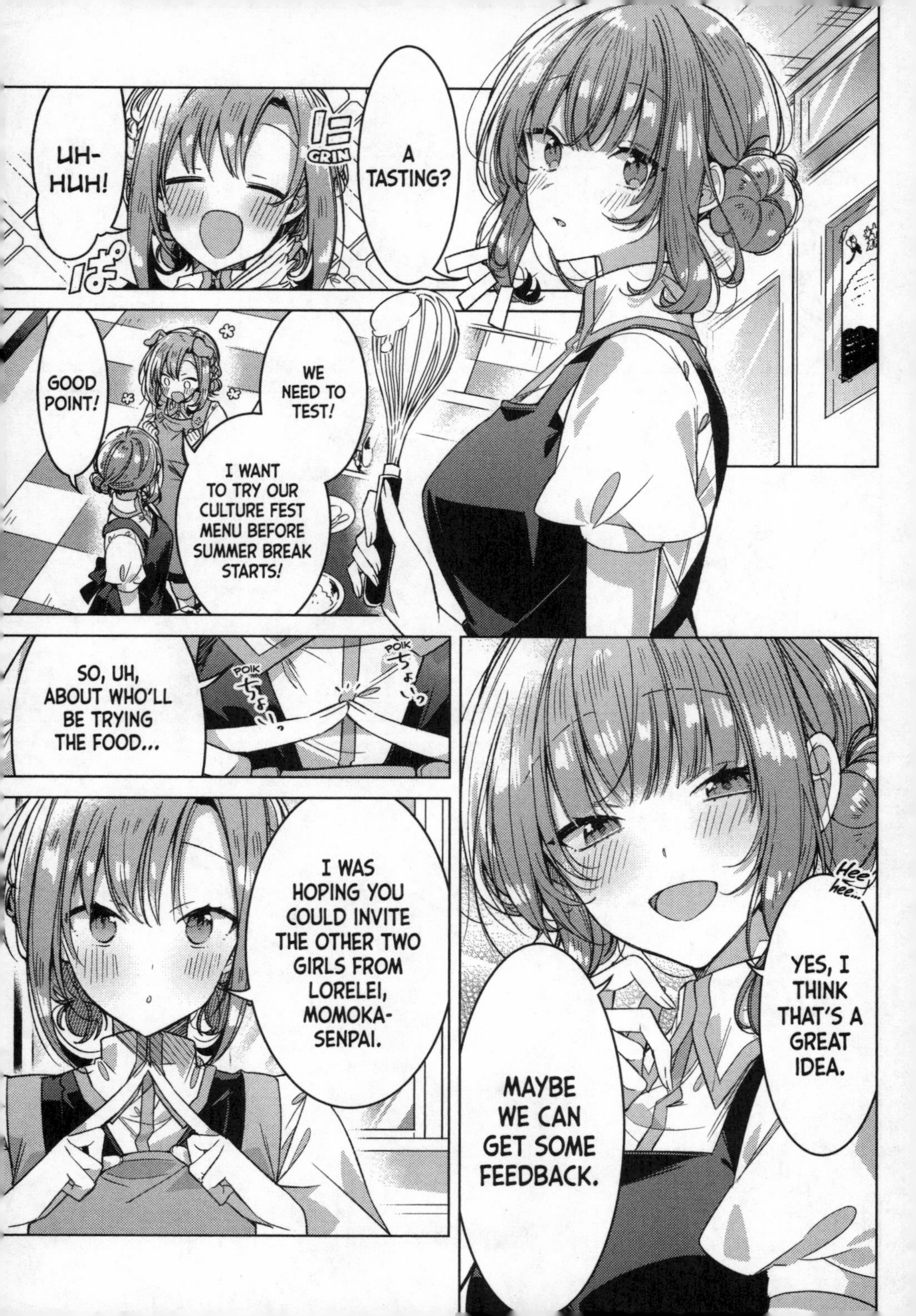
A TASTING?
ニッ
GRIN
UH-HUH!
ぱ
WE NEED TO TEST!
I WANT TO TRY OUR CULTURE FEST MENU BEFORE SUMMER BREAK STARTS!
GOOD POINT!
POIK ちょい
POIK ちょい
SO, UH, ABOUT WHO'LL BE TRYING THE FOOD...
I WAS HOPING YOU COULD INVITE THE OTHER TWO GIRLS FROM LORELEI, MOMOKA-SENPAI.
Hee hee...
YES, I THINK THAT'S A GREAT IDEA.
MAYBE WE CAN GET SOME FEEDBACK.

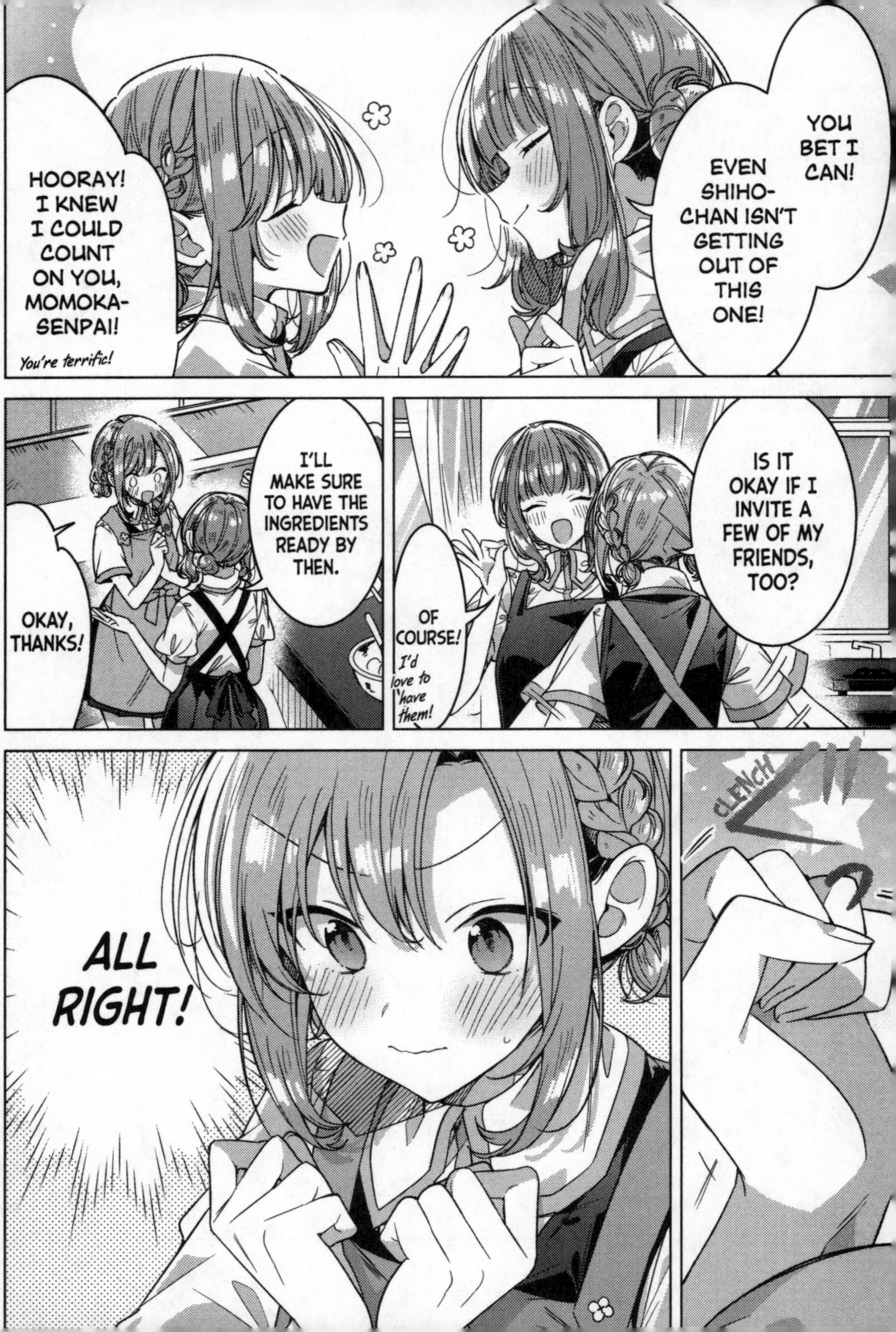
YOU BET I CAN!
EVEN SHIHO-CHAN ISN'T GETTING OUT OF THIS ONE!
HOORAY! I KNEW I COULD COUNT ON YOU, MOMOKA-SENPAI!
You're terrific!
IS IT OKAY IF I INVITE A FEW OF MY FRIENDS, TOO?
OF COURSE!
I'd love to have them!
I'LL MAKE SURE TO HAVE THE INGREDIENTS READY BY THEN.
OKAY, THANKS!
CLENCH
ALL RIGHT!

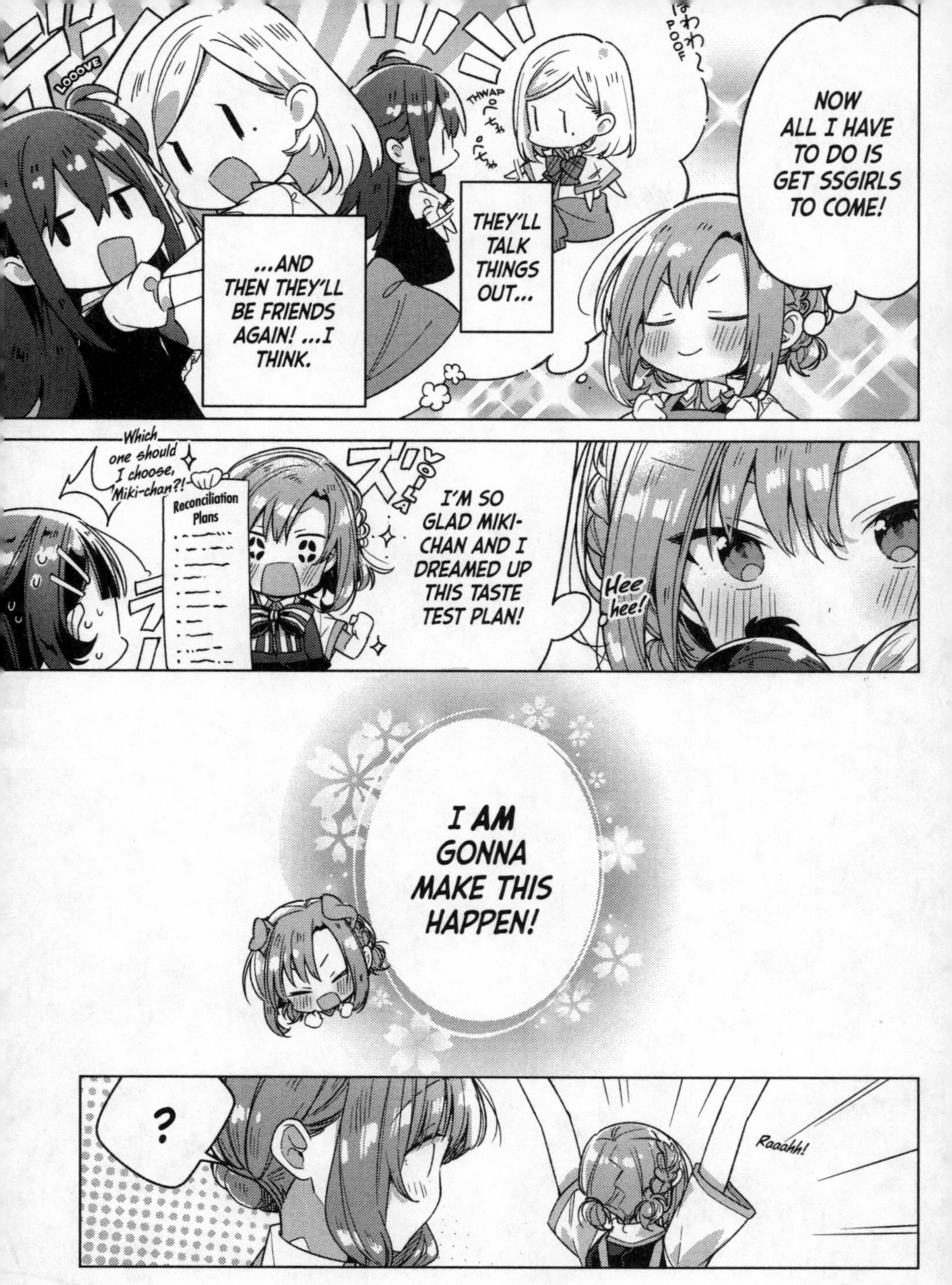
NOW ALL I HAVE TO DO IS GET SSGIRLS TO COME!
POOF
THEY'LL TALK THINGS OUT...
THWAP
...AND THEN THEY'LL BE FRIENDS AGAIN! ...I THINK.
LOOOVE
Hee hee!
I'M SO GLAD MIKI-CHAN AND I DREAMED UP THIS TASTE TEST PLAN!
VOILA
Which one should I choose, Miki-chan?!
Reconciliation Plans
I AM GONNA MAKE THIS HAPPEN!
Raaahh!
?

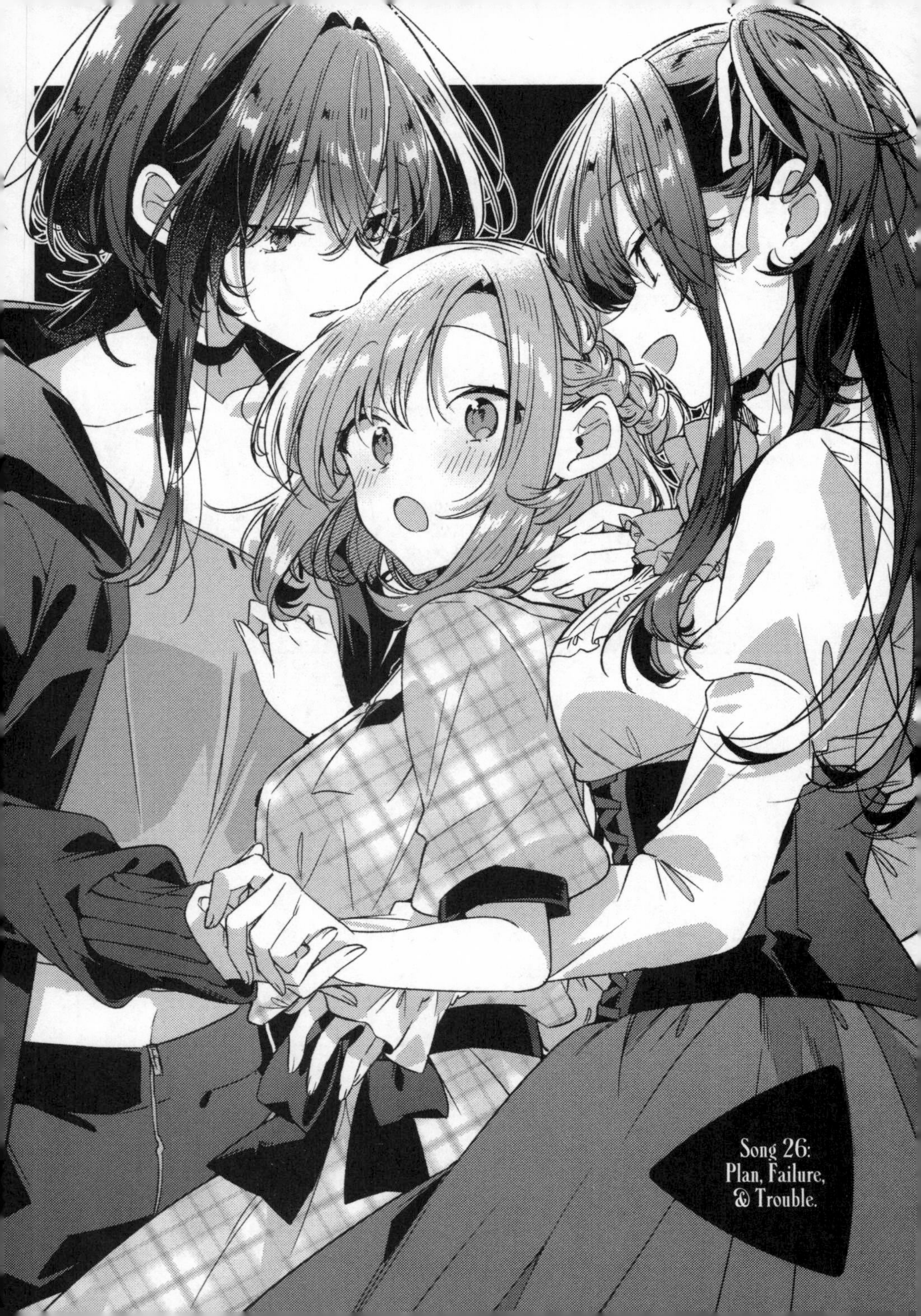
Song 26:
Plan, Failure,
& Trouble.

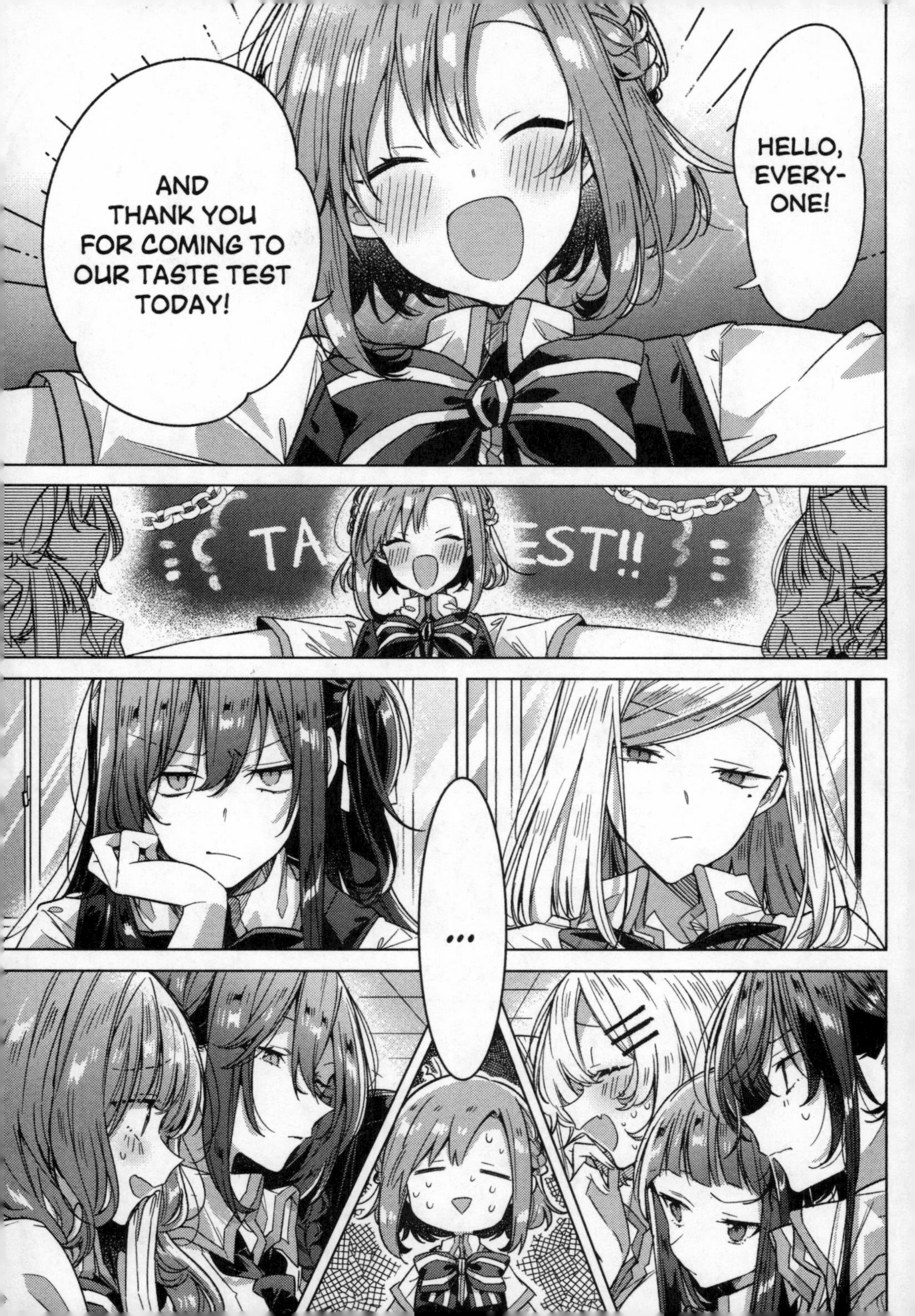
HELLO, EVERY-ONE!
AND THANK YOU FOR COMING TO OUR TASTE TEST TODAY!
TA
EST!!
...

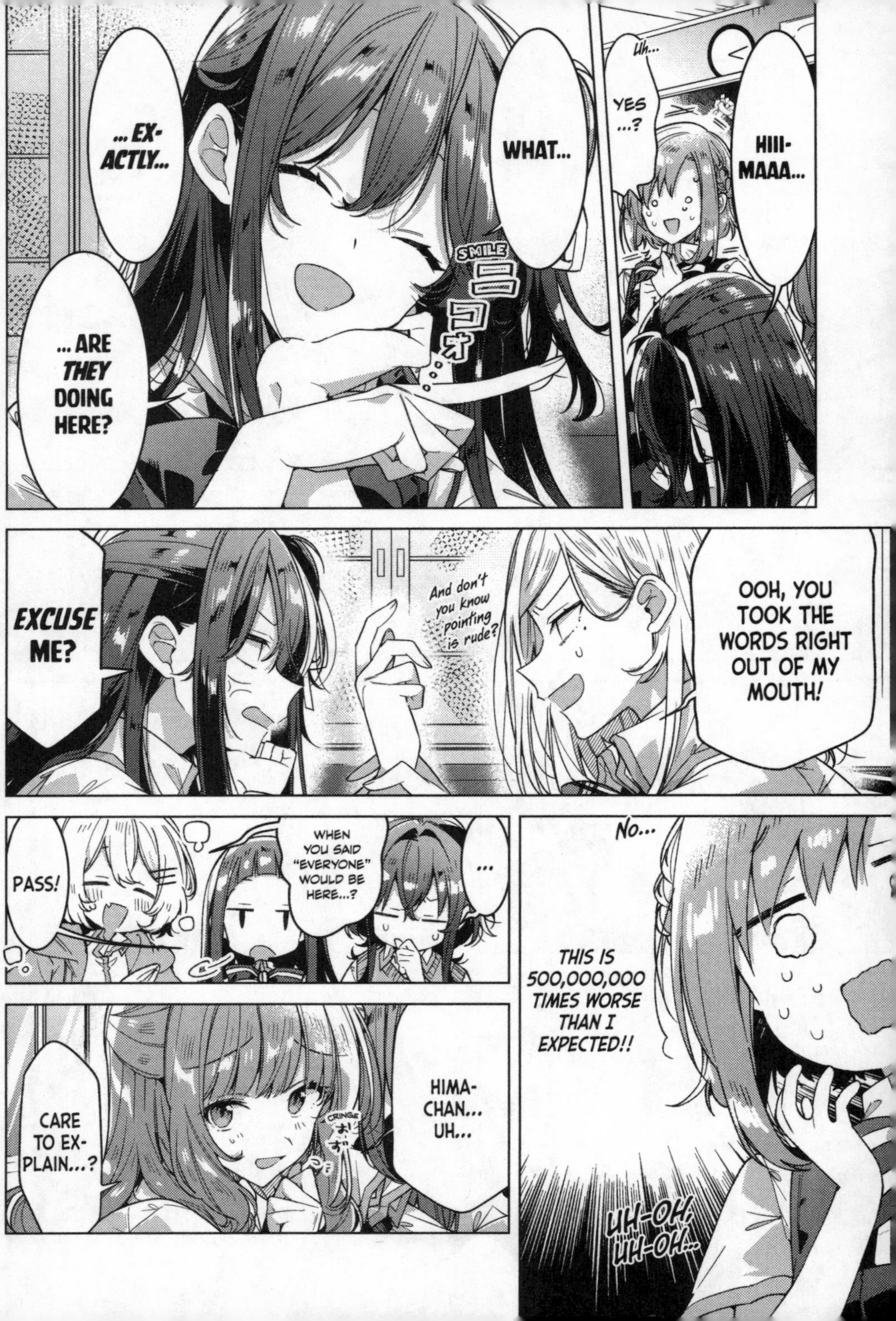
HIII-MAAA...
Uh...
YES ...?
WHAT...
... EX-ACTLY...
SMILE
... ARE THEY DOING HERE?
OOH, YOU TOOK THE WORDS RIGHT OUT OF MY MOUTH!
And don't you know pointing is rude?
EXCUSE ME?
No...
THIS IS 500,000,000 TIMES WORSE THAN I EXPECTED!!
UH-OH, UH-OH...
...
WHEN YOU SAID "EVERYONE" WOULD BE HERE...?
PASS!
HIMA-CHAN... UH...
CRINGE
CARE TO EX-PLAIN...?

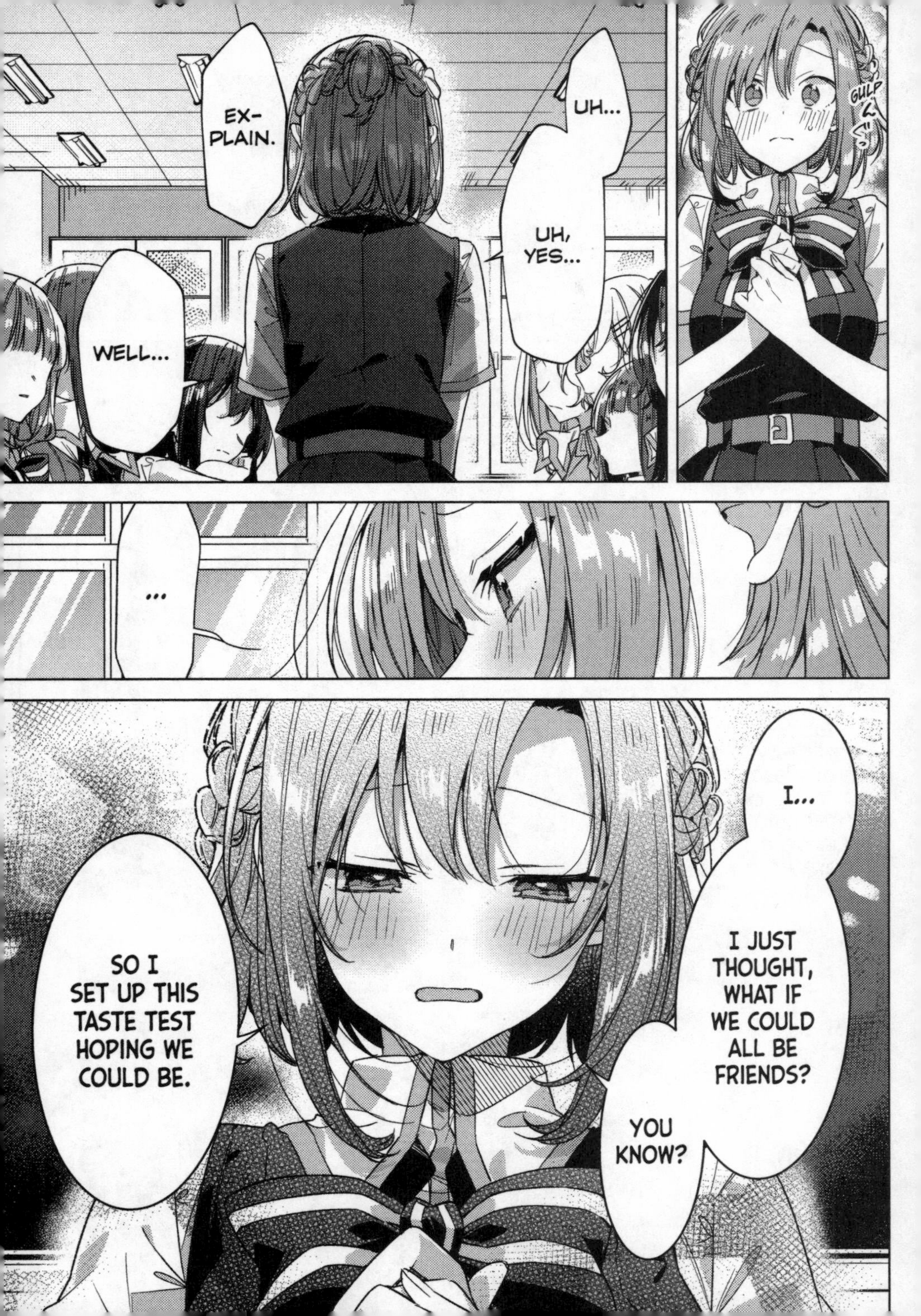
GULP
UH...
EX-PLAIN.
UH, YES...
WELL...
...
I...
I JUST THOUGHT, WHAT IF WE COULD ALL BE FRIENDS?
YOU KNOW?
SO I SET UP THIS TASTE TEST HOPING WE COULD BE.

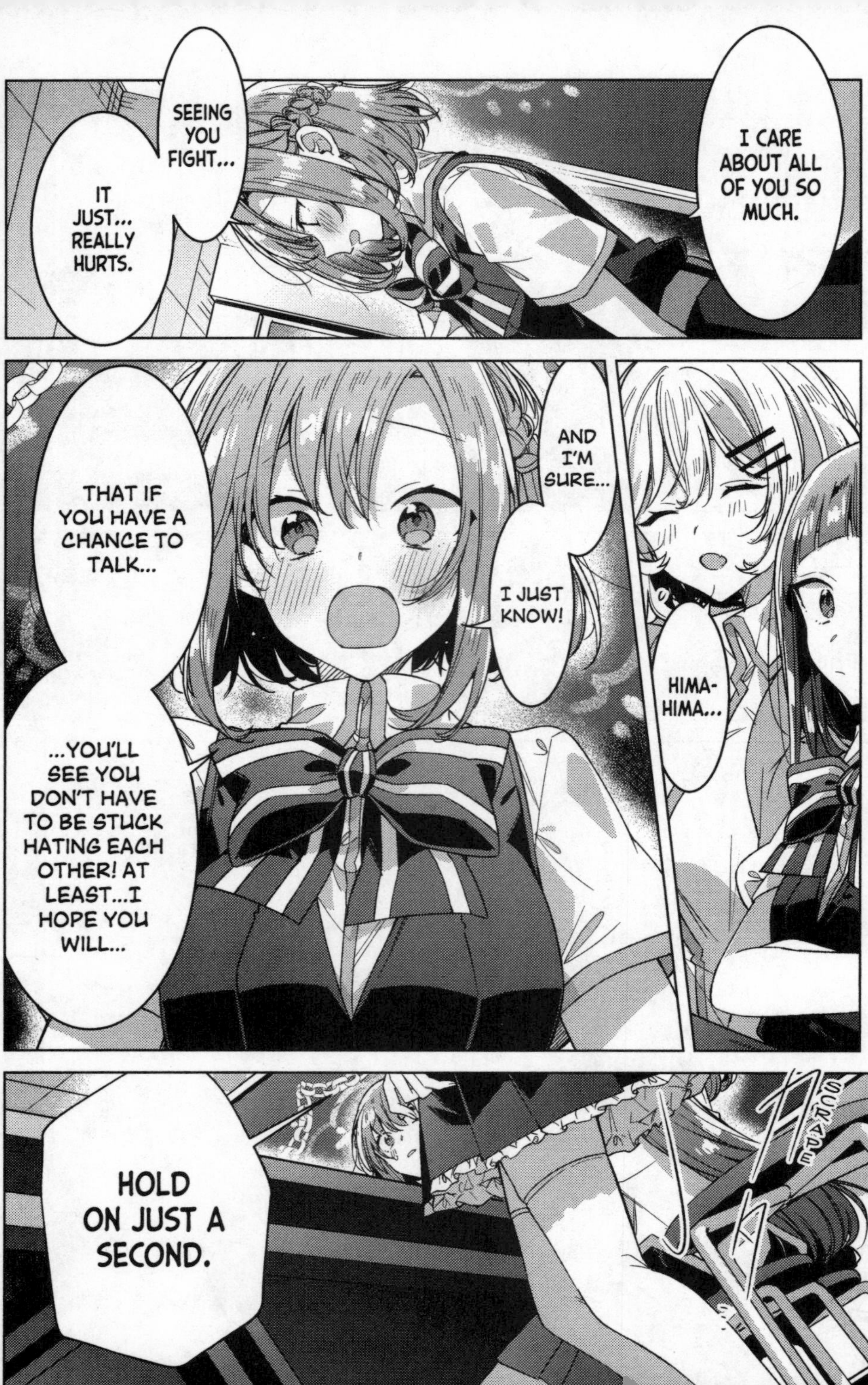
I CARE ABOUT ALL OF YOU SO MUCH.
SEEING YOU FIGHT...
IT JUST... REALLY HURTS.
AND I'M SURE...
I JUST KNOW!
HIMA-HIMA...
THAT IF YOU HAVE A CHANCE TO TALK...
...YOU'LL SEE YOU DON'T HAVE TO BE STUCK HATING EACH OTHER! AT LEAST...I HOPE YOU WILL...
SCRAPE
HOLD ON JUST A SECOND.

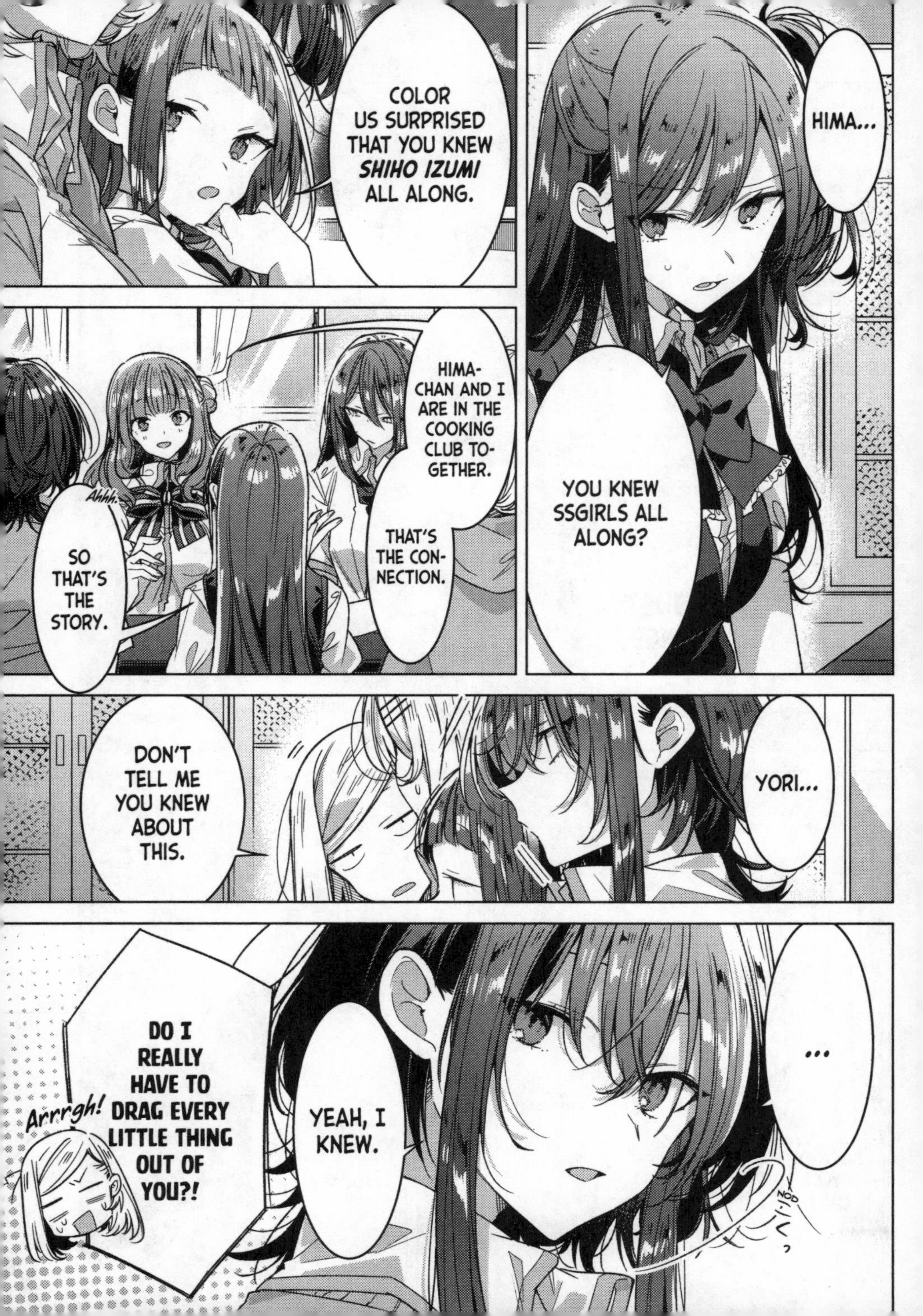
HIMA...
COLOR US SURPRISED THAT YOU KNEW *SHIHO IZUMI* ALL ALONG.
YOU KNEW SSGIRLS ALL ALONG?
HIMA-CHAN AND I ARE IN THE COOKING CLUB TOGETHER.
THAT'S THE CONNECTION.
Ahhh.
SO THAT'S THE STORY.
YORI...
DON'T TELL ME YOU KNEW ABOUT THIS.
...
NOD
YEAH, I KNEW.
DO I REALLY HAVE TO DRAG EVERY LITTLE THING OUT OF YOU?!
Arrrgh!

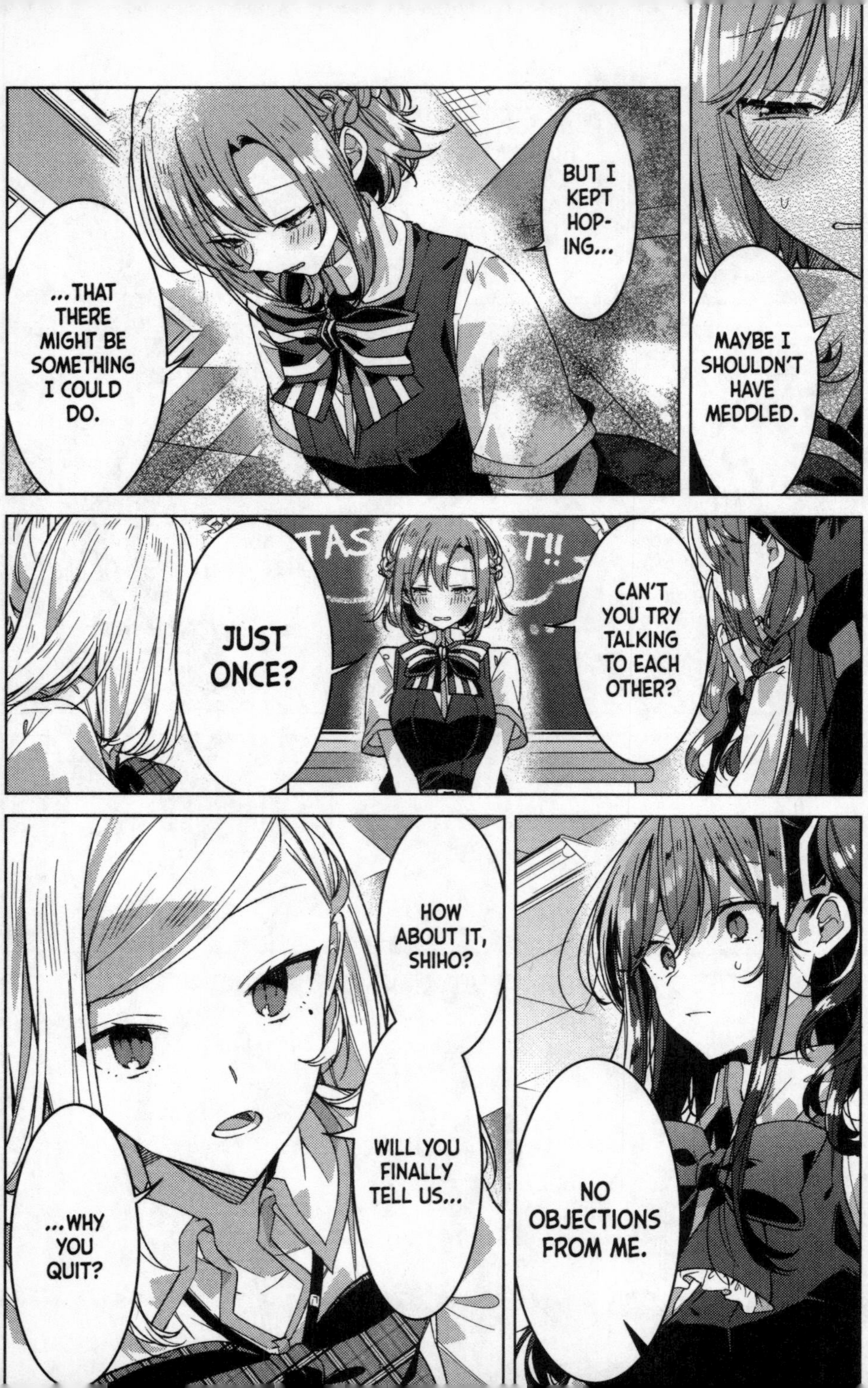
MAYBE I SHOULDN'T HAVE MEDDLED.
BUT I KEPT HOP-ING...
...THAT THERE MIGHT BE SOMETHING I COULD DO.
CAN'T YOU TRY TALKING TO EACH OTHER?
JUST ONCE?
NO OBJECTIONS FROM ME.
HOW ABOUT IT, SHIHO?
WILL YOU FINALLY TELL US...
...WHY YOU QUIT?

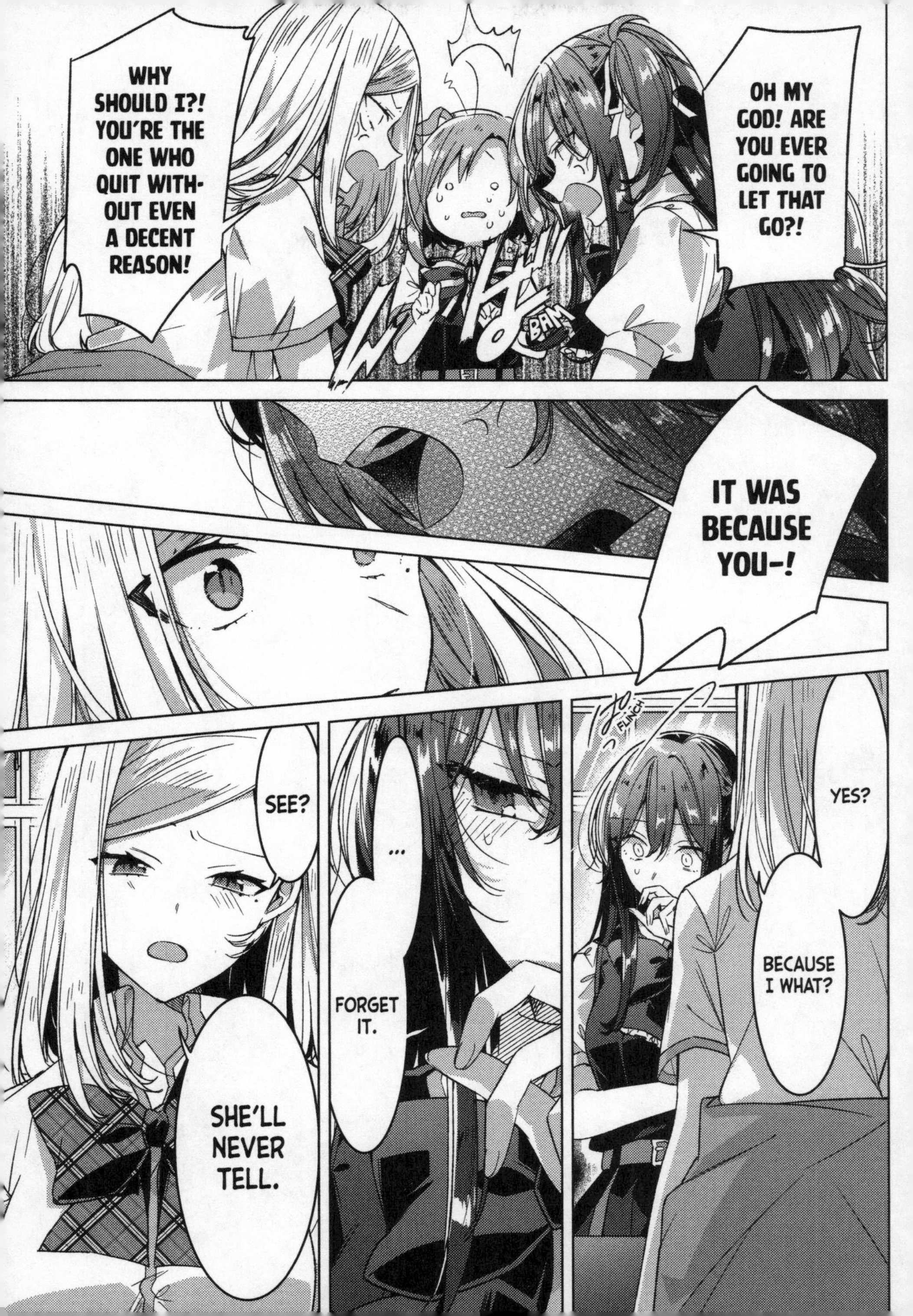
OH MY GOD! ARE YOU EVER GOING TO LET THAT GO?!
WHY SHOULD I?! YOU'RE THE ONE WHO QUIT WITH-OUT EVEN A DECENT REASON!
BAM
IT WAS BECAUSE YOU-!
FLINCH
YES?
BECAUSE I WHAT?
...
FORGET IT.
SEE?
SHE'LL NEVER TELL.

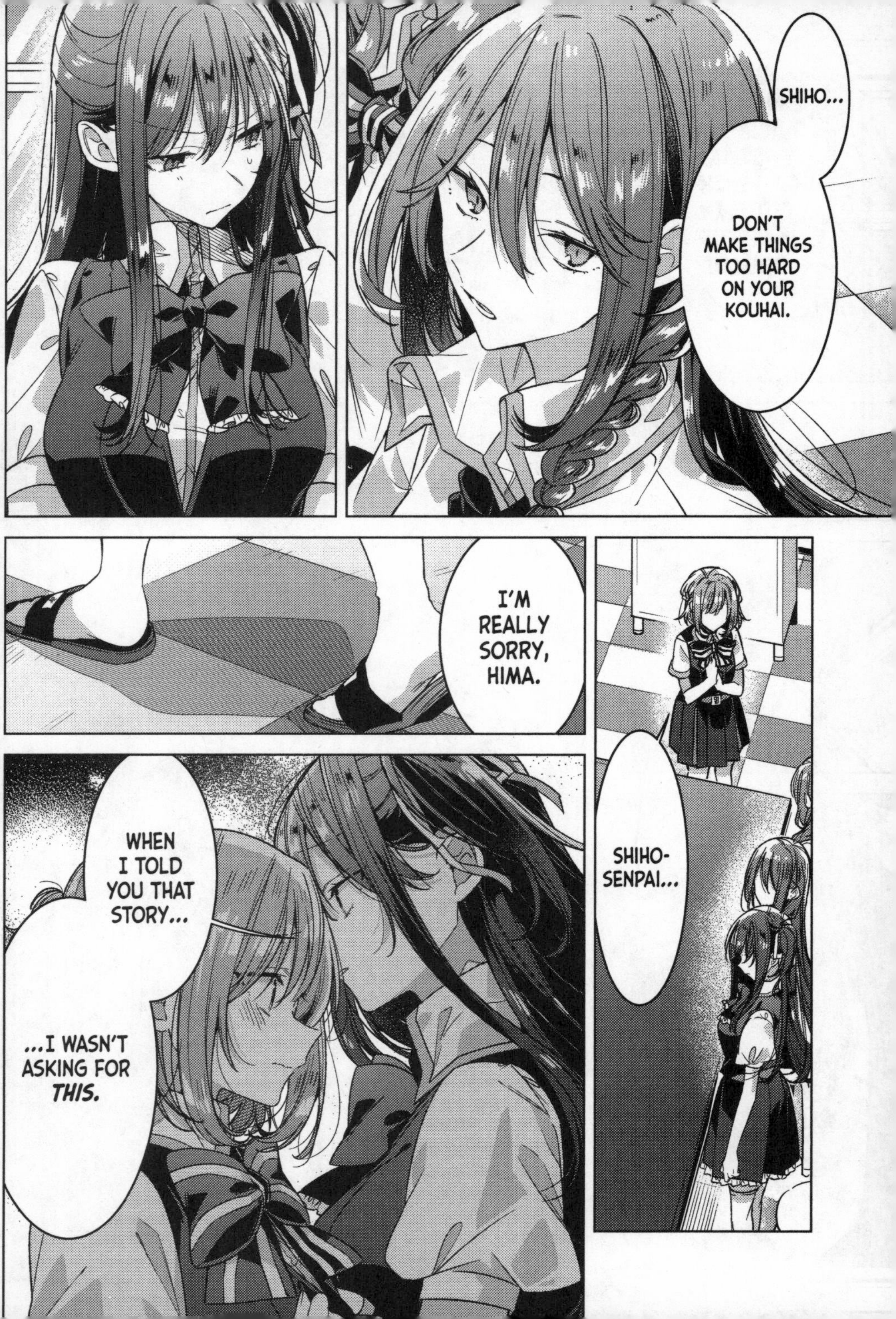
SHIHO...
DON'T MAKE THINGS TOO HARD ON YOUR KOUHAI.
SHIHO-SENPAI...
I'M REALLY SORRY, HIMA.
WHEN I TOLD YOU THAT STORY...
...I WASN'T ASKING FOR *THIS.*

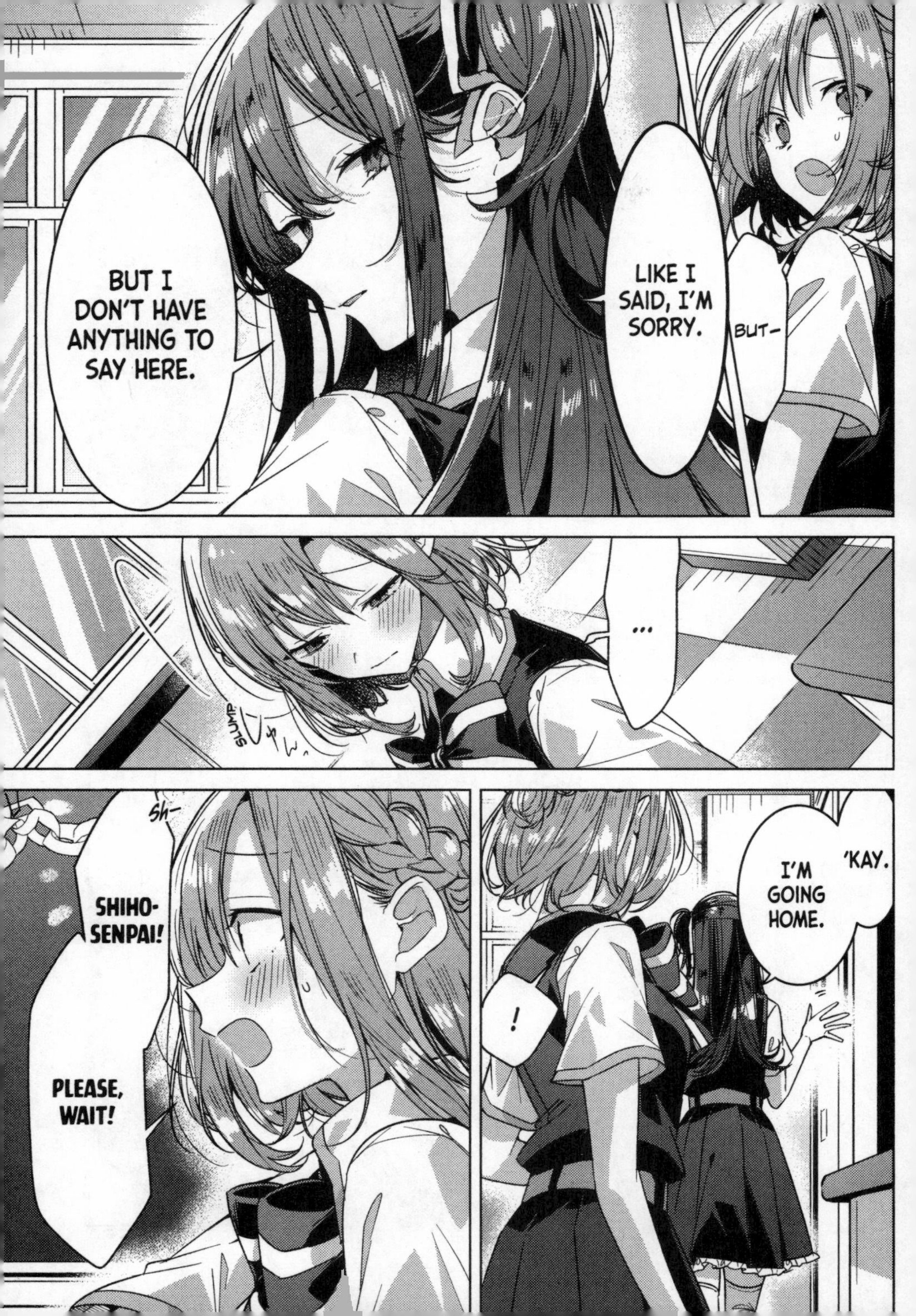
BUT–
LIKE I SAID, I'M SORRY.
BUT I DON'T HAVE ANYTHING TO SAY HERE.
...
SLUMP
'KAY.
I'M GOING HOME.
!
Sh–
SHIHO-SENPAI!
PLEASE, WAIT!

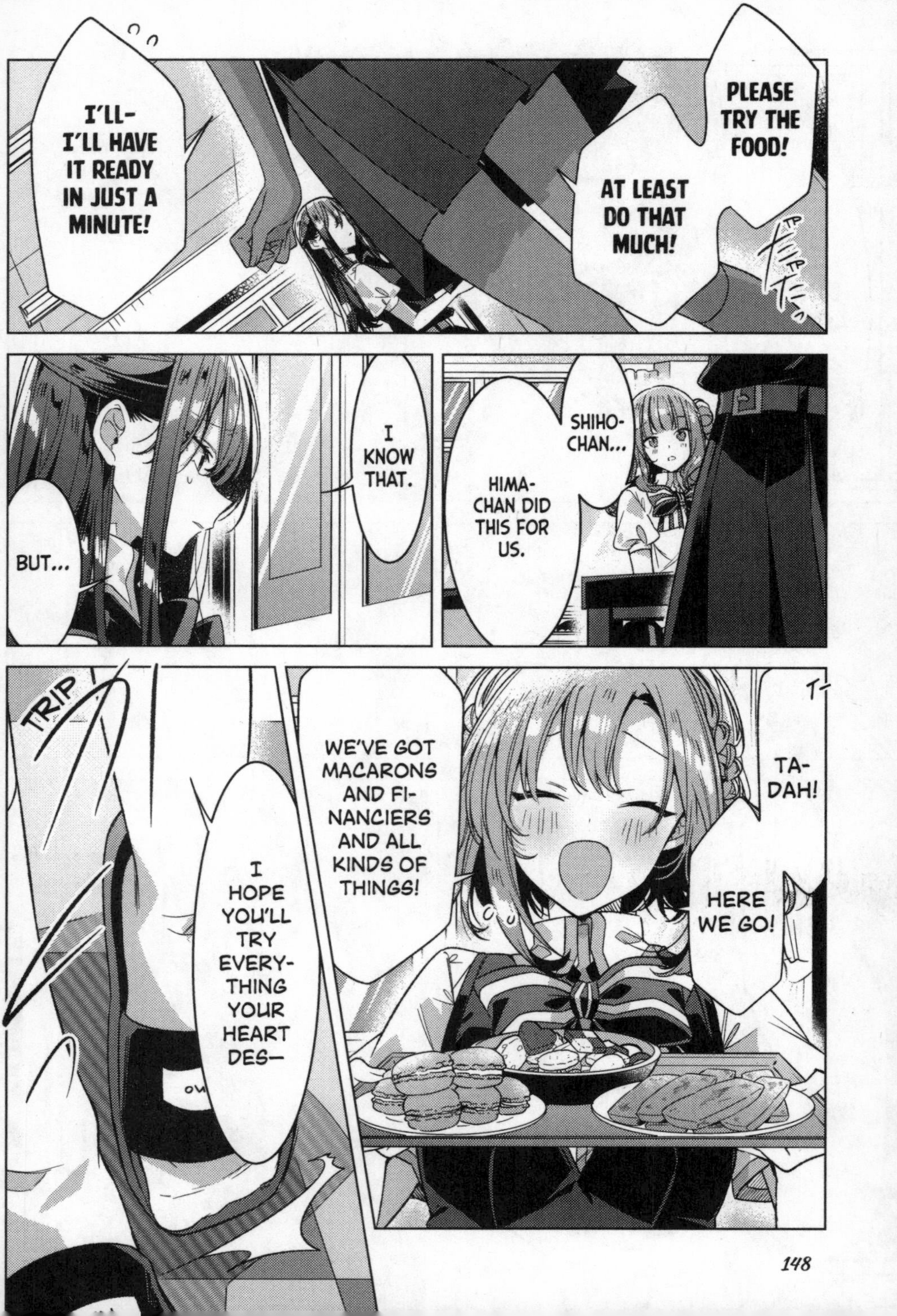
PLEASE TRY THE FOOD!
AT LEAST DO THAT MUCH!
TP TP
I'LL- I'LL HAVE IT READY IN JUST A MINUTE!
SHIHO-CHAN...
HIMA-CHAN DID THIS FOR US.
I KNOW THAT.
BUT...
TA-DAH!
HERE WE GO!
WE'VE GOT MACARONS AND FI-NANCIERS AND ALL KINDS OF THINGS!
I HOPE YOU'LL TRY EVERY-THING YOUR HEART DES—
TRIP

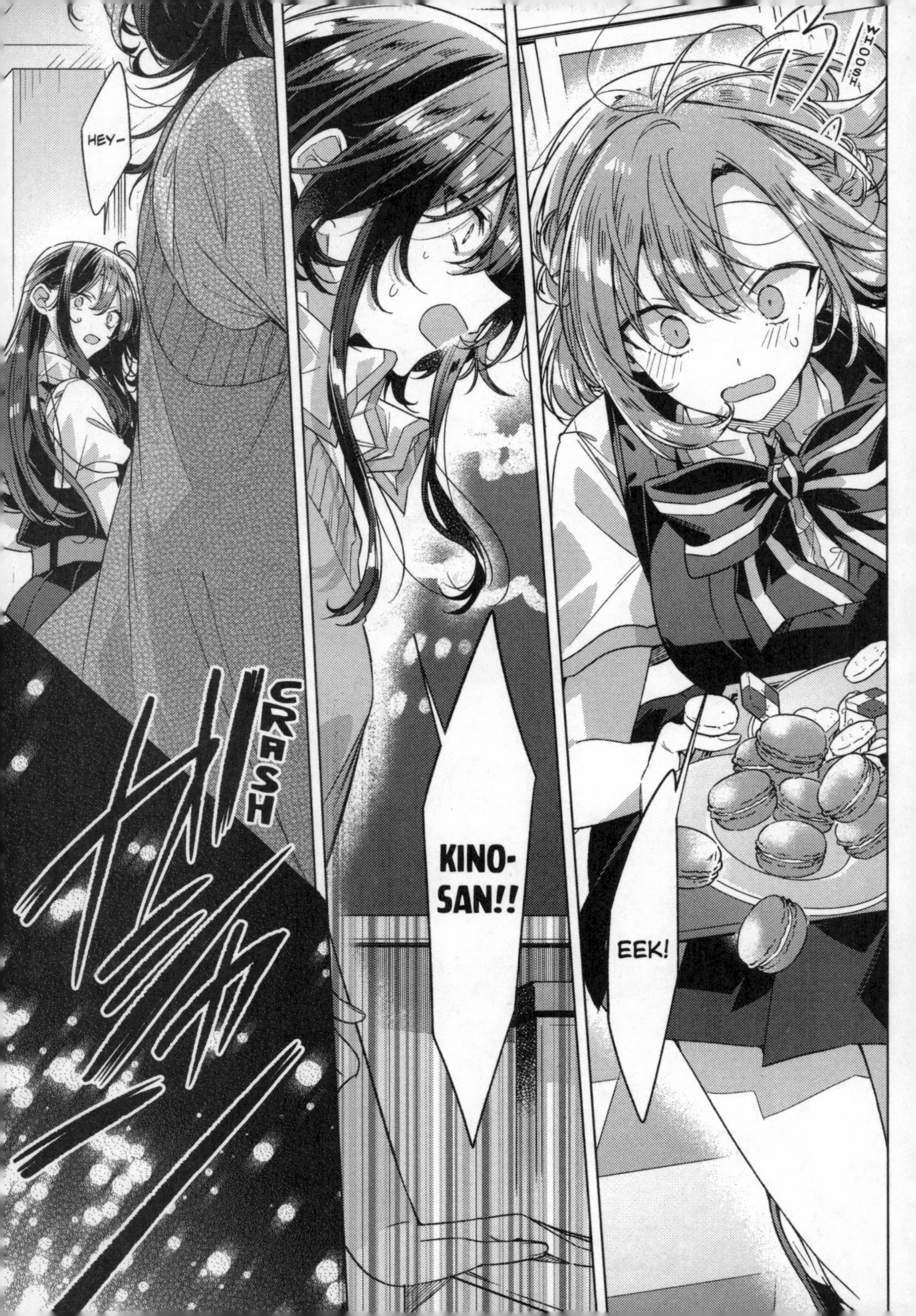
WHOOSH
EEK!
KINO-SAN!!
HEY—
CRASH

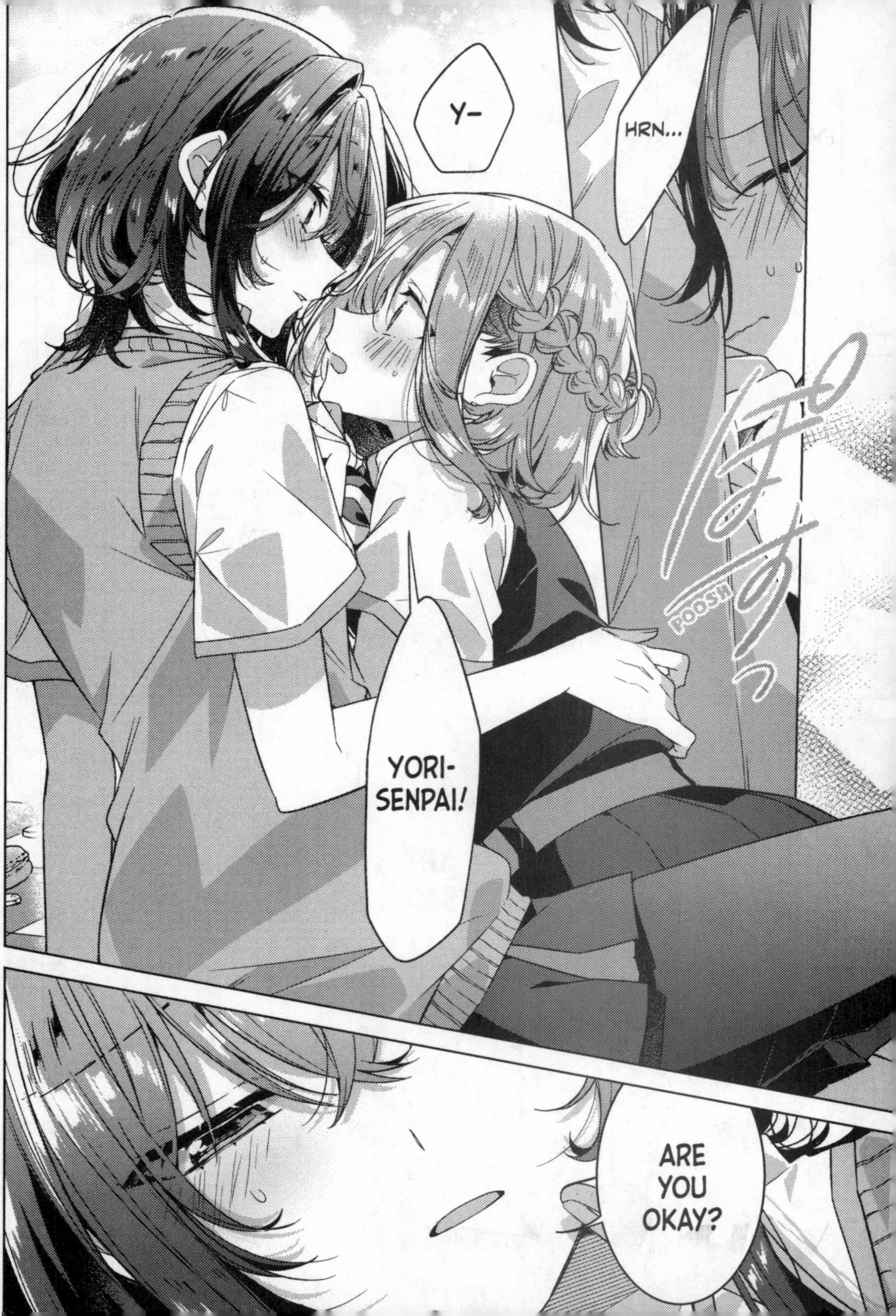
HRN...
Y-
POOSH
YORI-SENPAI!
ARE YOU OKAY?

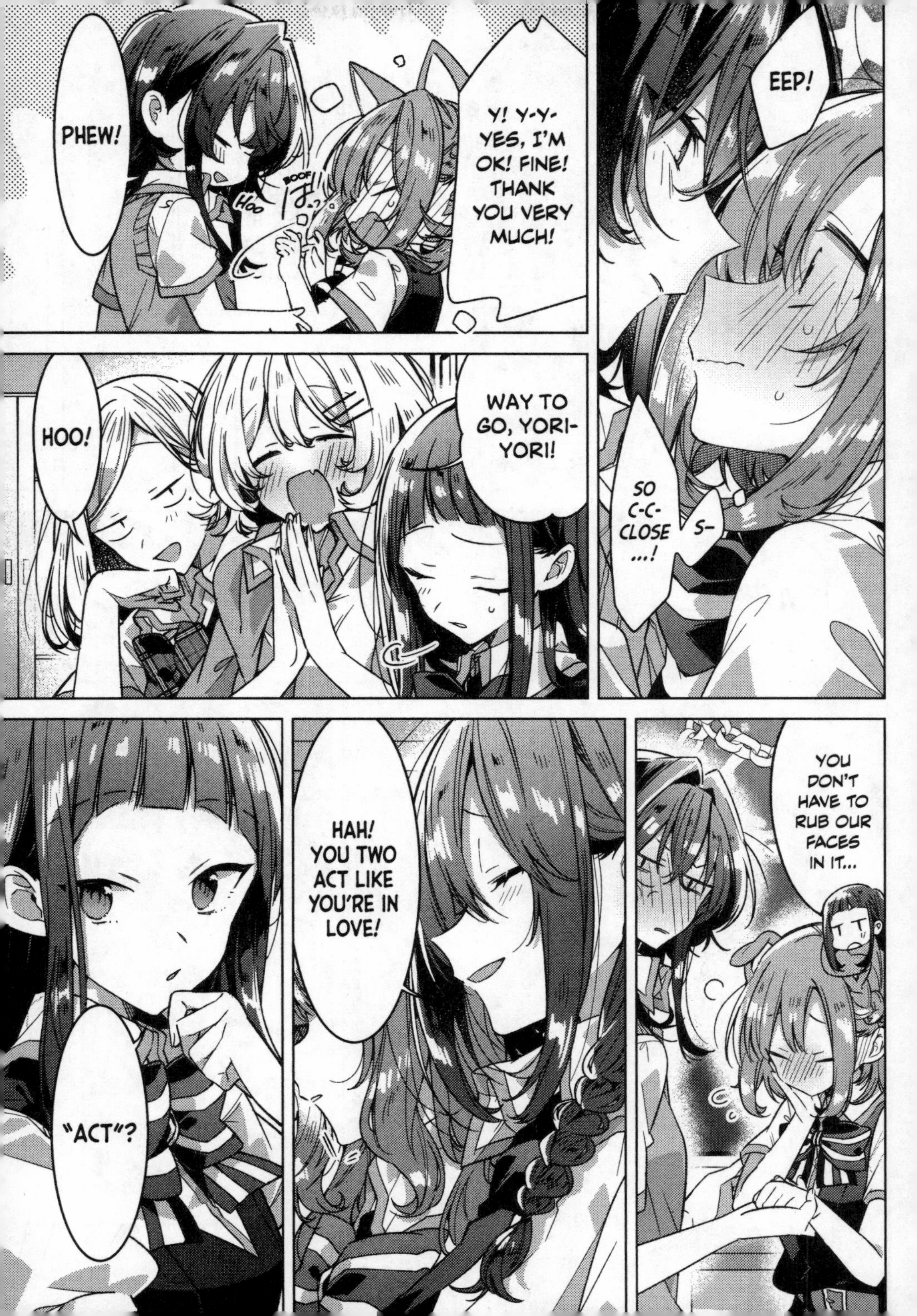

EEP!
S–
SO C-C-CLOSE ...!
Y! Y-Y-YES, I'M OK! FINE! THANK YOU VERY MUCH!
BOOF
HOO
PHEW!
WAY TO GO, YORI-YORI!
HOO!
YOU DON'T HAVE TO RUB OUR FACES IN IT...
HAH! YOU TWO ACT LIKE YOU'RE IN LOVE!
"ACT"?

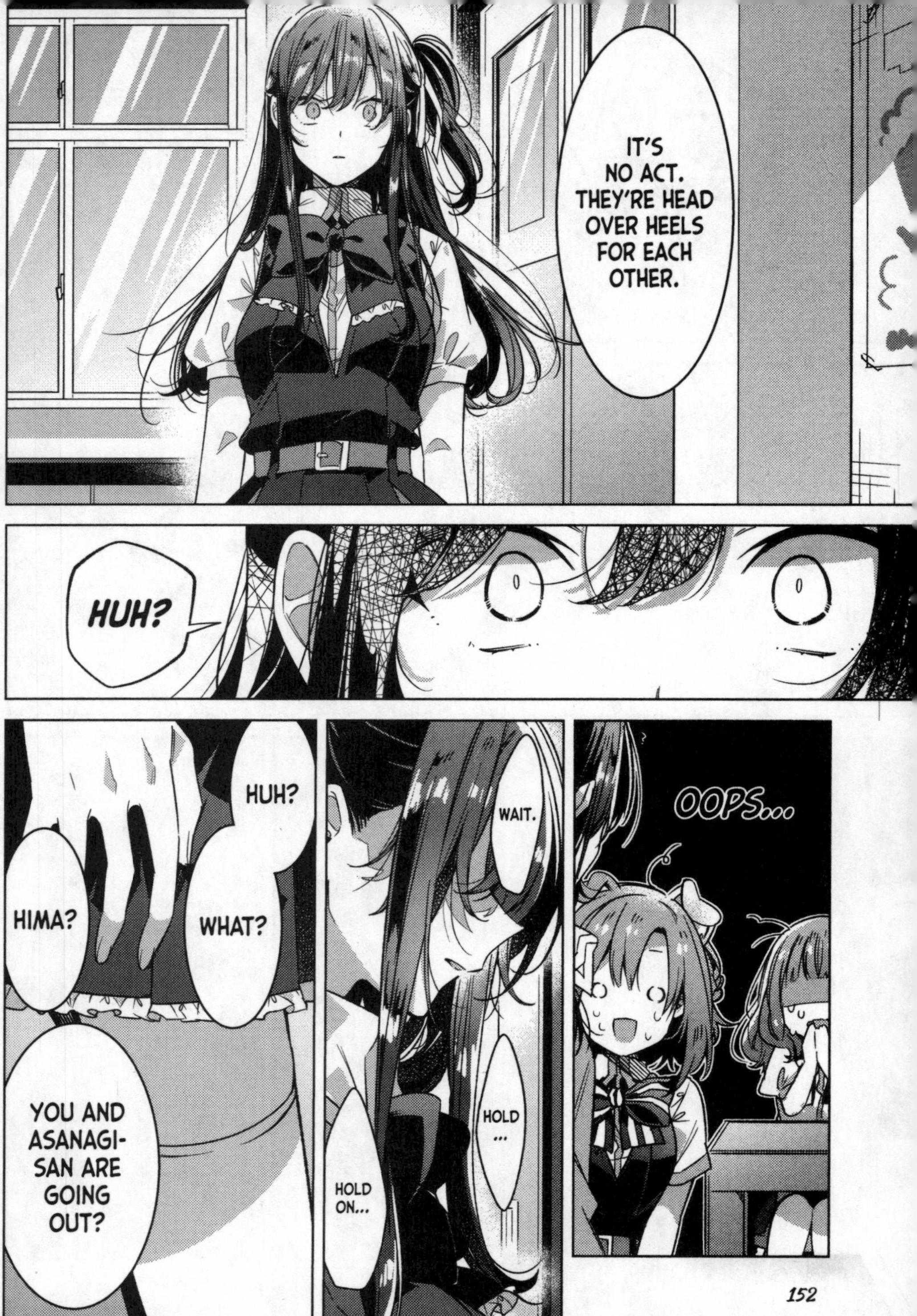
IT'S NO ACT. THEY'RE HEAD OVER HEELS FOR EACH OTHER.
HUH?
OOPS...
WAIT.
HOLD...
HOLD ON...
HUH?
WHAT?
HIMA?
YOU AND ASANAGI-SAN ARE GOING OUT?

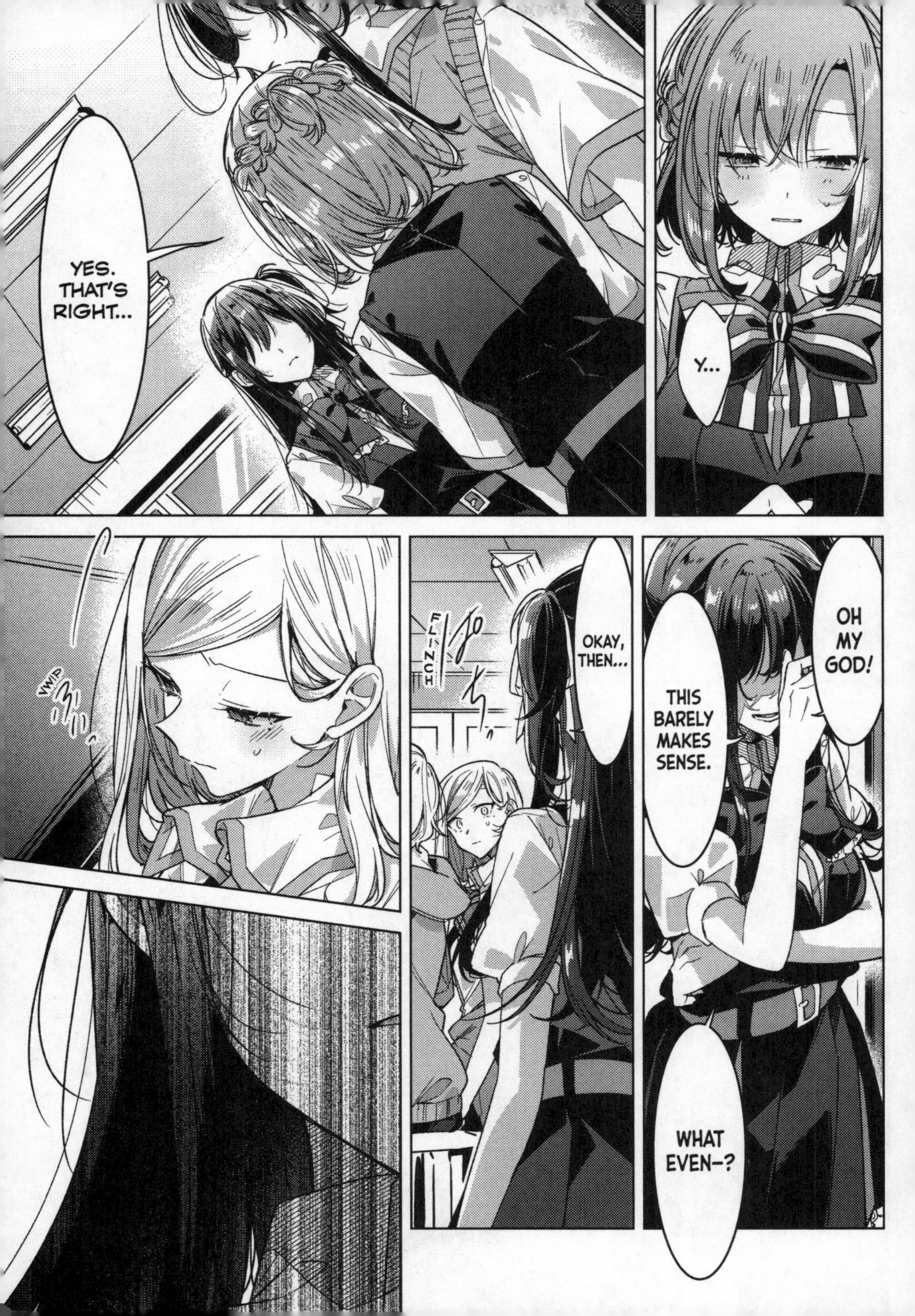
Y...
YES. THAT'S RIGHT...
OH MY GOD!
THIS BARELY MAKES SENSE.
WHAT EVEN-?
OKAY, THEN...
FLINCH
VWIP

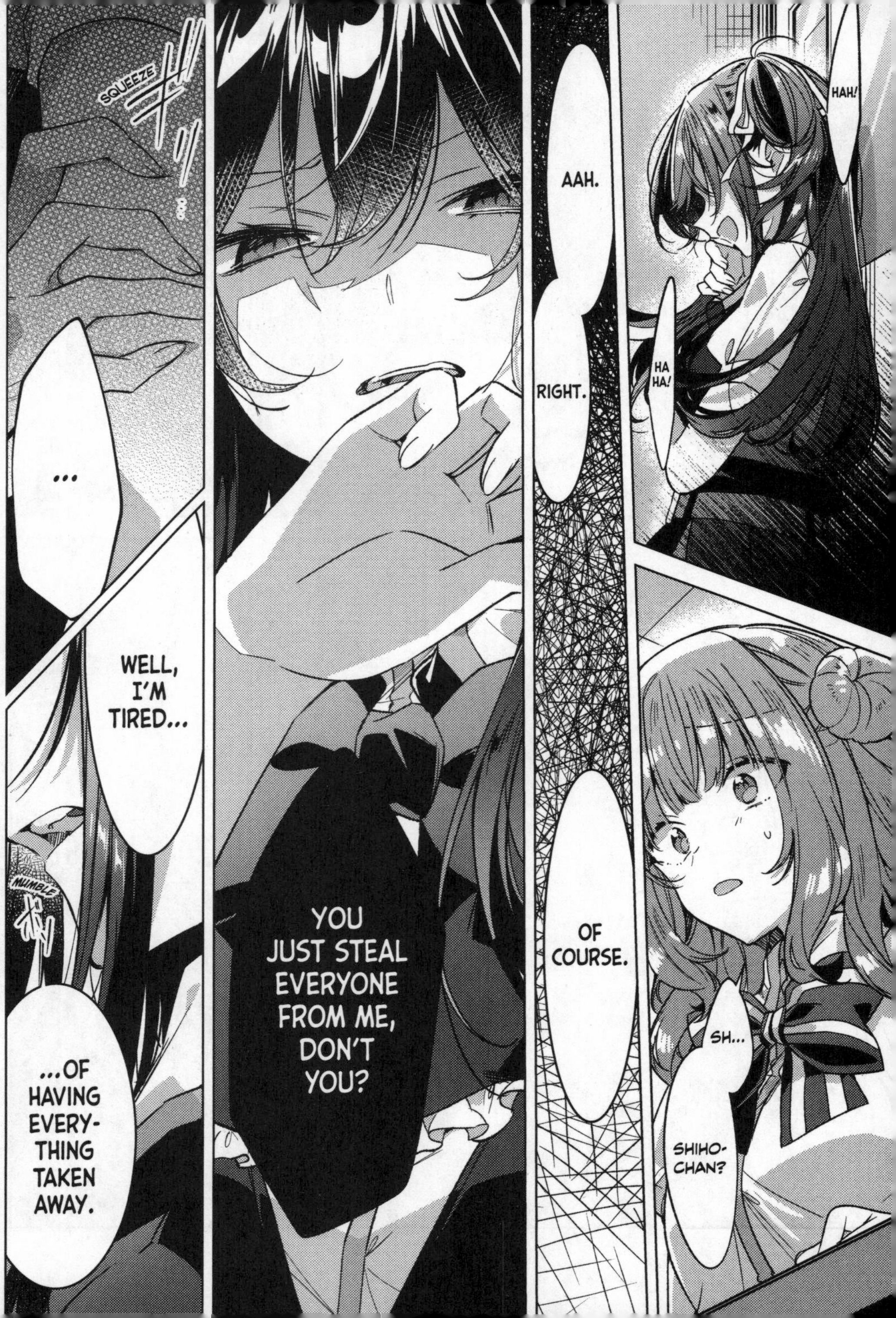
HAH!
HA HA!
AAH.
RIGHT.
SH...
SHIHO-CHAN?
OF COURSE.
YOU JUST STEAL EVERYONE FROM ME, DON'T YOU?
SQUEEZE
...
WELL, I'M TIRED...
MUMBLE
...OF HAVING EVERY-THING TAKEN AWAY.

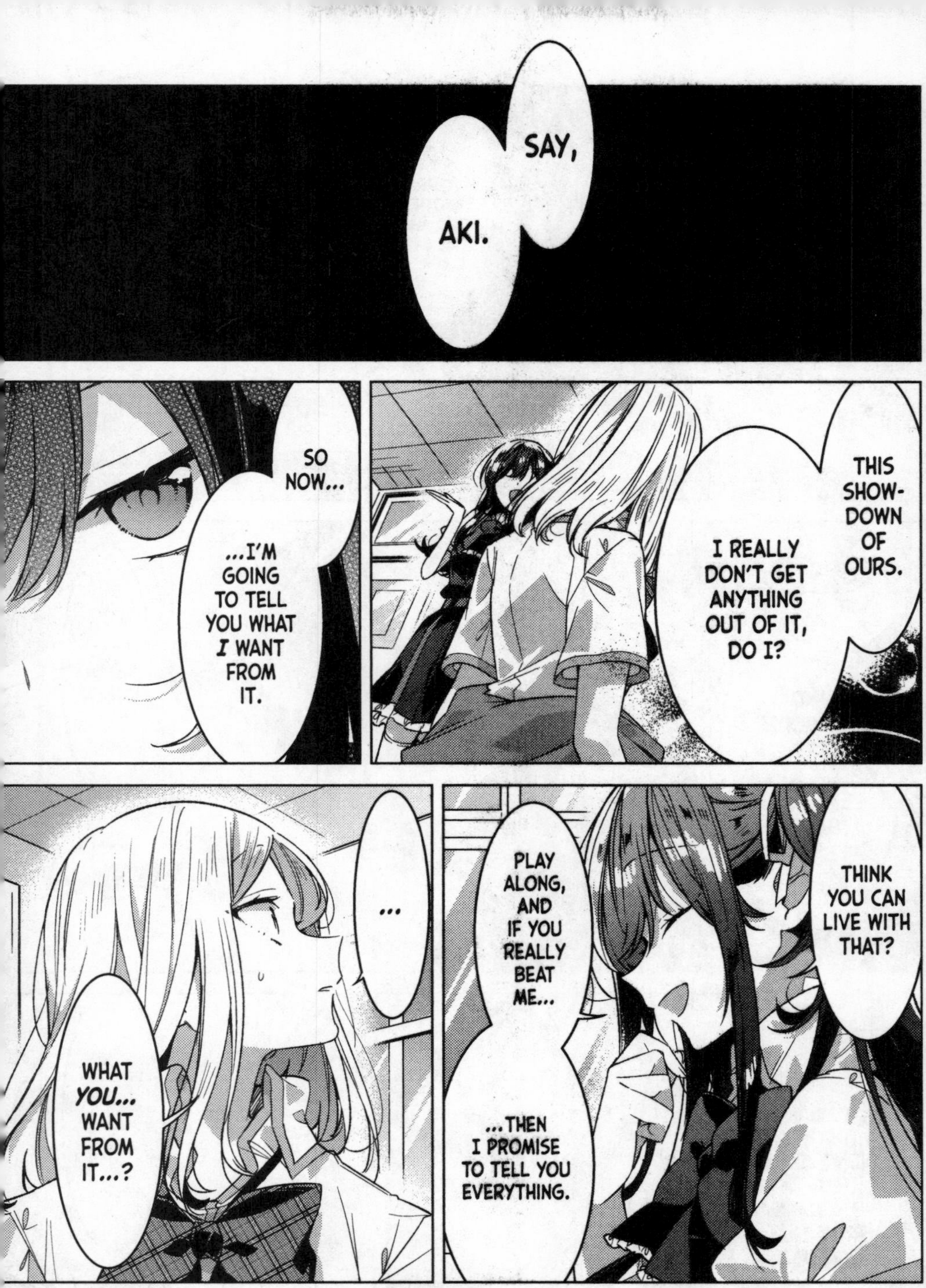
SAY,
AKI.
THIS SHOWDOWN OF OURS.
I REALLY DON'T GET ANYTHING OUT OF IT, DO I?
SO NOW...
...I'M GOING TO TELL YOU WHAT *I* WANT FROM IT.
THINK YOU CAN LIVE WITH THAT?
PLAY ALONG, AND IF YOU REALLY BEAT ME...
...THEN I PROMISE TO TELL YOU EVERYTHING.
...
WHAT *YOU...* WANT FROM IT...?

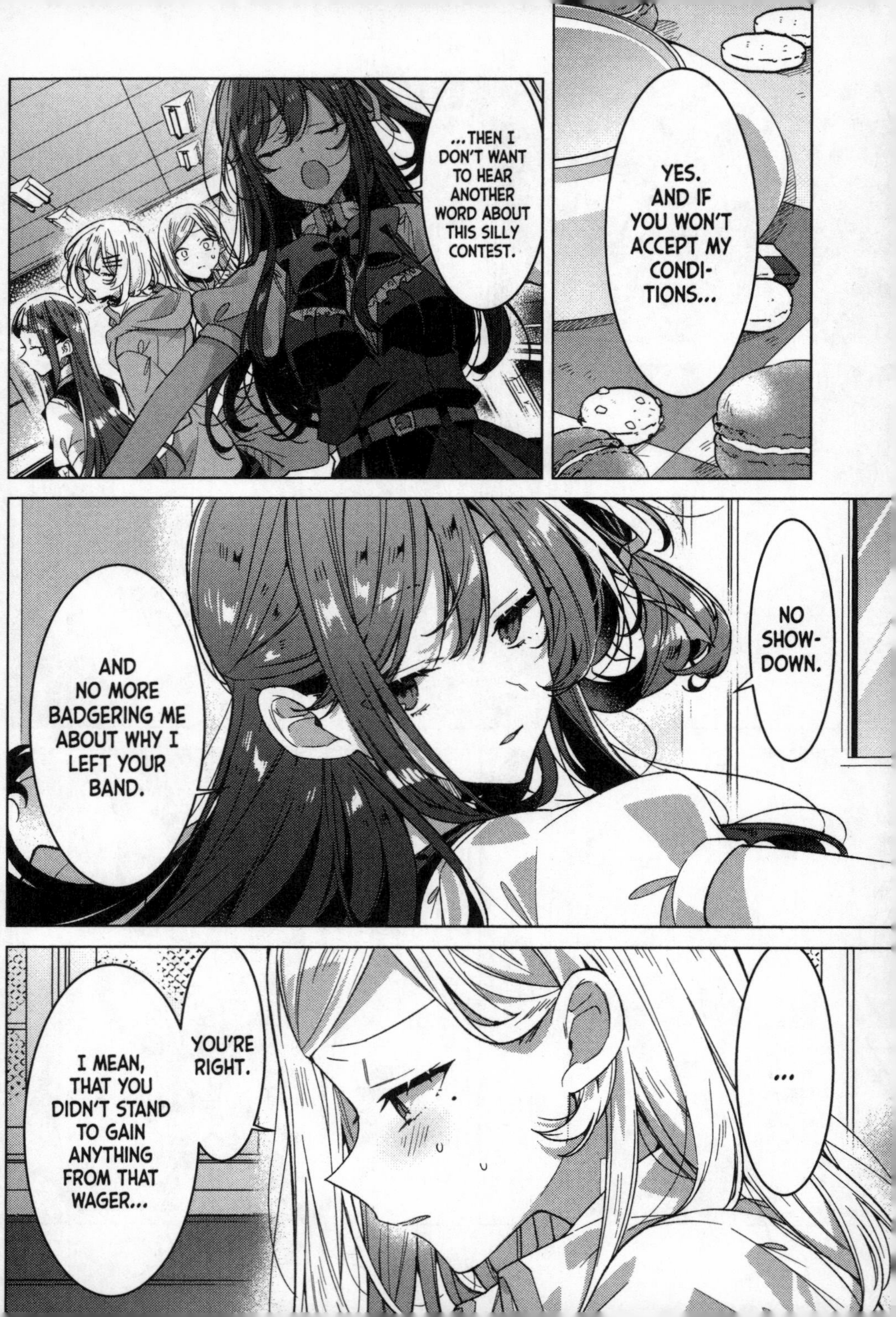
YES. AND IF YOU WON'T ACCEPT MY CONDITIONS...
...THEN I DON'T WANT TO HEAR ANOTHER WORD ABOUT THIS SILLY CONTEST.
NO SHOWDOWN.
AND NO MORE BADGERING ME ABOUT WHY I LEFT YOUR BAND.
...
YOU'RE RIGHT.
I MEAN, THAT YOU DIDN'T STAND TO GAIN ANYTHING FROM THAT WAGER...

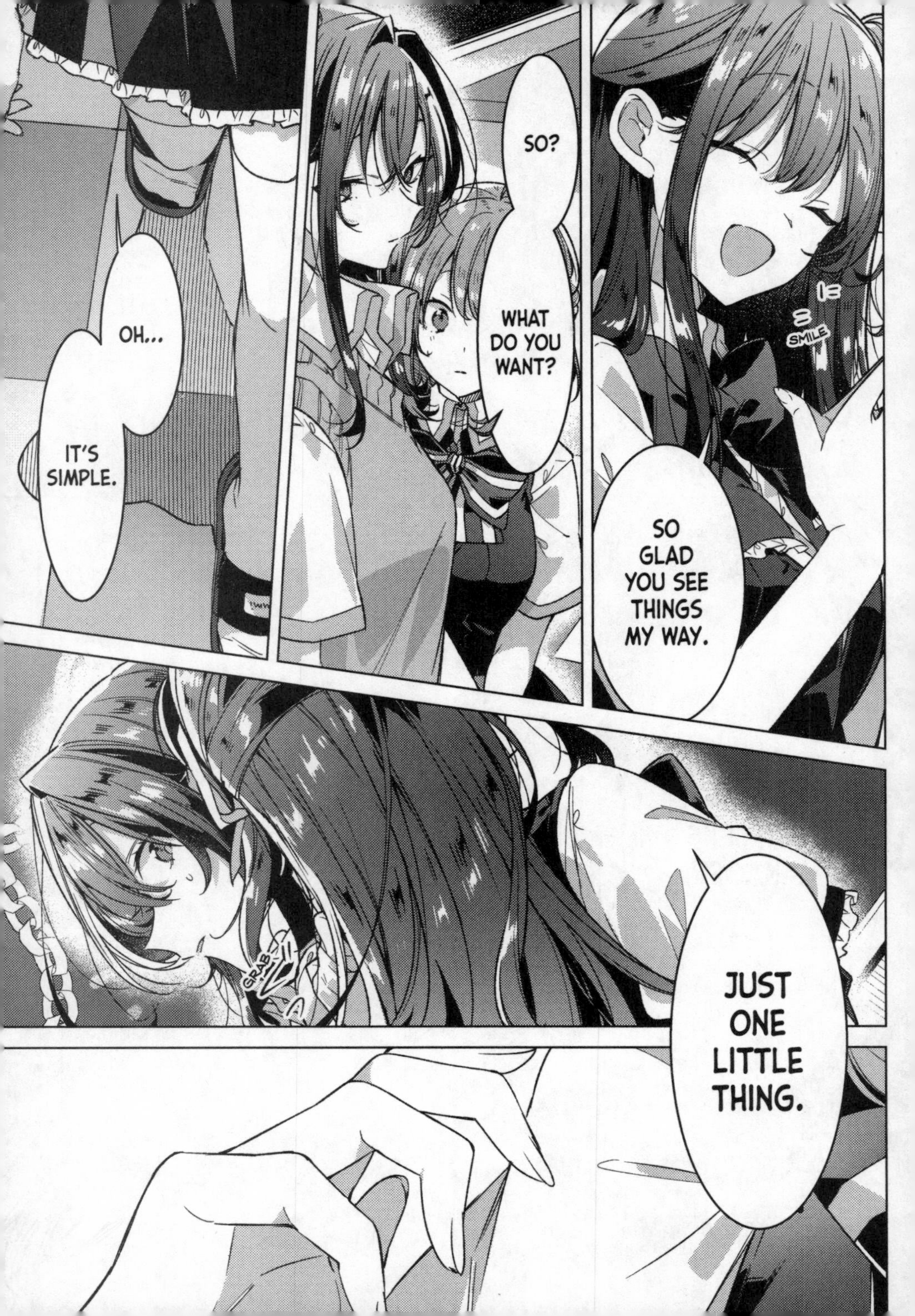
SMILE
SO GLAD YOU SEE THINGS MY WAY.
SO?
WHAT DO YOU WANT?
OH...
IT'S SIMPLE.
JUST ONE LITTLE THING.
GRAB

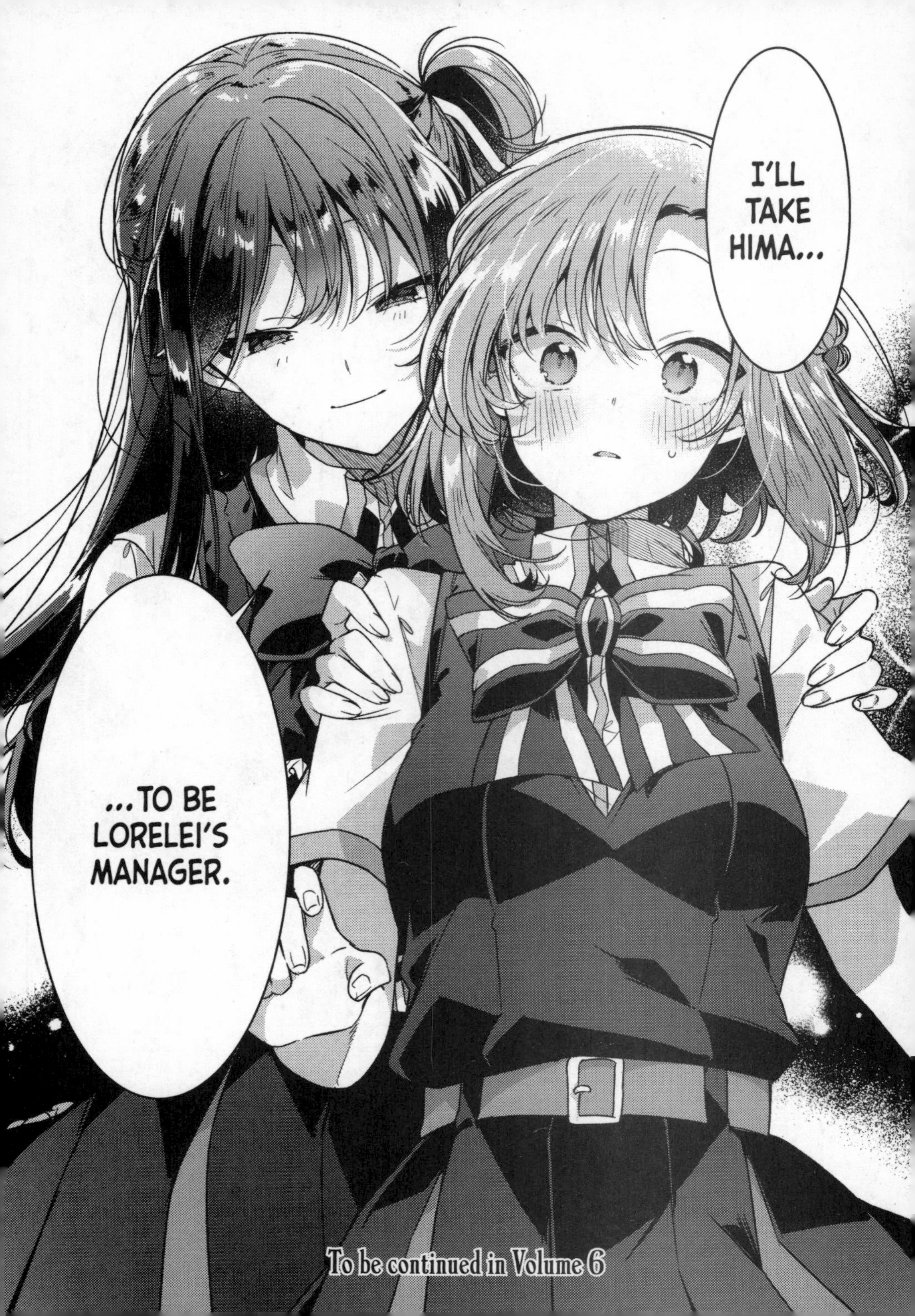
I'LL TAKE HIMA...
...TO BE LORELEI'S MANAGER.
To be continued in Volume 6

Whisper Me A Love Song

Eku
Takeshima

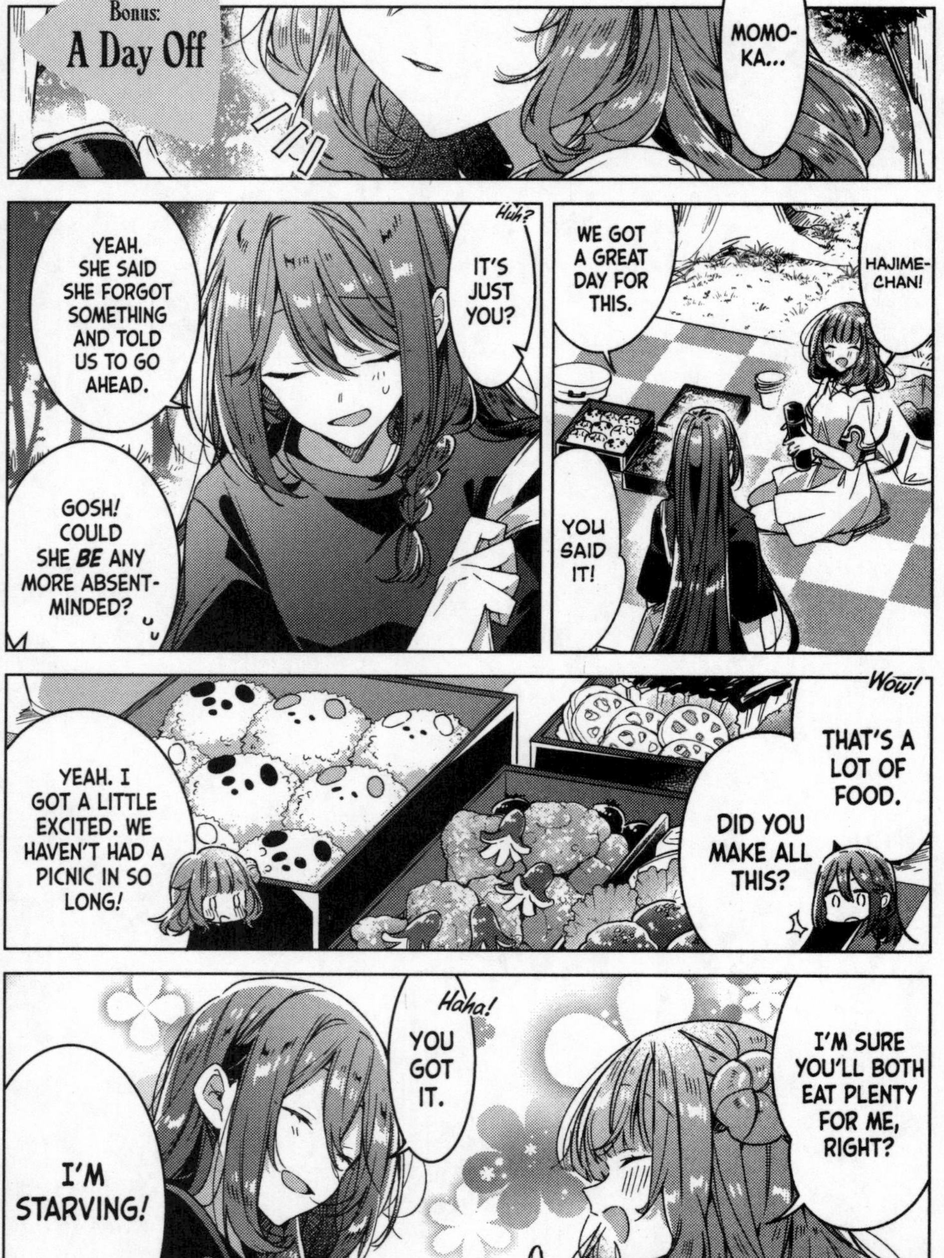
Bonus:
A Day Off
MOMO-KA...
HAJIME-CHAN!
WE GOT A GREAT DAY FOR THIS.
YOU SAID IT!
Huh?
IT'S JUST YOU?
YEAH. SHE SAID SHE FORGOT SOMETHING AND TOLD US TO GO AHEAD.
GOSH! COULD SHE *BE* ANY MORE ABSENT-MINDED?
Wow!
THAT'S A LOT OF FOOD.
DID YOU MAKE ALL THIS?
YEAH. I GOT A LITTLE EXCITED. WE HAVEN'T HAD A PICNIC IN SO LONG!
I'M SURE YOU'LL BOTH EAT PLENTY FOR ME, RIGHT?
Haha!
YOU GOT IT.
I'M STARVING!

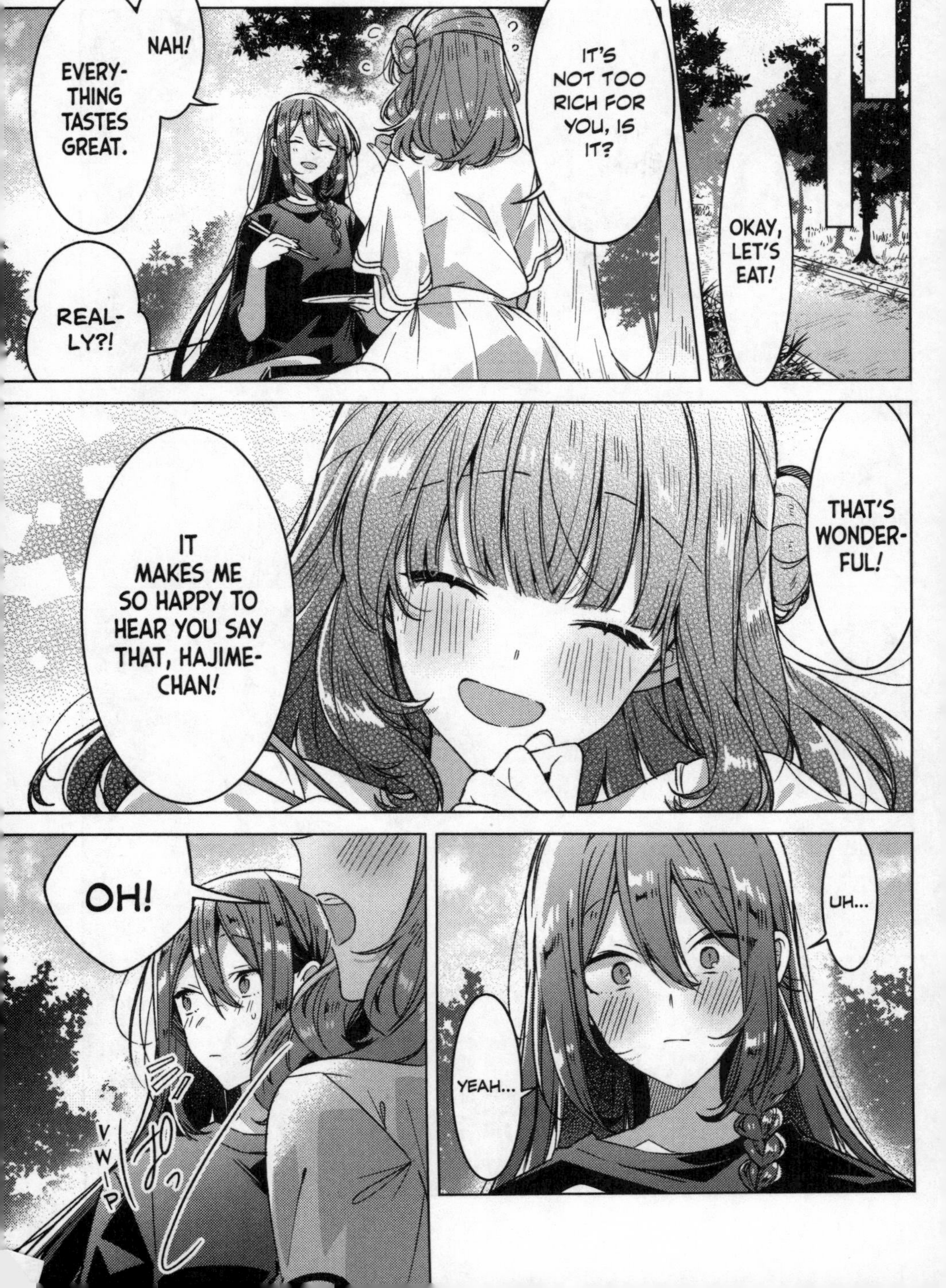
OKAY, LET'S EAT!
IT'S NOT TOO RICH FOR YOU, IS IT?
NAH! EVERYTHING TASTES GREAT.
REALLY?!
THAT'S WONDERFUL!
IT MAKES ME SO HAPPY TO HEAR YOU SAY THAT, HAJIME-CHAN!
UH...
YEAH...
OH!
VWIP

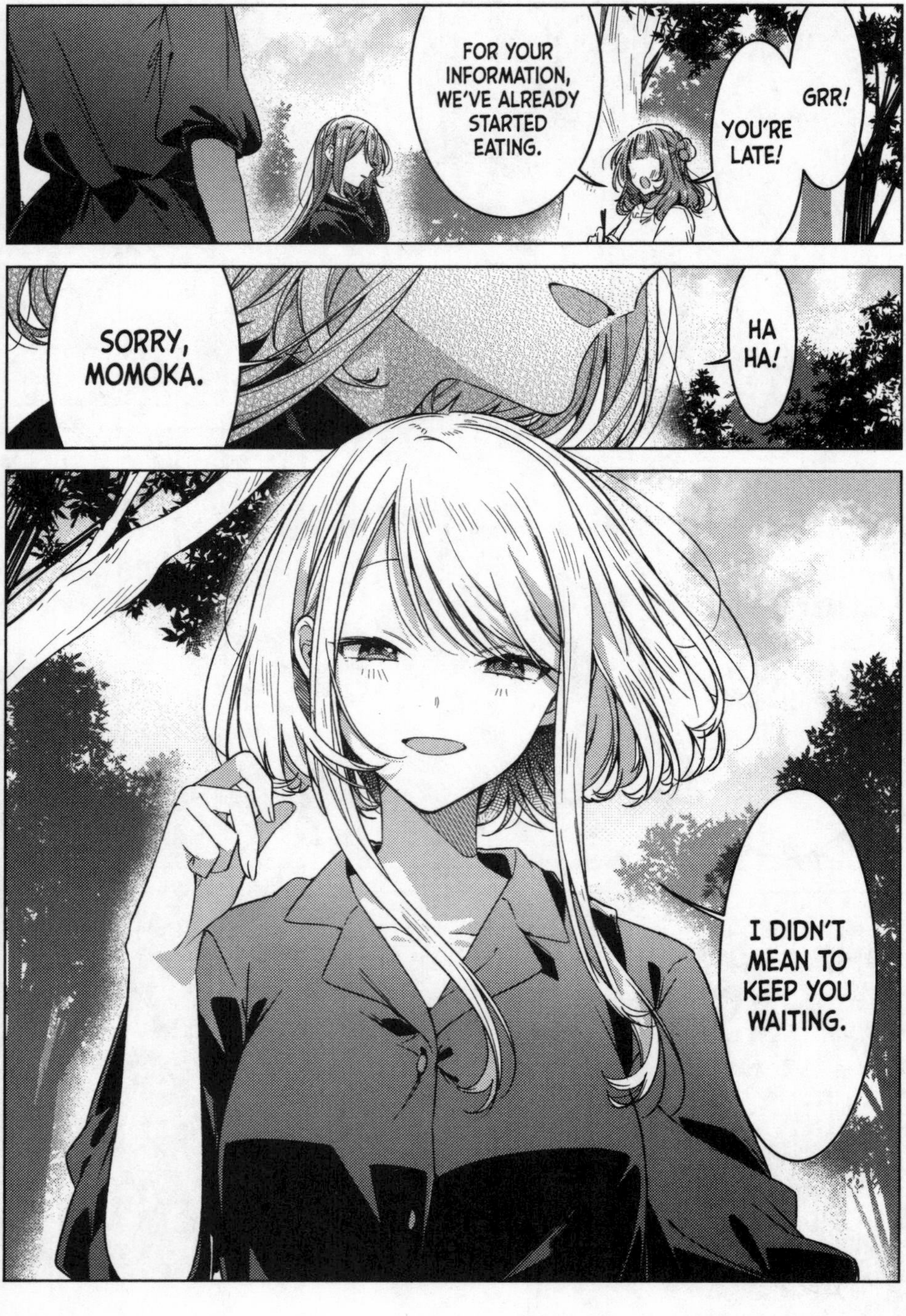
GRR! YOU'RE LATE!
FOR YOUR INFORMATION, WE'VE ALREADY STARTED EATING.
HA HA!
SORRY, MOMOKA.
I DIDN'T MEAN TO KEEP YOU WAITING.

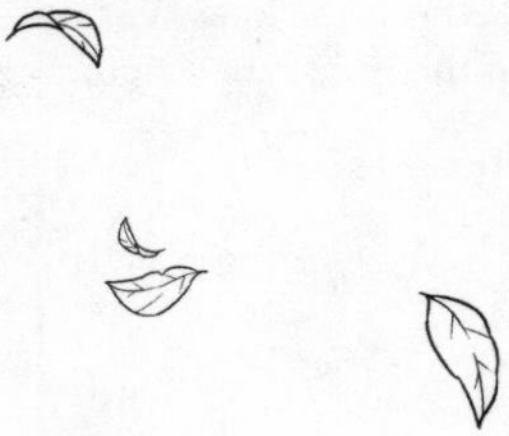

SPECIAL THANKS
Editor – Ten-san
Design – SALIDAS-sama
Assistant – Hirofumi Shino-san
&
Everyone who picked up this book!
Thank you all so much for all your support!!

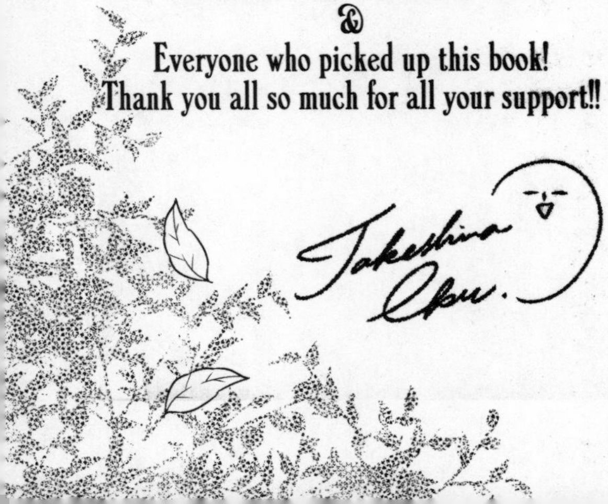

TRANSLATION NOTES

Cram School, page 88
Many Japanese students attend *juku,* or cram school, private institutions that provide additional instruction after the school day is over or on weekends. For high schoolers in particular, these classes are often aimed at mastering the material on the college entrance exams that students will soon have to take.

Bad Girl, page 93
High school students in Japan are often discouraged or outright forbidden from having jobs, the assumption being that it would distract them from their studies. That doesn't stop students from working part-time on the sly, but they run the risk of being discovered by their friends or acquaintances. (And in manga, they usually are...)

Summer Break, page 135
Japanese schools typically operate on a trimester system, with breaks after each trimester. The school year starts in April, so summer break, which usually runs from late July to the end of August, comes in the middle of the year, not at the end, as it does in the US. (The summer recess is the longest of the three; the winter break at the end of the calendar year and the spring break at the end of the school year are just a couple weeks each.)

Whisper Me
A Love Song
Eku
Takeshima

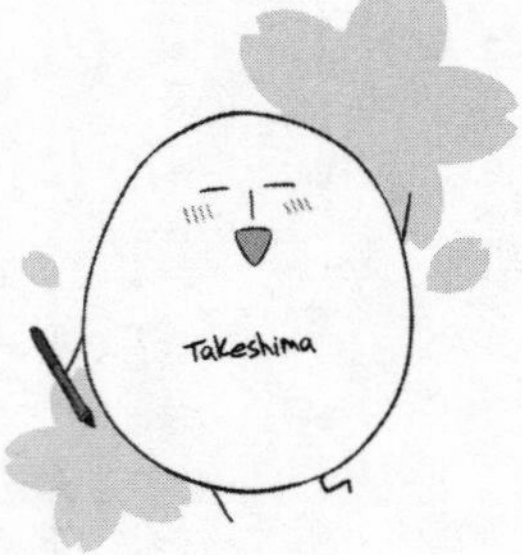
Takeshima

It's volume 5, and the emotions are starting to bubble to the surface. Our two bands are about to go head-to-head. I would be thrilled if you'd cheer both of them on.

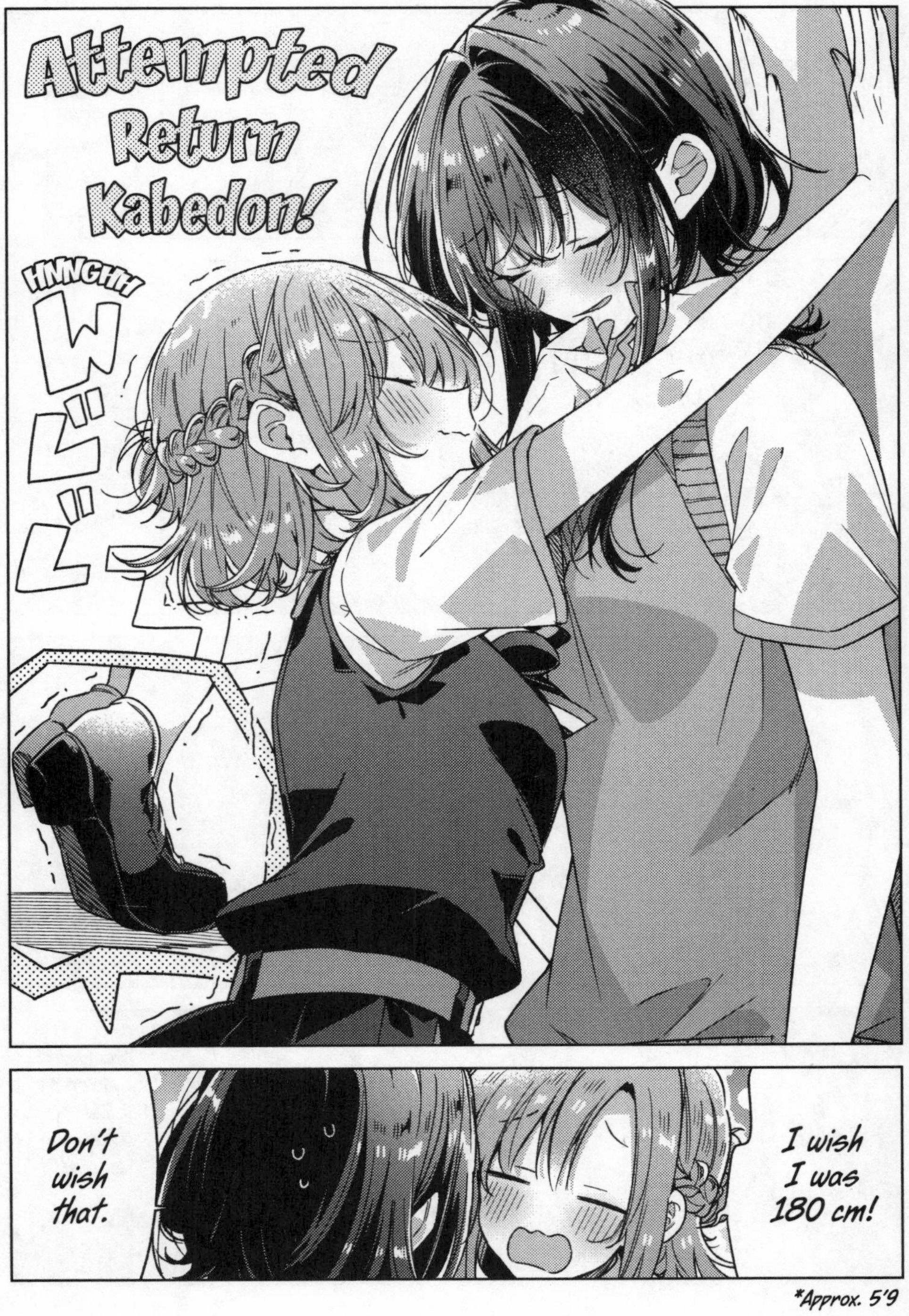
Attempted Return Kabedon!
HNNGHH
I wish I was 180 cm!
Don't wish that.

*Approx. 5'9

Kaori & Maa-chan, Together Again

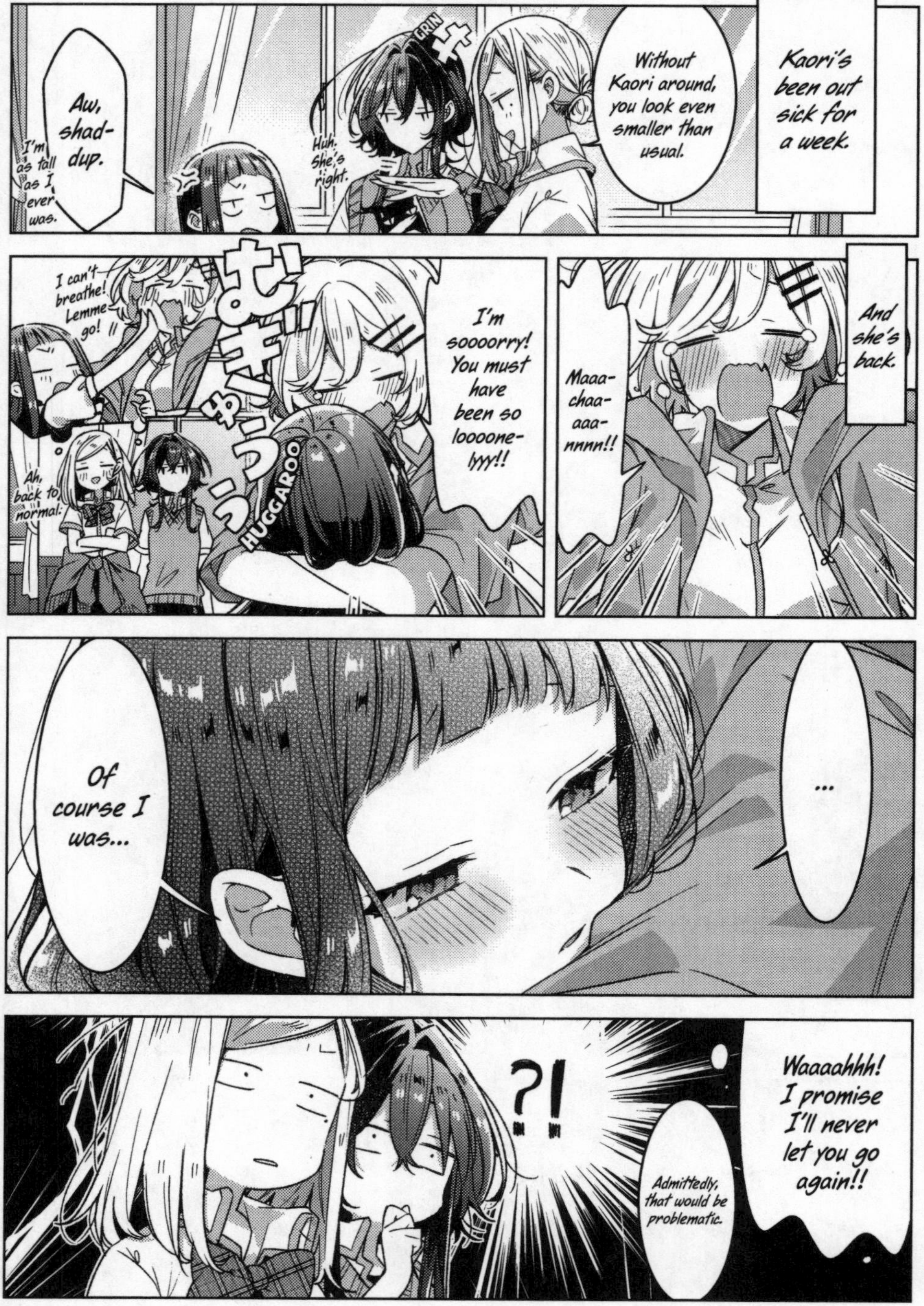
Kaori's been out sick for a week.
Without Kaori around, you look even smaller than usual.
GRIN
Huh. She's right.
Aw, shad-dup.
I'm as tall as I ever was.
And she's back.
Maaa-chaa-aaa-annnn!!
I'm soooorry! You must have been so loooone-lyyy!!
HUGGAROO
I can't breathe! Lemme go!
Ah, back to normal.
...
Of course I was...
Waaaahhh! I promise I'll never let you go again!!
Admittedly, that would be problematic.
?!

Whisper Me
A Love Song

Eku
Takeshima

A SMART, NEW ROMANTIC COMEDY FOR FANS OF *SHORTCAKE CAKE* AND *TERRACE HOUSE*!

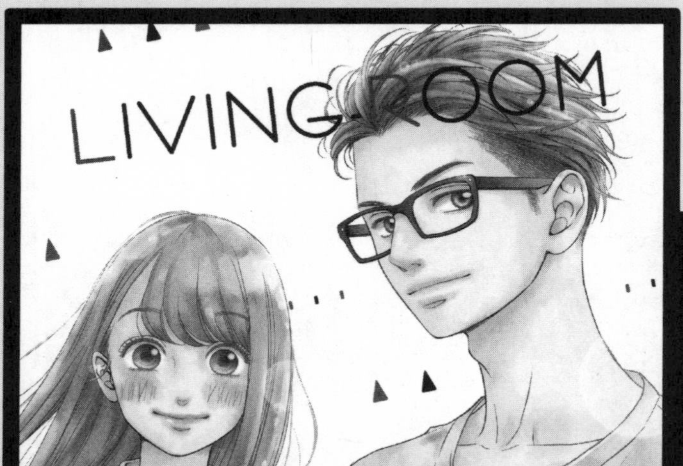
LIVING-ROOM
1
Keiko Iwashita
MATSUNAGA-SAN

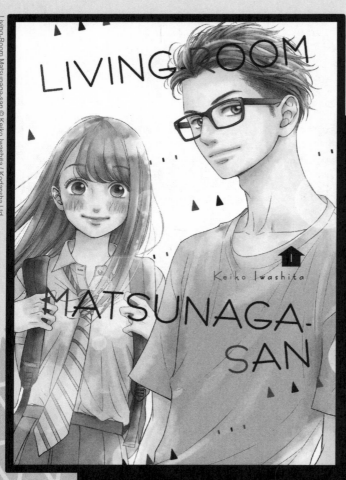

A romance manga starring high school girl Meeko, who learns to live on her own in a boarding house whose living room is home to the odd (but handsome) Matsunaga-san. She begins to adjust to her new life away from her parents, but Meeko soon learns that no matter how far away from home she is, she's still a young girl at heart — especially when she finds herself falling for Matsunaga-san.

PERFECT WORLD

Rie Aruga

A TOUCHING NEW SERIES ABOUT LOVE AND COPING WITH DISABILITY

An office party reunites Tsugumi with her high school crush Itsuki. He's realized his dream of becoming an architect, but along the way, he experienced a spinal injury that put him in a wheelchair. Now Tsugumi's rekindled feelings will butt up against prejudices she never considered — and Itsuki will have to decide if he's ready to let someone into his heart...

"Depicts with great delicacy and courage the difficulties some with disabilities experience getting involved in romantic relationships... Rie Aruga refuses to romanticize, pushing her heroine to face the reality of disability. She invites her readers to the same tasks of empathy, knowledge and recognition."
—Slate.fr

"An important entry [in manga romance]... The emotional core of both plot and characters indicates thoughtfulness... [Aruga's] research is readily apparent in the text and artwork, making this feel like a real story."
—Anime News Network

KC
KODANSHA
COMICS

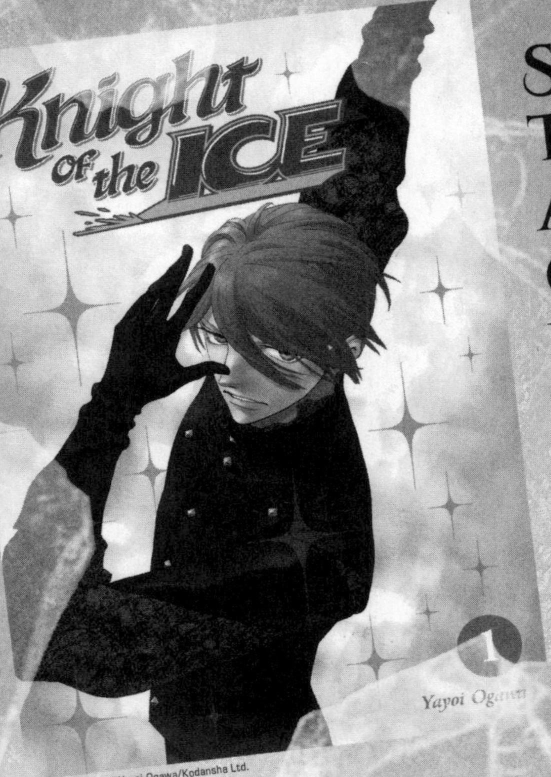
Knight of the ICE
1
Yayoi Ogawa

Knight of the Ice ©Yayoi Ogawa/Kodansha Ltd.

SKATING THRILLS AND ICY CHILLS WITH THIS NEW TINGLY ROMANCE SERIES!

A rom-com on ice, perfect for fans of *Princess Jellyfish* and *Wotakoi*. Kokoro is the talk of the figure-skating world, winning trophies and hearts. But little do they know... he's actually a huge nerd! From the beloved creator of *You're My Pet* (*Tramps Like Us*).

Chitose is a serious young woman, working for the health magazine *SASSO*. Or at least, she would be, if she wasn't constantly getting distracted by her childhood friend, international figure skating star Kokoro Kijinami! In the public eye and on the ice, Kokoro is a gallant, flawless knight, but behind his glittery costumes and breathtaking spins lies a secret: He's actually a hopelessly romantic otaku, who can only land his quad jumps when Chitose is on hand to recite a spell from his favorite magical girl anime!

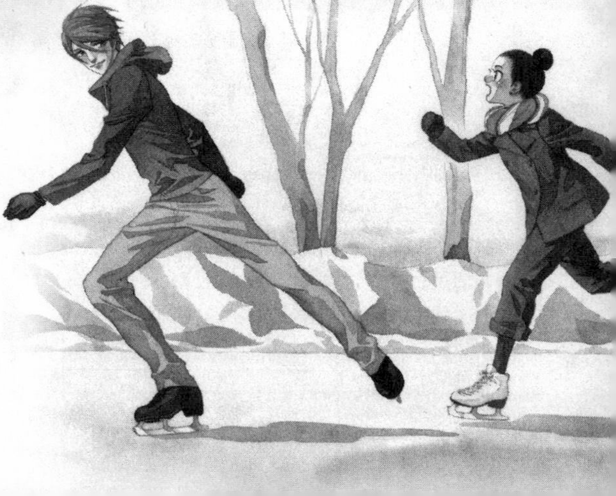

KC KODANSHA COMICS

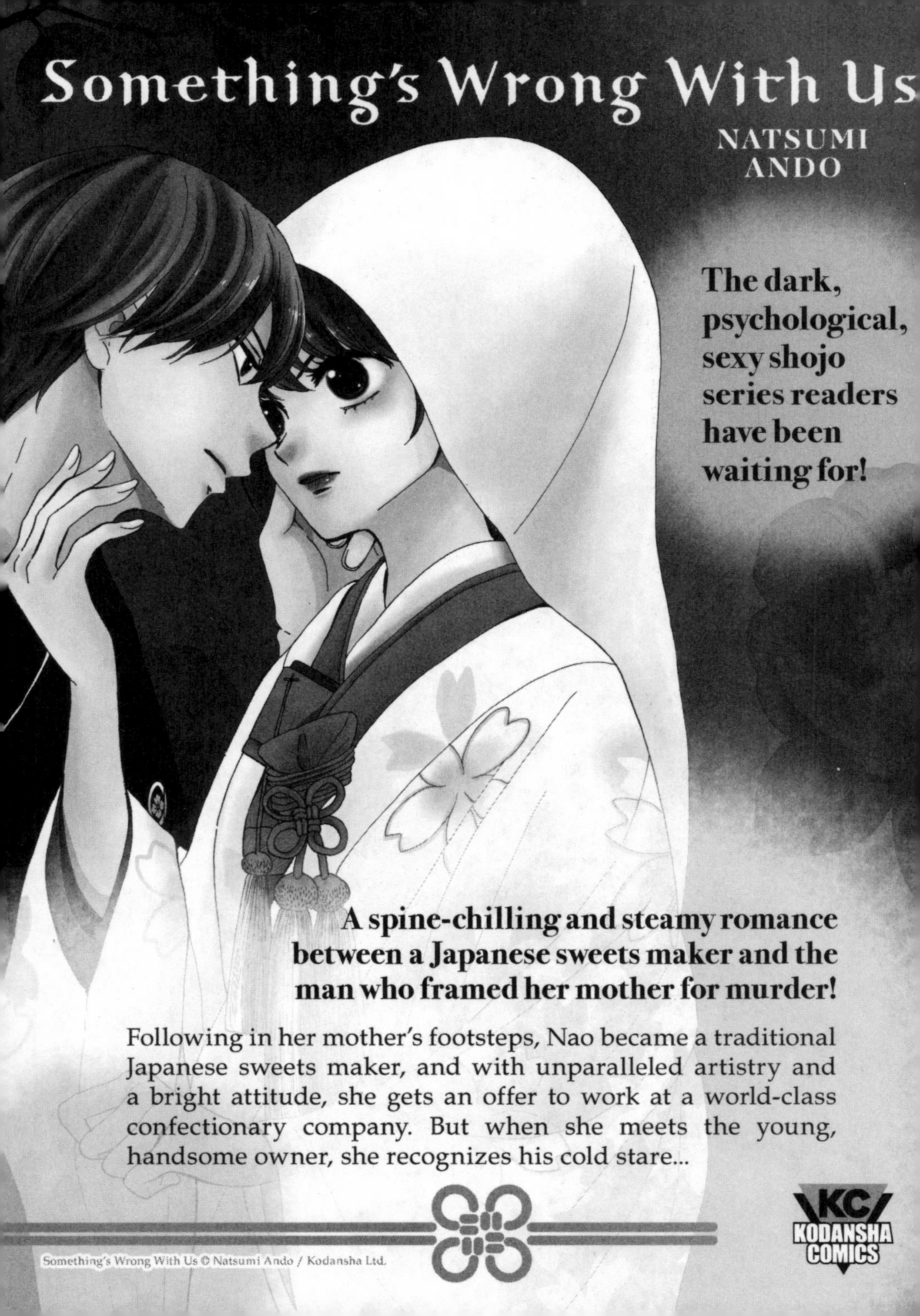
Something's Wrong With Us
NATSUMI ANDO
The dark, psychological, sexy shojo series readers have been waiting for!
A spine-chilling and steamy romance between a Japanese sweets maker and the man who framed her mother for murder!
Following in her mother's footsteps, Nao became a traditional Japanese sweets maker, and with unparalleled artistry and a bright attitude, she gets an offer to work at a world-class confectionary company. But when she meets the young, handsome owner, she recognizes his cold stare...
KC KODANSHA COMICS
Something's Wrong With Us © Natsumi Ando / Kodansha Ltd.

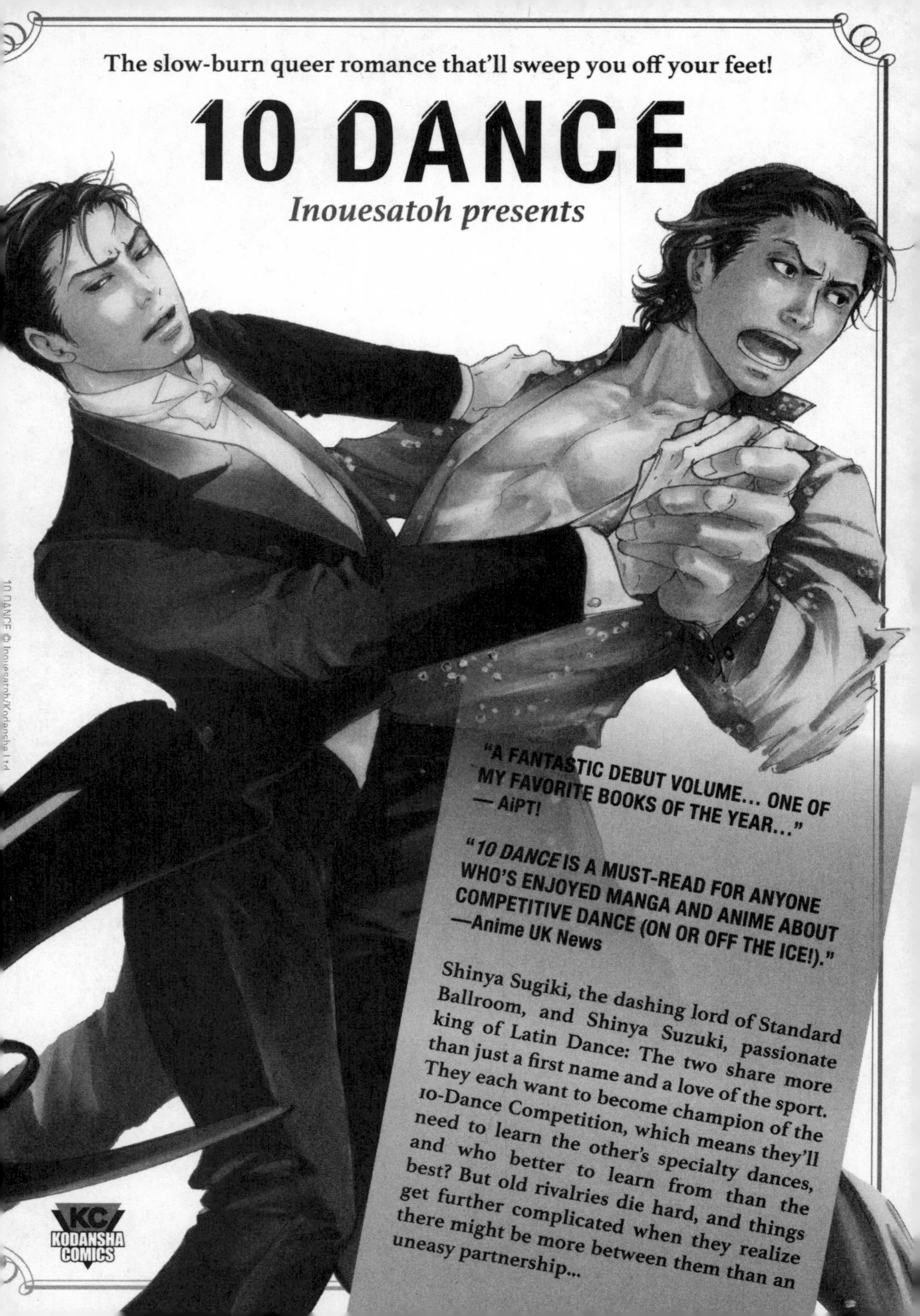
The slow-burn queer romance that'll sweep you off your feet!
10 DANCE
Inouesatoh presents
"A FANTASTIC DEBUT VOLUME… ONE OF MY FAVORITE BOOKS OF THE YEAR…"
— AiPT!
"10 DANCE IS A MUST-READ FOR ANYONE WHO'S ENJOYED MANGA AND ANIME ABOUT COMPETITIVE DANCE (ON OR OFF THE ICE!)."
—Anime UK News
Shinya Sugiki, the dashing lord of Standard Ballroom, and Shinya Suzuki, passionate king of Latin Dance: The two share more than just a first name and a love of the sport. They each want to become champion of the 10-Dance Competition, which means they'll need to learn the other's specialty dances, and who better to learn from than the best? But old rivalries die hard, and things get further complicated when they realize there might be more between them than an uneasy partnership...
KC KODANSHA COMICS
10 DANCE © Inouesatoh/Kodansha Ltd.

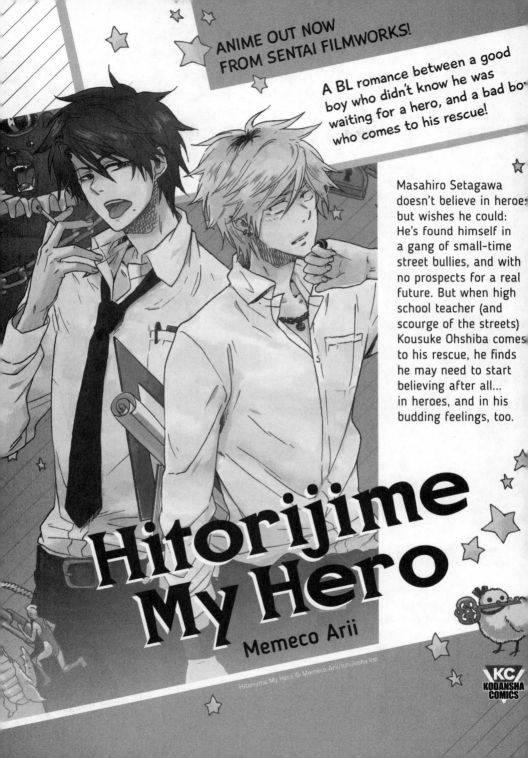

A BL romance between a good boy who didn't know he was waiting for a hero, and a bad boy who comes to his rescue!

Masahiro Setagawa doesn't believe in heroes but wishes he could: He's found himself in a gang of small-time street bullies, and with no prospects for a real future. But when high school teacher (and scourge of the streets) Kousuke Ohshiba comes to his rescue, he finds he may need to start believing after all... in heroes, and in his budding feelings, too.

Hitorijime My Hero

Memeco Arii

KC/ KODANSHA COMICS

One of CLAMP's biggest hits returns in this definitive, premium, hardcover 20th anniversary collector's edition!

Chobits © CLAMP·ShigatsuTsuitachi CO.,LTD./Kodansha Ltd.

Poor college student Hideki is down on his luck. All he wants is a good job, a girlfriend, and his very own "persocom"—the latest and greatest in humanoid computer technology. Hideki's luck changes one night when he finds Chi—a persocom thrown out in a pile of trash. But Hideki soon discovers that there's much more to his cute new persocom than meets the eye.

THE SWEET SCENT OF LOVE IS IN THE AIR! FOR FANS OF OFFBEAT ROMANCES LIKE *WOTAKOI*

Sweat and Soap © Kintetsu Yamada / Kodansha Ltd.

In an office romance, there's a fine line between sexy and awkward... and that line is where Asako — a woman who sweats copiously — meets Koutarou — a perfume developer who can't get enough of Asako's, er, scent. Don't miss a romcom manga like no other!

In love, there are
no save points.

ヲ
ヲ
ク
に
恋
は
難
し
い

NOW AN ANIME!

WOTAKOI:
LOVE IS HARD FOR OTAKU

by FUJITA

Narumi has had it rough: Every boyfriend she's had dumped her
once they found out she was an otaku, so she's gone to great
lengths to hide it. At her new job, she bumps into Hirotaka, her
childhood friend and fellow otaku. When Hirotaka almost gets
her secret outed at work, she comes up with a plan to keep him
quiet. But he comes up with a counter-proposal:
Why doesn't she just date him instead?

THE MAGICAL GIRL CLASSIC THAT BROUGHT A GENERATION OF READERS TO MANGA, NOW BACK IN A DEFINITIVE, HARDCOVER COLLECTOR'S EDITION!

CARDCAPTOR SAKURA
COLLECTOR'S EDITION
CLAMP

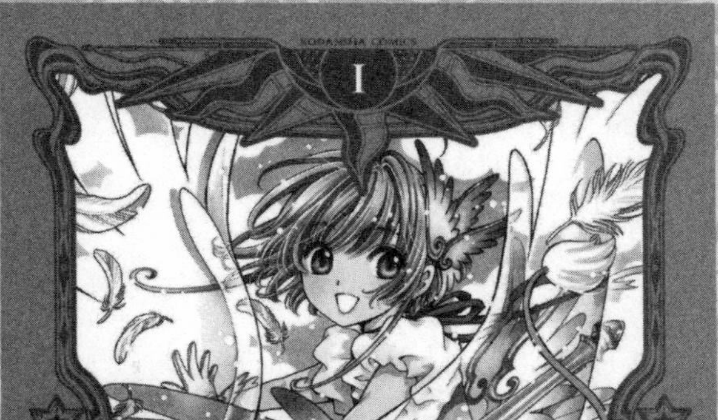
I
DELUXE·EDITION
Cardcaptor Sakura
CLAMP

Ten-year-old Sakura Kinomoto lives a pretty normal life with her older brother, Tōya, and widowed father, Fujitaka—until the day she discovers a strange book in her father's library, and her life takes a magical turn...

- A deluxe large-format hardcover edition of CLAMP's shojo manga classic
- All-new foil-stamped cover art on each volume
- Comes with exclusive collectible art card

KC KODANSHA COMICS

A Kodansha Comics Trade Paperback Original
Whisper Me a Love Song 5 copyright © 2021 Eku Takeshima
English translation copyright © 2022 Eku Takeshima

Published in the United States by Kodansha Comics, an imprint of
Kodansha USA Publishing, LLC, New York.

Publication rights for this English edition arranged through
Kodansha Ltd., Tokyo.

First published in Japan in 2021 by Ichijinsha Inc., Tokyo
as *Sayasaku you ni koi wo utau*, volume 5.

ISBN 978-1-64651-398-7

Original cover design by SALIDAS

Printed in the United States of America.

www.kodansha.us

1st Printing
Translation: Kevin Steinbach
Lettering: Jennifer Skarupa
Editing: Tiff Joshua TJ Ferentini
Kodansha Comics edition cover design: Matt Akuginow

Publisher: Kiichiro Sugawara

Director of publishing services: Ben Applegate
Associate director of publishing operations: Stephen Pakula
Publishing services managing editors: Alanna Ruse, Madison Salters
Production managers: Emi Lotto, Angela Zurlo
Logo and character art ©Kodansha USA Publishing, LLC